Todd Bolender, Janet Reed, and the Making of American Ballet

UNIVERSITY PRESS OF FLORIDA

Florida A&M University, Tallahassee
Florida Atlantic University, Boca Raton
Florida Gulf Coast University, Ft. Myers
Florida International University, Miami
Florida State University, Tallahassee
New College of Florida, Sarasota
University of Central Florida, Orlando
University of Florida, Gainesville
University of North Florida, Jacksonville
University of South Florida, Tampa
University of West Florida, Pensacola

Todd Bolender,

UNIVERSITY PRESS OF FLORIDA

Gainesville / Tallahassee / Tampa / Boca Raton / Pensacola / Orlando / Miami / Jacksonville / Ft. Myers / Sarasota

Janet Reed, and the Making of American Ballet

Martha Ullman West

FOREWORD BY FRANCIA RUSSELL

26 25 24 23 22 21   6 5 4 3 2 1

Library of Congress Cataloging-in-Publication Data
Names: West, Martha Ullman, author. | Russell, Francia, author of foreword.
Title: Todd Bolender, Janet Reed, and the making of American ballet /
    Martha Ullman West ; foreword by Francia Russell.
Description: Gainesville : University Press of Florida, 2021. | Includes
    bibliographical references and index.
Identifiers: LCCN 2020037883 (print) | LCCN 2020037884 (ebook) | ISBN
    9780813066776 (hardback) | ISBN 9780813057811 (pdf)
Subjects: LCSH: Bolender, Todd. | Reed, Janet, 1916–2000. |
    Ballet—America—History. | Ballet—America—Biography.
Classification: LCC GV1621 .W47 2021 (print) | LCC GV1621 (ebook) | DDC
    792.8/0973—dc23
LC record available at https://lccn.loc.gov/2020037883
LC ebook record available at https://lccn.loc.gov/2020037884

The University Press of Florida is the scholarly publishing agency for the
State University System of Florida, comprising Florida A&M University,
Florida Atlantic University, Florida Gulf Coast University, Florida
International University, Florida State University, New College of Florida,
University of Central Florida, University of Florida, University of North
Florida, University of South Florida, and University of West Florida.

University Press of Florida
2046 NE Waldo Road
Suite 2100
Gainesville, FL 32609
http://upress.ufl.edu

For Franklin C. West and our family, Alice West, Lewis Hess, and Feodor and Flora Hess West

Contents

Foreword

With the great surge of technology and the endless stream of films and photos that we all share now, much of the mid-twentieth-century history of dance in America has faded into the mists of time through lack of documentation. As a striking example, who, except dance writers, now talks about or has even heard of Diana Adams, my idol and friend?

I am grateful to Martha Ullman West for her years of devotion and the voluminous research she has done to remind us of the influence of two great American dance artists. Martha's book began as a biography of Janet Reed, grew into a dual account of the careers of Janet and her esteemed colleague Todd Bolender, and became a fascinating, in-depth view of the American dance world of their time.

Todd, born in Canton, Ohio, in 1914, began his career as a modern dancer; Janet, born in Tolo, Oregon, in 1916, was a ballet dancer first, last, and always. Both were powerful and uniquely individual performers, Todd for his distinctive movement style and intellectual approach to each role, Janet, the ultimate soubrette, for her sparkling personality, red-headed beauty, and innate gifts as an actor. And they shared a wicked sense of humor as performers and as friends.

Martha details the parallel careers of the two colleagues when classical ballet in America was in its toddler years and most dancers took jobs wherever they could find them, including on endless tours across the country. Todd made his way to New York to study modern dance and to attempt to make a living as a dancer in any way he could. Mary Wigman and Hanya Holm were profound influences on his artistic sensibilities. Janet, on the other hand, and when very young, was fortunate to become one of the favorite and most featured dancers in the San Francisco Opera Ballet, where she was cast as Odile (with Jacqueline Martin Schumacher as Odette) in

Willam Christensen's full-length production of *Swan Lake,* the first in the United States.

Todd's discovery of Balanchine precipitated a cataclysmic change in his life, and with his characteristic zeal, he plunged into classes at the School of American Ballet. In 1938, he joined Ballet Caravan, Lincoln Kirstein's early dream attempt to make ballet an American art form. Next for him was Ballet Society, which, in 1948, became the New York City Ballet. Janet appeared on the New York dance scene in 1942, performing stellar roles with the Dance Players, the Ballet Theatre, and, ultimately, the New York City Ballet, where she and Todd often performed together. To the end of their lives, they were admiring friends who supported each other in all ways.

Illuminating stories of their professional and personal lives fill Martha's book: their stunning successes as performers, Todd's early struggles to find himself as a choreographer, the painful task of achieving a balance of career and family life that preoccupied Janet. Both careers extended far beyond performance. Todd was a noted choreographer of ballets, operettas, and musicals and was the artistic director of four ballet companies, in Cologne, Istanbul, Frankfurt, and Kansas City. And Janet was a ballet master, a teacher, and a brilliant acting coach. Having worked with both of them over many years, I can attest to the fact that they were equally demanding and inspiring.

Martha includes two lovely quotes in her book that are illustrative of her subjects. Janet's credo: "I've never believed that a human being onstage could be abstract." (Some might be surprised to know that Balanchine expressed the same belief to me.) Certainly Janet was never for a moment abstract onstage or off. Also in these pages is a note to Todd from Tanaquil Le Clercq, which begins: "Dear Tootleie Poodlesie." They must have had more silly, clever, affectionate fun with friends in those days.

Adding vital contemporaneous descriptions and opinions of the artistry of both Janet and Todd, Martha quotes scores of reviews, the majority favorable to rapturous but a few doozies of negativity. The wealth of material she has unearthed and presented to us not only fills in an important chapter in American dance history but, almost more importantly, brings to vivid life the spectacular lives, careers, and legacies of two of our finest dance artists.

Francia Russell

Note on Sources

I have been collecting the material for this book for more than two decades. Interviews with Todd Bolender began in Kansas City in 2001; they ended with his death in 2006. Some of the transcripts for those interviews were lost; the recordings are in my possession, as are notes scribbled on pieces of paper. I have consulted archives in New York, at the New York Public Library for the Performing Arts and the New York City Ballet Society Archive, which a decade ago was housed in a sub-basement of a Wall Street bank and is currently somewhere in New Jersey. Some of Bolender's papers are to be found in the Jerome Robbins Dance Division at the New York Public Library for the Performing Arts, as are most of Janet Reed's. Kansas City Ballet houses the rest of Bolender's papers. I consulted many oral history interviews with Bolender and Reed's contemporaries in what we fondly call the Dance Collection at the New York Public Library, including one with Reed, and took notes but failed to make note of page numbers. Many of the San Francisco Ballet materials, including reviews of their pre–World War II tours and papers of the Christensen family, were housed at the Performing Arts Library and Museum, which closed several years ago.

I have had much e-mail correspondence with many people who knew both of my subjects and have quoted extensively from those e-mails. All errors are mine.

1

Todd Bolender and Janet Reed were dancing in *Pied Piper* when it happened, one of those unforeseen stage mishaps that can wreck a performance
completely. Set to Aaron Copland's jazzy *Concerto for Clarinet and String
Orchestra, Pied Piper* was Jerome Robbins's fourth work for New York City
Ballet. Its vocabulary was in the same vein as *Fancy Free* and *Interplay*, a
blend of classical steps, modern dance, and social dancing. For the finale,
he included a jitterbug move, in which Bolender had to swing Reed over
his head and around his neck, her legs in a wide second position, and from
there to the floor directly in front of him. In the early 1950s, when this performance took place, Bolender had begun wearing a wig over his thinning
hair that fit over his scalp like a hat. At this particular performance, all was
going well, until Bolender, after swinging Reed down to the floor, looked
down and thought, "My God, has she lost her tights" at the same moment
that Reed looked in the same direction. They both broke into uncontrollable laughter, fortunately just as the corps came rushing onto the stage and
covered their hasty exit, Bolender's much-loathed wig ("it had curls and
things," he told Deborah Jowitt) restored to his head.[1]

By 1952, when it's likely this performance took place,[2] Bolender and
Reed had been friends since Reed arrived in New York in January 1942.
They had been dancing together in Robbins's and Balanchine's work since
1949, when Reed joined City Ballet. They originated their roles in *Pied
Piper*; were partners in the restaged *Interplay*, in which Reed had been
first cast at Ballet Theatre; and had danced together in Balanchine's *À
la Françaix*, in *Symphony in C*; in the New York City Ballet revival of
Card Game, and in Bolender's own *Mother Goose Suite*. As dancers and
as people, they shared a passion for dancing, an openness to new ideas,
intelligence, musicality, a love of laughter, and a dogged determination

to get the job done no matter what it was. Although the specifics of their backgrounds were different, as Americans who came of age in hard, turbulent times, their lives onstage and off were guided by a point of view that was much the same.

Bolender was born in Canton, Ohio, on February 17, 1914. Canton was best known as the birthplace of William McKinley and professional football. It did not have a flourishing arts scene, but because Bolender came from a middle-class family (his father was a businessman and his mother a coloratura soprano who had passionately wanted a career as a singer), the arts, especially music and theater, were a part of family life. Bolender had vivid memories of accompanying his mother to her singing lessons when he was small and of her teacher, who wore extraordinary hats. No doubt those sessions and the piano lessons he had when he was older account for the acute musicality he showed later as a dancer and choreographer, at least in part.

Because he was constantly in motion, Bolender was dubbed the dancer of the family, and when he was 10 or 11, his energy was channeled into rudimentary ballet classes with a family friend. Lula Carter had been trained by Russian teachers in San Francisco, but her barre was quite basic and inconsistent, as was Bolender's attendance at her classes.

In 1932, at age 17, bored with high school (he was flunking algebra), Bolender left formal academic education behind and headed to New York, on what he described as a quest for knowledge about dancing that went beyond the inconsistent ballet training and the tap and acrobatics that were available to him in Canton. Eclectic as it was, that early training turned out to be important to his career as a dancer: what George Balanchine and Jerome Robbins choreographed on him later on capitalized on both those skills and his highly flexible, well-turned-out body.

New York, which he heard about from a friend, had for several decades been a magnet for American artists of every stripe. To the teenaged Bolender, all of its possibilities sounded like "a kind of heaven." However, three years after the 1929 crash, "heaven" featured bread lines, apple sellers on corners, and a lot of politically motivated modern dance. Between the time he arrived and 1936 or 37, when he began taking classes at the School of American Ballet (SAB), Bolender studied with several modern teachers, starting with Edwin Strawbridge, who had given him a scholarship before he left home. Erick Hawkins also studied with Strawbridge. In exchange for reduced tuition, he and Bolender would sweep out the studio when classes were over and occasionally walk Strawbridge's dog.

Tough as the 1930s were economically, it was a heady time to be young in New York, especially if you were interested in modern dance. Modern dancers, in fact, had a lock on the city's dance scene. Many, especially intellectuals and the connoisseurs of high art, considered ballet, which was often performed as a vaudeville act in movie theaters before the main feature was shown, to be popular art at best, cheap and tawdry at worst. Martha Graham, Doris Humphrey, Charles Weidman, and José Limón were all active in the city at the time. Hanya Holm, a disciple of German *Ausdruckstanz* practitioner Mary Wigman, opened a school on West 11th Street in Greenwich Village in 1931 to teach her technique. Wigman, Harald Kreutzberg, and Uday Shankar, the Indian modern dancer who for a time partnered Anna Pavlova, all performed in New York on tour in the early 1930s. Bolender took it all in and said later that Wigman and Shankar were the two most important influences on his choreography. Kreutzberg, that rare modern dancer with a gift for comedy, may also have influenced Bolender as a performer, for he too demonstrated comedic talents quite early in his career.

Bolender's studies with Strawbridge were brief. Once he saw Wigman perform, he was so overwhelmed by the blood-and-guts power of her dancing that he switched to Holm's school. There, where improvisation was an integral part of the classroom exercises, as was considerable interaction between the students and the percussionist who accompanied them, Bolender first became interested in choreographing. Photographs of a piece called "The Cry," which he made in that period, certainly show the Wigman-Holm influence, right down to the masks on the dancers. After a year's study with Holm, Bolender got a job with the Federal Dance Project (FDP), a short-lived offshoot of the Works Project Administration's Federal Theatre Project, which ironically, since it was dominated by modern dancers, led him to begin serious study of ballet. Classical dancer Arthur Mahoney, who was working for the FDP, insisted that Bolender take two ballet classes a day in addition to attending rehearsals for a show that toured around the city and its boroughs in an early form of outreach to people who couldn't afford tickets to performances. One class was with Mahoney, the other with a woman Bolender remembered as a "charming old Russian teacher who was so convinced I would become a ballet dancer, that she would teach me privately in her little basement apartment on the Upper West Side."[3]

The shift from modern to ballet wasn't difficult for Bolender at this point, because his compact body was highly flexible (he was five feet, eight inches tall) and he had natural turnout from the hips and a good jump. In her small studio, the Russian teacher began by teaching him *double tour en l'air* and *brisé volé,* good practice for the constricted spaces in which he would later perform on tour with Ballet Caravan.

At about the same time, Bolender began to hear talk of SAB, which Lincoln Kirstein and Edward Warburg had opened in 1934 in a building on the corner of Madison Avenue and 59th Street. He had seen Balanchine's *Serenade* and, struck by the easy flow of the movement, began to be interested in ballet. One day, curious about what the training was like, he climbed the four flights of stairs to SAB's studios to see what was going on there. The airy studios were certainly an improvement over the Russian teacher's low-ceilinged basement and he began to take classes regularly, receiving the structured training he had been hungering for. Paying for them was another matter. His FDP job having come to an end, he auditioned for an operetta called *Frederika,* which was to open on Broadway on February 4, 1937. The choreography was by Chester Hale, who later became a choreographer for the movies and had produced a lot of vaudeville numbers for a troupe known as the Chester Hale Girls in the 1920s.

Hale apparently was unimpressed by the brief audition, recognizing that Bolender's ballet technique still had a long way to go. But Bolender later recalled that as the tryout concluded, Hale told him he would give him the job "on one condition, that you will be in my class every morning for two and a half hours, so that I can keep an eye on your development."[4] Not wanting to give up his SAB classes, Bolender began yet another commute around New York, taking a Cecchetti-based class with Hale at his studio on Columbus Circle every morning and then zipping across town to receive a different form of classical training at SAB at noon, after which there were afternoon rehearsals and performances of *Frederika* at night. The show, Bolender's first professional job, had a four-month run.

Just before it closed, Bolender was taking class at SAB when "a tall, thin bullet-headed young man came in to watch Muriel Stuart's class." This of course was Lincoln Kirstein. "They talked a lot and at the finish Kirstein called me to his office and said, 'Where did you come from?' and then immediately, 'Would you like to join a small ballet group called Ballet Caravan?' It was a most timely invitation."[5]

There are several accounts of why and how Ballet Caravan was formed in the spring of 1936; each has more than a grain of truth. According to Lew Christensen, who was dancing with George Balanchine's American Ballet Ensemble at the Metropolitan Opera, where they had been in residence since the fall of 1935, the dancers needed summer employment when they were off contract and they also needed to stay in shape. As he remembered it in a 1984 interview with Francis Mason, "Harold [Christensen] and I got together and a few other dancers . . . and we would get a pianist, some music and play. We would do our own ballets. Lincoln heard about it and thought it would be a hell of a good idea. He organized us and got us booked into little dumps in New England."[6]

Some of the dancers were chosen because they also wanted to choreograph (all of them men, it should be noted). Ruthanna Boris, who was part of the troupe's female contingent, later became a choreographer of some note, creating one of Reed's most applauded roles as Hortense, Queen of the Swamp Lilies, in *Cakewalk*. Kirstein made plain what he thought of women choreographers, not to mention female artists of every discipline, in a 1953 essay titled "Alec, or the Future of Choreography": "A few male dancers have been grateful for dances by ladies," but "the male principle by instruction and design, has determined the executive prowess of girls and women."[7] This was something of a reversal of his positive opinion of Catherine Littlefield's *Terminal* and Ruth Page's *Frankie and Johnnie*, cited in a 1938 essay on *Billy the Kid*.[8] According to Yvonne Patterson, who danced with the American Ballet and with Ballet Caravan, which she called the "little company," for the four and a half years of its existence, a secondary purpose for the ensemble was to give male dancers more opportunities to perform lead roles. "The reason Ballet Caravan was formed I was told is that the men in our ballet went on a revolt against Balanchine for only using Bill [Dollar]. It was formed to give other male ballet dancers something to do."[9]

Patterson's explanation of why Ballet Caravan came into being makes a certain degree of sense when you look at the repertory Kirstein created for the company. A good deal of it centered on male protagonists, including *Yankee Clipper, Billy the Kid,* and *Filling Station*. If for Balanchine ballet was woman, for Kirstein ballet was man. All the Caravan dancers, men and women, had received at least some training at SAB and most were American born, hence Kirstein's inquiry about where Bolender came from.

Kirstein had long dreamed of making ballet American, with a company of native-born dancers who were trained in an American style (hence the founding of SAB in 1934) to perform a repertory that would reflect and express American culture and be created by composers, choreographers, and scenic and costume designers with American sensibilities, even though they might not have U.S. passports. He shrewdly brought Balanchine to the United States in the fall of 1933 in the service of this ambition. Several years later, in an interview with a reporter while Ballet Caravan was on tour, he was absolutely clear about why: "He continues to amplify the range of possibility in the classic dance to such an unfailing degree that he seems a mine of choreographic information. The more you take from his ideas of movement as model the more there is to be taken. He is here to be used by Americans of less experience, and from the moment I saw Les Ballets 1933, I knew he should be used by Americans in America."[10]

While Balanchine was born in Georgia and trained in Russia, he belonged to a generation of Russians and Europeans (Igor Stravinsky was another) for whom the United States, as it had presented itself to the world through movies, western novels, musical comedy, jazz, and blues, represented new and exciting territory, making it a sort of promised land for artists interested in innovation and the melding of contemporary and traditional forms. Balanchine, who left Soviet Russia for Europe in 1924, had seen American performers in Paris and London, and he was highly enamored of long-legged showgirls and the speed and unadorned athleticism he identified as qualities of American movement.

Without a company and with no work permit in England (Les Ballets 1933, which he directed, had just folded), Balanchine readily accepted Kirstein's invitation to come to the United States and not only choreograph on American dancers but also train them. The School of American Ballet came first, and the American Ballet became its performing arm. It was for this company Balanchine created *Serenade,* immediately democratizing ballet by giving the corps de ballet equal prominence with the soloists and making do with what he had: student dancers with mixed-level technique. As is well known, a late arrival to rehearsal and a fall by another dancer became part of the choreography. *Serenade* premiered in March 1935 at New York's Adelphi Theatre. Also on the program was *Errante* (which was originally made for Les Ballets 1933), with Tamara Geva, Balanchine's first wife, as guest artist; and *Alma Mater,* his first piece of Americana, a mercifully short-lived ballet. John Martin expressed considerable skepticism that it was a ballet at all but said that it was a pleasant enough revue-like entertainment.[11] Audiences, however, loved it. Another premiere, *Reminiscence,* which was set in a ballroom, closed the program.

Alma Mater was not the kind of serious Americana that Kirstein had in mind. Neither was the repertory Balanchine was creating for the American Ballet Ensemble, much as Kirstein admired it. So, logically, when he saw what the two Christensen brothers were up to, he took charge of the repertory and the bookings (although in practical terms, Frances Hawkins was responsible for the actual arrangements), which were not so much in "dumps" as in college towns. The company opened on July 17, 1936, on the Bennington College campus, a bastion of modern dance that had Kirstein shaking in his shoes. Moreover, the youthful impresario was finding that creating an entirely new ballet repertory was both difficult and complicated, especially for a troupe of around a dozen dancers.

Writing in the first of three pamphlets originally published in 1937, Kirstein said about the Caravan's repertory,

> The American subject matter gave me a lot of thought. I had only a small company, so that anything involving pictorial pageantry was out of the question. Trial and error had showed me the danger of competing with the Russians on any ground at all upon which they might choose to perform. Finally there must be no Spanish, Russian or Italian manual pantomime or character dancing. We needed something that would seem familiar to our hoped for audiences, something with which they could feel at home, and yet something in which our specifically American-styled dancers could be shown to their best advantage. The American classic style should never be dulled by a veneer of Russian glamour.[12]

The repertory that first season was scarcely replete with Americana. Only *Pocahontas,* set to a commissioned score by Elliott Carter with choreography by Lew Christensen and a scenario by Kirstein, met Kirstein's criteria for a ballet about an indigenous subject (and what's more indigenous than Pocahontas?) created entirely by American artists. Eugene Loring's *Harlequin for President,* again with a scenario by Kirstein, was based loosely on the Italian tradition of commedia dell'arte, accompanied by Domenico Scarlatti's music that was first played on one piano and later orchestrated by Adriana Mikeshina.[13] Keith Martin designed fairly elaborate costumes. Style notwithstanding, the ballet was created with a decidedly American sensibility, gleefully taking a form that satirized pomposity and pretension in medieval and Renaissance Italy and using it to send up democratic politics in an election year.

Other works included *Encounter*, Lew Christensen's first choreography, using Wolfgang Amadeus Mozart's music; Dollar's *Promenade*, choreographed to Maurice Ravel; and Doug Coudy's *Folk Dance*, choreographed to Emmanuel Chabrier. The choreographers were all American born, but the composers were European. There wasn't so much as a whisper of Russian music. The first season ended in December after thirty-eight performances, including one at the Kauffman Concert Hall at the 92nd Street YMHA in New York, another bastion of modern dance. *Dance Magazine* critic Anatole Chujoy's assessment was that despite the noteworthy efforts of the dancers, the work, perhaps because it was trying to prove a point, came across as "dry and cold." Clearly, with his commissioning of scores, decor, and costumes, Kirstein was emulating Sergei Diaghilev, whose productions were frequently controversial but not on the whole labeled either dry or cold. The comparison is instructive, because Diaghilev, at least in the early days of the Ballets Russes, also wanted to prove a point, namely that great and sophisticated art could come out of Russia, a country that Europeans perceived as rather more primitive than it actually was.

By the time Bolender joined the Caravan at the start of its second season, the repertory Kirstein had put together had expanded to include Loring's *Yankee Clipper*, a ballet about a young sailor on a whaling ship and the unpretentiously inauthentic dances he sees in ports of call such as Bali and Japan. It bears a structural resemblance to August Bournonville's *Far from Denmark*. While Loring could not have known about this ballet, which Bournonville had created in the nineteenth century in Copenhagen, Kirstein may well have been familiar with the form if not the work. The score was commissioned from the young American composer, Paul Bowles. Coudy, who doubled as company manager, contributed a second ballet, *The Soldier and the Gypsy*. It was based on *Carmen* but set to music by Manuel de Falla. "Erick Hawkins' ballet *Show Piece*," Bolender wrote, "was perhaps my favorite."[14]

Show Piece is set to a score commissioned from Bennington College faculty member Robert McBride, a contemporary of Aaron Copland and Virgil Thomson who, like them, incorporated jazz and American folk material into symphonic music. It was Hawkins's first choreographic effort and was designed to demonstrate the dancers' mastery of classical technique and bravura dancing with a series of variations that demanded some improvisation by individual performers. Like Bolender, Hawkins had been attracted to dancing by modernism: When he was an undergraduate majoring in classics at Harvard, he, too, had seen Kreutzberg perform and had been so inspired by him that he had spent a summer studying with him in Salzburg. Hawkins, a contemporary of Kirstein's at Harvard, knew that Balanchine was in New York and was asking to study with him before SAB had even opened its doors. Those studies and his studies with Strawbridge had prepared him to dance with both the American Ballet and Ballet Caravan, although his ballet career didn't last long. In 1938, he returned to modern dance as a guest artist with Martha Graham's company. The following year he was a company member on whom the feminist choreographer created her first male roles.

Given his modern dance background, Bolender clearly took more pleasure in putting his own spin on his role in *Show Piece* than Ruthanna Boris, who said of the experience, "I felt exploited. All I can remember is stomping around on my sore toes, banging castanets, with a little hat that kept slipping. I didn't realize I was getting a chance to do my own thing."[15]

While none of these works has endured, this repertory was at least a start toward fulfilling Kirstein's vision of a ballet canon that would express North American culture using a classically based style that could not be identified as anything but American. And while much of the music was by European composers, the choreographers built on the strengths of the dancers and the narrative was American to the core.

The press certainly recognized that. Although in most places critics were not particularly savvy about theatrical dancing (never mind ballet), they did know what American dancers were supposed to look like, as opposed to the Russians and the French. In a feature story that appeared in a Lowell, Massachusetts, paper on November 11, 1937, Frank Carey wrote in seeming wonder that the eight girls and seven boys who made up Ballet Caravan look like "normal" American kids, "although their routines are like Pavlova and Nijinsky. The boy dancers look more like football players than ballet men, and their favorite subject is scoffing against other men who think that the life of a male dancer is the life of a daisy." Harold Christensen had played football and track and attended West Point, Carey explained, adding that "Erick Hawkins, a Harvard grad . . . was dressed in black tights like Hamlet, but he is as shifty as Joe Louis, and has shoulders that would look good to any grid coach in the land."[16] The article was illustrated with photographs, including one of Bolender at the barre wearing shorts. Carey was also impressed by the democratic ethos of the company, particularly by the fact that the company men did considerable manual work, shifting scenery (mostly backdrops) and loading production trunks onto the tour bus. The women were also pressed into service, packing and unpacking costumes and often ironing them before putting them on for the next performance.

The dancers considered themselves fortunate when they traveled in buses, even though they could be slow. There was no air transportation for American tours in those days. "Trains," Bolender told an interviewer in 2002, "would go so far and they would stop and sometimes they would change and you get on the wrong track and go to the wrong place, so buses finally became the [preferred] mode of transportation."[17]

Kirstein viewed Ballet Caravan's first two seasons as experimental. The experimentation bore fruit in the 1938 season, with Lew Christensen's *Filling Station,* in which Bolender had his first featured role as the State Trooper, and in Loring's *Billy the Kid,* in which he was Alias, a role he loved. Both ballets were rooted in popular culture and the librettos, scores, decor, costumes, and choreography were created entirely by American artists.

Filling Station, an episodic work, with a score by Virgil Thomson and decor and costumes by easel painter Paul Cadmus, is not the masterpiece that Bolender and many others have judged *Billy* to be. However, it is that rare phenomenon, a ballet that is funny without being cute. While it can look dated, the likely explanation is its derivation from the popular culture of the first third of the twentieth century.

Kirstein wrote that "it has only a few characters, but each, either alone, or in combination, has its reason for being; each represented an actual facet of American civilization. Each was a recognizable social type, and each had its choreographic climax treated in a manner to heighten each individual dancer."[18] Those social types included a gas-station attendant, the hero of the piece, and various visitors to the gas station. These were a family lifted from the funny papers and short film comedies, such as those made by W. C. Fields; a pair of truck drivers; a state trooper; a rich couple (going home from a country club dance and feeling no pain); and a robber. Christensen originally danced the role of the gas-station attendant; later in revival, the exuberant Jacques d'Amboise danced the role. "Christensen's choreography," Kirstein wrote, "had a virtuosity and showmanship to which his long years of training in big-time vaudeville had accustomed him. The two truck-drivers' tumbling act was a surefire hit. The group dances in which he freely used the Big Apple were simplified past any actual resemblance to a dance fad which might date it in six months, as our repertory almost always must last us for many seasons."[19] The Big Apple, like most American social dances, was derived from Black culture, in this case the shout.

Over the years, Bolender performed several roles in *Filling Station*. His first program billing was as the State Trooper when it premiered in Hartford, Connecticut, in January 1938. He danced the Rich Boy on tour with Ballet Caravan and on the American Ballet Caravan tour of South America in 1941. As a principal dancer with New York City Ballet, he performed the role in the televised version of the 1953 revival, partnering Reed, who defined the role of the Rich Girl nearly fifteen years after the ballet's premiere. The timing of his performance was as impeccable as hers, right down to the goofily bemused expression on their faces as he ducked under her leg, which was extended in a perfect arabesque.

Although *Filling Station* has not endured in the way that *Billy the Kid* has, seven decades after its premiere it is still occasionally performed. It is in active repertory in the Kansas City Ballet and the San Francisco Ballet, and in 2010 the Nashville Ballet not only revived it but also reconstructed the original production's sets and costumes. The ballet was important to the careers of Bolender and Reed (who Bolender said "made it") and it was pivotal to Lew Christensen's career as a choreographer. "It was with *Filling Station* in 1938 that [Christensen] emerged as an American choreographer of the first rank, and showed his distinctive style—a commingling of the playfulness and sharp clarity that seem essentially American, with a sense of design and deportment derived from the classical tradition," historian Olga Maynard wrote.[20]

In addition to choreographing and performing for Ballet Caravan, Lew was the rehearsal director and ballet master, and Bolender found him very good indeed to work with. "[He was] very honest and very straightforward.

You always knew where you stood with him, which is a good thing in the theater because it's rather rare."[21] Bolender worked with him for more than three decades—on the 1941 tour of South America, in Ballet Society, at New York City Ballet, and minimally in the 1970s in Seattle and San Francisco.

Billy the Kid, Bolender wrote years later in notes for a memoir, "was a . . . masterpiece based on Kirstein's libretto and Aaron Copland's score [for which he won a Pulitzer Prize] in which I was cast as the ubiquitous Alias."[22] In Alias, Loring, aided by Kirstein, whose idea the ballet was, made a marvelous role for a dancer who would become known for his ability to create complex personalities with movement.[23] (Loring was the most experienced choreographer in Ballet Caravan, which isn't saying much; he'd arranged some dances for amateur theater performances in his native Milwaukee.) Bolender did that in the title role in the Balanchine-Stravinsky *Renard,* as Phlegmatic in Balanchine's *Four Temperaments,* as the husband in Jerome Robbins's *The Concert,* as the Mandarin in his own *Miraculous Mandarin,* and as the Man About Town in his own *Souvenirs.*

British dance historian Cyril Beaumont describes Alias as " a very important character, . . . who in various disguises symbolizes the variety and extent of Billy's victims, a cow-hand, a land agent, a sheriff, a jailer, an Indian guide, and so on."[24] Others, including Kirstein, viewed Alias as Nemesis in male guise. Kirstein provided Loring with an incredible amount of material about William Bonney, an outlaw of the Old West who became the stuff of legend, and cowboy ballads as Billy the Kid. Of Bolender's performance, Ballet Caravan dancer Fred Danieli said in a 1979 interview, "I think you have to go pretty far to beat [his] Alias. [It was] slinky, slimy, [and had a] dramatic quality."[25] In collaboration with Copland and artist Jared French, who became Bolender's friend, Loring succeeded in distilling the material into a 40-minute ballet that was as much about the settlement of the American West as it was about an unquestionably psychopathic young killer.

The ballet premiered on October 16, 1938, at the Civic Theater in Chicago, the second stop in a four-month tour that took the company to the West Coast for the first time. Previous tours had taken them to the Atlantic Seaboard; as Kirstein put it in a two-part "diary" for *Dance Magazine,* "from Skowhegan, Maine, to Havana, Cuba, but only as far west as Pittsburgh."[26] A photograph that George Platt Lynes took of Bolender while he was being fitted for a costume for Alias as sheriff shows a fresh-faced, rather innocent-looking young man with broad shoulders who is smiling patiently while the costumier adjusts the sleeve of a puffy shirt. He certainly doesn't look like Nemesis, the ancient punitive figure of doom, who Alias is meant to represent. The shape-changing character was Kirstein's practical solution to the problem of having a stage cluttered with the bodies of Billy's victims. Maynard rightly calls that choice a "stroke of genius, for the presence of this classic symbol gives Billy the same premonition of doom that the Ghost gives Hamlet."[27]

There is even less classical dancing in *Billy* than there was in *Filling Station*. Only the antihero is given bravura dancing to do, a double pirouette and a double air turn just before he kills someone that symbolizes a surge of rage and possibly replicates the spinning of a revolver's cylinder that can be seen in western movies of the period. The shootings are done in silence and without a prop gun; props in fact do not exist in the work. In the guise of a "good guy"—rancher, sheriff, land agent—Alias moves around the stage in a straightforward low, open jeté, or stride. As the Indian guide who betrays Billy, he moves sinuously, ingratiatingly, and sneakily, in a dated portrayal of the "Red man." Loring similarly differentiated between "good" women, such as ranchers' wives, and "bad," such as dance hall girls, the former moving calmly and deliberately, the latter swinging their hips and shaking their shoulders. Only Billy's Mexican sweetheart, the role originated by Marie-Jeanne, SAB's first graduate, dances on pointe; Loring said later she was meant to be a dream.[28]

A review of the Chicago premiere by Robert Pollak with the optimistic title "American Ballet Comes of Age" is worth quoting at length:

Lincoln Kirstein's Ballet Caravan, a young American troupe on exhibit for the first time in Chicago yesterday afternoon, should have proved to the full house at the Civic theater that the American dance movement is coming of age.

Kirstein, already familiar to us as the most provocative critic of the dance in America, now emerges as a director who will fight effectively and to the last ditch for native dancing, choreography and music. . . .

The bulk of yesterday's program, devoted to "Filling Station," a roadside document, and "Billy the Kid," the biography of a famous bandit, was cursed neither with the geometrical sterility of our "abstractionists," nor with the tinsel prettiness of the Russian ballet.

Kirstein is patently not afraid to be theatrical. His dancers, all well-grounded in the traditional ballet technique, use any form of physical expression for purposes of comedy and tragedy. The ballets are designed by his own people. Yesterday's "Billy the Kid" was not only a world premiere, with a first-rate score by Aaron Copeland [sic], but also an American adventure that suggests an early return engagement by Kirstein's corps."[29]

From Chicago, the Caravan traveled to Milwaukee. That it was Loring's birthplace made no difference to the sponsors, who, Kirstein wrote, refused to allow *Billy* to be performed because they felt that the outlaw was not an appropriate subject for a ballet. Here, Kirstein became increasingly aware of something he had known all along: that for most American sponsors and presenters, if it wasn't Russian, it just wasn't ballet. However, the company was permitted to perform *Yankee Clipper* (like *Billy*, an American subject, but the Farm Boy protagonist, danced by the choreographer, is a virtuous guy who yields not to the temptation of foreign dancing girls and returns to New England to marry his beloved, dragging her offstage, as one reviewer put it). The reviewer for the *Milwaukee News* gave Loring and Bolender special mention:

> As the enamored but bewildered farm boy, Eugene Loring rightly deserves first mention. Excellent in the art of miming and showing a style sincere and unassuming, this young Milwaukeean made a profound impression. Moreover, the choreography . . . is his. Interestingly varied and always "on the move," it is surely the work of one possessing outstanding talents.[30]

The sponsors, members of the Arion Musical Club, evidently paid attention to the critical praise, and they invited the company to return the following year and—what's more—to perform *Billy*.

Three weeks later, a critic for the *Seattle Times* was nothing like as favorably disposed as Pollak of Chicago had been toward *Billy* or *Filling Station*. The ballets were presented on a program at the Moore Theatre (a venue Kirstein loved so much he said he wished he owned it) along with Dollar's *Promenade* as the curtain raiser. "In the matter of technical proficiency and grace, American ballet dancers can hold up their heads and their toes with the best Europe has to offer," Gilbert Brown began, his opinion formed by earlier viewings of the fledgling San Francisco Opera Ballet, the Ballets Russes, and various European companies in the same theater.

The Ballet Caravan organization, making its first Seattle appearance Saturday night, demonstrated that theorem to the hilt. But when American dancers attempt to take over the American scene and express it in terms of the formal, mincing postures and pirouettes of the ballet, they crack up badly.

[They] provided two large samples of evidence to this effect, too, in their "ballet-document" *Filling Station* and their "character ballet" *Billy the Kid*.[31]

The former reminded Gilbert of the pantomime of a French music hall, "elaborated by intricate ballet steps which fitted ill with the spirit of the scene." He found the combination of classical and social dancing as "sterile as a mule" and had a similar view of *Billy*, "except for the seductive dancing of several dance hall girls and senoritas." *Promenade*, which had premiered at Bennington in 1936, fared far better: "The beautiful proficiency of these young American dancers found a happier medium in the opening ballet. Marie-Jeanne, Gisella Caccialanza, Lew Christensen, Todd Bolender and Eugene Loring shone individually in dancing roles." He liked the French Empire period costumes and the way Ravel's music was played. The audience, which was large, he reported, applauded warmly.

In San Francisco in early November, the company opened at the Opera House with Dollar's *Air and Variations* set to Trude Rittmann's arrangement of seventeen of Bach's *Goldberg Variations* for two pianos. The ballet had premiered the previous April at Winthrop College in Rock Hills, South Carolina. In a long review for the *San Francisco Chronicle*, Alfred Frankenstein, who was basically a music critic and a distinguished one at that, described it as "the straight, classic ballet, performed no doubt to show that the boys and girls knew how." Frankenstein identified an important direction of American choreography, particularly Balanchine's. "It was all movement, it was all pattern, it was all a play of lightly dynamic forces, and it had the good sense to avoid making its patterns too closely after those of the music."[32] Nevertheless, he found it lacking in energy.

Frankenstein predicted that American ballet would leave the classicism of Dollar's piece behind in favor of character ballets such as *Filling Station* and *Billy the Kid*. What he didn't allow for was the role Balanchine would play in creating an American classicism of musically based abstract patterns performed with precisely the kind of wired energy he found lacking in *Air and Variations*.

While the company was in San Francisco, Kirstein attended a dress rehearsal of Willam Christensen's *Romeo and Juliet*. All three Christensen brothers had been involved in Ballet Caravan's first tour and Lew was already becoming a cross-pollinator of East and West Coast American ballet. For example, his *Encounter* was on the program of the San Francisco Opera Ballet's first concert, under Willam's direction, in Oakland, in September 1937, with Lew partnering Reed in the adagio. Watching the *Romeo and Juliet* dress rehearsal, Kirstein was impressed with the quality of the dancers, "notably a charming red-haired girl[,] Janet Reed" and he liked Willam's "compact" version of *Romeo and Juliet*.[33] The Opera House was where the Caravan performed the next night, the San Francisco company having embarked on a tour of its own, and Kirstein found it "the finest theatrical plant in which I have ever worked." Since he had played a role in the American Ballet's performances at New York's Metropolitan Opera House, that was saying quite a lot. Moreover, it was in that elegant, European-style house that Kirstein felt "a real sense of the security of a strong working organism capable of producing a spectacular success."

From San Francisco, the troupe went on to less glamorous California towns, such as Fresno, where there was some letdown after the opera house success. There, Kirstein wrote, "Todd Bolender hurt his leg quite badly in *Yankee Clipper*, but cheerfully continued dancing while I was alarmed to see tears of pain continually plow through his makeup."[34] Bolender, ever the pro, was giving Kirstein a demonstration of dancer's discipline, something he had developed even this early in his career, and although he loathed the Christian Science approach to physical ailments his mother practiced, that may also have played a part.

The company performed in six more venues before it reached Los Angeles, where it had excellent advance publicity. The anonymous critic for the *Evening Herald* wrote of the performance, "Although the absence of boisterous enthusiasm argues that they didn't realize it at the time, Los Angeles dance lovers last night saw the finest contemporary dance troupe America has produced when the Ballet Caravan gave their concert at the Philharmonic Auditorium." The critic lauded "its typically American themes, . . . the high excellence of individual dancers and the brilliant manner in which they have freed the classic ballet technic [*sic*] from the shackles of Ballet Russe formalism and combined it with some of the best things in the strictly modern dance."[35] He gave particularly high marks to Lew Christensen's performance in *Filling Station* and hoped that the next time they came they would be accompanied by a full orchestra.

The next port of call was Phoenix, Arizona, where the company manager had to cope with a floor so slick that Kirstein compared it to a skating rink. She did so by mopping it with water laced with lye, a technique used well into the late 1940s by touring musical comedies and dance companies. In Phoenix, the audience loved *Billy*, and from there the company had a "thrilling" ride over the mountains by bus to a mining town where ballet was being seen for the first time. Of this experience Kirstein wrote, "I'd rather dance for a completely unprejudiced, even ignorant, audience than for the kind who feels outraged if there are no white tarlatans in sight."[36] In El Paso, Texas, real Billy the Kid country, the Texas champion square dance team showed the company various dances and a good time was had by all.

From Austin, their last stop in Texas, the Caravan traveled by bus to Fayetteville, Arkansas, where the audience, Kirstein wrote, was "rowdy," and the performance was disrupted by football players whistling at couples dancing together. In Tulsa, where alumni of Wassily de Basil's Ballets Russes would start the Tulsa Ballet in 1956, Kirstein ran into an acquaintance on the street, who, much to his surprise, was working as a critic for the *Tulsa World*. Kirstein was justifiably pleased by his response to *Filling Station* and Caccialanza and Danieli's performance as the Rich Couple: "The dance of the drunken couple was as superb an example of ballet humor as one may expect to see, yet it never descended into clowning nor did it lack a certain sodden grace."[37] His opposite number at the *Tulsa Tribune* agreed, commenting that burlesque in ballet is "even more difficult" than ballet technique itself.

The tour ended in the middle of December in Kirstein's native Rochester, New York, where the program was in many ways both a critical and popular success. At the end of his tour journal, Kirstein talked about what he had learned, most compellingly "not only that New York is not America, but that Americans genuinely love good dancing if they are allowed to see it."[38] Press notices for Ballet Caravan's dancers and accounts of the enthusiastic applause they received in various places are also proof that Americans could and did identify with dancers named Hawkins, Bolender, and

Loring (who had actually changed his name from Le Roy Kerpestein to Eugene Loring), although Caccialanza, who was not American born, and Marie-Jeanne, who was born Marie-Jeanne Pelus in New York, were the company's leading ballerinas.

Janet Reed, however, had a name as American as peach cobbler and was the descendant of pioneers on her father's side, the same people Loring depicted traveling across the stage in *Billy the Kid.* She was born on September 15, 1916, on her maternal grandparents' farm northwest of Medford, Oregon, in a large house that had been a stagecoach inn. Reed was intensely proud of her ancestors. "I'm from pioneer stock," she said in 1978 in an oral history interview with critic and historian Tobi Tobias.[39] "From the ones who went west. We were always seeking new frontiers, or I think my ancestors always sought new frontiers."[40] Reed, like Bolender, went east, to New York, looking for new ways of dancing.

She spent the first decade of her life in rural Oregon as the 1920s roared toward the 1929 Depression. It was marked by hard work, family upheaval, financial problems, and (unlikely as it may seem) an introduction to ballet. Her parents were in their teens when Reed was born and the marriage didn't last beyond her babyhood, when her father departed for San Francisco, leaving Reed and her mother on the family farm. A few years later, Reed's mother left for Portland to work as a beautician and the grandparents' marriage was disintegrating; Reed recalled in an unpublished memoir that "there was not much laughter or gaiety."[41]

Laughter and gaiety fed her soul ("Janet loved to laugh," Bolender said of his lifelong friend) and she cherished an early memory of dancing while her mother played the piano. What she did not cherish was the memory of being taken at age six or so to a ballet teacher. "It's one of those cases of the mother taking the child for ballet classes," Reed told Tobias. "When I first started I didn't really like it at all and fought like a steer. But then the next time I got started in Portland, Oregon, was sort of under my own steam."[42]

That was just a few years later, when Reed was 9 or 10, and her mother came to Medford, where she was living with her grandmother, and illegally removed her from the grandmother's custody. The child's life hadn't been easy in Medford; she had worked hard helping her grandmother with her boarding house. But her life in Portland with her single mother wasn't much easier. Esther Reed had her own beauty shop, and Janet studied with several Portland teachers. They gave her eclectic training: in addition to ballet, she studied acrobatic dancing and tap. These early teachers, whose background we do not know, had some expertise in spotting talent and gave Reed numerous opportunities to perform, "for any and all occasions," Janet recalled. She speculated that it helped them build their schools. Reed was good box office throughout her career, and although her teachers may well have been using her, the exposure she received from them led her at age 16 to Willam Christensen. He had come to Portland in 1932 to help his aunt run her dancing school and to establish a ballet component. The latter was no easy task at the height of the Depression and, furthermore, was against his aunt's wishes. She specialized in teaching ballroom dancing to the daughters of Portland society. Her nephew, Richard Billings, whose specialty was teaching tap, was also opposed to adding classical dancing to the curriculum.

Willam, who needed badly to recruit students for the fledgling program, saw Reed dance in a school performance and immediately invited her to study with him. "I said I can't afford it," Reed told Tobias.[43] Willam had a solution. Knowing that Reed's mother was a beautician—the Esther Reed Beauty Parlor was located in downtown Portland close to his school—he employed the barter system, suggesting that Esther Reed could do the Christensen women's hair in exchange for Janet's lessons with him. They must have been the best coiffed women in Portland; Reed took a lot of lessons and "they had to have their hair done a lot."[44]

In this period, Esther Reed frequently couldn't pay her rent, and mother and daughter would sneak out of apartments in the dark of night, carrying their belongings in a suitcase. Reed's cousin recalled a time when she and her mother (Esther's sister) lived with them in a cold, damp house on Portland's Canyon Road, which, because there was no wood for fuel, they heated by burning rubber tires the two girls scavenged.

At one point, Reed did acrobatic dancing in a speakeasy, creating her own costume and sewing multiple rows of glittering bugle beads on it. She was escorted home each night by the bootlegger's bodyguard. Ultimately, she had to quit: her studies with Christensen coupled with the attempt to keep up her schoolwork at Portland's Lincoln High School (where a home economics teacher who had seen her dance gave her the passing grade to graduate that she had not actually earned) took a heavy toll on her health. She may well have been malnourished; all her life she struggled with anemia.

Both Reed and her friend Jacqueline Martin, who, along with seven of their classmates, went with Willam to San Francisco, remembered their teacher as immensely passionate about ballet and highly inspirational. And Reed vividly recalled working extremely hard. "We were a group that hadn't seen much ballet," she said. "We didn't know that much and yet he instilled in us this love of dance." Taking class was only the beginning. "We would come early and work. We would stay *after* and work by ourselves. We kept challenging each other. Then he would choreograph and we would have rehearsals and we weren't paid."[45]

Christensen's passion and personality worked their magic on many members of the Portland community. Willam assembled the students who would become the nucleus of Portland's first ballet company. He started small, with only three students, and with a disaster. Shortly after classes began and just as he was ending a lesson, the building caught fire. While there was little damage to the structure itself, the firemen had to destroy part of the ballroom floor, where most classes took place, in order to save the building. Undeterred by small enrollment and disaster, Willam continued to court Portland's leading citizens and to recruit students such as Reed and Robert Irwin. (A few years later in San Francisco, Léonide Massine asked Irwin to join the Ballet Russe de Monte Carlo.) Irwin hadn't had a lick of ballet training when Christensen took him on, but he had a great deal of physical strength and a good body for ballet and, as it turned out, considerable talent. He and Reed became the poster students for the school; their photographs adorned flyers for classes and performances.

Remarkably quickly, Willam was sufficiently successful to break from the family business and establish studios of his own on the top floor of Portland's Selling-Hirsch Building. He used marketing strategies such as free lecture demonstrations to introduce ballet to an ignorant public and performances of a visitors' night program for which he charged twenty-five cents. When he moved to his own studio, he took Billings and their students with them. They were joined by a music teacher and a theater director and the Portland Creative Theatre and School of Music and Dance was born. Unlike SAB, where the faculty in the early years was primarily Russian, Reed's first serious training ground had American teachers. She learned a little bit of everything at Christensen's school, in addition to ballet technique.

In 1934, the year that Bolender moved to New York permanently, Reed was featured as the Sugar Plum Fairy in Willam's first attempt at the *Nutcracker*, although the suite of plotless dances he created to the Tchaikovsky score bore little resemblance to the Petipa-Ivanov classic, which he had never seen. The performance, which took place in June as part of Portland's annual Rose Festival, came about through the intervention of the mother of Natalie Lauterstein, another talented student who went to New York in 1935 and danced two seasons with Balanchine's American Ballet at the Met. Mrs. Lauterstein had introduced Willam to Jacques Gershkovitch, the conductor of Portland's Junior Symphony. Gershkovitch claimed to have toured with Pavlova and was to have a significant influence on Reed's career; he later suggested to Christensen that *Coppélia* would be an ideal vehicle for her. On this occasion, he suggested they perform selections from *The Nutcracker* in celebration of the coronation of the Rose Festival queen. Gershkovitch was familiar with Tchaikovsky's score and Willam set to work creating dances for the ballet's second-act divertissements: the Russian trepak, Arabian coffee, Chinese tea, the Waltz of the Flowers, and the Mirlitons reed pipes. These were group dances with large casts (publicity claimed there were more than 100 dancers in the company) with one pas de deux for Willam and Reed, as "Sugar Plum Fairy, Queen of Jam Mountain." The Waltz of the Flowers closed the show; the dancers wore costumes appliquéd with images of American Beauty roses, the symbol of the city.

A group photograph taken at the time shows Willam in a vaguely military tunic and Reed in what looks to be more a tunic than a tutu, a leafy ruffle around her neck and a headpiece that somewhat resembles Napoleon's hat. Asked years later by a New York journalist what her most thrilling experience had been, Reed cited this *Nutcracker* because it was her first performance with a symphony orchestra.

Reed had been studying dance and performing for almost eleven years without ever seeing a professional ballet company (although she had read Tamara Karsavina's evocative and informative memoir *Theatre Street*) when the Ballets Russes de Monte Carlo came to town in January 1935. The 19-year-old saw her first live performance, mostly from the wings of the Civic Auditorium, since she and Lauterstein were supernumeraries in Massine's *La Boutique Fantasque*. Reed tells the story in a filmed interview done by her son and daughter-in-law, Reed and Maren Erskine, in 1997.

Because they were small, Reed, who was just over five feet tall, and Lauterstein, who Reed remembered as tiny, were cast as children in the Russian family, shopping on Christmas Eve in the "fantastic" toy store. Alexandra Danilova was the Fairy Doll, and the two students were directed to stand on either side of her, in an admiring pose, and, on a musical cue, lift one of her impeccable legs. Neither had ever seen the ballet and they didn't know the Rossini-Respighi score. Anxious not to make a mistake, and well ahead of their cue, they "started tugging. The leg wouldn't budge. [When the cue finally came,] of course the leg went right up."[46]

Danilova's influence on Reed was profound. "[She] was my first real inspiration," she told Tobias. "She was so alive and so—she just projected vitality and more than any of them she stood out in my mind. That and her beautiful feet and legs. . . . then I *knew*. You see, before I had been dancing, but when I saw [her dance] then I knew it was ballet that I wanted to do."[47]

It wasn't Danilova that influenced Willam so much as the repertory in which Danilova danced—the one-act story ballets of Léonide Massine, David Lichine, and Michel Fokine and their focus on characterization, narrative, and the dancers' personalities. Willam's experience as a vaudeville performer whose first priority was to entertain an audience of ordinary people and the Ballets Russes's approach of presenting such eminently accessible and audience-pleasing ballets as *Boutique, Petrouchka, Gaîté Parisienne,* and *Graduation Ball* provided a model for his choreography and artistic direction. For the first Visitor's Night of ballet excerpts, Willam choreographed bits of the Dance of the Hours from *La Gioconda.* For a 1935 school performance, he staged a version of *Les Sylphides* that he called *Chopiniana* (when it was restaged in San Francisco it was titled *Chopinade*); in it, he featured Reed and Irwin, his most gifted students. Fokine's solos were not included; Willam replaced them with group dances for his pupils, making it a recital piece.

Gershkovitch suggested *Coppélia* for the 1935 Rose Festival celebration. Willam had seen it performed in San Francisco in Anna Pavlova's one-act version during one of her American tours. Gershkovitch thought it would make a good showcase for Reed, as indeed it did, both in the one-act distillation, in which Reed danced Willam's reconceived title role and Lauterstein danced the role of Swanhilda, and in the complete ballet that Willam staged in 1939 in San Francisco. It was the San Francisco Opera Ballet's first independent production in the War Memorial Opera House; Reed was Swanhilda and Willam was her Frantz.

Willam may have claimed that he had Russian training (and he did take class with Fokine in New York, which he said changed his approach to ballet technique), but he had a very pragmatic (arguably American) attitude toward staging the classics. He scaled them down for practical reasons, tailoring roles to his dancers' capabilities (in his first *Coppélia* the doll's role was expanded as a vehicle for Reed), and adjusting their plots for the same reason. In program notes and advance publicity Willam was careful to focus on audience education; for the one-act *Coppélia* he managed to whip up enough excitement for this abbreviated rendition of an evening-length classic that ticket sales were so good a second performance was added.

Willam's younger brothers Lew and Harold and other family members were present for these concerts, and, later in the summer, they went with the student company to Seattle, where they participated in a performance at the Moore Theatre, adding parts of their vaudeville act to a bill that included *Coppélia*. They also taught in Willam's school, which he renamed the William F. Christensen Ballet School in the fall of 1935.

Willam shrewdly allied himself with the most prominent people in the cities where he established ballet companies—Portland, San Francisco, and Salt Lake City. But he could also be ruthless. For the Moore Theatre performance, he shunned Gershkovitch as conductor in favor of the assistant conductor of the more prestigious Portland Symphony. It was a smart move; two months later he was asked to perform at a benefit with the orchestra, which garnered him considerable backing from symphony supporters.

Good notices in Seattle certainly helped as well, especially reviews of Reed's performances. "Janet Reed [is] a danseuse whose presentations are marked by a joy in dancing which is more than merely apparent. *Coppélia* is a rare combination of technical and creative excellence," wrote one reviewer, adding that this was "ballet as entertainment, not just proof of technical ability."

That was a pretty good summation of Willam's philosophy at the time, and, except for the use of the Ballets Russes de Monte Carlo as his model, it wasn't all that different from Kirstein's philosophy for Ballet Caravan. And while Kirstein vocally and at times angrily eschewed the Old World flavor of the Ballets Russes repertory, ballets such as Dollar's *Promenade* and his 1939 *Air and Variations* were a definite link to the European tradition. Kirstein programmed them to warm up audiences for Loring's *Yankee Clipper* and Lew Christensen's *Filling Station*. In stark contrast to the modern composers his younger brother was using for those ballets (Bowles and

Thomson, respectively), Willam, working on the West Coast, spent two years creating a repertory for his student company that was heavily flavored with Spanish paprika and Viennese *schlag*, as was the music. (He later took much of this repertory to San Francisco.) As a librettist, however, he had none of Kirstein's literary skills or sophistication, which may be why, looking back on it, some of the dancers judged the narrative to be on the corny side.[48] It's fair to say that nobody ever accused Kirstein of being corny.

The program for a Willam Christensen concert in early 1936 included three demi-caractère ballets with different national themes, the costumes largely created by the mothers of his students (as still happens in regional ballet schools). The plots were easy to follow. *Les Visions de Massenet*, for example, featured the choreographer as the composer and lead male dancer, performing with company members portraying various musical instruments, their quite smashing Art Deco headdresses signaling to the audience which instrument in particular an individual dancer was. The next ballet took the dancers to Spain; Reed and Martin alternated as a ballerina whose dancing is so distracting it breaks up a "fight" between two jealous ladies in a café. The music was Rimsky-Korsakov's *Capriccio Espagnol*. *Rumanian Wedding Festival* set to George Enesco's eminently danceable *Rumanian Rhapsody* closed this program and, according to dance historian Debra Hickenlooper Sowell's account, seems to have included every sentimental dance cliché known to humankind. "All three works were populated with broadly drawn figures and depended upon Willam's ability to establish characterization through movement."[49]

That ability, and his talent for passing it on, served Reed well, even when she was dancing in Balanchine's so-called abstract ballets. "I've never believed that a human being on stage can be abstract," she told writer Mindy Aloff in 1978. "When you get people on stage they're already implying motivation. It's especially interesting and subtle in Balanchine's ballets. . . . When he says that he doesn't want acting in a ballet, he's talking about layered-on or ham acting. In truth, everything that is going on inside you affects movement, even what you had for dinner. It's a matter of body and mind. Sometimes the music gives you the quality and sometimes the character you are portraying, but the expression must still come out of the *movement*."[50]

By 1936, Willam had established Portland's first ballet company and had a roster of competent to extremely talented men and women that included Reed, Irwin, Lauterstein, Martin (who was still in high school), Earl Riggins, Fred Staver, and Mary Carruthers (who would go on to dance with Ballet Theatre). Some Willam had trained himself; others had been sent to him by his uncle, who was teaching in Salt Lake City. Never reticent about beating his own drum, Willam sent out press releases announcing that within the next year he would have a company "equal to any ballet in the country."[51] At the time, such an achievement was not outside the realm of possibility. His chief competition, of course, was de Basil's Ballets Russes, which had already had two successful American tours by 1936. Willam decided that he, too, would tour, and he hired a tour manager.

However, bookings were not forthcoming and instead, in August 1937, Willam headed south to San Francisco to take over the directorship of the Oakland branch of the San Francisco Opera Ballet School, bringing with him his repertory of ballets and his most talented students, packed into a caravan of cars. Through his connections in Portland's classical music world, Willam had learned that Adolph Bolm's contract as ballet master of the San Francisco Opera was not being renewed and that Serge Oukrainsky would replace him temporarily. Willam's students auditioned for the Russian, who accepted them, although he wanted them to "Russianize" their names. Martin, who had dropped out of high school, and Reed, who was finally going to be paid for dancing and expand her repertory of American "firsts," declined; they thought it was kind of silly. Needless to say, they were not paid well. They earned $25 a week during the opera season and when on tour. The women had to buy their own pointe shoes, which they made durable by painting them with shellac. However, two people helped the impoverished dancers in very important ways. One was the stage doorman at the opera house, who kept doughnuts and pastries on hand for them when they came to rehearsals and, according to Martin, for a time permitted Harold Lang to camp out in a backstage area when he was too broke to pay rent.[52] The other was their landlady, Madeleine Carlton, who rented them rooms in her apartment, which was located near the ballet studios. She helped them in every way she could, accepting late rent payments and on a crucial occasion for Reed, lending her the train fare to New York, when Loring offered her a contract as a principal dancer with his newly formed (and short-lived) Dance Players.

It was a hand-to-mouth existence. Between opera performances, 21-year-old Reed, who was so small she looked no more than 14, earned money teaching children to dance, just as she had in Portland, dressing in the most sophisticated way she could in order to convince their parents that she was a genuine grown-up who could be trusted to teach them well. At the same time, Willam was rehearsing the dancers in his Portland repertory. Very soon after his arrival in San Francisco, he staged his first concert for the ballet and then took the company on its first California tour.

"We toured around the Bay Area by bus," Reed wrote. "The men in the company hung curtains and installed lighting equipment, and the women took care of the wardrobe. Eventually we were able to hire a wardrobe woman and a stagehand, and we were accompanied by two wonderful pianists."[53] The following year, when the Opera Ballet was reorganized and Willam was appointed the ballet master in place of Oukrainsky, he finally got his wish for an extensive tour. The *New York Times* announced that this was the first time a western ballet company would support itself through western touring. Right after the fall opera season concluded, they embarked for the Pacific Northwest, dancing in cities and towns where ballet had never before been seen.

"The place I particularly remember was Burns, Oregon," Reed wrote. "The streets were not paved; there were wooden sidewalks. The theater, if you could call it that, had the smallest stage I had ever seen. Our local sponsor was a Catholic priest, who wore a ten-gallon hat and cowboy boots. He had the most piercing blue eyes that looked as though they were used to looking great distances."[54] The company, made up of the Portland contingent and dancers who had worked first under Adolph Bolm and then under Oukrainsky, went as far as Seattle and Vancouver, British Columbia, performing repertory programs of short ballets. Most of the ballets were Willam's, but some programs contained Lew's *Encounter,* which he had created on Ballet Caravan in 1937.

The following year, Willam created a one-act version of *Romeo and Juliet* to the Tchaikovsky score, which premiered in Sacramento in March and in San Francisco in April. A photograph of Reed in costume as Juliet shows the flexible upper body of a modern dancer. Her feet nevertheless are firmly placed on pointe, as, arm raised over her head, she curves over to the side. She looks young and vulnerable, as befits the role, and despite her vaguely Renaissance costume, she looks like the American girl that she was. Audiences and critics loved her as usual, and Reed had the opportunity to develop her range as a dramatic dancer.

Romeo and Juliet remained in the company's repertory for some time, and, in 1939, Willam revisited *Coppélia* in the Opera Ballet's first evening-length production to be mounted on the opera house stage. For the opera lovers, *I Pagliacci* rounded out the evening. Reed, of course, had already danced in one version of *Coppélia* in Portland, the role of the doll expanded for her benefit. This time she danced Swanhilda, the feisty village girl. It was a role that typecast her as a soubrette for the rest of her career. Much to her amusement, members of San Francisco's Russian community told her that she looked extremely European in the ballet. She had never, at that point, been out of the Pacific Northwest.

As she told Tobias in 1978, she knew at the time that Danilova had danced the role but she had never seen her, or anyone else, perform it. "So it was my own interpretation. However, in San Francisco, there were many people who had seen it in Europe and said that I was very European. I had never been out of California and Oregon. But it's one of those things too where I saw pictures and coupled with Willam Christensen's choreography and his direction and my own imagination and pictures I'd seen of dancers I had this to build it on."[55]

In the fall of 1939, on tour in Seattle, where she danced Swanhilda in front of an audience that included members of Ballet Caravan, she met Bolender for the first time. Bolender never forgot the impression she made on him and his fellow dancers as Fred Danieli escorted her into a restaurant where they had gone for a post-rehearsal meal. "And some of us thought . . . God[,] Freddie's fast, he's already picked up a girl! And then later one of the dancers said . . . that must be Janet Reed[,] that famous redhead from the San Francisco Ballet, so it made sense, because it meant that Freddie hadn't actually been out just picking up girls but actually had met her probably through [Lew] Christensen, so we all made a big point of going to the table and saying, Hi Freddie, how are you?"[56] The "famous redhead" was already known to dancers on the East Coast, if not the public. In three years' time this performance in Seattle would take her to that coast as a member of Loring's Dance Players.

2

When Bolender and Reed met in that Seattle restaurant in 1939, she was the principal ballerina of San Francisco Opera Ballet. She had originated leading roles in most of Willam Christensen's ballets, including Juliet in his *Romeo and Juliet* and Swanhilda in *Coppélia*. In the tour diary he kept for Ballet Caravan's 1938 tour, Kirstein had admired her dancing and her red hair. West coast critics had praised her to the skies. Bolender was just beginning to get featured roles, but even in small parts he was frequently singled out by critics wherever Ballet Caravan toured.

Nevertheless, neither the critical acclaim nor her experience as a performer kept Reed from having the worst case of stage fright of her career when, as she took her place on stage as Swanhilda at the Moore Theatre on November 18, she realized that many of the Ballet Caravan dancers were sitting in the audience. *Coppélia* had already been responsible for giving her a bad attack of jitters when it opened in San Francisco. While the dancers had had several weeks of stage rehearsals before the premiere, the front curtain had been kept closed. On opening night, standing alone on stage while the curtain rose, she had a moment of sheer panic as she gazed out into the "shadowy cavern" of the opera house. The Ballet Caravan dancers were in attendance in Seattle because their run had ended and they had the night off before they hit the road again. They scared her almost as much as that "shadowy cavern."

She needn't have worried. The Seattle critics raved about her opening-night performance. "Janet Reed Wildly Applauded in Ballet," headlined Gil Brown's column in the *Seattle Star* the following Monday. "In red-headed Janet Reed," he stated, "the San Francisco Ballet has a prima ballerina as glamorously attractive as Nini Theilade, No. 1 beauty of the Ballet Russe and almost as sumptuous a dancer (and beauty) as Irina Baronova. . . . Miss

Reed's dancing of Swanhilda Saturday night seemed quite as competent as that of the Ballet Russe's Alicia Markova, and I can't even remember Pavlowa [sic] giving the role anything that Reed left out."[1]

Brown also gave other cast members high marks, including Willam Christensen, whose "leaps and entrechats . . . are superb to watch, tho he is perhaps a shade less fine as a dancer than his brother . . . Lew Christensen of the Ballet Caravan."[2]

The Seattle appearance was part of the most extensive travels the company had undertaken. The 1939–1940 tour lasted three and a half months with a four-week intermission back in San Francisco to celebrate the holidays, rehearse, and recharge their batteries before heading to the Southwest and Midwest. Immediately after *Coppélia*'s San Francisco premiere, twenty-seven dancers, two pianists, a wardrobe mistress, a stage manager, and two other non-dancers (one to sell the company's first souvenir program, which featured Reed on the cover) boarded a chartered Greyhound bus. Several productions had been refurbished with new sets and costumes, and *Coppélia* was the centerpiece of the tour.

With the exception of *Impromptu, Chopinade,* and *Romeo and Juliet,* the repertory was a lighthearted one, geared more toward entertainment than enlightenment, although it also contained Willam's first assay at Americana, called at various times *Red Tape, American Interlude,* and *And Now the Brides.* Christensen's biographer characterized the work as social satire and Jacqueline Martin, who danced in it, "awful." Judging from various reports and descriptions of the day, it was certainly no *Billy the Kid* or even *Filling Station,* although *Oregonian* music critic Hilmar Grondahl, writing of its world premiere in Portland's Mayfair Theater, called it a "balletic yarn, part and parcel of the American scene and the American sense of humor."[3] A program note proclaims the ballet to be about "the sometimes dull lives of we the people in America." The libretto was loosely based on Aristophanes' *Lysistrata,* transported to the United States of Franklin Delano Roosevelt's New Deal. As in *Filling Station,* which featured a truck drivers' tumbling act and a Keystone Cops chase, *American Interlude* borrowed from popular culture and vaudeville. Willam himself played for laughs as the town drunk whose unsuccessful attempts to light his cigar evidently brought down the house.

Reed, whose role in *And Now the Brides* had little significance compared with the roles of Juliet and Swanhilda, was the linchpin of the company, so much so that when a minor illness sidelined her for a day or two at the start of the second part of the tour, dancer Frederick Lee Staver wrote of her recovery that "we all breathed easier, so indispensable she is to the company both as a person and a dancer."[4]

With her small stature (on a publicity form some years later she said she was five foot, one and a quarter), pretty face, and the red hair she considered both a curse and a blessing, Reed looked like a dancer from central casting. She was, Bolender said, very good on pointe, and "capable of making the technique look proper, and the most entrancing personality on stage."[5] In Klamath Falls, Oregon, where the tour began, the critic for the *Klamath Falls News and Herald* said of her, "Reed, so admired on her appearance here before gives the part of Swanhilda something more than the conventional interpretation, for she is a superb dancer and a consummate actress and pantomimist."[6]

Then it was on to Portland, with some stops en route, where Mr. C, as the dancers called him, had chosen to premiere *American Interlude* in a matinee performance at the Mayfair Theater on November 17, a wise decision, since he and many of the dancers already had a well-established reputation in the city. Grondahl gave rather short shrift to the evening's program, which included the three-act *Coppélia, In Vienna,* and *Ballet Impromptu,* all of which had been seen before in less polished versions when Christensen and many of the company members were still based in Portland. He did mention his pleasure in watching "some of this company's principal dancers rise from student efforts to an eminence of artistic consequence."[7]

From Seattle, the company went north to Vancouver and Victoria in British Columbia and then doubled back to Oregon. In Baker, a small town close to the Idaho border, Reed started a letter to her mother in a clear, legible hand, describing the highs and lows of being on the road, including the encounter with Ballet Caravan:

Dear Mother,

Just arrived in Baker after riding all day from Seattle. Haven't danced since I left Vancouver. I'm really having too much fun[;] this is more like a vacation than a tour. We had a terrible orchestra in Victoria. The cellist went mad during the performance. It seems he had been shell shocked in [World War I]. The whole orchestra was tight! [meaning drunk] We got on the boat after the performance to go to Vancouver and Mary [probably Carruthers] and I had a stateroom so small that when we got our bags in *we* couldn't get in, then the orchestra fellows continued their party next door but we were so tired it didn't make any difference. We stayed in a beautiful hotel in Vancouver. I had turkey Thanksgiving but it wasn't Thanksgiving there. It was just another day. Met lots of interesting people. My write-ups have been marvelous all the way.

Ballet Caravan was at Morris Hotel while we were, so they saw our performance. Lew came backstage and said that I was the greatest ballerina in America today. That's all!! But that is something coming from him, especially when his girl friend Gisella Caccialanza is supposed to be such a wonderful dancer."[8]

Several days later, the company was in Utah, Christensen's home state. In Salt Lake City, the writer for the *Deseret News* provided what must have been heartwarming validation for his endeavor: "For those who believe in the American artists' right to a place in the sun, the San Francisco Opera supplies overwhelming justification."[9] The company went on to smaller towns in Utah and Idaho, ending the first part of the tour in early December in Reno, where, according to Staver, the dancers couldn't resist having a flutter at the gambling tables and slot machines. Fortunately, they didn't lose much of their tour pay, which they would need to live on during the four-week break in San Francisco. While they were in rehearsal for much of that time, pay when they were not on tour or performing in the opera house was limited or nonexistent. These were the days before dancers joined unions and decades before they were so bold as to go on strike.

The holidays over, and a new year begun, San Francisco Opera Ballet headed for the warmth of southern California and performances in Long Beach, El Centro, and Ontario. Then the company wended its way across the country, stopping in many of the same cities as Ballet Caravan had; Chicago was their easternmost destination.

Both the climate and the reception in Tucson and Phoenix continued to be warm and the dancers had every reason to expect balmy temperatures in El Paso, Texas, their next stop. There they were in for a chilly surprise: having arrived late at night after a long bus ride, the dancers awakened on a Sunday morning to find that a blizzard had covered the city in its first snowfall in three decades. When they danced, Reed recalled: "there were about ten people in the audience, but never mind; they got the best performance we could give."[10] Audiences were bigger as they traveled across Texas and then to Oklahoma City and Tulsa, performing a repertory that included *Coppélia* and *Bach Suite* (as *Ballet Impromptu* was now called), which Staver described as a "ballet chef d'oeuvre for the palates of the initiate," no doubt because it was plotless.[11] Audiences in general, Staver noted, responded positively to *Chopinade,* Christensen's reconfiguration of Fokine's *Sylphides.*

When *Coppélia* wasn't on the program, *Romeo and Juliet* was. Staver's description of Christensen's 21-minute compression of Shakespeare's five-act tragedy indicates that it worked well and that, moreover, Reed was just as gifted at tragedy as comedy. "The movement, closely correlated with the music, is styled to convey the feeling of jealousy and conflict. Only the adagio between the lovers affords relief, with its softly passionate eloquence, its vivid tenderness of appeal." He added that "[Reed] brought to [Juliet] an exquisite subtlety of delineation in strict accordance with the finest dramatic tradition."[12]

In Little Rock, the company enjoyed inaugurating a new auditorium that was better equipped than many of the professional venues they had been dancing in. Reed lost her temper in an interview for a human interest story that appeared in the *Arkansas Democrat* on February 2: "Do you know what irks me to distraction?" she demanded. "For people to come backstage after a performance and greet me with, My, what gorgeous hair you have! And then mention my dancing. After I've danced myself to exhaustion this is too much." Asked about her likes and dislikes, she emphasized how hard she worked, and, in response to a question about her love life (she was, after all, a stunningly pretty woman) said she had "no time for love or marriage. Not just yet. My career comes before everything and I want nothing to interfere."[13]

While Reed undeniably worked harder than most stevedores at whatever she was doing, that last statement was a little disingenuous. In San Francisco she had a number of male friends. One was quite wealthy and another gave her flying lessons long before she learned to drive a car. But, at this stage of her life—she was 23—dancing did indeed "come before everything."

They had a welcome break from the snow until they reached Cedar Rapids, Iowa, but from there to Chicago they were traveling through a full-fledged midwestern winter that made sightseeing from frost-covered bus windows difficult. Moreover, it's unlikely that they were equipped with sufficiently warm clothing. Nevertheless, following successful appearances in St. Louis and Milwaukee, they arrived in Chicago in the third week in February eager to show that dancers from the West Coast could perform classical ballet.

In that week, they performed in the city's Civic Opera House, which had an enormous stage and was sold to capacity. As usual, Reed was a hit: the critic for the *Chicago Tribune* called her "a roguish Swanhilda. Everything she did whether it seemed to classify as miming or dancing, increased the audience's understanding of the spoiled little beauty" (an odd description of the feisty peasant girl).[14] The reviewer for the *Daily News* dubbed her "an artist of the first rank."[15] Writing in the *Chicago Herald-American*, music critic Herman Devries created some music of his own: "These young people from the West are well-versed in their métier. They seem to enjoy their work and go about it with an élan and enthusiasm that project far over the footlights until one wonders at their stamina and strength."[16] Clearly they had succeeded in showing what dancers from the West Coast could do. In his tour log, Staver gave Christensen full credit for it:

> Nothing pertaining to the success of the ballets escaped his attention. Like a ghost he would move about backstage and was likely to materialize from any quarter at the most unforeseen times. Stage discipline was rigidly enforced. No performer was permitted to speak to another before his or her entrance. Through such practices the minds of everyone [were] kept focused upon the stage action from the wings.[17]

The return to San Francisco from Laramie, Wyoming, the final stop on the tour, was marked by "fair weather," Staver reported in his journal. He proclaimed that the company had grown as a result of their three months of barnstorming and, just as important, had found new audiences not only for themselves but for ballet itself.

Back in San Francisco, emboldened by the success of *Coppélia* and the company's first national tour, Willam Christensen began work on a full production of *Swan Lake,* another staple of the nineteenth-century classical repertory that he—and most Americans—had never seen, although de Basil's Ballets Russes had toured with a truncated version of the second, "white" act. Clearly he was confident in the ability of his dancers to sustain an evening-length, four-act ballet. In contrast to Kirstein, who had admonished his countrymen not to compete with the Russians on their own ground, Willam was eager to rise above the achievements of Adolph Bolm and Serge Oukrainsky, the two Russians he had succeeded as director of the San Francisco Opera Ballet, who had wanted the American dancers to Russianize their names.

He was also determined to prove that he could render an authentically American version of a ballet that was considered the epitome of Russian soul. Since this was as much due to Tchaikovsky's lushly operatic music as the ballet itself and 1940 was the centenary of the composer's birth, what better way to celebrate than with a new, New World production of his first, groundbreaking ballet score?

Unfortunately, the director of the San Francisco Opera didn't see it that way. In 1940, the ballet company was not the autonomous organization it became after World War II, and unless the dancers were needed for an interlude in *Faust* or *Aida,* it was definitely not a priority for him. Moreover, Willam wanted to present the ballet in the Opera House before the regular opera season officially began. The director refused the necessary permission, so Christensen, who could be both reckless and ruthless in pursuing his dreams, went over his head to the chair of the board of trustees, requesting a two-week run and promising to "take full artistic and financial responsibility." The board chair, after some hesitation, gave him the go-ahead, and Willam, who in his Portland years had learned how to make maximum use of community resources, went straight to people he had been cultivating in San Francisco's considerable Russian colony. These were White Russians, members of the former ruling class who had fled the 1917 Bolshevik Revolution and landed, famously, in Paris, and less famously in San Francisco and elsewhere around the world. They became a tremendous resource for Christensen both artistically and financially. They sponsored the production and were equally generous in sharing their memories of the Petipa-Ivanov staging in 1895.

"When I decided to do *Swan Lake,*" Willam said at a conference in 1988, "I picked everyone's brains. First, I read everything I could find on the ballet, and then I got San Francisco's large colony of Russian émigrés to help me. They would say, 'So-and-so goes here, and so-and-so goes there,' and I would work it out choreographically with the music. If I had not been a musician, I would never have dared to stage such a large production. The main thing I wanted was the right style and the placement of the dancers."[18]

In fact, the Russians gave him much more than that. Two of them wrote the libretto. Another two designed the nostalgic scenery and built it themselves to save money. (This later turned out to be a prime example of the perils of penny-pinching.) The Tchaikovsky Centennial Committee, which was the official sponsoring organization, not only underwrote the production but also took care of publicity and advertising. This freed Willam to combine Russian reminiscences of style and placement, his own knowledge of the music, and the story itself, and, Reed remembered, "just put it together."[19]

Willam was steadfastly grateful to the Russians for their help, but he did maintain artistic control of the choreography and the casting. Like many who came after him in the United States and around the world, he was not afraid to tailor tradition, in this instance the 1895 Petipa-Ivanov *Swan Lake,* nipping here, tucking there, adding and subtracting in ways that would maximize the individual talents of the dancers and minimize the limitations imposed by the company's small size.

As had been done in the earliest productions, he cast different dancers as Odette and Odile, making dark-haired Jacqueline Martin, whose five-foot-five-inch height made her one of the tallest women in the company, the first American Odette, and Reed, her physical opposite, the first Odile. Martin remembered a considerable amount of byplay between her boss and the Russians, who were present in the studio during rehearsals. Some of them wanted her to perform both roles because she looked like a classical ballerina—tall, dark-haired, and with beautiful line, as a Klamath Falls critic pointed out in 1938, when the company was there on tour. However, in a number of interviews over the years, Reed said she danced Odile because she could do the requisite thirty-two *fouettés* in the third act. She also remembered the Russians in the studio and how seriously they took the bravura turn: "They insisted it was the high point of the third act. Technically I did not have a problem with [them]—I was strong on beats and turns. In order to be sure that I could do thirty-two on the stage, I always did sixty-four in the studio, so there would be no fumbling in performance."[20]

The *fouettés* were not exactly the only reason for the casting; Martin has said that she could do them, too, and in fact did, after Reed sprained her ankle before the Pacific Northwest tour that followed the ballet's première. More important, virtually every ballet Willam created for both the Portland company and the San Francisco company contained a starring role for

Reed. She was as much his muse as Marie-Jeanne was Balanchine's, and she was an audience favorite and a box-office draw. He had every reason to cast her as Odile, von Rothbart's seductive daughter, who whips Siegfried into shape with every *fouetté*, sealing his sad fate. And as Reed astutely pointed out years later, this particular casting changed the interpretation because the dancers were physically so different. Reed was costumed differently, too: she wore a gold-colored tutu to define her as Rothbart's daughter, so it was the red-headed woman of American blues who made a fool out of Siegfried, not the traditional black swan princess pretending to be Odette. The aristocratic Prince Siegfried thus becomes an easily distracted, testosterone-driven, post-adolescent male and not the tragic hero of European Romantic tradition. In Christensen's version of the story, Siegfried dies and Odette remains a swan.

Reed and Martin may have been onstage rivals for Siegfried's attention and both loved dancing with Lew Christensen, who under Balanchine's tutelage had become a superb partner, but they had been friends since they first met at Christensen's Portland school. They shared living quarters and much else as long as they were in San Francisco. Both were rehearsed in the dual role and Martin did end up dancing it multiple times when Reed sprained her ankle. Reed danced the White Swan pas de deux at a number of benefits in San Francisco and she gave one performance of both roles at the Moore Theatre in Seattle.

Not only did the San Francisco Russians have their fingerprints all over this first American *Swan Lake* but Willam's brothers also played a role: Lew quite literally as Siegfried, but also as the conveyor of Balanchine's compressed, experimental staging of the ballet for the Hollywood film *I Was an Adventuress*, in which he had partnered Vera Zorina.

Like Lew, Harold Christensen was in San Francisco following the dissolution of Ballet Caravan, performing with the company and assisting in the rehearsal studio. "We had been told that in the Russian version [in the third act ballroom scene] the six brides dance first by themselves and then with Siegfried. But we decided to do it differently. One of the six gals would come out. Siegfried would bow to her very courteously, dance with her, but then he would turn around to find there's another gal, also waiting. And pretty soon there's another one and another one and another. They're all swarming like bees around him. In other words, the *pas de sept* ended up like a series of short pas de deux."[21] This sounds a good deal more like

American barn dancing when there aren't enough men to go around than the dances of the European courts, and in practical terms it gave some of the corps members a moment in the spotlight.

After months of rehearsal, *Swan Lake* opened at the opera house on September 25, 1940. Prince and Princess Vasili Romanoff, who headed the Tchaikovsky Centennial Committee of San Francisco, gave the production an "imperial" seal. Critics, such as Frankenstein of the *Chronicle*, who had been skeptical of Willam's abilities to stage a great classic he had never seen, responded positively. Calling the production the "surprise of the season," his colleague at the *San Francisco Call-Bulletin* wrote that "the music was Russian and the dancing was in the Russian idiom, but the figurants were as American as a turkey dinner. And what a performance they turned in, especially the mercurial Janet Reed and Lew Christensen, as nimble as a young Nijinsky and far more personable. If San Francisco Ballet can sustain the high order of artistry set last night at the Opera House we are independent of Messrs. S. Hurok and others who make a great ballyhoo about bringing the original 'Russian' classics to the wild west."[22]

Once again the San Francisco Opera Ballet hit the road, taking a Pacific Northwest tour before Christmas in which they performed both *Coppélia* and *Swan Lake* and, as they had the previous year, heading for the middle of the country after a holiday and rehearsal break. Most of their audiences were seeing *Swan Lake* in its entirety for the first time and they were eager to do so. In Seattle, where they performed at the end of November, the Moore Theatre had to turn hundreds away for lack of space. Richard Hays, writing for the *Seattle Times*, announced that "Russia must look to its ballet or America will take it away, and so completely that only tradition will remain."[23]

In January 1941, the company was on the road again, traveling through the Midwest and as far east as Detroit. While *Coppélia* was in the tour repertory at least in part as a more suitable ballet for children than *Swan Lake*, it was fortunate indeed that Christensen had programmed it because the *Swan Lake* backdrops, which had been executed by inexperienced scenic designers rather than professional union painters who knew something about the exigencies of touring, soon began to self-destruct, the paint flaking and the canvas wrinkling when folded up after a performance.

The reviews were favorable in cities where audiences were seeing the program-length ballet for the first time. Critics were clearly more interested in the dancing than in the mise-en-scène. In Kansas City, for example, one writer announced that Reed "joins the company of great artists which America is producing," and in Detroit, where they gave a single performance accompanied by two pianos, a reviewer for the *Detroit News* called her a *ballerina assoluta* and predicted that she would go far and fare wondrously in show business if her heart does not remain faithful to ballet for she has these striking attributes: "an extraordinary talent, a sense of unusual good looks, an electric charge quickening sort of personality," and of course, red hair.[24]

The company returned to San Francisco in the spring and opened an independent season of dance with *Swan Lake*. The *Chronicle*'s Frankenstein couldn't get enough of Reed, Martin, and Norman Thompson, who had replaced Lew Christensen as Siegfried when the latter left the tour to choreograph a musical in New York: "While Miss Reed's range of technique and expression is practically unlimited, she reaches a particularly sensational height when she [does] several thousand fouettés to the enormous applause of the audience." However, the house was not filled in the same way it had been for performances by the Ballets Russes earlier in the season, causing a critic for the *San Francisco News* to comment, "This city has one of the best looking and best dancing ballets on the American stage today. Critics to the north, south, and east have so acclaimed it. Let it no longer be the prophet without honor in its own city."[25]

Meanwhile, although the first part of Ballet Caravan's 1939 tour had finished in early spring, Bolender and the rest of the dancers were still employed to rehearse for appearances in May with the American Lyric Theater, an organization that, like Kirstein's, had been established to promote American performing arts. In mid-May, they warmed up the audience with *Filling Station,* then premiered Douglas Moore's opera *The Devil and Daniel Webster.* Later in the month, they danced *Billy the Kid* for the first time in New York, along with *Air and Variations* and *Pocahontas*, accompanied by a full orchestra, led by Fritz Kitzinger, the former conductor of the Berlin Staatsoper. In urban New York, *Billy* was a hit, just as it had been in rural San Angelo, Texas, much to Kirstein's surprise at the time: he had worried that working ranchers would sneer at the dramatization of their daily lives. Instead, they were glad to see a ballet with Western themes.

In New York, John Martin, who was not on the whole an admirer of classical ballet at this time, dismissed the first two ballets of the evening "as only middling at best. . . . But *Billy the Kid,* with music by Aaron Copland, is a perfectly delightful piece of work. More than that, it falls inescapably into that category which, in spite of the implications of the term, must be called significant. For one thing, it opens up new possibilities of theatre dancing, and for another, it makes doubly certain the conviction that in [choreographer Eugene] Loring the American dance has a young creative talent of genuine importance." Summing it up, he said, "Here is a choreography with blood in its veins, a keen imagination and a fine sense of theatre."[26]

After a summer layoff, during which Bolender returned to Canton for a visit and then returned to New York to take classes and teach, Ballet Caravan embarked on its last cross-country tour. In ten weeks, they went as far south as Los Angeles. There were now twenty-five dancers in the company, and by the time they returned to New York in December, Loring had left for the new Ballet Theatre and been replaced by Michael Kidd. Two new ballets had been taken into the repertory, his *City Portrait* (in which Bolender had performed a prominent role and in which Reed would later appear with Dance Players) and Lew Christensen's *Charade,* a romp of a ballet.

When Ballet Caravan performed *Charade* in New York at a Holiday Dance Festival that Frances Hawkins had put together and that included presentations by Martha Graham and the Korean dancer Sai Shoki, Martin compared it somewhat less than favorably to *Filling Station,* giving high marks, however, to Gisella Caccialanza, who performed in both.[27] *Dance Magazine* critic Anatole Chujoy felt that while the company was dancing better than ever, choreographically it was becoming less interesting. (He didn't like *City Portrait,* which, he speculated, was the result of Kirstein's boredom and frustration.)

More to the point, the Caravan and its constant tours were a drain on Kirstein's personal resources, which were far from unlimited. They also took a physical toll on both him and the dancers. He was, moreover, an uneasy impresario; all his life he worried (sometimes to the point of panic) about every performance and how critics and audiences would receive it. Nevertheless, he felt responsible for the dancers, and when industrial designer Walter Dorwin Teague of the Ford Motor Company came to him to request a theatrical spectacle in the service of selling Ford's 1940–1941 model cars at the 500-seat theater in the corporation's pavilion at the New York World's Fair, he could not bring himself to refuse. The fair, which had opened in April 1939, had two six-month seasons; it closed for good at the end of October 1940. Kirstein, and no doubt many others, was skeptical about the efficacy of such an international exposition in the same years that Hitler invaded five countries, including France. However, dancing in the Ford pavilion's quite elegant and well-equipped theater, which had a turntable stage, more than adequate dressing rooms, and a place where the dancers could eat between performances, served to postpone penury and unemployment for forty-two dancers from Ballet Caravan, Ballet Theatre, and the School of American Ballet.

Bolender had a principal role and Nicholas Magallanes his first paid job in *A Thousand Times Neigh*, which Dollar choreographed to a jazzy score by Tom Bennett, staff composer for NBC radio. The thrust of the piece was that far from being made obsolete by the automobile, the horse would become a beast of leisure, no longer needed to pull carriages, or worse yet, plows, but still very much a performer and athlete. Horses have figured in dance for centuries; there were horse ballets at the court of Louis XIV, and the Viennese Lipizzaners still put on a good show on several continents. The equine star of *A Thousand Times Neigh* was a two-man horse that performed a sort of soft shoe and, at one point, sat down in so feline a manner you expected it to wash its face with one hoof.

While Kirstein dismissed the work as commercial fluff and hardly a contribution to ballet history, Chujoy dubbed it "imaginative, amusing and in good taste."[28] No one knows if it sold any cars, but it gave a half-year of job security to the dancers, even if it was (appropriately enough) assembly-line work. The ballet ran eighteen minutes and was performed twelve times a day, on the hour; each company member performed six times a day, since there were two shifts. It is estimated that two million people had an opportunity to see Dollar performing triple pirouettes and Marie-Jeanne speeding her way through multiple entrechats, all in the service of commerce and, not incidentally, keeping dancers housed, fed and in shape.

A Thousand Times Neigh was not the only employment opportunity for dancers at the 1940 fair; seventy-five were hired to participate in *American Jubilee*, billed as a "spectacular musical panorama of American history," for which Catherine Littlefield was commissioned to choreograph five dance numbers. This extravaganza was performed outdoors on an enormous stage with a concrete floor, a common physical trial for dancers.

By the time Littlefield made *American Jubilee*, she was an experienced choreographer, having created dances for two opera companies in Philadelphia and the Philadelphia Civic Ballet. She had also choreographed the stage shows of the prestigious Roxy Movie Theater in New York City, which frequently had live performances before film showings. In 1932, when she was 27, she created a dance for a ballet symphony by Carlos Chavez titled *H. P. (Horse Power)* that was presented at the Philadelphia Metropolitan Opera House, the first piece of choreography with her name on it; Diego Rivera designed the sets and Leopold Stokowski conducted the orchestra. *H. P.* was intended to show the commercial interdependence of Mexico and the United States. While no manufacturer was named, it could easily have been about the Ford Motor Company's dependence on Mexican minerals to make cars.

Littlefield had trained in classical ballet in Paris and New York and with her mother, Caroline, who founded the Littlefield School of Ballet in Philadelphia in 1908, when Catherine was 3. In the 1920s, students were taken regularly to Paris as part of the school's summer program, not only to study ballet with European and Russian teachers but also to soak up continental culture. On one of those trips, Catherine and her younger sister, Dorothie, met Balanchine. When Balanchine opened the School of American Ballet in 1934, he recruited students from the Littlefield School for his first American company. He hired Dorothie to head the school's junior division. A year later, in 1935, Catherine, who at 15 made her professional debut in a Ziegfeld musical on Broadway, founded the Littlefield Ballet Company; her extremely capable mother was the director. However, Catherine, a savvy programmer, did not start making ballets with American themes until after her first season, during which she established the company's classical foundation with her own versions of *The Fairy Doll, The Snow Queen,* and the work she regarded as her best, *Daphnis and Chloe,* set to the same Ravel score Fokine had used for the Diaghilev company.

For her second season at Philadelphia's Academy of Music, she choreographed an evening-length *Sleeping Beauty;* she was the first American choreographer to do so. The lavish production was funded with a $10,000 gift from Philip Leidy, a wealthy attorney Catherine had married in 1933. In the fifteen years of their marriage, Leidy underwrote the majority of Catherine's ballets. Littlefield's *Beauty* had a cast of ten dancers, most of whom were American, and eight hunting dogs for the "Vision" scene; it was accompanied by a full orchestra of eighty-five musicians. Littlefield was familiar with the Petipa choreography from her summer trips to Europe and studies in Paris with Lubov Egorova, who had danced Aurora in Diaghilev's 1921 production. While she made no effort to re-create Petipa's steps for the entire ballet, she did use them for the "Wedding Pas de Deux" in the third act. She also danced the lead role, "cleanly and classically," according to an anonymous music reviewer in *Time* magazine.[29] The reviewer, however, did not think highly of either the production or any other cast member.

Littlefield's *Beauty* was so expensive to mount that it had only six performances, but that and her first season gave the renamed Philadelphia Ballet credibility as a classical company. It also made enough profit to permit her to take the troupe on a European tour the following summer. This was the first American ballet company to perform in Europe. It was invited to unofficially represent the United States with a week's run at the Théâtre des Champs Élysées, in conjunction with the Paris Exposition of 1937. The tour continued in Brussels and The Hague and finished with three weeks in London. Audiences loved Littlefield's Americana ballets, particularly *Barn Dance* and *Terminal;* both had premiered in 1936. Her *Terminal* mixed classical technique and jazz dancing with physical comedy. It takes place in a railway station with a cast that consists of commuters, a Hollywood starlet, porters, shoeshine boys, and other American stock characters, similar to the characters in Lew Christensen's *Filling Station,* made in the same year.

Barn Dance had a score by David Guion, L. M. Gottschalk, and John Powell.[30] It was a series of vignettes that, according to one source, "are mainly—and exuberantly—danced . . . square dances, reels, rounds and other American community dances, broadened, strengthened and organized for theatrical effect while preserving their inherent form and spirit."[31] What little plot it had involved the return to the rural fold of a country girl gone wrong in the big city. Littlefield had considerable skill in tapping into an American ethos—city bad, country good—that she likely didn't share herself in order to make audience-pleasing ballets. Some of her titles were marvelous: *Café Society, Ladies' Better Dresses,* and *Let the Righteous Be Glad* were all works about Americans from various strata of American society. They were decidedly not peasants and dukes, swans and princesses. When British critic Arnold Haskell saw *Barn Dance* in London, he called it the first chapter in American ballet.[32]

For the bicycle ballet in *American Jubilee,* fifty women and twenty-five men, a mix of former Littlefield School students and dancers from Ballet Theatre, most of whom had never ridden a two-wheeler, were asked to do a great many stunts in a piece for which Littlefield evidently created the kind of group formations and floor patterns she would later make for skaters in several of Sonja Henie's ice shows.

Other dance sections of *American Jubilee* included a flag drill to represent the Teddy Roosevelt era, a waltz for the Civil War period, a "Tennessee Fish Fry" with a cakewalk (performed by the only solo dancer, Paul Haakon, who had danced with Pavlova and had been trained at the School of the Royal Danish Ballet), and a concluding number created around the upcoming presidential election, in which FDR made a controversial run for his third term.[33]

The fair closed at the end of October 1940, and once again dancers were scrambling for jobs so they could pay their rent. Opportunities had narrowed; Ballet Caravan no longer existed and Balanchine and his American Ballet (the only permutation of the Balanchine-Kirstein enterprise in which Bolender never danced) had been ejected from the Metropolitan Opera in 1938; the company folded shortly thereafter. Littlefield's Philadelphia Ballet, however, was still operating, and in January 1941, it embarked on an eight-week tour that took it to theaters and college auditoriums throughout the Midwest and the South. The tour ended in Washington, DC. The company roster was expanded to include Bolender, Nicholas Magallanes, and Zachary Solov. *Aurora's Wedding* was programmed and there was one performance of *Daphnis and Chloe.*

The tour was grueling. The company traveled mostly by bus; sometimes they traveled all night in order to reach the next town in time to warm up and perform both a matinee and an evening show. Frequently, Bolender would sit up with Littlefield and they would talk through the night. That made the exigencies of that particular tour a pleasure for a young Midwesterner who was thirsty for knowledge of the world. Littlefield was a sophisticated and witty woman and Bolender enjoyed her company very much. And because *Aurora's Wedding,* the third-act excerpt from Littlefield's *Sleeping Beauty,* was programmed on the tour, he received valuable experience in more traditional ballets than the Ballet Caravan repertory had offered.

They didn't always travel by bus. After the company's performances in Chicago, where it was well known from its stints as the Chicago Opera Ballet, they traveled by train to St. Louis and Oklahoma, where they had the pleasure of dancing in sold-out civic and college venues in several cities.

Because of Works Project Administration funding for accompaniment by the Oklahoma Symphony Orchestra, the company (which must have been exhausted by that point) rehearsed and remounted *Daphnis and Chloe,* which was not part of the original tour repertory.

Trains took them as far as Texas, where they shifted to Greyhound buses, which, following performances in several cities, took them to North Carolina. There, on February 27, the Page Auditorium at Duke University was filled to near capacity for a bill that included *Aurora's Wedding, Café Society,* and *Barn Dance.* According to one report, the dancers, far from being worn out by the exigencies of the tour, "radiate[d] the joy of living and physical perfection. . . . and more than justified their place on the Duke concert series."

The tour ended in Washington, DC, where the dancers received an ovation for their performance of their standard mixed bill. One critic, writing of *Café Society,* praised it as "the wittiest satire . . . in many a year. [It] was a study in expert exaggeration, with every accent overstressed. Yet all the time it was a sustained and varied exhibition of the dance that had every virtue of grace and technical resource." More important, perhaps, he assessed Catherine Littlefield's version of *Aurora's Wedding,* another version of which he had seen de Basil's Original Ballets Russes dance recently enough to be fresh in his mind, as "superior in choreography and performance quality."

The company returned to Philadelphia on March 9. Bolender returned to Canton for a brief visit before rehearsals started in New York at the end of the month for American Ballet Caravan's goodwill tour of South America. Magallanes, John Dunphy, Doug Coudy, and John Taras also joined the South American tour. Other male dancers in the Philadelphia Ballet were drafted into the army, and by the end of the year, the company had disbanded.

It's a wonder that Reed and Bolender didn't have a second serendipitous meeting somewhere in the United States in 1941, for San Francisco Opera Ballet and the Philadelphia company performed in many of the same places, including Chicago. Back in San Francisco, in the spring, Willam Christensen opened an independent season of dance with *Swan Lake,* but audiences were sparse.

Although *Swan Lake* had been given a new production, it is possible the San Francisco audience was getting bored with the company's basically one-man repertory. Additionally, the company tour manager was finding it increasingly difficult to market it on the road, and after finding Christensen resistant to the idea of commissioning other choreographers, he quit. Reed was definitely beginning to get tired of dancing the same things over and over; she was also feeling that there were not enough opportunities to perform. Through the dancer grapevine, specifically Lew Christensen, she had also been hearing about new developments on the East Coast, including "marvelous stories about Balanchine," and she was starting to feel curious.[34]

And restless. She began taking flying lessons with a beau who was a flight instructor with an eye toward possibly becoming a professional pilot, and, by her own account, was doing quite well. On Sunday, December 7, 1941, she went to the airfield expecting to make the solo flight that would qualify her for her pilot's license. World events put that particular plan on hold: the Japanese had bombed Pearl Harbor and all private airports on the Pacific coast were closed to civilian flying. "End of flying career," she said.[35]

It was also the end of her tenure with San Francisco Opera Ballet. At about the same time, she received a telegram from Loring inviting her to join Dance Players, the company he had formed to create ballets with American themes on American dancers. "I had a job if I could get there," she remembered. "I didn't have money for the train fare, but I had a wonderful landlady who believed in me. She went to her bank and borrowed a hundred dollars [and] I bought a coach fare ticket and rode for four days and three nights curled up in a seat [and] I was able to pay her back as soon as I started working."[36]

The prima ballerina of San Francisco Opera Ballet was, as she wrote, "starting all over again."[37] Her name was known by dancers, especially the Ballet Caravan dancers, and of course Lew Christensen had been friends with her since the early days of his brother's school in Portland. One summer, it is said, they were more than friends. Her anonymity in New York, which even then seems to have regarded itself as the epicenter of American arts, didn't bother her. Faithful to her pioneer roots, she said she "viewed it as a new adventure."[38]

Reed and Bolender would meet again, in New York, early in 1942, after American Ballet Caravan returned from its South American tour. They were to work together in several capacities in several companies for the next forty years, and their friendship endured until Reed's death fifty-eight years later.

3

At midnight on June 6, 1941, the *Argentina*, a large passenger ship owned by the Moore-McCormack Lines, chugged its way out of New York harbor, carrying Bolender, Balanchine, and thirty-five members of the newly constituted American Ballet Caravan. The company was primed to take South America by storm. It was headed first to Rio de Janeiro on a short-term mission for the U.S. government to counter Nazi propaganda in the region, but also, more significantly in the long term, to show that classical ballet was as viable a form of cultural expression in North America as it was in Europe and Russia. By the time they returned to New York on November 12, they had given over 100 performances in seven countries in venues ranging from European-style opera houses with raked stages to tatty movie theaters with splintered floors.

Also on board were 135 pieces of personal luggage and sixty-eight large trunks containing backdrops, props, lights, and costumes for thirteen ballets. (A fourteenth, Balanchine's *Fantasia Brasileira,* would be created on the tour.) Company personnel included conductor Emanuel Balaban, who would lead existing opera-house orchestras; pianists Trude Rittmann, Simon Sadoff, and James Doyle, who accompanied rehearsals and performances in smaller venues; tour manager Michael Rainer Horwitz; wardrobe mistress Eudokia Miranova; stage manager Douglas Coudy; technical director Jean Rosenthal; support staff (including a CPA) for Lincoln Kirstein, general director; someone Kirstein referred to as a "nanny" from the U.S. State Department; and, listed as a guest, the former Fidelma Cadmus, who Kirstein had recently married. Kirstein himself was not on board, having stayed behind in New York to finish up SAB business. He arrived in Rio by air a few days ahead of the ship.

"We were full of beans and wanted to get going," Bolender recalled sixty years later, although they hadn't a clue as to what to expect.[1] Bolender had not been out of the country before except for three days in Cuba as part of Ballet Caravan's last tour. That was the case for most of the company, except for those from the Littlefield company who had toured Europe. What they did know was that with an extensive repertoire and performances scheduled in every South American country except Paraguay, they had a lot of ground to cover and plenty of dancing to do, much of it under conditions that were daunting to say the least. In theory they knew it would not be easy. Accommodations would be less than luxurious and transportation schedules would be iffy (although how iffy they would turn out to be never occurred to anyone involved), and while the entire company had been vaccinated against every conceivable disease, including yellow fever, the threat of illness certainly was a concern. A Park Avenue doctor had issued instructions not to eat unwashed produce or ice cream or drink unboiled water or iced drinks.

State Department officials, Kirstein, and his assistants had made careful plans for getting all this personnel and luggage around the continent, but they were consistently stymied by bad weather, breakdowns of trains and buses, the exigencies of wartime travel, and bureaucratic hassles with the various customs and immigration officials. At times, it was extremely hard on the dancers, but they were young and adaptable and their excitement and curiosity about seeing new places and reaching new audiences gave them considerable resilience. The impact of this tour on Bolender was huge. The itch to travel lasted until the end of his life, when he considered his most significant achievement to be the roles he played in disseminating American ballet abroad as a dancer, a choreographer, a teacher, and a director, all of which he did worldwide with a passion bordering on religious fervor.

The threat of war was also in the air. Although the United States would not be officially involved for another six months, World War II was already well under way in Europe and Asia. German U-boats had begun attacking merchant ships in the Atlantic in July 1940. On September 16, Congress passed a national conscription law. Bolender, Lew Christensen (the ballet master and principal dancer), Kirstein, and several other men in the company had all been declared fit for service. Involvement in the war seemed inevitable, but the dancers were ready for adventure and glad to have a dancing job in the late days of the Great Depression.

"[It] was a wonderful experience," Bolender told an interviewer in 2002. "And it was a hellish tour because we went all the way down and around and up the west coast of South America. [We took] anything that had wheels or that was able to ride on water that didn't sink."[2] The nine-day trip to Rio was probably the easiest part of the tour. By the time they returned to the United States, they had indeed traveled in the conveyances Bolender described, but they had also traveled on foot and had flown through the Andes in a snowstorm. For those who had never flown before, this was considerably more unnerving than a possible U-boat attack. And practice drills on board the *Argentina* in case the Germans directed a torpedo at the ship were less than reassuring.

Staying in shape to perform had its challenges. "We used to walk the decks a great deal and dance, ballroom dance," Bolender recalled. "The trip was really quite smooth. We didn't have any really rough weather, [but] we all [were] a little bit anxiety-ridden at times because of the U-boats."[3] Bolender never sighted one himself, but some of his shipmates did, making the trip, he said, "a little hair-raising." Mary Jane Shea, who, like him, was from Canton and had also been a member of the New York World's Fair company, upped the emotional ante one night, standing on deck to look at the moon. "[It was] a marvelous night, beautiful sky and everything," Bolender recalled. "And then she said, dreamily, 'You know, it's just possible we might not make it.' A very dramatic character, she was."

Company class, which Christensen led, was not particularly useful. Some dancers got seasick, and, because the ship was never really still, it was difficult for them to get their balance and maintain it. "If you're in a fifth position and you're [in] *développé*," Bolender said, "you can be thrown, you feel the weight being shifted under you." Class therefore became considerably simplified. "It was just barre and jumps and I don't think we did any middle of the floor, [maybe] a few little *ronds de jambe,* anything that would work that we could control easily."

Fortunately, funding for a two-month rehearsal period before departure had been part of the arrangement Kirstein had worked out with Nelson Rockefeller, who President Roosevelt had appointed as coordinator of inter-American affairs. He headed the new United States Office for Coordination of Commercial and Cultural Relations between the American Republics at the State Department. The purpose was to revive FDR's faltering Good Neighbor Policy, which emphasized economic aid and cultural exchange rather than the political and military intervention of previous and later administrations. Because of the mutually beneficial friendship Kirstein and Rockefeller had forged in the early 1930s, when both were involved in the founding of New York's Museum of Modern Art, American Ballet Caravan was the first dance troupe to receive sponsorship from the United States government for anything, never mind touring. It was also the first North American ballet company to be seen on a continent where Anna Pavlova and Diaghilev's Ballets Russes had toured in the early part of the twentieth century and de Basil's company had toured more recently.

When Rockefeller was appointed, Kirstein had been quick to tell him that dance could easily cross language barriers, making it an ideal vehicle for cultural exchange. Collaboration with South American musicians and visual artists was part of Kirstein's mandate, as was recording South American music for the Library of Congress. Additionally, American Ballet Caravan's dancers, who were performing a varied repertoire with the energy and speed that was already characteristic of American classicism, would surely help counter any suggestion that North Americans were uncultured barbarians, upstarts whose efforts as artists were beneath the notice of the civilized world. And, not incidentally, Kirstein would be able to keep his eyes and ears open for the anti-American propaganda the Axis powers had been disseminating in the region for some time.

On April 12, 1941, Kirstein signed a contract that had actually taken effect in mid-March. It stipulated that Rockefeller's office would underwrite all expenses for a six-month tour of South America, including an eight-week rehearsal period (which became nine) for Balanchine and the dancers, while the company would pick up any deficit associated with the cost of production. The budget for the tour was $95,000, a substantial chunk from the agency's $3.5 million allocation.

On June 12, before he headed to Rio de Janeiro to prepare for the company's arrival there, Kirstein reported to Rockefeller what had been accomplished since March. "Our dancers," he wrote, "while unquestionably younger and less experienced than the Europeans, have been drawn from six American dancing organizations from here to California, and are representative, by their talent, training and appearance of the best in American dancing."[4] While most had come from the American Ballet and Ballet Caravan, others, such as John Dunphy, had danced with the Philadelphia Ballet. John Kriza was a guest artist, on leave from the newly founded Ballet Theatre, which had neither a home nor a regular season at that point. Others came from the Metropolitan Opera Ballet and the cast of *A Thousand Times Neigh*. Many, including Bolender, were to become the founding linchpins of New York City Ballet in 1948. Not everyone remained a professional dancer. Dunphy later gave up ballet for literature and Bolender for Truman Capote.

The four principals had all been with Ballet Caravan and Bolender knew them well. Lew Christensen and Gisella Caccialanza had recently married. Marie-Jeanne, one of the youngest company members, had trained at SAB and was Balanchine's first North American ballerina muse; her program biography stated that she was the inspiration for several choreographers and that she was considered to be North America's prima ballerina. Dollar was Marie-Jeanne's most consistent partner and, in Bolender's assessment, one of the finest classical dancers of his generation.

During the rehearsal period, which ended in three open dress rehearsals in late May at Hunter College, Balanchine choreographed *Concerto Barocco* and *Ballet Imperial* (later retitled *Tchaikovsky Piano Concerto No. 2*), in part to showcase Marie-Jeanne's fleet, precise technique. Eight hundred people who might be useful in creating advance press for the tour (including journalists from both Americas) were invited to the preview. The reception for *Apollon Musagète* (now *Apollo*) was disappointing, as, to a lesser degree, was the reception for *Pastorela*, a work based on a Mexican Indian nativity play that Rockefeller had commissioned with choreography by Christensen and music by Paul Bowles. Antony Tudor's *Time Table*, the British émigré's first ballet created in the United States, was also shown at Hunter College, as was Dollar's *Juke Box*, which, like *Barocco* and *Imperial*, was made specifically for the tour. *Pastorela* and *Juke Box* fell by the wayside after the tour (fun to dance but not a good ballet, Bolender said); *Barocco* and *Imperial* remain in active repertory all over the world.

"Both [ballets]," wrote Bolender in 1955 in an unpublished memoir, "[were Balanchine's] first steps into the new phase, toward which he had been headed for a long time. *Concerto Barocco* in those far off days . . . was termed a dancer's ballet, meaning presumably a ballet only to be enjoyed by the elect. . . . It has an importance," he continued, "that puts it into a class completely removed from any other Balanchine ballet with the possible exception of *Four Temperaments*. [It] obviously was composed by one as deeply in love with music as movement."[5]

Earlier Balanchine ballets were also in the repertory, providing a retro-spective of his work to date. They included *Serenade, Errante* (which tour programs listed as *Alma Errante*), and *The Bat*. "*Barocco* and *Apollo* were the [ballets] that made us an outstanding company at that time," Bolender told Nancy Reynolds. While he never much liked *Ballet Imperial*, it was nevertheless in his view "justified in the performance of Marie-Jeanne. She was an extraordinary instrument—she was like greased lightning, and she was not like some dancers who look well in this, and not in that—she was beautiful, perfection, . . . startlingly well-placed, and her whole line was always right. That was an excellent reason to do it—she had an extremely powerful technique."[6] So powerful, in fact, that at age 15, when Bolender first encountered her at SAB, "she could perform *entrechat-huit* too fast to count them." She also possessed all the qualities that Balanchine looked for in American dancers: speed, athleticism, musicality, and daring—the willingness to try anything asked of her. Caccialanza, who was no slouch either, was cast in *Ballet Imperial*'s second ballerina role, dancing with two male partners, and Bolender was the understudy for one of them. "[This] really excited me very much, though the chance of performing with Gisella wouldn't be that frequent—she was such an inspiration to be with on stage."

Balanchine made two more ballets specifically for the tour, *Fantasia Brasileira* and *Divertimento*. Both were *pièces d'occasion*. Neither was deemed worthy of later revival. *Brasileira*, despite its title, premiered in Santiago, Chile, and was created while the company was actually en route. *Divertimento*, a series of variations set to an arrangement of Gioachino Rossini's music by Benjamin Britten, was made to be what Balanchine later called an "applause machine," offering a foretaste of such closers as *Stars and Stripes*. It featured a bravura Tyrolean solo for Marie-Jeanne that she never forgot. "It was one of the most brilliant things I have ever done," she told Reynolds. "All on toe, very sharp, very exciting. I used to have to do encores; that was something new—and sometimes almost impossible."[7] Particularly at high altitudes. *Divertimento*, which Bolender said had costumes from every work Balanchine had done to date, ended in "a chase [by] a large hoop-skirted creature wearing a large mouse's head, caught and pounced on by the dancers. From the melee, out springs an acrobat who does a few tricks. The entire cast joins in; curtain. One night, Balanchine [casting himself rather than the dancer scheduled to perform] popped out, jumped high in the air, whipped off some good pirouettes and high, clean double air-turns and finished his stint with the authority of a premier danseur." The mouse's head may well have come from *Les Songes*, created for Ballets 1933, the short-lived company Balanchine headed in London. In Marie-Jeanne's recollection, all the costumes came from that ballet.

Kirstein met the ship when it arrived in Rio to help the company negotiate customs and immigration and to get the production trunks from the dock to the Teatro Municipal. "Filtering [them] through customs officials onto a fleet of trucks into a theatre is no cinch," Kirstein reported in a four-part travel diary that was published in the October 1941 issue of *The American Dancer*. Bolender remembered the process being lengthy and complex; it took most of a day to get everything unloaded and through customs and then to the hotel where they were staying. The hotel was a ten-minute drive from the opera house on a curvy coastal road with views of the ocean. Remembering how terrifying Brazilian drivers were on that road, taking its curves at breakneck speed, Bolender noticed quite quickly how temperamentally different they were from their northern neighbors. "It's either all energy [as in driving] or very slow [as in bureaucratic procedures]," he recalled. Ultimately, Bolender, who was an experienced driver (he had driven trucks for the Canton, Ohio, Parks Department as a youth) and who loved fast cars, became so frightened by the Brazilians' recklessness that he declined to ride with them.

Nevertheless, he was enchanted by Rio's beautiful parks and gardens, which the company had three days to explore while the scenery was being put up and the stage was being prepared for a run in which they would dance every night for a week. Evening performances throughout the tour began at eleven, and matinees, when they had them, began at six, which took some getting used to. "It's like being in a nightclub," Bolender said. "But it's a little hard to dance, you know, *Concerto Barocco* at midnight."

The opening night repertory on June 25 did not include *Barocco*; it premiered two nights later. Kirstein carefully programmed the company's introduction to South American audiences with *Serenade; Ballet Imperial*, to demonstrate that ballet from North America was still rooted in the tradition of Petipa and Ivanov; and, as a closer, Christensen's *Filling Station*, its characters based on images from popular culture.

Serenade had a new backdrop commissioned from Brazilian easel painter Candido Portinari (Balanchine had given the original to the Ballets Russes de Monte Carlo). Portinari had painted murals for the 1939 New York World's Fair and had also shown his work in a one-man exhibition at the Museum of Modern Art. While Kirstein liked the backdrop, which he described as "a free interpretation of the sky over the Southern Hemisphere with the stars of the Southern Cross intertwined with two meteors," the audience found it merely adequate because, he speculated, they were looking for something less subtle.[8] Both the backdrop and the new costumes had been made in the opera house shop in less than a week, which impressed him mightily.

Filling Station, which Kirstein remembered as the middle ballet on the opening program (the reviews state otherwise) wasn't entirely a success either, because of the audience's unfamiliarity with Virgil Thomson's music and the inability of several orchestra members to deal with the composer's jazzy rhythms. *Ballet Imperial,* however, was received with great enthusiasm, making the evening a triumph. That was a relief to Kirstein, who had had his doubts about putting two works accompanied by Tchaikovsky's music on the same program. Kirstein described it as "a Russian ballet danced by an American company. And yet it was perfect to cap the evening on our initial appearance in South America. For, first of all, it proved to a packed house of skeptics that Americans born and bred all over the Northern Continent . . . and trained in New York in our own school, could really dance. This needed proving."[9] The company received eighteen curtain calls and bouquets galore.

Marie-Jeanne not only danced brilliantly in *Imperial,* with some help from Balanchine and a Brazilian admirer; she also had the all the glamour audiences associated with such Ballets Russes stars as Alexandra Danilova, Mia Slavenska, and Irina Baranova. Balanchine had designed an aristocratic coronet of diamonds as part of her costume and the Brazilian admirer had given her two large aquamarines to wear while performing. The Ballets Russes had toured South America the previous summer, performing in the major cities but not the small venues where the American Ballet was to perform for audiences that in some cases had never seen ballet at all, never mind ballet from the United States.

In Rio, the American ambassador was particularly pleased by *Imperial* (mostly he and his colleagues in other cities wanted to see *Swan Lake*) and Kirstein was gratified by the comment of the impresario of the theater that not since Pavlova had performed there had a ballet appearance been so successful.

The anonymous critic for the *Jornal do Brasil* was enthusiastic about the opening program, calling it "an inspiring sight—an impressive manifestation of friendship, mingled with admiration for the great country of the North. The 'American Ballet,'" the reviewer continued, "conforms strictly to the principles of classical Russian Ballet. However, influenced by its wonderful spirit, it does not follow that technique blindly. It only uses it as a basis, discovering new aspects and leaving much room to imagination. At the same time it shows understanding of modern life and makes the dance beautifully human." Of Balanchine, the critic said perceptively, if somewhat inaccurately, "trained at the Imperial Ballet Academy in St. Petersburg and Diagilef's [sic] School, . . . [he] has created a synthesis filling the old, classical principles with new spirit." About *Serenade* and *Ballet Imperial*, he wrote, "The performance was filled with purity and harmony and reached a climax of greatest beauty. Everything was penetrated by its own life and by no means was limited to the mere presentation of traditional dance steps."[10]

The critic for the *Diario Coriola* considered *Filling Station* to be the best ballet of the evening, "transmitting most poignantly the impression of the American art of dance," and "typical of American life."[11] And writing for the *Jornal do Commercio,* another anonymous reviewer thanked Balanchine for "this beautiful evening, which was 'modern' not only in the usual sense, but which brought us really something entirely new."[12] Small wonder Kirstein wrote home of his deep respect for the Brazilian critics, who he considered among the best informed he had ever encountered.

In his account of the Rio run, Kirstein omitted any commentary about *Pastorela,* the ballet Rockefeller had commissioned to show the company's attentiveness to South American culture. Since the ballet, which had a score that was an arrangement of Mexican folk music by Paul Bowles, was based on a Mexican rather than a South American morality play, it did not in the end particularly resonate with audiences or critics in most of the countries where it was performed, possibly because their cultures were markedly different both from Mexico's and from one another's. The exception was Buenos Aires, where, Kirstein speculated, discerning intellectuals were impressed by the respect with which *Pastorela's* creators treated the folk material. One of them was dancer José Martínez, a Mexican native whose father had performed in such morality plays.

For Bolender, who dismissed the work as a sop to cultural exchange, the premier of *Pastorela* on June 27 was painfully memorable because he nearly ruined it. A luscious-looking salad he was served on the company's first night in Rio in their hotel's rooftop restaurant seduced him into throwing caution to the wind. In defiance of medical instructions to steer clear of raw vegetables, he ate every bite. "[It] was so exquisite you cannot believe it," he said. "The green, the leaves were so beautiful and the tomatoes were to die over. As I ate it I thought, "Well, this is pure heaven." Pure heaven soon turned into pure hell, as "Just like that I was suddenly overwhelmed [by] dysentery." And with it a very high fever, which meant he was unable to get out of bed, let alone dance, for several days. He was so ill it was feared he had come down with something really serious, so a doctor was called who gave him medication. It was not effective enough to enable him to attend *Pastorela's* dress rehearsal, but it deceived him into thinking he would be able to perform at its premiere.

Pastorela began with the curtain rising on Bolender and Caccialanza posed in what he remembered as a sort of tableau. Since that was pretty much all that was required of him, Bolender thought he could perform even in his weak, dehydrated state. Company members took him to the theater in a taxi, and once he was in his dressing room, conductor Emanuel Balaban came to his door and said, "Now, I want you to tell me exactly when you're ready and when you're ready . . . they will send me down [to the pit] and then they will give me a sign that I can go . . . but it's up to you. You have to tell us how you feel."

The dancers, in Bolender's account, took their places center stage, but, as it happened, just as the lights came on and the curtain went up, nature called, and doubled over with cramps, Bolender scuttled off stage. Christensen was furious, and while Bolender did manage to recover sufficiently to perform Alias, the role he originated in *Billy the Kid,* in the third concert of the run, for the rest of the trip—indeed the rest of his life—he was exceedingly careful about what he ate.

Errante, titled *Alma Errante* (*Wandering Soul*) for this tour (all titles were translated into Spanish, which didn't do a lot of good in Brazil, where they speak Portuguese) proved immensely popular with South American audiences; it appealed to their sense of drama and romance. Originally created for the star of Balanchine's Les Ballets 1933, Austrian dancer Tilly Losch, who was more of a ballet character dancer than a classical technician (she performed barefoot), it had its first New York performance in 1935 with Tamara Geva, Balanchine's first wife, in the lead role. In South America, it was performed by Marjorie Moore, except in Medellín, where an infected wisdom tooth kept her from dancing.

By and large, the Rio performances were a critical success and Kirstein was pleased. Following the third repertory program, the critic for *Correio da Notte* summed up the evening as "a perfect synthesis of the classical and modern ballet; this is what we couldn't get neither from the classical ballet of Monte Carlo or from the extremely modern Ballet Joost [*sic*]. [It] showed us new direction of the art of dance and we are glad to applaud them heartily."[13] Since Kirstein regarded the Ballets Russes as American Ballet Caravan's chief competition in both South America and the United States, this unsigned review pleased him greatly and reinforced his respect for South American critics generally.

Convincing Jefferson Caffery, the U.S. ambassador in Rio, of the viability of American ballet was another matter. Had he been given advance notice of such works as *Billy the Kid* and *Filling Station* before the company's arrival, he would have forbidden their performance, Caffery told Kirstein. Despite his approval of *Ballet Imperial,* he essentially had his staff boycott the performances and did not himself attend any of the three embassy receptions to which the company had been invited. One can only wonder at the appointment of ambassadors who are ashamed of their own culture, although it should be remembered that ballet as an American art form was at the time taking its first baby steps, much like Balanchine's toddling *Apollo.* At the first reception, in honor of sculptor Jo Davidson, Kirstein, who, as an intellectual, had a rare respect for the intelligence of dancers, was both bemused and disgusted by a comment from someone that it was a shame the dancers had been unable to attend. In fact, they were there, justifying, Kirstein wrote, "for the first time all the overweight of their personal baggage by appearing in the latest New York summer magnificence, the smartest people at the party." Evidently, Kirstein mused, the embassy secretary who expressed his regret "had no idea they ever appeared out of tutus, off point, or spoke in a voice [below] a scream."[14]

The company gave their last performance in Rio on July 1 in an all-Balanchine program. Christensen danced the title role in *Apollo,* and he was an enormous success in it throughout the tour. Not long before he died, Bolender said that he thought Christensen might have been the best Apollo he had seen in six decades of watching the ballet.[15] Also on the program were *Alma Errante* and *The Bat,* a balletic reduction of *Die Fledermaus* to the Johann Strauss score that had premiered at the Metropolitan Opera when the company was in residence there.

Antony Tudor's *Time Table* (in Rio titled *Good Luck and Goodbye* and on the rest of the tour called *Despidido*) premiered on this program. A wartime ballet based on Tudor's observations during World War I in England, *Time Table* was revived once by City Ballet in 1949, but it was deemed slight by the New York critics in comparison with Jerome Robbins's *Fancy Free* (1944) and Tudor's own *Pillar of Fire* (1942).

Like *Pastorela*, *Time Table* was commissioned for the tour. Reportedly, Tudor was still working on it while the company went up the gangplank of the *Argentina*. "I was not in [it]," Bolender said, "but I thought [it] was a very beautiful ballet, very touching." Set in a railway station on the eve of war, the ballet opens so that the "the audience sees the station as though [they were looking at it from] across the tracks. The action would bring people onto the platform to look in the direction of the approaching train. It was filled with hesitation, anxiety, and resignation from the various characters."[16] The cast was small, mostly men in military uniforms and their female family members costumed in dresses, hats, and gloves, carrying purses, presaging the costuming of *Fancy Free*. Robbins, like Tudor, was interested in making ballets about ordinary people.

Danced to Aaron Copland's "Music for the Theatre," *Time Table* featured a central pas de deux performed by Caccialanza and Christensen. "It was one of parting," Bolender wrote. "He [was] on his way to war and she [was] attempting to hide her anxiety and grief. Gisella was an extraordinary dancer-actress who could break your heart or be hilarious."[17] Christensen was to depart for the war in Europe very soon after the company returned to the United States, a likelihood that may well have infused the newlyweds' performance with the edgy psychological atmosphere that is a constant in Tudor ballets. In *Time Table* there was also the usual triangle, with Christensen as Caccialanza's lover going off to war and another dancer portraying her husband returning on an incoming train.

From Rio the company went to São Paulo, a city that reminded Kirstein of Seattle, where, he reported, the orchestra was confused by the scores for *Billy the Kid* (Copland), *Juke Box* (Alec Wilder), and *Apollon Musagète* (Stravinsky). *Juke Box*, as narrow a representation of North American culture as *Pastorela* was of South American, turned out to be an audience favorite, just as it had been in Rio, no doubt because it was a romp for the dancers. Its social dance–based choreography was something they could just let go and have fun performing.

What wasn't fun was getting from São Paulo, high in the Serra do Mar, to Santos, roughly a 40-mile drive on steep mountain roads, where the company boarded a ship for Buenos Aires, the next stop on the tour and an important proving ground for them. Since the war in Europe had severely disrupted shipping schedules, it took some maneuvering on the part of the American vice consul in São Paulo and Kirstein and his staff to find enough space on a boat for the company and its cargo. Eventually, arrangements were made for first-class passage on the *Cabo de Buena Esperanza* (which they hadn't budgeted for and couldn't afford) for forty-six people, not to mention their personal luggage and those sixty-eight production trunks. Like the voyage from New York on the *Argentina,* with its threat of U-boat attacks, traveling on the *Cabo de Buena Esperanza* heightened Bolender's awareness of the war in Europe because it was one of the infamous "White Sepulchre" ships.[18] These were ships that carried Jewish refugees fleeing Nazi persecution on routes from Spain and Portugal to ports in both Americas which began after Kristallnacht (Night of Broken Glass) in Germany on November 9–10, 1938. Shamefully, they were repeatedly refused entry in the Americas, including the United States. Bolender was well aware of Kristallnacht and its ramifications, but he knew nothing about the White Sepulchre ships until he boarded the *Cabo de Buena Esperanza,* after the first of what would be many grueling drives in rickety vehicles on undeveloped roads.

"[We went] in a caravan of automobiles," Bolender remembered. "The whole company and luggage and everything, over a huge mountain range. It was hair-raising, but we got there and by degrees we got on the ship."[19] When he and Kriza, with whom he was rooming, looked around their assigned stateroom, they realized immediately that the first-class designation was more like steerage, or worse. "The beds looked all right," he said, "but then we went into the bathroom and the towels were all brown." Worse yet, so was the water in the sink. If Bolender was repelled by the condition of his quarters, he was appalled by what he saw when he went on deck. While the records show that there were no more than eighty-three refugees on board, it seemed to Bolender that there were far more, huddled around little makeshift cookstoves, preparing their own food, and sleeping in "little knots all over the deck. The look in their faces was tragic," he told Reynolds.[20] With good reason: Bolender believed that by the time the ship reached Santos, the refugees had already been refused entry into every one of the ports in South America and the Caribbean and had been back to Portugal and returned. This time around, according to a story in *Time* magazine, they were given ninety days' grace and admitted to the country, but they ended up returning to Europe on the *Cabo de Hornos*, landing in Curaçao, where the Dutch finally granted them asylum.[21]

Not all were sleeping on deck. Bolender became friendly with an elderly German woman he met in the ship's lounge whose fingers were covered in rings, primarily diamonds. A charming woman with memorably good manners, she told Bolender that she had escaped from Germany to Spain, selling most of her jewelry so that she could get passage on the ship and go to America. Bolender was so charmed by her that he spent much of the four-day trip to Buenos Aires in her company. When they disembarked, she wept. Bolender never knew what happened to her, but he never forgot her. "It was like leaving my grandmother," he said.

It is a little odd that Bolender said he had known nothing about the White Sepulchre ships until that trip, since Rittmann, who was one of his friends, was a German refugee of Jewish descent. She had left Germany, where she had been a concert pianist, in 1932, after she was instructed to list on programs which composers were Jewish. She spent over four years trying to get to the United States. She arrived there in 1937, with a letter of introduction to Kirstein from Kurt Jooss. Kirstein, ever helpful to artists of every stripe, first gave her a job as an accompanist at the SAB and then hired her as music director of Ballet Caravan. She went on to have a stellar career as an arranger and composer, working closely with, among others, Agnes de Mille and Jerome Robbins on Broadway and with Lew Christensen, for whom she created the score for *Charade*, a comic work intended to represent an aspect of North American popular culture to South American audiences. Bolender deemed the role Christensen created for Caccialanza in *Charade* quite amusing. Rittmann pronounced both Christensen and Kirstein to be unmusical, particularly compared to Balanchine, who she claimed to have worked with note by note, phrase by phrase, refining *Concerto Barocco* while on the ship to Rio.[22]

Kirstein flew to Buenos Aires ahead of the company to pave the way for opening night and get the feel of a city that considers itself to be the Paris of South America. In 1941, the city had an opera-house public that was accustomed to seeing Russian ballet, starting with Pavlova before World War I, and de Basil's Ballets Russes. While the American Ballet was in the city, Kirstein heard Arturo Toscanini conduct the NBC Symphony Orchestra in a stirring performance of the Verdi *Requiem* at the Teatro Colón.

As in Rio, Kirstein was on the dock to meet the ship. And a good thing, too, for Marie-Jeanne, Nicholas Magallanes, and a couple of other dancers were told they could not be admitted to the country to work, since they were under the age of 22. Although they were carrying the necessary parental authorizations, they were still detained and quarantined on a small island off the coast of the city. Balanchine insisted on going with them until Kirstein and American officials could straighten out the paperwork. Since it was a weekend and a magistrate couldn't be found, they all spent two days and nights in jail. In due course, they were released. Their reports of their accommodations were so awful, however, that Bolender deliberately put the details out of his mind. Kirstein wrote in his journal, "All girls under eighteen were arrested and removed to a local jail; work permits don't apply. We were importing dancers for purposes of prostitution. Some sort of German-inspired plot?"[23] He didn't mention Magallanes, who Bolender recalled as also being detained. At age 19, Magallanes, who had been born in 1922 in Mexico and was one of the Spanish-speaking members of the tour, was, of course, eligible for arrest.

Although the Buenos Aires season was cut short by the delay in arrival, the company gave nineteen performances in twelve days at the Teatro Politeama, which Bolender described as a "hideous movie house," the first of several in which they would dance. The audiences were made up of snooty socialites, intellectuals and critics, and, in the higher reaches of the balconies, young arts aficionados. The latter were by far the most enthusiastic. Much to Kirstein's annoyance, the socialites were more interested in being seen by their peers than in actually looking at the ballet. This was manifested in a request from the director of the theater to make the intermissions longer so they could promenade in the lobby and talk with their friends.

In Buenos Aires, Kirstein got to know literary translator Maria Rosa Oliver (who was the first to translate the plays of Eugene O'Neill into Spanish), who advised him to program ballets that would distinguish the company from the European and Russian companies that had preceded it. Oliver turned out to be correct: the most popular ballets in Buenos Aires were *Billy the Kid, Juke Box,* and, much to Kirstein's surprise, *Pastorela,* about which he had a higher artistic opinion than Bolender. He had had two concerns about presenting the ballet: first, its religious theme, and second, its North American take on a Central American subject. "Perhaps Latin Americans would resent it," he wrote, "in the way we resented the Russian Ballet's 'American numbers' like *The New Yorker* or *Union Pacific.*"[24] Or the way people raised in the American West still resent ballets such as Agnes de Mille's *Rodeo* and Balanchine's *Western Symphony,* created by city folks whose experience of ranching and cowboys was confined to popular culture and observation rather than participation in the dirty work on the range.

From Buenos Aires, the company traveled to Montevideo, Uruguay, where they gave five performances in four days at the Auditorio de Sodre, a white marble building with a resplendent classical frieze over its columned entrance. Unlike in Rio and Buenos Aires, ticket sales were fairly good, yet the critical reception turned out to be the least favorable of the tour. There was, however, a company wedding in Montevideo, when former Littlefield dancer June Graham, another friend of Bolender's, married Joe Johnson. From there, the company traveled in what Rittmann described as a caravan of old, wobbly cars to Rosario, a medium-sized Argentinean city that in the twenty-first century is a center for the arts.[25] Bolender recalled neither what they performed nor how many concerts they gave there (it was only two or three), but he vividly remembered Marie-Jeanne bringing the start of a performance to a grinding halt. Prone to treating menstrual cramps with alcohol, the best remedy available in those days, the company's prima ballerina drank a bit too much at dinner on their first night in town and was visibly inebriated when she got on stage. The curtain was immediately pulled down and the program quickly rearranged with understudies sent in where needed.

Córdoba, the next stop, Argentina's second largest city, was also unmemorable as far as Bolender was concerned, although Kirstein reported to Rockefeller's office that performances there and in Rosario had been a success. What Bolender did remember was Mendoza, because an "appalling" series of blizzards trapped them there for what he recalled as two or three days but was actually nine. The dancers performed every night in a small municipal theater attached to the Mendoza gambling casino, but they missed their scheduled subscription opening in Santiago de Chile. It was impossible to get across the Andes by train, as they had been scheduled to do, or by a highway, which had been so badly hit by avalanches it was shut down for the next six months.

Ultimately, after appeals to the American embassy in Lima, Peru, their destination following Santiago, "the entire American Ballet, complete with scenery [except for Apollo's chariot], costumes, lights and personnel of fifty-one people," Kirstein wrote in his travel diary, "climbed into four Pan Air Boeing transport planes which flew between the two highest peaks in the Western hemisphere."[26] This account isn't quite accurate, since several of the dancers had been sent ahead to Bolivia with some of the scenery and the dancers' personal baggage, which, Rittmann recalled quite vividly, they were not to see again for quite a while. "Nobody had a stitch to wear but what we had on," she said. "We stank."[27] And one of the dancers recalled in an unpublished memoir that when they flew from Medellin to Bogotá, "[John] Taras and many others had their first experience of being above the clouds."[28]

While Kirstein was thrilled by the beautiful weather and the plane's-eye view of Mt. Aconcagua (at 22,841 feet the highest peak in the Western Hemisphere), not everyone on board shared his delight. The cabins weren't pressurized and oxygen masks had to be used, something that particularly bothered wardrobe mistress Miranova, who for fifteen years had traveled all over the world with Pavlova. Fred Danieli, who had never flown before, was nervous as a cat, even though, according to Kirstein, the plane "crossed as flat as if it had been on a stage floor at about 19,000 feet." That was quite high in an era when jet engines were not in widespread use. In a little over an hour they landed in Santiago, "surrounded by a cheering crowd of wholly incredulous spectators. It must have been the first time in history that bombers had flown a ballet."[29]

On August 27, *Brasileira*, Balanchine's last addition to the tour repertoire, premiered at the Teatro Municipal in Santiago de Chile. The idea for the ballet had come from a critic who reviewed the company's second performance in Rio: "The American Ballet should do well if it would include in the repertoire a Brazilian ballet; our composers have written a great many works which would fit in, but this is only a suggestion."[30] Balanchine apparently wasn't enthusiastic about doing such a *pièce d'occasion* (*Pastorela*, according to Christensen's biographer, was given to the less experienced choreographer because Balanchine wasn't interested in it), but

Kirstein took the suggestion seriously as part of their goodwill mission and hired Brazilian composer Francisco Mignone to write the music and set and costume designer Enrico Bianco to create décor and costumes for a work that Balanchine evidently whipped up while the company was on the road. Mignone incorporated Brazilian dance forms, such as the samba, into the score, and the ballet was well received by the Chilean audience. The company, one critic wrote, "interprets in felicitous fashion moments of great beauty based on the customs of the country. It received a careful interpretation, full of beauty and emotion."[31] Olga Suarez, one of several Spanish-speaking company members; Magallanes; and Danieli danced the leads backed by the ensemble, but the dancers didn't find it particularly memorable (Danieli couldn't remember the plot) and it was dropped after the tour. In Kirstein's assessment, "*Brasileira,* which takes place in a jungle, was about as Brazilian as *Prince Igor* is early Russian," leaving open to question whether the Brazilian critics would have been as favorably disposed toward it as those in Santiago.[32]

Kirstein left the tour after the week's run in Santiago, claiming urgent business in New York and a very real need to report to Rockefeller in Washington. According to his biographer, he was thoroughly sick of dealing with both North and South American bureaucracies—few State Department officials regarded the ballet company as anything but a nuisance, although there were some exceptions—and he was tired of traveling. But there was considerable justification in his reporting directly to Washington: due to unanticipated cost overruns, some lukewarm reviews, and accusations from members of the U.S. Congress that Rockefeller was favoring "ballet over bullets" (i.e., allocating resources for the former that would have been put to better use for the latter), Washington was wanting to bring the tour to a halt.

Without their leader but eager to see at least part of the west coast of South America, the company was on the move again.[33] Following a single performance in Viña del Mar, the company departed on the S.S. *Maipocho,* arriving in Valparaiso in time to open on September 10 at the Teatro Municipal.

They were a hit in Lima, but, as so often happened on this tour, it was the journey and not the arrival that stood out most vividly in Bolender's memory. Kirstein, who wasn't, of course, on board, called the *Maipocho* "the yacht of the American Ballet, for besides the hundreds of head of cattle in the hold, the members of the Ballet had the boat to themselves."[34] Bolender, who thought the trip from Valparaiso to Lima took three weeks (it actually took less than two), recalled stopping every night to offload the cattle on board and take on more, plus wheat and, as he put it, "everything else." The dancers tried, in his account, to do their barre on board, but in the end they substituted a walk around whatever port they had stopped in. Another dancer remembered the cattle keeping them awake at night, bawling in the hold, not exactly the kind of night music one expects on a yacht.

Lima, however, turned out quite unexpectedly to be a triumph for American ballet. On September 11, Kirstein forwarded to Walter Prendergast, Rockefeller's assistant, the following jubilant telegram:

> Just received following:
> Quote in sold out house premiere American Ballet Lima, Peru, present President of the Republic, Dr. Manuel Prado, first vice president Rafael Largo Herrera, Minister of Justice, Director of Cultural Artistic Relations, Ambassadors of the United States, Argentina, Colombia, Mexico, Minister of Bolivia, Consul of Norway, British Legation with all press and propaganda attachés, Mayor of Lima, ex Ambassador of Poland Count Potocka [sic] etc. First time this president ever attended any unofficial performance. No other theatrical company domestic or foreign ever created such interest here. Aaron Copland conducted his cowboy ballet Billy the Kid. Over half house sold for remaining four subscription programs, unquote. What more can you want, best wishes, Lincoln.[35]

Copland was also on a goodwill tour of South America, funded by the Guggenheim Foundation and under the auspices of the Committee for Inter-American Artistic and Intellectual Relations. His tour took him in the opposite direction from that of the American Ballet Caravan. It began in Mexico in August, then went down the west coast and came back through Argentina, Brazil, and Cuba, from which he returned to the United States in December. Copland's diary entry for September 7 states: "Preceding me had been successful performances of *Billy the Kid* by Ballet Caravan and the film version [probably the one starring Robert Taylor, made in 1940] was being shown in local movie houses. The Orquestra Sinfonic[a] Nacional invited me to conduct *Billy* on 10 September. The players left much to be desired technically, but they were lively and enthusiastic."[36] Since the

American Ballet didn't open in Lima until September 10, when he conducted, it seems likely that he was referring to American Ballet Caravan's performances of the ballet in Cuba in the late 1930s. In any case, his conducting contributed to the American Ballet's highly successful run in Lima, something that came as a very welcome surprise.

In Lima, Bolender acquired a camera; he documented the rest of the tour with snapshots of his friends, prominent among them Marie-Jeanne, Dunphy, Kriza, Adelaide (Addie) Varricchio, Taras, and Rittmann. He took many photographs of the company on the *Santa Elena*, a Grace Line steamer that took the company to Colombia. Compared to the S.S. *Maipocho* it was a luxury liner that gave the dancers a bit of a holiday and some well-earned relaxation. It had a swimming pool and plenty of space on deck to lounge or sew ribbons onto pointe shoes. Most important, by holding onto the deck rail, the dancers were able to stay in shape by doing their daily barre. On September 30, the *Santa Elena* docked in Buenaventura, Colombia's major port, having made stops in Guayaquil and Esmeraldas along the way (Bolender took pictures of his shipmates making purchases from local vendors in both towns). The company did not perform again until they reached Cali on October 1, in time to open for a three-day run.

In Cali, as Beatrice Tompkins wrote Kirstein, who was back in Washington reporting to Rockefeller's office, they "gave three performances under very interesting conditions." It was the dry season, water pressure was low, and that made the lighting (driven by hydroelectric power) dim, to say the least. "Trying to put on a good stage makeup in semidarkness was a real problem," she wrote. "However, the stage lights were also affected, and I imagine our audience couldn't see whether the makeup was good or bad."[37]

Since no ballet company had performed in Cali for the past sixteen years, there were some concerns about how good their reception would be. "Much to our delighted surprise," Tompkins reported, "the audience evidenced great enthusiasm, and expressed the hope that we would return ere long."

From Cali they traveled by train for twelve hours to reach Manizales, arriving with "white hair and eyelashes" due to the dustiness of the dry season. Bolender took photographs of the scenery, of naked children standing by the tracks, and of the dancers trying to get some rest on the hard, bench-like seating of the train.

In Manizales, they performed in an old movie house where the stage was small, the dressing rooms were square boxes made of tin, and the floor was dangerous. Not only was it full of holes but it was also extremely slippery. The dancers survived with no injuries, and the audience, which had never seen ballet before, loved the performances. It was scarcely an elite, black-tie crowd; "there were men in ponchos, with machetes and bare feet," wrote Tompkins to Kirstein.[38]

The company stayed in the small La Pension Latina in Manzinales; it may have been here that they slept three to a bed. Bolender remembered that he had shared one with two of the women. "I slept in the middle," he said demurely. He didn't mention, however, that they were awakened early by the cathedral bells opposite the *pension,* or that there wasn't enough water to flush the toilets, or even that "since there was an election in progress, five bombs were let off." According to one source, "Taras watched the crowd chase a man up the steps of a church and beat him until the police came to his rescue. After a frightening afternoon of noise and flag-waving the American Ballet danced *Serenade.*" And "the audience was enthusiastic."[39]

Medellín was the company's next destination. All but Billie Wynn, an ensemble member who had been taken ill, and Franklyn Weinberg, the CPA on Kirstein's staff, were transported there in yet another caravan of cars, ten of them, over what Tompkins described as "a magnificent though hair-raising drive over precipitous dirt roads."[40] Bolender was sufficiently impressed by the skill of their drivers to take pictures of them and of a bridge that had partially collapsed and was under rather dilatory repair when they reached it, causing a two-hour delay. Some of the dancers had a cooling swim in the river, and most of them, not trusting the repairs, elected to walk across the bridge, but, in the end it held and everyone, cars included, made it across.

It was a long and exhausting trip, Michael Horowitz wrote in a letter he typed to Franklyn Weinberg on stationery from the Hotel Europa in Medellín. Weinberg and Wynn had gone directly to Bogotá, the company's next destination. "You did not miss much by not coming to Medellín," Horowitz said, where the hotels and the food had been bad. But the company had recuperated quickly from the arduous trip there and, in his assessment, "gave excellent performances, with little signs of tiredness."[41] What he didn't mention was that in Medellín, where they gave three performances, the Catholic Church had banned them sight unseen.

This didn't stop them from having "a marvelous house" on opening night, "2200 people and gross receipt of 3200 Pesos (more than 500 we had to pay for taxes, however)."[42] But because Marjorie Moore, who had made the lead role in *Alma Errante* her own on this tour, was hors de combat, her face swollen from an infected wisdom tooth, Horowitz substituted *Billy the Kid* and, as he put it, made the mistake of having two modern American ballets on the program instead of one. When the substitution was announced before the curtain went up, "everyone began booing or hissing or whistling or shouting 'Malo,' all through *Billy*, scaring us all out of our wits."[43] In spite of the commotion and the controversy, the sponsors agreed with Horowitz's assessment of the quality of the dancing and presented each dancer with an orchid before the company departed for Bogotá, the next stop.

The flight to Bogotá, this time in three planes, got them there in time to adjust somewhat to the altitude before they opened a week-long run on October 14 at the Teatro Municipal, a new theater that was the pride of the city. Tompkins characterized it as a "smaller Radio City Music Hall" and Bolender's snapshot of the marquee, with "American Ballet" in big letters, supports this impression. "The altitude of 8,500 feet bothered us quite a lot," Tompkins wrote, "but we managed somehow although I'm sure the audiences could hear us heaving our way through the various ballets."[44]

In Bogotá, the company stayed at the Hotel Victoria, where Bolender and Kriza had a room with a terrace from which Bolender took pictures of the view of Monserrate (he labeled it Mt. Serrate), and of Lucille, the maid, bringing a breakfast tray that included a large box of cornflakes. There was time to do considerable sightseeing, as Bolender's album reveals with its photographs of a laden burro in the market, several shots of the cathedral, and compelling views of the German Embassy flying a huge, swastika-bearing flag.[45]

They left Bogotá on October 21, having, as usual, received favorable reviews from the critics, and headed for the Colombian-Venezuelan border town of Cúcuta in a caravan of coaches that had seating with no upholstery that, Bolender told Reynolds, "you wouldn't even use for school buses." They would ride from six or seven in the morning until midnight, and "get to a place, and then they would try to find us a place to sleep (and most of us slept in the buses) and then . . . we got to Cúcuta, where they did have little hotels the company could stay in."[46] In Cúcuta, they switched to a dozen automobiles, according to Tompkins, and, once again were on frightening, undeveloped terrain. She wrote to Kirstein that they crossed "three branches of the Andes, along dirt roads, really just narrow ledges hewn out of the sides of mountains. Twisting and turning up and down, for three days. Our drivers were amazing. We stopped for a few minutes' rest at various little towns, but the food was not edible for us from the effete U.S.A. So we lived on what we had bought in Cúcuta in case of such an emergency. When we stopped at these villages we'd take our various baskets and bundles to the village square, sit under the trees, and pool our store of cheese, crackers, etc. In every village we were encircled by dozens of natives."[47]

Bolender's album shows a couple of the rest stops, including a shack he ironically captioned a Colombian Howard Johnson, and Cúcuta itself. Struck throughout the tour by the poverty he saw everywhere, he also recorded a couple of very thin children standing by the road. There are shots of Horowitz with a sheep and one of Trude Rittmann "[taking] too many pills."[48] In Caracas, Bolender began to understand just why she took so many pills and had so many headaches when he and Georgia Hiden went with her to stay at "a wonderful rustic Swiss-chalet-type hotel" on the outskirts of the city," according to the memoir. "As they sat on the terrace to drink coffee after dinner, Trude suddenly whispered, 'Do you realize this place is full of Nazis?'" To find herself in what indeed must have been a nest of Nazi agents "turned her inside out," and she paid her bill and looked for other accommodations, as did Bolender and Hiden.[49] This may have been the Hotel Spies, which Bolender photographed for his album: Spies himself was a Nazi, Bolender said.[50]

After a week of reasonably successful performances at the Teatro Municipal in Caracas, the company departed on the *Santa Paula* for New York on November 6, arriving six days later. Bolender took what he captioned a classic picture of the Statue of Liberty as they sailed into the harbor. Marie-Jeanne was not on board, having married her first husband in a church ceremony in Buenos Aires; their official marriage took place in 1942.

After giving over 100 performances in seven countries, the company was disbanded. Bolender danced in two Balanchine Broadway musicals, Kriza returned to Ballet Theatre, and others were drafted into the army. Bolender said of the tour, "It was important in a great many ways to the establishment of American ballet, because this was virtually the first time that an American company had ever ventured beyond its borders to perform ballet." For Kirstein, it was a success because of the cultural exchange and because it enhanced Balanchine's reputation. While the company was in Buenos Aires, Balanchine was invited to take over the direction of the ballet at the Teatro Colón. He turned that job down, but he later returned to set a work on the company, as did Bolender, decades later.

Bolender certainly made no bones about the discomforts of the tour, and he cast a clear eye on the quality of the repertory they took to South America. However, he said that "one marvelous thing was the casual rubbing of shoulders so to speak with Lincoln Kirstein and George Balanchine—there was an unusual democratic we're-all-in-this-together principle at work."

4

When Reed, rumpled and tired from spending four days and three nights curled up in a coach seat, got off the transcontinental train at Grand Central Station, Eugene Loring's secretary was there to meet her at the information booth. She easily identified her by her red hair and her lack of a heavy winter coat. Reed knew virtually no one in New York. It's possible that she met Loring in Seattle in 1939, when she danced *Coppélia* before an audience that included the Ballet Caravan dancers, but she didn't know him any better than she did the woman who met her train. Her only friend in New York was Lew Christensen, who was also a member of Loring's new company. But at age 26, starting fresh held few terrors for the descendant of pioneers. Moreover, she had a principal dancer's contract, and in New York, she would have far more resources to develop her talent and technique and feed her ever-curious mind.

Apart from a warm coat, the first thing she needed was a place to live. Housing, particularly affordable housing, has always been a problem for New York artists. In the first few months, Reed lived in a hotel on Manhattan's West Side. It was conveniently located near Loring's studio, which was on West 56th Street in back of Carnegie Hall. There, she got to know Loring very well and learned an approach to ballet that was new to her in some ways and familiar in others. Willam Christensen had looked toward Europe for the raw material and the music for his ballets (with the exception of *And Now the Brides*), focusing on theatrical values, the expression of character and narrative, and the vocabulary of *l'école de danse*. While Loring was just as interested in telling stories, he quite deliberately looked to American material—pioneers, the urban poor, a famous outlaw—and, while he certainly made some use of the classical vocabulary in all his ballets, he also tapped into modern movement and popular dance, even equestrian gaits in *Billy the Kid,* mixing them all up with enormous success. He was fearless in combining genres and techniques, perhaps because the first concert dance he saw, when he was a teenager in Milwaukee, was performed by Diaghilev's Ballets Russes and Uday Shankar, the great Indian modernist, who also influenced Bolender. "I didn't know the difference between ballet and anything else," Loring said in 1976, "[and] except [for] tap, dance was dance."[1]

On the strength of *Billy,* which is still regarded as his most successful ballet, Loring was asked to head what was then called the American wing at Ballet Theatre, which he joined as both a dancer and a choreographer right after the Caravan's 1939 tour. For the company's debut program in January 1940, he created *The Great American Goof,* which audiences loathed and critics loved. In collaboration with writer William Saroyan, Loring used a musical score by Henry Brant, the composer of *City Portrait;* spoken text; and sliding stage screens in a work that was far ahead of its time and confusing for an audience primed to expect an evening of romantic ballet. A year later, Ballet Theatre had one of its chronic financial crises and Loring used his layoff time to found a company that would be the logical extension of Ballet Caravan, an all-American company that offered choreographies based on American themes.

Like Ballet Caravan, Dance Players was underwritten by a cultivated, wealthy patron, a woman who was a writer and poet with an interest in creating librettos for dance. Winthrop Palmer, the descendant of early Massachusetts settlers, was deeply involved in the programs of the New Deal, such as the music, dance, and literary projects of the Works Project Administration that kept so many artists and the arts they practiced alive during the Depression. Palmer was not just a supporter of the arts, dance in particular, she also helped individual artists. When Dance Players folded, she gave Reed money to help tide her over until she got another job.

Loring drew on his connections to Ballet Caravan to assemble a roster of fifteen dancers (sixteen including himself) that Lew Christensen and Reed led as principals. Michael Kidd, who had replaced Loring when he left Ballet Caravan, was also his rehearsal director. Former Littlefield dancers Joan McCracken and Zachary Solov were also company members. They were handpicked to perform a repertory of what Loring called "dance plays." *Billy, Harlequin for President* and a very much reworked *City Portrait* were remounted. Christensen created *Jinx* for the company and Loring added

Prairie, based on the eponymous Carl Sandburg poem. *The Man from Midian* (which had a libretto by Palmer and was inspired by the Old Testament account of the life of Moses) and *The Duke of Sacramento* (which was based on Native American folktales from the Southwest and was performed only once) were also part of a repertory that gave Reed and the other dancers some wonderful roles.

The Dance Players repertory increased Reed's range immensely as a performer. Much of it prepared her to work with Antony Tudor after she joined Ballet Theatre in 1943. Except for *Harlequin* and the *Duke of Sacramento,* little of the repertory was cheerful or comic. Most of it called for the dramatic skills she had employed in Willam Christensen's *Romeo and Juliet*—specifically *Prairie, City Portrait* (the last piece Loring made for the Caravan), and *Jinx,* which premiered in Schenectady on April 9, 1942, a work some critics think the best Lew Christensen ever made. All of them provided Reed with very different roles, shifting her from the portrayal of a European peasant girl (Swanhilda) and a Veronese aristocrat (Juliet) in Willam Christensen's work to a woman in *Prairie* who could have been one of her own pioneering ancestors and an impoverished girl of the tenements in *City Portrait,* who surely reminded her of the tough times in Portland when she danced in a speakeasy and scavenged for rubber tires to burn for fuel.

Reed always thought Loring hired her because she was short, and she was partly correct. "She was a perfect partner for me," Loring said in 1976, because he was also short, a physical attribute that kept him from classical roles. While he didn't remember seeing her live on stage in *Coppélia* when Ballet Caravan and San Francisco Opera Ballet crossed paths in Seattle in 1939, he did recall seeing film of her probably taken by Ann Barzel in Chicago. In general terms, Loring hired Reed and the other members of Dance Players because he needed "people who had a good technique but, primarily, those who could perform the repertoire that I would be presenting. I was looking for something more than just technique. Naturally one tries to get the people who are most technically developed because . . . [it] makes it possible for them to express ideas."[2]

As principal dancer, Reed learned the role of the Sweetheart in *Billy* and the little sister in *City Portrait,* and she originated leading roles in *The Man from Midian,* in which she danced barefoot, and in *Prairie,* the first ballet she remembered working on with the meticulously organized choreographer: "He made charts and was very methodical in everything. Everything was very carefully studied, [and] he worked fairly quickly. I think he went in a studio by himself and really worked out the movement and when he came [in] he gave it to you." This was quite different from the process of such choreographers as Tudor, Jerome Robbins, Balanchine, and Agnes de Mille, who created on Reed later on. "[They had] a framework and then within that they [were] more flexible."[3]

Prairie, which had music by Norman Dello Joio, who later composed for Martha Graham, can be viewed as a sequel to *Billy,* which is as much about the westward migration as it is about the outlaw. In the first of *Prairie's* four parts, homesteaders settle east of Billy's territory, in the Midwest, establishing communities, planting crops, and raising families. The second part, about the next generation, features a prodigal daughter (Reed's role) who, bored with the daily routine, leads an exodus to the cities, where she and her companions find the same hardscrabble life as on the prairie, mixed with some urban grit. In the third movement, a man rescues the prodigal daughter and takes her back to her parents and the land. In the finale, to quote the synopsis, "they return to [it] not as homesteaders but as enlightened people who have learned the source of their strength and the cradle of their wisdom."[4]

According to Reed, "*Prairie* was the story of families moving west, not a particular family, but a symbolic one. In a way," she said, "it was like an American *Les Sylphides,* in that we wore a modification of Western dress in the shape of a long tutu. The costume was wool, with long sleeves, a high-necked frontierswoman's dress, and it changed the look of our movement [which was on pointe], but it was right for a frontierswoman." It was also remarkably uncomfortable to dance in. Beyond the costuming, Reed thought *Prairie* was similar to *Sylphides* because Loring chose to do it "in classical form, with a corps, pas de deux and pas de quatre."[5]

Cities get a bad rap in *Prairie* and an even worse one in *City Portrait,* which is set in Depression-era New York, and, by all accounts, was laced with the bitterness and degradation of the times. It is about the disintegration of a family of five that is confined to too-close quarters in a tenement apartment under the Third Avenue El. Brant's score contained quotations from Beethoven's *Moonlight Sonata* and what John Martin, who admired it, described as street music. Reed recalled the ballet being "rough and tough. I was the younger sister and I did it on pointe . . . a little girl playing in the streets with a tough, mean older brother." (Loring said the ballet was first done in slippers, then, for Dance Players, in heeled shoes.) Kidd was the mean brother, dancing like "one of the guys in *West Side Story*. . . . A lost little sister, a tough hard-boiled brother—the older sister already beginning to hit the streets and you knew she would become a prostitute." This was not a piece destined to be a crowd-pleaser.[6]

Neither was Lew Christensen's *Jinx,* which New York City Ballet revived in 1949 (both Bolender and Reed performed leading roles in it there), the same year it went into San Francisco Ballet's repertory. Reed originated the Girl in Pink, a tightrope walker who is the object of the title character's affections. Jinx is a clown who always seems to be present when some kind of disaster befalls the circus people. The only person who loves him, let alone likes him, is the Bearded Lady, whose attentions he rejects. It's a complex work with a decidedly dark side. Benjamin Britten, who wrote the score, gave permission for composer Colin McPhee to transcribe it for the two pianos that were the customary accompaniment for Dance Players. Some writers have called *Jinx* an American *Petrouchka;* one critic compared it to Leoncavallo's opera *I Pagliacci,* to which, in terms of plot at least, it bears a far closer resemblance.

After a fairly lengthy rehearsal period, Dance Players went on a short tour of the Northeast, performing in Baltimore, New Haven, and upstate New York. On April 21, they opened at the National Theatre in Manhattan, ending their sole New York season on May 3.

The *New York Times*'s John Martin reviewed the second week of the season quite favorably, treating the much-changed *City Portrait* as a new ballet, writing approvingly of its more sympathetic tone and "greater feeling of unity. Its episodes are outstandingly imaginative of movement and create atmosphere eloquently." Of the score, he wrote: "Brant's music is both atmospheric and sardonic, and its use of polytonality succeeds in projecting a psychological state quite remarkably." The principal dancers, including Reed and Kidd, he judged to be capable, concluding that "the company has found itself and got into its stride in a remarkably short time for a new organization, and its final week finds it a lively and highly interesting little outfit."[7] Anatole Chujoy was disappointed in the revised *City Portrait,* although he gave Reed high marks for her performance as the desperate little sister who tries and fails to keep the family together.

Critical response from Walter Terry and George Amberg was also quite mixed, although the latter gave Loring high marks for "[a] creative imagination [which] endows all his work with the quality of an immediate human experience."[8] All three found the ensemble dancers weaker on the whole than the principals, although Terry singled out McCracken as the Sweetheart in *Billy*.

Their New York season over, the Dance Players spent the summer in New Hope, Pennsylvania, where, according to a feature story in the local paper, they played Monopoly and Reed poured shellac into her pointe shoes to make them last longer, a task in which she was as well practiced as doing the daily barre. In the course of the summer, the Players presented *The Duke of Sacramento* at the Bucks County Playhouse (it was its only performance) and Reed taught ballet. What critics had deemed to be an extremely promising company disbanded in the late fall; the Dance Players gave their final performance in Trenton, New Jersey, on November 12. Loring returned to Ballet Theatre, which was up and running again, taking several of the dancers with him, including Kidd. He didn't stay long; management declined to let him continue with experimental works like *The Great American Goof* in favor of more commercially viable ballets, requesting instead that he make a ballet based on *Show Boat*. Loring declined and departed for Broadway and Hollywood, where he could make considerably more money.

A few months before Reed's arrival in New York, Bolender returned from South America with American Ballet Caravan and headed home to Canton for a family visit in a pattern he would follow for many years, this time traveling with fellow Cantonese Mary Jane Shea. While he had tried to persuade Catherine Littlefield, who was working on Broadway at this time, to do another multicity tour, she had disbanded her company, in part because most of her male dancers had been drafted. Bolender, who was classified 1A before he went to South America, was also subject to the draft, but in an interview with his draft board after his return he was asked a routine question about homosexual encounters. Like Jerome Robbins, he answered in the affirmative, which got his classification changed to 4F, which meant the armed services did not want him.

Balanchine always had employment for his dancers in mind, and he quickly arranged for Bolender and several other Caravan dancers to appear in the New Opera Company's *Rosalinda*, for which he was the choreographer, assisted by William Dollar as ballet master. "His dances for this production were elegant and charming," Bolender said, and the show was an immediate hit.

Rosalinda was based heavily on Johann Strauss's *Die Fledermaus*, excerpts from which Balanchine had used for *The Bat*; Bolender had performed half the title role for the latter on the South American tour. Balanchine had created the title part for a man and a woman who "separated and 'covered everybody' with one giant wing each, then got back together again at the end." It premiered at the Forty-Fourth Street Theatre on October 28, 1942, and had a thirteen-month run, closing in November of the following year.

Bolender, Dollar, and Yvonne Patterson, who Bolender partnered in the operetta, were all living in an apartment house at 1246 Second Avenue. All three were working extremely hard, but they were also having what Bolender loved to refer to as a "*wonder*ful time," onstage and off. Modern dancer José Limón had the male dancing lead in *Rosalinda* (it would be his last performance on Broadway), and Bolender and Patterson did everything they could to upstage him. During a ballroom scene in one performance, Bolender poured champagne down Patterson's bosom. Conductor Erich Korngold, an Austro-Hungarian émigré who had already won an Oscar for film music (in which he was a pioneering composer), evidently egged them on from the podium. In a letter Bolender wrote to Patterson in March 1991, mostly about the success of that year's Kansas City Ballet Ball, Bolender reminisced happily about their shenanigans in the operetta: "I haven't worn tails and white tie since *Rosalinda,* when you and I used to kick up our heels as Korngold conducted the orchestra delighted with our performance and egging us on to higher and higher champagne antics."[9]

In another letter, written two months later, after Bolender and Patterson had a face-to-face meeting in New York, Bolender writes of the South American tour when "[he] was a corps de ballet boy and you were an uppity soloist" that "[their] great romance didn't begin until *Rosalinda* when the Germans got a lot more than they ever expected when you and I would burst upon the stage nightly (I would fire the two of us on the spot) tho I must admit we certainly did our best to enliven that bunch of dead and boring chorus singers who oddly enough seemed to object to our clarion voices joining in 'Brother mine, sister mine . . . etc.' . . . and ANYWAY, just thought I'd give your memory a jog to see if you happened to think of those ghastly days by any chance. We should have a champagne toast to the fact we've got this far, n'est-ce pas?"[10]

When the theater was dark, they would go to what they called the "bare-assed" beach, a section of Jones Beach on Long Island that was reserved for those who liked to swim and sunbathe nude. They also delighted in picking up French sailors, with whom wartime New York abounded, and taking them home to Patterson's mother, who had lived in France and was pleased to practice her French by flirting with them. New York, a great liberty port during World War II, was crawling with sailors of all nationalities; more than one ballet was made about them.[11]

Dancers in New York in the 1940s worked hard, none harder than Reed and Bolender. Both were taking classes at the School of American Ballet; Bolender was teaching here and there, including at the Fokine School; Reed, in the period before she joined Ballet Theatre, was rushing around New York, teaching ballet at The New School and tap dancing in a studio over the Apollo Theater in Harlem.[12] In the summer before the opening of *Rosalinda*, Bolender put together a summer workshop on a farm in East Stroudsburg in the Poconos, not far from where Dance Players was having its summer program. A very young Patricia Wilde was a participant and she recalled that Bolender had converted part of a barn to a dance studio with his own hands and was usually the person who cooked breakfast for everyone.[13]

In the fall of 1943, with Balanchine's name and blessing, a loan from Winthrop Palmer of $600 (which was fully repaid), and Doug Coudy as stage manager and dancer, Bolender, Shea, and Dollar formed the American Concert Ballet as a vehicle for creating their own work. They gave their debut performance on October 31 at the Central Needle Trades High School, where Ballet Society would have its debut performances in 1946. The Concert Ballet was even shorter-lived than Dance Players: nearly everyone involved was already dancing in musical comedies. After the group's debut, it performed only two more times, once at the 92nd Street YMHA and once at Amherst College. However, it was extremely important as a petri dish for new work, as Edwin Denby pointed out in his review for the *Herald Tribune*. For would-be choreographers who were performing with the touring companies—the Ballet Russe de Monte Carlo and Ballet Theatre—and who had little free time or rehearsal space, it offered a chance to try their hand at making movement and an opportunity to hone their choreographic skills.[14]

There was an attempt to make the Concert Ballet into a permanent touring company as an alternative to the big companies. According to an unsigned and undated mission statement (probably written in 1944), it would be "one in which ballet will once again be presented as an expressive art," something the larger companies were failing at because of their need for box-office attractions that would reach a popular audience. "[They] have transformed American ballet into Broadway big business, because they dare not gamble on experimental work." The document includes a proposal for a tour of small cities with fifteen dancers performing work by Balanchine, Robbins, Dollar, Shea, Bolender, and Taras. There would be no star system and the proposed salary for the entire company, including staff and musicians, would be $41 a week.

For Bolender, the Concert Ballet, not to mention the use of studio space at SAB, was crucial to his development as a choreographer, in part because of the skills and talents of the dancers who made up the sixteen-member roster. A few years later, he told writer Baird Hastings that he had always been fortunate in the dancers he worked with. In this instance, they included, among others, Gisella Caccialanza Christensen, Leda Anchutina Eglevsky, Yvonne Patterson, Dorothie Littlefield, and Reed.

The only ballet that was not a premiere at the first performance was Balanchine's *Concerto Barocco*, which was experimental only in the sense that it had no plot. As titular head of the company, Balanchine lent his name and his ballet to show his support. Dollar had choreographed for Ballet Caravan and the South American tour, using both classical steps (*Air and Variations*) and social dances (*Juke Box*). Bolender, who had had some practice in creating dances when he studied with Hanya Holm, wasn't a complete novice, either. His *Mother Goose Suite,* set to Maurice Ravel's charming score, was basically a series of classical divertissements linked by a woman's memories. It was his first work using the steps of *l'école de la danse,* and it was remarkably successful.

"All of my ballets are about the human condition," Bolender said toward the end of his life, and that is certainly true of the first one he made.[15] The ballet is a reverie in which an older woman watches her younger self dancing with fairy tale characters that represent events from her past. The meditation on youth and its vulnerabilities is a theme Bolender would return to thirteen years later with *At the Still Point* and the "wallflower" section of *Souvenirs. Mother Goose,* for which Bolender rearranged the order of

Ravel's score to suit his narrative purposes, has five distinct segments, beginning with a young girl surrounded by clouds (represented by dancers on pointe swirling white fabric around their heads, an idea he may have gotten from Balanchine's *Errante,* with its rippling satin skirt) who is dancing quietly, seemingly for herself. As she dances, a second woman costumed in an evening gown crosses the stage and seats herself in a replica of an opera-house box to watch a series of divertissements that begins with the music for the "Enchanted Garden."

In this section, the girl is left out of a dance for four couples; she's an outsider, not part of the group, as is made clear by its conclusion, in which the men lift the women and carry them off stage, over the young girl's head. The vocabulary is classical, but in the following section—about the miniature Hop O' My Thumb and a bird who seduces him with her long, long hair, capturing him by draping it over him—there are movement details that echo the modernists of the day. (Bolender expanded the pas de deux with the bird in 1949, when he reworked the ballet because Una Kai, who had "very good hair," in her words, was performing the role.)[16] The bird leaves the boy and he dances a tentative pas de deux with the young girl, but like most first loves, it does not end well, and the boy returns to his captor.

Of the next two sections—the first, an attempt at a lavish "oriental" spectacle to the "Pagodas" music in which the girl dances with a golden prince and the second about Beauty and the Beast, with the girl as Beauty—John Martin wrote, "[the ballet] exhibits some excellent and original ideas. Even in the less successful passages, the work possesses a feeling of mood and style all to its credit."[17]

Thanks to a magical ring and a godmother, the dream part of the ballet ends happily when the Beast, transformed to a handsome prince, carries the girl offstage into a presumably rosy future. But the world-weary spectator turns her back on the dream, exiting slowly as the "clouds" continue to dance. As Bolender said, this was not a ballet for children. *Mother Goose's* divertissements with a twist could conceivably be interpreted as a rejection of nineteenth-century classicism by someone who wanted to create ballets that expressed a twentieth-century American point of view.

In 1950, Baird Hastings published an article that gave equal weight to the choreographic artistry of Bolender, Robbins, and Aurel Milloss. Hastings wrote of *Mother Goose* that it was "tender, evocative and captivating, extremely sincere, while its nobility of movement as well as its satire make for vitality and compulsion."[18] Walter Terry found the ballet appealing in its revival by New York City Ballet seven years later, giving accolades to Reed's performance as the young girl. "[It] is a haunting reverie," he wrote in the *Herald Tribune*, "a woman's dream of the half-forgotten but wholly-sensed adventures of her childhood. This dance is fragile, even evanescent in quality, but its very intangibles give it a hypnotic beauty and rare power. As the young girl . . . Janet Reed was utterly lovely in a part which made full use of her lightness of motion, her delicacy of gesture, her girlishness and her masterful command of the dramatic values of dance."[19]

For his contribution to the Concert Ballet's opening program, Dollar turned to American literature. *The Five Gifts of Life* is based on a fable by Mark Twain that Martin thought "cynical to the point of being adolescent."[20] In the fable, a Fairy offers a youth (danced by Bolender) five gifts—Love, Fame, Riches, Pleasure, and Death—each of which has its perils. What's American about this fable is that Youth keeps getting another chance to make the right choice, which he fails to do in the end. Death is the prize, and the Fairy gives it to a young child (this is Mark Twain, after all) For the Youth's folly, the Fairy gives him Old Age.

It's an odd choice for a ballet, and the critical response was mixed. One critic disliked the music, Ernst von Dohnányi's *Variations on a Nursery Rhyme*. But Martin thought it was Dollar's "most interesting piece so far. He makes terrific demands upon his dancers, especially upon Mr. Bolender in the central role, for he is uncompromising in his use of rapid and brilliant passages." Martin thought the score "excellent for his purposes" and said that "[Dollar] exhibits a fine musical sense."[21]

For Martin, Shea's *Sailor Bar* was a failure, although Bolender, who Coudy thought had captured the essence of the American sailor in his performance in it, thought it "not bad" as a predecessor of *Fancy Free*. From Denby's description, it's quite close, at least in its libretto, to Robbins's groundbreaking work, which premiered the following year. Denby thought the ballet was the most interesting of the new works presented. "It is a realistic scene in a sailor bar," he wrote, "where sailors come in, meet their girls, they dance, they fight, they leave again."[22] He commended the choreographer for creating credible psychological action and "realistic gestures [that] look astonishingly familiar. What is interesting is that they have not been stylized to fit into a definite dance style, they keep their natural contour and impulse; what has been stylized is the weight, the flow and tempo of the motion."[23] *Mother Goose* and *Five Gifts* were taken, briefly, into the repertory of New York City Ballet, but *Sailor Bar* had only a few performances. Shea's promise as a choreographer was not to be fulfilled. The war intervened—she joined the USO in a production of *Rosalinda*—and the few women choreographers who succeeded in the ballet world in the 1940s were the exceptions, not the rule.

American Concert Ballet offered Reed her first opportunity to dance in Balanchine's work. While she was not cast in *Concerto Barocco* for the opening concert, she distinctly remembered performing it "as a workshop thing" in the studio at SAB, partnered by Nicholas Magallanes with Balanchine and violinist Nathan Milstein watching. They danced in their own practice clothes rather than the fussy tutus and tunics replete with curlicues designer Eugene Berman created to represent the baroque period for the original production. "We did it several places here in New York, [when] I had a few months of unemployment where I rushed around frantically."[24]

Balanchine knew Reed needed a job, and at one point in this period—when he was working with Lorenz Hart on a new musical that never happened because of Hart's untimely death a few months later, he arranged for her to meet him. Reed dressed as she thought appropriate for an audition, with her hair pulled back in a ballerina bun. Hart took one look at her and said she couldn't possibly be the sultry cast member he had in mind. "I can be anything I want," Reed retorted, stung by his rudeness not only to her but to Balanchine, who was present.[25] Not long after that, she joined Ballet Theatre, first as a guest artist to be the Sweetheart in *Billy the Kid,* then as a soloist and principal, replacing Anabelle Lyon, another petite dancer. For the next six years, Reed danced roles ranging from the nasty Youngest Sister in Tudor's *Pillar of Fire* to the Second Passerby in Robbins's *Fancy Free,* a part she originated and defined.

Getting into Ballet Theatre in its early days was not a simple matter, as is clear from Reed's recollection of how she did it. Dance critic and editor Anatole Chujoy, like Balanchine and Kirstein, was interested in helping dancers he liked find paid employment. While holding court at a table in the Russian Tea Room one day, he advised Reed to get in touch with Lucia Chase about joining the company. This turned out to be a bum steer (Reed's words) she told him later, because at the time, Chase—the financial angel behind the company—wanted to be regarded as just another dancer. "I am not the director of the company," Chase said angrily, when Reed telephoned her. "I have nothing to do with hiring dancers."[26] The person who did was Ballet Theatre's business manager, Gerald (Gerry) Sevastianov and it was he, as far as Reed knew, who hired her, although Chase may well have had the final say.

When Reed was still a guest artist, Tudor saw her dance and asked if she could learn the French ballerina in *Gala Performance,* his satirical look at dancing divas set to Prokofiev. The role called for constant motion, as La Fille de Terpsichore, as she was called, plays catch-me-if-you-can with her frustrated partner.[27] There was so little time for Reed to learn the role before she performed it on the stage of the Metropolitan Opera House that she heard the orchestra for the first time as she waited in the wings to make her entrance. Tudor, however, was sufficiently pleased with her performance that he next put her in his *Judgment of Paris* as Juno, which, with *Billy*'s Sweetheart, gave Reed three principal roles as a guest artist. In time, she signed a company contract, went on the summer tour to the West Coast, and then, without anything to dance, "just sort of sat around." Much as she needed the money, something in the neighborhood of $35 a week, she thought it was very unfair "to be collecting a salary and not performing."[28] Since she took company class and watched many rehearsals in order to learn parts that she hoped to dance, she wasn't exactly twiddling her thumbs, but her need to be on stage was such that dancer Hugh Laing had to persuade her not to volunteer to dance in the corps, fearing that she would never get out of it, as has happened to many dancers.[29] Patience paid off, and Anton Dolin cast her in his version of *Pas de Quatre,* which he had set on the company two years earlier.

"Then little by little, I began to do a little more. The Page in *Bluebeard, Graduation Ball,* after Riabouchinska did the opening. One thing led to another and then I was dancing in lots of ballets, two ballets a night on one-night stands. Three sometimes," she said in an interview with Tobi Tobias.[30]

On October 12, 1943, Reed danced Fanny Cerrito in *Pas de Quatre* and the Youngest Sister in *Pillar of Fire,* two very different roles, the first calling for charm and nineteenth-century technique, the second requiring adolescent impatience and sneaky seductiveness, rendered in Tudor's modern classicism. Learning the Youngest Sister was a grueling process that was emotionally demanding in ways that none of her previous roles had been, although in Loring's work Reed had begun to analyze them much like a Method actor. Tudor, the master of the psychological narrative, forced her to dig far deeper into both her own psyche and the Youngest Sister's. "He had to really work quite hard with me to strip off, oh, some veneer or concepts [in order to] get down to the nitty-gritty of [her character]." Reed did not originate the role—Annabelle Lyon did—but Tudor "treated it almost as though it was from scratch and spent hours and hours in rehearsal, and *nothing* was right and it just went on and on and on digging, digging, digging until I simply blew up. Burst into tears and fled." She blocked from her memory exactly what Tudor had said to her, pulled herself together, dried her eyes, and returned to rehearsal. After many performances, Tudor, who was never completely satisfied at last began to say, "Yes, we're on the right path."[31]

There were both personal and professional challenges in *Pillar*. Offstage, Reed and Nora Kaye, who danced Hagar, were friends, close enough for Kaye to be Reed's matron of honor in 1946, when, at age 30, she was ready to pay some attention to her private life and get married. Onstage, they were nothing of the kind. Tudor's choreography called for Reed, as the malicious Youngest Sister, to make a physical attack on Kaye as the moody, sexually repressed Hagar, who disgraces her New England family with loveless sex on a hot summer night:

> There's one point where I'm supposed to run and she's right in the middle of a jeté, and I'm supposed to hit her in the back and knock her. I was afraid I would hit her too hard and she'd fall and hurt herself. [Tudor] kept goading me into this and setting up this relationship of really I must feel this way about this stupid sister—why does she mope around and act like that? Finally I went all out. And with great *glee* I hit her in the back [when she was] in mid-air and knocked her all the way into the wings.

Kaye evidently didn't hold it against her, amusing Reed by observing in the aftermath that she was really beginning to feel the role. What she might have resented, however, was Reed's compliance with instructions from Tudor to tell Kaye to "'watch her back' in a section of the ballet where she had to kneel with her back turned to the audience:

I'd go on and mutter out of the corner of my mouth, "Watch your back! Hold your back!" I didn't notice it—she seemed strong to me—but it may have been tiring and he was constantly needling her from the wings. That was one moment when she could rest, but not *really*. She was not moving but she was not resting. She had to hold and keep the tension in the body. And her nose was running and all the uncomfortable things were happening.

Dancing for Tudor, as had been the case with Willam Christensen, required the performers' undivided attention: "There was no kidding around and walking into the wings at the last minute. You prepared and you were in the character an hour before you made your entrance."

Getting into character well before going on stage is what Method actors do. For Reed, and in some respects also for Bolender, acting was as intertwined with ballet as music was for Balanchine. "Although I love to just dance, just pure movement," she told Tobias, "even in doing just [that] there's an acting thing that happens too. I just never feel anything is completely abstract. It's you and you're not abstract; you're a human being and whatever you do, you emerge."[32]

Early in her San Francisco career, Reed had acted intuitively, without much analysis of what she was doing as the feisty Swanhilda in *Coppélia* or the doomed Juliet in Christensen's reduction of Shakespeare's play. The analysis began with Dance Players, particularly with *Man from Midian*, with Palmer discussing her libretto and her intentions in retelling the story of Moses. Working with Tudor went way beyond that, particularly in *Pillar*, where she not only had to become a teenager fed up with her older sister (which was probably not easy for an only child), she also had to be completely immersed in the ethos of a small town in New England in the dog days of summer. "The movement, the business of it being a New England town, a hot summer's afternoon, and I'm the pretty one that all the boys like, and we go down to the corner for an ice cream soda. And the way you move on a hot, sticky afternoon in a small New England town. . . . Also her character was feline. The movement was cat-like. So I must have had a hard time getting it right for him because he worked and worked and worked."[33]

On the other hand, in an interview with Judith Chazin-Bennahum, Reed characterized Tudor's use of "imagery to help the dancer create a role," as wonderful: "For the kittenish younger sister in *Pillar of Fire* he told me she never looked at anyone directly; it was always from down and under. She never went straight to anything; her movements were all curly. In *Jardin aux Lilas* he told me to move as if I were stepping on grass; in *Gala Performance* it was a red velvet carpet. He never worked on character as a thing apart from dance; the character was in the movement."[34]

Roles in Tudor ballets that Reed took over or shared with others held different dramatic challenges. As Juno, in Tudor's seedy version of the *Judgment of Paris* (the goddesses are prostitutes), she was a world-weary lady of the night. In *Gala Performance*, she was a nineteenth-century French ballerina in a takeoff on the art form she had fallen in love with in her teens. In *Dim Lustre*, a ballet filled with Proustian *nostalgie*, she originated one of three Who Was Shes, and in Tudor's Freudian-soaked ballet *Undertow*, which premiered almost exactly a year after *Fancy Free*, on April 10, 1945, she originated the role of Hera and performed a bridal pas de deux with Richard Beard. Beard remembered Tudor telling them only that "we were a lascivious couple underneath our wedding costumes, barely able to wait for the bedroom when they would come off."[35] *Undertow* was a highly controversial ballet for its raw and seedy characters, the violence presented on stage (there is a murder and a gang rape), and for the graphic portrayal of the psychologically damaged protagonist's birth, when his mother rejects him the moment he emerges from the womb. A photograph of Reed in an extraordinary picture spread in the May 7, 1945, issue of *Life* magazine shows her in full bridal regalia, laughing as the Groom lifts her high in the air.

In a summary review of Ballet Theatre's 1943–1944 season, Reed's first full season as a company member, Martin singled out dancers for special bouquets. He tossed one her way, describing her as "delightful and versatile" and "a distinct addition to the organization."[36] In the course of the season, she had shown that versatility in leading and soloist roles in *Billy*, *Pillar*, Agnes de Mille's *Tally-Ho* (as a neglected lady of the French court) and *Three Virgins and a Devil*, and Fokine's *Bluebeard* and *Petrouchka*, for which Balanchine, coming upon her rehearsing by herself, gave her some valuable coaching in the difficult role of the Ballerina. She also played leading roles in *Pas de Quatre*, *Princess Aurora* (Bluebird Pas de Deux), and *Fancy Free*, in which Robbins, who Martin cited in the same review as a promising addition to Ballet Theatre, gave her the chance to be no one other than herself.

April 18, 1944, the opening night of *Fancy Free,* Robbins's first ballet, was the stuff of artists' dreams. Nobody, least of all Robbins; Leonard Bernstein, whose first theatrical score it was; or any of the cast members, including Reed, imagined they would take more than twenty curtain calls and make American ballet history. "We all knew something very special had just happened," Bolender, who was in the audience, said decades later. Denby described the scene at the Metropolitan Opera House:

> Jerome Robbins' *Fancy Free,* the world premiere given by Ballet Theatre last night at the Metropolitan, was so big a hit the young participants all looked a little dazed as they took their bows. But besides being a smash hit, *Fancy Free* is a very remarkable comedy piece. Its sentiment of how people live in this country is completely intelligent and completely realistic. Its pantomime and its dances are witty, exuberant, and at every moment they feel natural. It is a direct, manly piece: there isn't any of that coy showing off of material that dancers are doing so much nowadays. The whole number is as sound as a superb vaudeville turn; in ballet terminology it is a perfect American character ballet.[37]

Fancy Free is the story of three sailors on shore leave in New York and three girls (called passersby in Robbins's libretto) who have an encounter that begins and ends outside a Broadway bar, with action aplenty inside it in between. Kermit Love designed the costumes, 1940s-style dresses with short, flippy skirts and summer-white sailor suits, and the set was designed by Oliver Smith, who, like Robbins and Bernstein, was only 25 years old.[38] Robbins's 27-minute ballet contains steps from such social dances of the day as a *danzón,* a rhumba-like Latin American dance, for a solo he himself originally performed; the Lindy; the Shorty George; and, according to Robbins in an interview published in *Dance Magazine* in 1980, "a lot of theatrical dancing, you know, like waltz clogs, time steps, Shuffle Off to Buffalo."[39]

To cast the ballet, which was not performed on pointe but contained a good many classical steps, like grands jetés and tours en l'air, and a central pas de deux, Robbins chose his friends: Reed, Muriel Bentley, and Shirley Eckl as the three girls; John Kriza, Harold Lang, and himself as the sailors. In part, he chose them for their technical versatility. As dance historian Nancy Reynolds writes, they were "five impertinent youngsters, all American born and trained, for whom the switch from vaudeville tricks to the jitterbug to classical ballet pyrotechnics posed no problems; they could wiggle, they could sway, they could somersault and they could execute a grand pirouette with the best of the classical princes. That kind of versatility was American."[40] Bentley, who was a tall brunette with the confident sophistication of the city girl, was cast as the First Passerby; Reed, who, in 1943, when Robbins first conceived the ballet, had only been in New York a short time, had the petite prettiness and image of country freshness that was a natural for the Second Passerby. "Muriel's movement was more big city . . . sharp and staccato; she was a real rhythmic virtuoso," Reed said in 1980. "I guess my girl was a little softer, sweeter. Long red hair hanging loose. Every girl I saw do it after me I thought was too tough and hard, consciously trying to be sexy. Which I didn't think was right . . . I never really thought of that girl as anyone but myself."[41]

Robbins had first seen Reed perform in Dance Players and, like most of the people who saw her at the time, thought she was wonderful. Many of the reviewers of *Fancy Free* pegged her as an unknown, a young soloist with the company, even though by 1944, at age 28 she was highly experienced, having performed professionally in principal and soloist roles for nearly a decade on both sides of the continent and on tour all over the United States. Robbins, who had watched her in the work of other choreographers for Ballet Theatre, was well aware of Reed's talents as a theatrical dancer. He knew she was capable of giving fine-tuned, highly detailed performances, which is why he "knew that there was material I wanted to work with. And I used her a lot while she was in the company. I did *Interplay* with her. *Fancy Free*. And then when she joined New York City Ballet I used her there."[42]

Fancy Free was created under the most grueling conditions. Robbins seized every free moment on a tour that began in January 1944, taking the company by train and bus to Tennessee, Texas, California, Minnesota, Ohio, the Pacific Northwest, and Vancouver, British Columbia. Not only did he have to persuade his friends to rehearse when they were exhausted from dancing in four ballets the night before, in Ballet Theatre's "ham and eggs" programming, they also "rehearsed whenever and wherever they could, sometimes for little more than a half hour. *Fancy Free* was hammered out coast to coast on stages, in rehearsal studios, in hotel lobbies, in nightclubs during daytime hours, and on trains."[43]

Robbins observed sailors and their rolling walk, their sense of entitle-ment as they sauntered down New York's Broadway or in cities where Ballet Theatre was on tour as they prowled in and out of bars and night-clubs. "Jerry picked up on everything that was going on all around us," Reed remembered. "I didn't actually witness this, but someone, Johnny [Kriza] or Jerry, told me that the little episode in Jerry's solo, the rhumba, where he pretends to dance with a girl who isn't there . . . he got the idea from seeing a drunken soldier pick up a chair in a bar and dance with it as though it were a girl. Then once, on tour, looking out a train window, we saw planes flying in a shifting, triangular formation, and Jerry cho-reographed that into the opening sailors' dance. And one time we were in Bloomington, Indiana, walking down the street on the way to the theater, and Jerry said, 'I wonder what would happen if' and he described the girl running and suddenly jumping and the boy catching her. He just talked his image of it as we were walking. I let him walk on ahead a little ways and I said, 'You mean like this?' and I ran down the street and jumped at him. And he had to drop his bag to catch me. That's in the pas de deux we did together."[44]

Reed and Robbins left the tour in Cincinnati to return to New York and work directly in the studio with Bernstein, who had been corresponding with Robbins and sending him wax recordings of a piano reduction of the score. The slowness of the communication frustrated both collaborators. The goal was to create the central pas de deux, which Reed would perform first with the choreographer and later on with Kriza. The process was the most collaborative Reed had been involved in, and she found it highly sat-isfying. "I think when we were in a studio working we were really impro-vising and Leonard Bernstein was improvising, and we did this back and forth thing. Then once he got something then he'd go home and work on it. But we experimented and it was an *exhausting* time of trial and error and experiment. . . . I enjoyed it even though it was tiring. It was really very exciting, very stimulating. Because as a dancer I felt a part of the creative thing because I was contributing, too."[45]

The duet is tender and ephemeral. It has many high lifts, separations, and reunions and ends with a feathery kiss and Reed's character gently wiping the lipstick from the sailor's mouth. This is clearly not a relationship with a future; the ballet was made at the height of American involvement in World War II, as Reed comments:

The whole attitude of so many young people at that time was very disoriented. And we were living right in the middle of it: On tour, when we could get a train, the Ballet Theatre cars would be hooked up to the troop cars. All those soldiers and sailors and ballet troupes, in strange places and different towns. We were uprooted, and although we had a very carefree attitude, we were also very tentative about relationships. There was a certain brashness . . . mixed with a sensitive, almost timid quality. We were all so terribly young, not necessarily young in years, but kind of innocent, and rather lonely. Our attitude was one of wanting to be close to one another, but knowing that it couldn't last. So that there was this constant reaching out, but knowing that it was only temporary. Can you see that in the choreography, in the pas de deux?[46]

And of course you can, perhaps not as clearly as when the ballet was first made and perhaps not as clearly with twenty-first-century dancers, but the ephemeral nature of chance meetings is inherent in the choreography, as is Reed's precise characterization when pretty girl and sailor come to a parting of the ways. Even in grainy black-and-white film clips, the polished dramatic quality of Reed's performance is clearly visible along with the gestural details—a hip cocked, a hand flexed, a wistful facial expression.

Denby returned to the Metropolitan Opera House a few nights after the opening and paid tribute to the cast in a review titled "Fancy Free: A Second Time." "They dance it with a direct vitality and a sense of real life that are even more remarkable than their dance brilliance. The three sailors . . . of course have the best roles. But Janet Reed's transition from the stiffness she first gives her hardboiled part to the later natural abandon is superb."[47]

While Reed never viewed her character as hardboiled, Denby picked up on her ability to look natural in all the character ballets she performed in. On May 2, after watching her in three out of four ballets (*Pas de Quatre, Fancy Free,* and *Tally-Ho*) at the Met the night before, he made Reed the centerpiece of his review, further defining her as a soubrette in not entirely positive terms. "It was a tour de force," he wrote, and "redheaded Miss Reed carried it off with determination."[48]

He continued, "As a dancer she is a born soubrette: petite, active, bounding, sharp, malicious and strong. She is in her element in character parts where the gesture counts and the speed makes a point. Her fault on the stage is that she often has a tendency to force both in her movement and in her projection; the first breaks the continuity, the second isolates her own part from the general atmosphere and meaning of a ballet. Forcing, except in farce, destroys the dancer's dignity."[49] That is true enough, although both *Pas de Quatre* and *Tally-Ho* could easily be classified as balletic farces. When Denby saw her in *Tally-Ho* for the first time, he judged her "dance technique . . . superior to Miss de Mille's—the steps are more distinct and rapid, she is more at ease in the lifts." But he missed "the sense of legato phrasing that Miss de Mille showed."[50] Tellingly, Denby suggests that "a quieter approach, and movements timed just a trifle behind the beat, might help Miss Reed." Denby had been looking at the way Balanchine choreographed rhythm to reveal the music.

For the 1944–1945 season, David Lichine revived *Graduation Ball*, his 1940 creampuff of a ballet about Viennese cadets, debutantes, and their teachers, originally made for de Basil's Ballets Russes. Chicago critic Ann Barzel gave Reed high praise for her performance as the Junior Girl for "[making her] a charming unsophisticated adolescent. . . . Opposite her dances Harold Lang who has similarly treated the role of the Junior Cadet. Together they make parts of *Graduation Ball* less a farce and more a young party than it has ever been before." Reed was once again proving herself a soubrette to be reckoned with.[51]

Bolender joined Ballet Theatre in June 1944, just in time to participate in rehearsals for a West Coast tour that took the company to Seattle, San Francisco, and Los Angeles, then to Montreal, where Lichine's ballet premiered the end of September. His American Guild of Musical Artists contract, which paid him $70 a week while performing and half that when merely rehearsing, was a good one; $35 a week went quite a long way in the mid-1940s. Nevertheless, this was not a good experience for him. He didn't like the repertory (he characterized it as boring); nor did he care for the training, which seems to have been erratic—company class was not part of the daily routine. Bolender very much enjoyed dancing with his friends—Reed, Kriza, Bentley, Taras, Miriam Golden, and Albia Kavan, who, he said, had a tongue like a whip and always knew all the gossip—and remembered with pleasure the amusing parties they attended during the month they spent in Los Angeles. But he recalled with no pleasure whatsoever the way Lichine treated him and other male dancers: "[He] would stand in front of you and shout in your face, and I thought if I have to put up with this kind of crap I'm going back to modern dance. Ego is very essential in theater people, [but not the kind when] they're trying to kill you. His whole interest was in denigrating the male, any male.[52] Lichine, who was a charismatic performer with both the Ballet Russe and Ballet Theatre and an audience favorite, was nevertheless insecure about his body (by one account he padded his calves with cotton wool so they would look better muscled in tights) and he didn't have good turnout. This might in part account for his attitude toward dancers like Bolender, who was so well turned out naturally that he was able to make the shift from modern to classical technique with considerable ease.

In Montreal, an injury incurred during the dress rehearsal of *Aurora's Wedding*, in which Bolender actually enjoyed dancing one of the Cavaliers, turned out to be a lucky break. Unaware that he had hurt himself badly, Bolender finished the *Aurora* rehearsal and then got himself together for the next ballet on the program, which was probably *Graduation Ball*, in which he danced a pas de trois with Reed and Roy Tobias. "At one point we had to lift Janet, the two of us, and I remember that I was in deep pain from the hand, [and thought] God what was that?" After rehearsal was over, Bolender, still oblivious to the seriousness of his injury, even though his hand was throbbing and swollen, went out to dinner with a group of his friends. A couple of drinks later, one of the stage people came to talk about a technical problem and he excused himself to go to the bathroom. "I stood up and fainted right onto the table, and Miriam got me up, and she put me over her shoulder, said we've got to get you out of here, get you some air and she carried me down the steps, so who was partnering whom?" Golden, who had been on the 1941 South American tour and had the kind of tall, leggy body Balanchine loved, took him to the hospital, where it was determined he had broken his wrist. That, much to his relief, ended his career with Ballet Theatre.

Back in New York, Bolender was able to take barre at SAB, the cast on his wrist notwithstanding, and do some work with Balanchine, including a few rehearsals of *Waltz Academy* which he danced in with Reed. Balanchine was choreographing for Broadway and Hollywood and, without a company of his own, was making work for SAB students and preparing for the 1946 inauguration of Ballet Society. One such work was *Symphonie Concertante*, set to Mozart's Piano Sonata no. 4 in E-flat Major. It was first presented on November 12, 1945, at Carnegie Hall, in collaboration with the National

Orchestra Association (the equivalent of a youth symphony), which was directed by Léon Barzin, who conducted. Bolender, who was listed as guest artist in a program titled "Adventure in Ballet," was the lone male in a cast that included fourteen-year-old Tanaquil Le Clercq. While Bolender thought the plotless ballet one of Balanchine's masterpieces, a "lovely" work, Martin found it "boring" and unrewarding to watch when Ballet Society presented it at New York City Center in 1947, with Le Clercq, Maria Tallchief, and Bolender in the leads. *New Yorker* music critic Robert A. Simon, however, who reviewed the student performance, referred to the ballet as Mr. Balanchine's "fetching version of the [music]." Simon was also pleased with the orchestra's performance of Tchaikovsky's Orchestral Suite no. 2 in C Major, Op. 53, for which Bolender had "neatly choreographed" some sections and Balanchine the others. "All told, this adventure in ballet was a pleasantly stimulating one. It had a few informal moments, especially for early arrivals, who could watch Mr. Balanchine himself dusting the Carnegie Hall stage with resin [*sic*; rosin], or whatever it is they use to keep dancers from slipping and making unscheduled landings on the platform."[53]

Denby, too, was respectful of Bolender's segment of the Tchaikovsky: "Bolender's crisscrossing crowds of dancers in the Valse, though not so limpid as the crowds in Balanchine numbers, was very interesting too, in its romantic expression."[54] Bolender said years later that he had simply done Balanchine's *Serenade* in waltz time and, with typical self-deprecating humor, thought himself terrific!

Clearly, Balanchine, who never explicitly taught a choreography class or workshop, had his eye on Bolender as a potential maker of ballets or he wouldn't have asked him to do the Tchaikovsky segments. A bit later, Bolender "was working on little things" in an SAB studio, which Balanchine had told him to use any time, with Ruthanna Boris and Leon Danielian. They were friends from the Caravan days who were dancing with the Ballet Russe de Monte Carlo and took class at SAB whenever they were in town. This was nothing new: by 1945, SAB had become an informal center for dance in New York. Professional dancers from several companies took class there, and not just ballet. Muriel Stuart, who had been trained by Pavlova and danced in her company, had also studied with German expressionist dancer Harald Kreutzberg and with composer and teacher of musical forms Louis Horst. In addition to classical technique, Stuart taught "plastique," which Doug Coudy said "was really modern dance. Stretching exercises, floor movements—barefoot, an inspiration and very fine teacher." Coudy, who was one of the first male students in the School, recalled in an oral history interview that in the 1930s, soon after it opened, "[De Basil's] Ballet Russe dancers descended on SAB and took class, Lichine, Shabelevski, Baronova, Toumanova, the whole slew." The young American dancers were singularly unimpressed with them and their repertory, which "we didn't think too highly of, because it didn't touch us as Americans. We had no rapport with that repertoire: *Gods Go a-Begging* [by Balanchine at that] and Massine's symphonic ballets. We had no feeling, in a sense, for them." Coudy, who was with Ballet Caravan and also on the South American tour, said that Balanchine provided "a flag to follow. . . . The flag he waved to us was that we were Americans and he had faith in us that we could dance. That's why many came from all over to work with him."

While the conventional wisdom was that there was a deep, unbreachable division between the modern dance and ballet communities in New York in this period (Bolender himself said so in several interviews), like most rules, it had its exceptions. Martha Graham sent young members of her company to SAB to take ballet fundamentals, and Merce Cunningham taught there in the mid-1940s, with John Cage accompanying classes.

Stuart, who was an ideal teacher for Bolender because she had backgrounds in both classical and modern technique, asked him one day if he would like to do a ballet for Ted Shawn's theater at Jacob's Pillow, where she was teaching in the summer program. He said he would try and began working with Boris, Danieli, Le Clercq, Beatrice Tompkins, and Lillian Lanese to make a piece to Stravinsky's *Pulcinella* suite. He was just polishing it up when Balanchine came into the studio, curious about what was going on, and asked to see it. After they ran through it, "Balanchine said, 'very nice, very nice, very nice.' And he . . . left and about an hour later, I got a call from Serge Denham and he said, 'I want you to come over here to Ballet Russe [de Monte Carlo] and discuss your ballet.'" Bolender went immediately to talk to Denham and the next day the whole company came to SAB and "watched us as an audition. We were shaking in our boots."

The result of the audition was a contract for Bolender as guest choreographer and dancer with the company for the 1945–1946 season, on condition that he allow his ballet to be called *Comédia Balletica,* Denham's title and one the choreographer rightly resisted. It was performed at Jacob's Pillow in June with a set piece by Robert Davison, before its September premiere in New York. At the Pillow it was called, far more appropriately, *Musical Chairs.* That's because the ballet, which is performed in simple traditional costume against a backdrop by Robert Davison, involves five dancers, who after performing a solo, duet, or ensemble section, switch seats in what could be described as a balletic version of the "chair dances" that proliferated in the contemporary dance community in the 1960s and 1970s.

The Ballet Russe souvenir program for the 1946–1947 season described it thus:

> Against a harlequinade screen, five dancers appear in conventional ballet costumes. They present themselves to the audience, sit down on stools, take turns in solos, duets and ensembles, changing seats at each conclusion. It is a sort of party, a party of professionals, where each does his or her turn as an entertainer. The style is straight ballet with an iconic sharpness and quickness in timing suited to the acerbity of the orchestra. The choreography has skill, humor, imagination.[55]

Denby reviewed the New York premiere, in which Marie-Jeanne replaced Lanese, not entirely positively; he wrote that although "it was applauded by the audience with enthusiasm" and "was danced with frequent brilliance, and though a promising work, I thought the piece as a whole an unsatisfactory ballet. It marks, however, the big-time debut of a young local choreographer, Todd Bolender, in whose gifts many young dancers have great confidence." Of the title, which, in New York, had reverted to Denham's idea, the ever-astute Denby said, "[it] is a fancy one for a work that is so unpretentious in manner." After commending individual performances, including Bolender's, he concluded that "Mr. Bolender is highly inventive in many details but it strikes me he has missed the Neapolitan amiability, the naturalness of Pergolesi's flow which Stravinsky's score embroiders in such violent and witty color. The music is a pretty fancy joke, but it is a larger joke than the ballet."[56]

Like Denby, Martin objected to the title in not one but two reviews of New York performances, and he also cited Balanchine's influence, with considerable understanding: "[It] is manifestly influenced by Balanchine, and that is natural under the circumstances. . . . But in spite of this obvious debt to a teacher, the choreography has its own skill, its own humor and strong evidence of its own latent style. Toward the end, beginning with Mr.

Bolender's solo, "Vivo," and continuing through the minuet and finale, it breaks away considerably from influences and speaks with an authentic voice. . . . there is genuine promise here. The craftsmanship is good, the imagination is alive."[57]

Following its performance in May in Boston, *Christian Science Monitor* critic Margaret Lloyd also criticized the title, saying that, had *Musical Chairs* been retained, "[the ballet] could pass for good American ballet; for it shows five American ballet dancers just dancing (in a highly technical way) and having fun."[58] Remi Gassmann, however, writing for the *Chicago Times,* was highly dismissive, referring to "commonplaces and precious bits of coy borrowing. . . . And though it might be nice to predict that a second piece by Mr. Bolender will be better than the first, it would be hard to suggest in great detail, just why *Comedia Balletica* promises so little."[59] Gassmann, a composer (he later collaborated with Oskar Sala on the score for Balanchine's *Electronics* in 1961, a rare Balanchine failure) was the paper's music critic and possibly expected something a little more avant-garde than the misnamed *Comédia,* or, alternatively, a more explicit narrative.

Bolender got several positive reviews for his performance in *Comédia.* William Leonard, who, like Gassmann, found the ballet deeply flawed, called him "quite a dancer." This was not his only opportunity to dance: because Frederic Franklin was *hors de combat* for much of the season with a back injury, Bolender danced his role in Balanchine's *Baiser de la fée,* performing with Maria Tallchief and Alexandra Danilova. While Martin announced in the *Times* that he danced it for the first time in New York on March 21, Bolender recalled that his first crack at it was in Toronto, where some of the company men were less than pleased. "At that time I had gained just a little bit of weight . . . and this guy came up behind me and said, 'do all leading dancers have a big ass?' . . . The son of a bitch." The tensions between the American and non-American dancers in the Ballet Russe have been well documented by, among others, Agnes de Mille in *Dance to the Piper.* When she was creating *Rodeo* in 1942, in which she herself danced the Cowgirl, some of the Russian men refused to work with her. George Zoritch was one of them; in his memoir, he referred to the choreographer's derrière in the same terms. Balanchine had warned him about working with Ballet Russe, asking him why he wanted to be with those "terrible dancers," but just as Balanchine had when he took the position of that company's artistic director, Bolender needed a job.

Comédia stayed in the Ballet Russe repertory through the 1946–1947 season, although Bolender was no longer dancing with the company. Bolender revived it twice, first for a concert of his work at the 92nd Street YW-YMHA in February 1949 and a decade later for Robbins's Ballets: U.S.A., when the title changed again, this time to *Games*.

In the mid-1940s, Bolender was becoming an active participant in New York's intellectual and arts circles. He was known for his wit and intelligence and the free-wheeling open-minded curiosity that is the mark of the true intellectual. Reed also possessed these attributes; both were passionate readers who were well informed about current events and were always advocates for the underdog and the outsider. Bolender was also continuing to establish himself as a choreographer and teacher, consciously or subconsciously preparing himself for the time when he could no longer dance.

Toward the end of 1945, he was performing both roles at Katherine Dunham's school on West 43rd Street, part of a roster of faculty that included Franziska Boas, the daughter of anthropologist Franz Boas, with whom Bolender had studied in the 1930s when he was focusing on modern dance and Franziska was teaching at Hanya Holm's School. According to Bolender, she was a wonderful teacher and a powerful dancer, but her famous father was less than encouraging about her professional ambitions. She managed to combine both dance and anthropology in 1942, when she led a seminar at Columbia University on the "Function of Dance in Society." The participants were her father; Geoffrey Gorer, whose *Africa Dances* remains a wonderfully descriptive study of West African tribal dancing; Harold Courlander, an expert on Haitian music; and Claire Holt and Gregory Bateson, whose studies of Balinese dance remain among the best available.

Dunham herself had studied anthropology at the University of Chicago and Northwestern University and had done field work in the Caribbean, chiefly Haiti, a country with which she had a lifelong love affair. A charismatic performer with a beautiful face and a body designed for dancing, she developed a distinctive technique that later would be labeled fusion—Afro-Caribbean movement melded with American modern dance. The school was set up to produce dancers with a well-rounded education that included social science, liberal arts (philosophy and foreign languages, specifically French and Spanish), music, and theater arts (which included scenic design and makeup, along with several dance techniques). Margaret Mead, whose career had been nurtured by Boas *père*, was a guest lecturer. So was Antony Tudor.

Several faculty members were European refugees with PhDs. Columbia University accepted credits from the school and returning veterans could take classes there funded by the GI Bill. Bolender, who might well have loved attending the school as a student had it existed when he first arrived in New York, was part of the ballet faculty and taught in the summer school. Toward the end of 1945, Dunham's representative wrote a letter to the Galaxy Music Company requesting performance rights to Stravinsky's *L'Histoire du Soldat;* Dunham wanted to collaborate with Bolender on a piece for her company. She planned to give at least one performance in New York and then take the work on tour. As soon as she obtained the rights, Dunham planned to ask Leonard Bernstein to conduct, with members of the New York Philharmonic playing the music. There is no evidence that this work was ever made or that she received the rights. However, in October 1946, at her request, Bolender made a pointe piece on her that was set to Mozart's Piano Sonata no. 2 in F Major.

Dunham, who, according to Bolender, had very beautiful feet, had studied ballet with former Moscow Theater dancer Ludmila Speranzava in Chicago, but Speranzava advised her to shift to modern dance and develop her own technique She later followed that advice with considerable success. Nevertheless, for years Dunham, whose early dance training was in ballet, had wanted to dance on point, so Bolender devised a *Pas de Cinque* for her in which four men carried her around fetchingly posed in attitude, set her down briefly, and then carried her around again. As far as Bolender could remember, the piece was never performed before an audience. It was called *Concerto.*

In January 1946, Bolender went on the record as a passionate advocate of Dunham's work. He was outraged by an article in *Dance Observer* that seemed to denigrate Dunham as a serious artist. In the 1940s and later, even African American dancers tended to look upon successful artists of their race as exotic, or entertainers, or both. Written by Eunice Brown, herself an African American modern dancer, the article was about a Black modern dance company in Minneapolis, and began with the following:

> When thinking about the Negro and the dance, one inevitably turns to such well-known dancers as Bill Robinson, Snake-Hips Tucker, Josephine Baker, Avon Long and Katherine Dunham. These dancers are top-notch entertainers and without equals in their fields. But they are primarily tap, step, acrobatic, or eccentric dancers.[60]

They were not, she implied in the next sentence, to be taken seriously as concert dancers.

Bolender was quick to respond. In a letter dated January 9, 1946, he dismissed the entertainment pigeonhole as "incorrect for one who is the first well-known Negro concert dancer in American culture, an artist whose interpretation of Negro culture in dance is based on thorough anthropo-sociological training and field study . . . in the United States and Caribbean. . . . To group Miss Dunham and her company as Miss Brown does incorrectly evaluates the only permanent Negro concert dance group in the world, in fact, one of the very few permanent dance theatres that is entirely unsubsidized."[61]

After pointing out the Dunham company's new permanent studios and the ongoing rehearsals for a March concert series, Bolender continued, "I will leave it to your readers to decide whether a concert program based on the following music is worthy of the classification 'serious': Aaron Copland, Ravel, Mozart, . . . Darius Milhaud and Igor Stravinsky."

While the opportunity to make a dance on Dunham's company never materialized, in the same period, Bolender was learning to choreograph for the television cameras, most notably a production of *An American in Paris* presented by the School of American Ballet, directed by Paul Belanger. The American in question, complete with bewildered expression and a Baedeker, was danced by John Kriza; the Dancing Girl, whose image he first sees on a poster, was performed by Marie-Jeanne, and her very aggressive Apache partner by Frank Moncion. There are also a couple of sailors. This may have been another choreographic chore that Balanchine passed on; he was extremely busy preparing for Ballet Society, the seedbed from which New York City Ballet would grow—and Bolender's career as a dancer and choreographer would flourish.

5

In postwar New York, talk was the talk of the town. Uptown, downtown, midtown, out in the boroughs, people talked. Intellectuals talked about what constituted art and about each other. At Columbia University, where Ruth Benedict headed a project called Culture at a Distance, anthropological "informants" talked about their homelands. Composers made music and talked about why; painters and sculptors talked about themselves while they drank at the Cedar Tavern; critics, literary and otherwise, talked about "schools" and art and artists *en passant*. Everyone, seemingly, including Bolender and Robbins, talked to their analysts.

Nationally, the self-protective isolationism of the late 1930s had been replaced with considerable pride in the country's contribution to the defeat of the Axis powers and the rebuilding of Europe, tempered by a jittery awareness that the nuclear bombing of Hiroshima and Nagasaki had created a new, much more insecure world.[1] The country's newfound self-esteem, coupled with a certain degree of angst, made New York and other large cities fertile ground for the creation of American art of all kinds, not only by native artists, such as painter Jackson Pollock and choreographer Jerome Robbins, but also by European émigrés, such as Surrealist painter Esteban Francés, who designed the sets and costumes for Balanchine's *Renard* and, less successfully, for Bolender's *Zodiac*.

Into this creatively self-confident climate, a demobilized Kirstein returned in September 1945 and at once plunged into the pursuit of his biggest dreams, the creation of an American ballet and choreographic home for Balanchine, the support of modern visual artists, and writing. Ballet Society, founded in 1946, was basically modeled on Diaghilev's Ballets Russes, in which choreographers worked in collaboration with easel painters and composers. However, the attempt to focus on all at once was to meet with only limited success. The publications, recordings, film, and opera presentations that the announcement about the new company promised soon fell by the wayside, and, according to several observers, the contributions by visual artists (with one or two noteworthy exceptions) tended to overwhelm the choreography. For Bolender, the emphasis on easel painters as full partners in creating the ballets was more destructive than not. "The interesting thing was that Lincoln, who really was doing something magnificent for American dance," he told Nancy Reynolds in 1974, "was [establishing] it with painters. In other words, he was making music, paint, choreography such a strong trio of creativity [that] in a way [it] almost choked the lot of us."[2]

Nevertheless, two brilliant works in the Balanchine canon were created under the auspices of Ballet Society: *The Four Temperaments,* which reflected the edgy emotional atmosphere of its time and place, and *Orpheus,* a note-by-note, step-by-step collaboration with Stravinsky, with set and costume design by Isamu Noguchi. *Time* named the first a masterpiece of modern art; the second led to the creation of New York City Ballet and a permanent home for the Balanchine-Kirstein enterprise.[3]

To perform these ballets and a dozen others, including Merce Cunningham's *The Seasons* and Bolender's *Zodiac,* Balanchine and Kirstein once again assembled a roster of dancers gleaned from the companies they had formed—together and separately—and from the Ballet Russe de Monte Carlo, Ballet Theatre, and the School of American Ballet. A total of seventy-nine dancers was listed for the first season, a few of them as guest artists. Among the American Guild of Musical Artists (AGMA) professionals were Bolender, Gisella Caccialanza, Lew Christensen (as dancer and ballet master) Fred Danieli, Bill Dollar, José Martínez, John Taras, and Beatrice Tompkins, all of whom had been on the 1941 tour, joined by Betty Nichols, Edward Bigelow, Francisco Moncion, and Mary Ellen Moylan. The union issued special work permits to the apprentices from SAB, including Jacques d'Amboise, who was twelve, and Tanaquil Le Clercq, who was fifteen. Many, such as Talley Beatty, who had just left the Dunham company, had the chance to perform only once; others became founding members of City Ballet and had lengthy and stellar careers with the company. Léon Barzin, who Balanchine had worked with on the 1945 Carnegie Hall showcase for SAB, was the musical director, a position he continued with City Ballet, and Jean Rosenthal, who had been on the South American tour, was in charge of technical supervision.

In mid-September, Balanchine began choreographing *The Four Temperaments,* working evenings in SAB's studios on Madison Avenue, which was when they were available. This was his second attempt at making a ballet set to a score he had commissioned in 1940 from Paul Hindemith for his personal use, when he found himself with an extra $500 from his work on Broadway. What he asked for was something that could be performed during the musical evenings he held with friends (Barzin was one of them) in his New York apartment, where he had two pianos. What he got was a composition with a three-part theme with four variations. Its title and the variations were based on the medieval idea that personality was driven by the four "humors" of the body: Melancholic, Sanguinic, Phlegmatic, and Choleric.

The first version was called *Cave of Sleep,* which Balanchine had intended for the 1941 tour. The project was abandoned in part because of Hindemith's fear that the costumes and décor, designed by Pavel Tchelitchew (who, in collaboration with Balanchine, had sketched out the scenario), would detract from the music. This was no small matter because of their potential cost. Bolender had seen the designs for the men, which he recalled "were very elaborate, in great taste, with wonderful capes hanging off backs, gold things on the legs and arms."[4] To produce them, he quipped, "Lincoln would have had to sell another part of Bloomingdale's." (Kirstein's family money actually came from Filene's of Boston.)

Kurt Seligmann, another émigré painter who interested Kirstein, was Tchelitchew's replacement. On the surface at least, he was ideal for the project since he was deeply interested in medieval history, black magic, Surrealism, and psychoanalysis. His designs for both the set and the costumes amounted to a visual artist's takeover of the ballet, however: not only did the mise-en-scène make the choreography nearly invisible to the audience, the costumes, particularly the headdresses, made it impossible for the dancers to see where they were going. Full, fussily trimmed skirts for the women and the elaborate suede patchwork on the men's tunics and tights obscured the line, sometimes restricted their movement, and more often gave it a different meaning. Painter and choreographer, in short, had conflicting points of view. Seligmann's designs were expressive of his idea of how dancers representing medieval "temperaments" in the mid-twentieth century needed to look, full of symbols (Bolender had an arrow appliquéd to his tunic), while Balanchine approached the temperaments as musical directions, claiming many years after the premiere that Hindemith had simply substituted their names for andante, presto, and the like.

That being said, both the very tricky rhythms and the tempi for each of the four variations are highly suggestive of the personalities that were theoretically created by an excess of one of the humors. This was most clear for Choleric, which Le Clercq danced with adolescent fury and fearlessness, and Phlegmatic, which Bolender originated and was arguably the most difficult of the four to express in movement terms.

Balanchine, as usual, gave few if any verbal cues when he began work on it one evening with only Bolender and pianist John Colman in the SAB studios. Instead, the master of nonverbal communication showed, with unusual emotion, the movement he associated with a medieval concept of personality that comes quite close to the modern psychoanalytic definition of ambivalence.

"I shall always remember when George was beginning to outline the variation," Bolender wrote in 2004 in a letter to Una Kai, who joined Ballet Society in its second season and became a lifelong friend and colleague. "I shall always remember with amazement how passionate [he] was as he choreographed [it] and how in the final 32 measures it built to a kind of violence before collapsing back into the passive state. . . . Much as [in] the score, [there is] a pulling forward and a hesitation followed by a surge of energy [which] is how the variation concludes—with the almost groveling repetition of movement going back to the very studied exact step, which brought the variation onto the stage, now sends it off—an explosion of passion from lethargy back to lethargy."[5]

Balanchine completed the solo quite quickly and then, apparently, got stuck. "All right, that's enough," Bolender remembered him saying, and Colman, so brilliant as a rehearsal pianist that Balanchine would work with no one else, protested: "What do you mean that's enough?" Balanchine replied he was finished with the variation and Colman told him he couldn't be, that the music "that's coming up here is so gorgeous, you can't just stop here."[6] And soon thereafter (in one interview Bolender said it was the next day, in another he said it took some time) four tall women were brought into the studio and the variation was completed.

Dancing a character was one thing, and Bolender, now 32, had proved himself to be good at it, particularly as Alias in *Billy the Kid* and as the State Trooper and the Rich Boy in *Filling Station*. But, as he pointed out frequently in interviews, in *The Four Temperaments* Balanchine was choreographing an idea, and in the case of Phlegmatic, a pretty complicated one at that. In Bolender, Balanchine had a dancer who could and did develop the role. Bolender had a background in modern dance, which focused on self-expression; he had trained in classical dance with Anatole Oboukhoff and Felia Doubrovska at SAB; he had an acute sense of musicality; and he had strong analytical skills. His compact, loose-jointed, highly flexible body also contributed to the choreography: the lifting of his foot and examination of it at the beginning of the variation, the sweeping gestures at the floor, executed while bent almost double, the enervated affect his seemingly boneless body gave the audience, and his powerful jump all contributed to a performance that no one else has been able to match.

In the same letter to Kai, which he wrote following a public appearance at the Guggenheim Museum's Works and Process series, in which he had coached a New York City Ballet dancer in the first minute or so of Phlegmatic, Bolender spoke of the importance of analyzing the role to make it interesting. "I think analysis is personal," he wrote. "Certainly George never ever even whispered a direction to me as to how I should do it, except at the one developing point midway when the tempo shifts abruptly."

Throughout his career, analysis was essential to the performance of any role for Bolender. "For myself," he told Nancy Reynolds in the mid-1970s, "I had to find out why I went out on the stage, and what it was that I was creating—not the image in Balanchine's mind, but what I felt in relation to the dance that I was doing and the people surrounding me. . . . In *Four Temperaments* I had a terribly difficult time and I finally would say to myself: 'well, OK, so you don't have an idea, just go on stage, and you're going to tell a story, improvise a story, so that when you get there the whole thing will suddenly happen.' And [I'd] start to tell the story and go on from there, and there would be just a relationship with you and the audience. And sometimes I would start walking out and I would say: 'Here I go. Now let me see, what am I going to say . . . ' and then I would just let the movement take over. . . . It was as though the story had to come from the movement . . . and then I remember, often afterwards, I would feel that I had told my story as well as I had wanted to . . . that there had been a connection with the music . . . because when it was right, it was as though I had been at one with the music—it couldn't have been any different."[7]

The Four Temperaments, which was preceded by Ravel's short opera *The*

Spellbound Child (Balanchine did his first version in 1925 for the Monte Carlo Opera; this one was the second, with different choreography), opened on November 20, 1946, on the abysmally cramped stage of the Needle Trades High School auditorium. The costumes were somewhat pared down by the choreographer wielding a pair of scissors a mere half hour before the dancers went on stage. According to Danieli, who partnered a "liquid" Mary Ellen Moylan in Sanguinic, Balanchine was "snipping everywhere," not only on the costumes but metaphorically, at least, what Reynolds later dubbed the easel painter as tyrant.[8]

Sitting in the audience was Jacques d'Amboise, on hand in part because he was the understudy for singer Joseph Connolly in the title role of *The Spellbound Child.* In his autobiography, he conjured up some vivid descriptions of the evening's second ballet. Of the Choleric variation, he writes of

> Tanny flaying her mile-long limbs in a circle, reminding [him] of [his mother's] eggbeater whipping up heavy cream; as Melancholic the pantherish Bill Dollar all amorphous softness. . . . But Todd Bolender took the crown. In the Phlegmatic section, he stole the show. Among the many great artists who have subsequently danced this role, none can touch Todd's slinky, feline magic. His face, covered in pale white makeup, was bisected by a giant painted slash of a mouth, drawn with one side curling downward in a sneer and the other upward in a smirk. A lavender floppy hat crowned his bizarre face. Every night seated in the audience, I awaited my favorite moment. . . . [when] he leans over and in slow motion, wraps his right hand around his ankle as if it were a snake slithering around the stem of a flowering plant. Then, slowly, he lifts his foot toward his face. Motionless, balancing on his other leg, he stares unblinkingly at the foot. Others enter and dance around him; he doesn't quiver, breathless in his stillness for what seems like hours. Suddenly, without taking his eyes off the foot, he places it back on the floor and explodes into a high stepping, spinning dance. . . . In seconds this complicated movement evolves into a simple prance, performed with a nonchalant saucy air.[9]

By referring to "every night," d'Amboise was likely conflating several performances over time. Ballet Society programmed *Four Temperaments* only once more, with a new finale, in February 1947, when it was on a bill with Balanchine's *The Triumph of Bacchus and Ariadne* and *Divertimento* (music by Alexei Haieff), a strictly classical ballet that had premiered in the first season, when it was paired with the Balanchine-Stravinsky *Renard*. After the company became New York City Ballet, in 1948, *Four Ts*, as it came to be called, was performed in the Seligmann production with the costumes streamlined. It was then put on hiatus until 1951 (except for the 1950 British tour), when Balanchine revived it without the scenery and costumes, at which point, according to Bolender, the City Center audience, which had previously been indifferent to the work, went crazy with applause.

For him, the first performance in rehearsal garb proved to be something of an ordeal, although he and the other dancers had welcomed the elimination of the unwieldy costumes. "I went on stage, and I walked across and I did this whole thing, and I lifted up my leg, and I was standing there—and suddenly felt absolutely naked. . . . And I really had the most awful panic, because I thought, my God—it was this terrible thing, that I'd forgotten my costume. I was really shattered. It had never occurred to me that I would have a reaction like that."[10]

While the broader City Center audience was unable to see past Seligmann's elaborate production, which Bolender suggested changed the meaning of the movement, it bothered neither the Ballet Society cognoscenti nor Edwin Denby, the critic who best understood Balanchine in those days. In his December review for *Dance News*, the focus was entirely on the movement, with no mention at all of the costumes or décor.

Anatole Chujoy, on the other hand, complained that the set and costumes overwhelmed the dancing, a complaint he was to repeat about several ballets over the course of Ballet Society's two seasons with considerable justification. He also didn't warm to the presentation of opera ballets, such as *Spellbound Child* and the ballet-burlesque *Renard*, which opened Ballet Society's second concert, on January 13, 1947, although the flyer announcing Ballet Society made it clear that opera would be a part of its mission. In fact, Gian Carlo Menotti's *The Medium* and *The Telephone* both premiered under its auspices.

Renard, which had a delicious, rhythmically complex score by Igor Stravinsky, was created in 1916 with a libretto based on a Russian folk tale written by the composer, and gave Bolender a part he loved, the title role of the wily Fox, who, first disguised as a nun, lures down the Rooster (originally performed by Lew Christensen) from an eight-foot perch to confess his sins, and, then, minus the wimple and rosary beads, persuades him to descend for a second time for some corn. At this point, the Rooster's friends, the Cat (danced by Danieli) and the Ram (performed by Taras) gang up on Renard and do him in. The piece elicits the *skomorokhi,* the Russian answer to the strolling players of Italian commedia dell' arte, and it begins and ends with the four characters marching jauntily onto the stage, carrying their masks. Esteban Francés, a Spanish Surrealist painter living in New York, did a charming, highly detailed job with the costumes and a swirling, abstract backdrop. Barbara Karinska was able to make the costumes work so well that Bolender said they almost did the dancing on their own.[11] "In *Renard,*" d'Amboise recalled, "I adored the undulating tail of the Fox's costume and the way Todd played with that tail as if it were another limb, at times kissing it fondly on its tip. Todd's performance . . . was full of tongue-in-cheek humor and pepper-spiced."[12]

Balanchine, who was the third choreographer to tackle the piece, worked quickly, according to Bolender, rehearsing most of the time on the stage of the Hunter College Auditorium, which was small and less than ideal but better than the Needle Trades auditorium.[13] He made some deceptively simple movements, including running steps with bent knees, executed so fast the dancers come close to falling. The choreography was not on the whole classical, although Renard does several high pas de chats. All of the steps are dependent on the performers' abilities to imagine how an animal might actually dance. At one point, when he was restoring it for Kansas City Ballet, Bolender directed a dancer to run high on half-toe, "as if you have claws."[14]

Some critics, Walter Terry included, felt there was a paucity of steps and that *Renard* looked as amateurish as a Sunday school performance, but this was no more a children's ballet than Bolender's *Mother Goose Suite.* In contrast, Martin recognized it as "an important event, for here is a work extremely difficult to produce, destined always to be unpopular, and yet of the greatest interest" because "it marks Stravinsky's transition from a merely progressive force in the lyric theatre to a radical one." He also called it "a kind of historical milestone in the modern ballet" and gave kudos to Francés for his "extraordinarily beautiful" setting and costumes, [which made] for a pictorial unity that is rare in the ballet."[15]

Speaking about *Renard* not long before he died, Bolender judged it to be "the most playful ballet Balanchine ever did," adding that "[it ought] to be in active repertory at City Ballet and most ballet companies." Kirstein wrote that he considered it to be Ballet Society's most completely realized production: "On its small scale it was as perfect a production as might be imagined."[16] As it happens, Balanchine's version has had very few performances over the years: there were two at Hunter in 1947 and Bolender, at Balanchine's request, set it in Boston in 1957, when it was accompanied by the Boston Symphony for one performance at a summer festival held on the Boston Commons. Lew Christensen revived it "after Balanchine" for San Francisco Ballet in 1955, rebuilding the original set and costumes since they had been destroyed in a warehouse fire in 1953, and taking it on the company's first international tour in 1957. Kansas City Ballet performed Bolender's restoration in a Stravinsky Festival in 2001 and again in New York at Symphony Space, in 2004 in a twelve-hour celebration of Balanchine's centenary.

Ballet Society's third program, on March 26, 1947, contained no choreography by Balanchine, who was in Paris creating *Le Palais de Cristal* (later called *Symphony in C*) on the Opéra Ballet, which gave critics further grounds for complaint. Chujoy and several others did, however, acknowledge the program's importance in giving opportunities to three young choreographers to work with composers and painters, Bolender among them. None of the works endured. The program opened with *The Minotaur* to a commissioned score by Elliott Carter; Taras, substituting for Balanchine, choreographed it. It was memorable primarily for Le Clercq's dancing and was quite likely trumped by Graham's *Errand into the Maze*, which had premiered a month earlier. Dollar's *Highland Fling*, in which Bolender danced the lead role of the groom, was the most popular and the least experimental, a mid-twentieth-century American no-nonsense take on *La Sylphide* in which the groom resists the Sylph and all ends happily. *Zodiac*, Bolender's contribution, was retired after a single performance, in part because the elaborate setting by Francés overwhelmed the choreography and dim lighting obscured it. In addition, several critics deemed the music, composer Rudi Revil's first large orchestral work (Kirstein described it as in "the style of international jazz"), indifferent at best, and Bolender's reach pretty clearly exceeded his grasp. Revil, who Kirstein had assigned to Bolender, turned out to have an ego that was as hard to deal with as any of the visual artists'; the score had some interesting parts and was adequate, but Revil was nearly impossible to work with.[17]

Over the years, Bolender's choreography tended to veer between the personal (in *Mother Goose* an older woman looks back on her life) and the intellectual. In *Zodiac,* he was attempting to choreograph an idea, specifically what he viewed as the potential loss of a moral center in postwar society. Although he was not a religious man in any way—his distaste for institutionalized religion was well known in later years—or a believer in astrology, the signs of the zodiac were nevertheless a useful metaphor and organizing principle for a piece about the human condition at a specific point in American history.

In his article on Bolender in *Chrysalis,* Baird Hastings described the story (no one seems to have taken credit for the libretto) and the dancing thus:

> The scales were kidnapped by gemini (danced acrobatically by William Dollar and Todd Bolender); all was thrown out of whack and everything became legitimate. This led the girls to become whores and the men bandits. The geminis masqueraded as the Sun and the Moon, and assumed the prerogatives of dictators. Now the twins were split, and no order was possible until after they were reunited. Personality, rather than guns was the instrument of force and The Earth (Gisella Caccialanza) was at the mercy of the gemini. Decay and chaos set in as Gisella and Todd performed a pas de deux, but then the Earth took hold of herself and with great effort returned all to normality. Betty Nichols danced the Black Virgin with a haunting beauty.[18]

In a note in the Ballet Society yearbook, Kirstein stood by *Zodiac* as an example of his commitment to new work, pointing out that "no other ballet company would have undertaken it, with its combination of unfamiliar subject and collaboration of young musician, painter and dancer. Restudied and revised, it will find a permanent place in repertory."[19] A year later, Bolender did remake it, with new music (by Samuel Barber) and the *Zodiac* designs, titling the ballet *Capricorn Concerto.* It, too, was not a success; Terry found the choreography cold and Martin thought it monotonous, although Chujoy cited excellent dancing. In 1951, while considering repertory to take to London on a second New York City Ballet tour that actually didn't take place, Kirstein listed *Zodiac* along with *Filling Station* and Cunningham's *The Seasons* as potential programming.[20]

While Bolender claimed in 1974 that he could barely remember *Zodiac,* that it was "a step along the way" to becoming a choreographer, it is worth looking at as an indicator of some recurring themes in his work (the need for balance in society, empathy for the outsider, the human condition generally) and for his dependence on a good score to make a good ballet.[21] It was, after all, listening to a recording of Stravinsky's *Firebird* as a young boy in Canton, Ohio, that made him want to choreograph in the first place. *Mother Goose Suite,* his first ballet, is set to Ravel's dreamy eponymous score, and *The Still Point,* considered his masterpiece,[22] was made in the early 1950s to Debussy's String Quartet in G Minor. For *Voyager,* the "space ballet" that four decades later grew out of *Zodiac,* he used Leonard Bernstein's powerful *Serenade After Plato's Symposium.*

Zodiac, with Betty Nichols cast as Virgo (it was Hastings who called her the Black Virgin, not Bolender), is an example of Bolender's lifelong advocacy of Black dancers, outsiders in the ballet world not only in the 1940s but, in the case of women in particular, in the twenty-first century as well. While some might question his creation of a blackamoor role in the 1948 *Seraglio* or his casting of Richard Tanner and Arthur Mitchell as the elevator operator in the 1955 *Souvenirs,* both of which were done in the service of historical authenticity, there is no record of either man objecting to these roles. Moreover, Nichols's memories of dancing in *Zodiac* were nothing but positive, as she made clear in a 1983 interview with Joel Lobenthal that was published in *Ballet Review* in 2013 and as a participant in a 1996 symposium on Blacks in ballet. On both occasions, she spoke glowingly of her happiness when she learned she had been cast as Virgo, something she had not expected at all. In the interview with Lobenthal, she described the excitement in the SAB studios when the various choreographers for Ballet Society came in to observe the professional classes, which evidently substituted for auditions for their ballets. "I remember when Todd Bolender came in to do *Zodiac,*" she said. "Obviously everyone wanted to be in the ballet. Great effervescence, nervousness. I thought, I am the only one who is not going to be nervous in this class because I know I am not going to be chosen. It never occurred to me. So I did my class quite normally, and when we came out, everybody was going to the water cooler to see the names that were posted. Someone said, 'Betty your name's here; you're in it.'" Nichols didn't believe it until she went and looked for herself. "It was wonderful working with Todd," she said. "Bill Dollar danced. We were Gemini, the Twins that upset the Zodiac. I was a virgin. . . . [and then] became the sort of *fille de joie* [lady of the night] when everything was reversed."[23]

Nichols didn't specify why she didn't expect to be cast in Bolender's ballet, whether it was because of the color of her skin, her erratic classical training, or some other reason. She had been one of legions of American children who fell in love with ballet in the 1940s and 1950s after seeing a performance by the Ballet Russe de Monte Carlo and had been inspired to become professional dancers; Alvin Ailey and Allegra Kent were two others. When she was very young, her mother took her to see the Ballet Russe perform at the Philadelphia Academy of Music and she was immediately seduced by what she later called the "beauty and the spectacle," so much so that she at once told her mother that was what she wanted to do. "Do you see one colored dancer on stage?" her mother asked, and of course she didn't.[24] Undeterred by the obvious obstacles, after some training in her home town, she went to New York in 1943, where she was first in a summer program run by Hanya Holm and then in the fall was admitted to SAB as the first Black student in the school. She took two classes a week and from time to time was steered by people at SAB toward Broadway shows. As a result, she appeared in *Carmen Jones* from December 1943 to February 1945, which was exhausting but paid the rent. At about that time, Balanchine decided to give her a full scholarship on the condition that she stop working on Broadway so she could focus on her classical training. It is quite likely that the combination of classical and modern schooling; her experience as a performer in *Carmen Jones,* which Eugene Loring choreographed; and her elegantly proportioned body made Bolender believe her to be ideal for his developing expressive classicism.

While participating in the class that Bolender observed didn't make Nichols nervous, Francés's set and costume design had the opposite effect. She well remembered her fearfulness at performing in a wig made of long metallic ribbons to represent her hair in choreography that demanded that she smoke a cigarette while she danced on the ropes that made up the set. "I'd never smoked a cigarette before, and I was worried. I thought that the hair could go up in flames." She also remembered dancing in a netting-covered leotard that had been dyed to match her skin color, which may well have been Bolender's idea: in the later *Voyager,* he also had costumes that were intended to make the dancers look nude.[25]

For Ballet Society's May program, which was performed at the Ziegfeld Theater, a vast improvement over both the Needle Trades and Hunter College auditoriums, Lew Christensen also turned his attention to racial issues, casting Nichols and Beatty in *Blackface,* with music by Carter Harmon, in which the composer laced the score with such Stephen Foster melodies as "Camptown Races" and "Sewanee River." The costumes and décor by Robert Drew were later recycled for Ruthanna Boris's *Cakewalk.*

Blackface was the direct result of Christensen's war service, in which his awareness of the ill treatment of African Americans had been heightened considerably. "I had just gotten out of the Army," he told Reynolds, "and I had all kinds of emotional things about the black man and helping him out. I tried to put this into a minstrel show. It would probably work better in the seventies, but at the time it fell flat."[26] It certainly fell flat with Terry,[27] who found it "consistently dull," although literary translator James Graham-Lujan, who was in the audience, remembered a chilling moment when one of the minstrels tried to rub the "paint" off another and realized that it would not come off.[28] The ballet was a failure, both as art and as social commentary, a difficult mix to pull off at any time, especially using the classical vocabulary. However, it did give Nichols and Beatty a rare opportunity to perform classical dance.

Symphonie Concertante, the *ballet blanc* Balanchine originally made for a cast of SAB students with Bolender in the only male role, premiered professionally on November 12. This time, Bolender, still the only man on stage with a corps of twenty-two women, again partnered Le Clercq, now a company member, and Maria Tallchief, whom Balanchine had married the previous year. The piece is a "teaching" ballet, technically so demanding that Tallchief said dancing it was like "taking your medicine every day."[29] Audiences and some critics found it dry and uninteresting, but it is another example, like *Ballet Imperial,* of a Petipa-based ballet that was choreographed with American dancers in mind.

By that time, Balanchine's resolve to create an American ballet was as strong as Kirstein's. His experiences in Paris with the Opéra Ballet, where he worked for six months, served to reinforce it. They were less than pleasant, in part because of a lax work ethic, at least in comparison with that of American dancers, that was to plague Bolender decades later in Germany and Turkey. There were also the invidious comparisons critics made to the choreography of Serge Lifar, the Opéra Ballet's former director. At one point, Balanchine wrote Kirstein that he wanted "to devote all my time towards making a good American company." Europe, he felt, "was centuries behind us."[30] Balanchine had become a citizen of the United States in 1939, six years after his arrival in New York, and possibly because of his work on Broadway and the movies and his marriage to Tallchief, who was half Osage, had begun to identify himself as American. It was in these years that he began to wear the string ties, western shirts, and a silver and turquoise bracelet one of his Osage in-laws had given him (he wore the bracelet for the rest of his life).

Before he went to Paris, Balanchine had begun teaching the Ballet Society dancers on a regular basis, something he had not done in the past, relying on the excellent staff at SAB to give them their technical training and only occasionally giving a class on the South American tour. This, too, represented a commitment to building an American company with consistent and uniform training, although Balanchine was, given his own training, a rather unorthodox teacher, frequently spending most of class time on one step or combination. Bolender, who had observed his classes at SAB before he became a student there, fondly recalled one that was completely devoted to running. "In those years, only modern dance used running movement as dance. Balanchine had only begun to shake the nineteenth century out of twentieth century dance. I began to realize he had a much wider awareness of movement possibilities than I had imagined, but then that was a period of immense importance to all dancers, choreographers, and artists."

Bolender was doing considerable teaching in this period—several classes at the Fokine School in the Carnegie Hall building and at Dunham's school—developing skills that would prepare him to teach all over the world after he retired from dancing.

In 1947, for Ballet Society's fifth (and last) season, Balanchine started work on *Orpheus,* his first step-by-step, note-by-note collaboration with Stravinsky, another Russian émigré enamored of American culture. With costume and scenic design by Isamu Noguchi and lighting design by Rosenthal, *Orpheus* was undeniably the most successful collaboration Ballet Society produced, not only aesthetically but practically. Morton Baum, then head of the executive board of New York City Center, a city-subsidized performance hall that originally was built as a Masonic temple, was so impressed by what he saw when he dropped in on a rehearsal that, quite soon after the premiere, he invited Ballet Society to make City Center their permanent home and to change their name to New York City Ballet. *Orpheus* premiered at City Center on April 28, 1948.

By and large, Balanchine's *Orpheus* choreography did not call for the speed, daring, and athleticism he admired in American dancers, except for the Bacchanale, which Bolender, who wasn't in the ballet, later described as "a powerful, terrifying climax."[31] It called for both physical and emotional restraint in a mixture of classical and modern technique. What Balanchine and Stravinsky, who conducted opening night, did require, however, was acute and precise musicality; Tallchief, who was cast as Eurydice, had to die in precisely five beats. She found this difficult.[32]

The cast was as multicultural in nature as Graham's company. In addition to Tallchief, who had a Native American background, Nicholas Magallanes, born in Mexico, danced the title role, and Francisco Moncion, born in the Dominican Republic, lent his dramatic powers to the crucial role of the Dark Angel. Nobody seems to have remarked on the cultural diversity at the time and it's doubtful it was deliberate on Balanchine's part, but it is nevertheless emblematic of the pluralistic society that was part of what attracted many European artists and intellectuals of the time to the United States, including Balanchine and Stravinsky.

Noguchi's designs contributed to the modern aspects of the work, which is not surprising, since he had been working with Graham since 1935, when he used minimal sculpture—in that instance, wooden rails and long pieces of rope—to define the vast open spaces of the American prairie for *Frontier*. By 1947, his set pieces and props were very much part of the choreography in Graham's *Errand into the Maze* and *Cave of the Heart*, and for Ballet Society, he had already created sets for Cunningham's *The Seasons*. For *Orpheus*, he used balsa wood to make the lyre that would become the symbol for the New York City Ballet and rope to bind together Orpheus and the Dark Angel in a pas de deux. Bolender described as "beautiful, in which the Dark Angel ever supports the unsure Orpheus, giving him the warmth of companionship to enable him to speak for Eurydice, in a confrontation with Pluto, whose arrogance Balanchine refers to as [like] a Nazi politician, who refuses contact except by force."

Noguchi was not Balanchine or Kirstein's first choice to design the ballet. That was Pavel Tchelitchew, but he turned them down. This was fortunate. What Noguchi brought to the collaboration turned out to be a shared aesthetic sensibility and enthusiasm for the work itself. "Never was I more personally involved in creation than with this piece which is the story of the artist. I interpreted Orpheus as the story of the artist blinded by his vision (the mask). Even inanimate objects move at his touch—as do the rocks, at the pluck of his lyre."[33] Noguchi brought to his designs elements of Japanese culture and theater, specifically the mask for Orpheus, whose shape is based on the way towels are folded to disguise characters in folk dances, and a point of view based on a Japanese myth that is close to the one from ancient Greece. This was completely appropriate, since Stravinsky, in particular, had not wanted the ballet to "look" Greek, even to the limited degree that *Apollo* does.

There was no conventional backdrop for *Orpheus* and no way to separate the action in the real world from the underworld until Balanchine solved the problem by using yards of pure silk in the same way Tchelitchew had done in *Errante*. Rosenthal then projected lights on the ever-moving fabric in her own visualization of Stravinsky's atmospheric score. Balanchine viewed this very expensive silk as so essential to the production that when Kirstein told him at the last minute that there was no money to pay for it, Balanchine said he would personally find the money, and, in short order, returned to the theater with $1,000 in cash. All he would say about where he got it was that he hadn't robbed a bank.

"*Orpheus*," wrote Bolender, "met with the windy bravos of an opening night audience in 1948 and superb reviews."[34] Several came from the hard-to-please Martin, who wrote glowingly of Stravinsky's score in his review of the premiere and commended Balanchine for the "directness" with which he told the story and for his minimal use of ornamentation in his choreography. "There is nothing at all of virtuosity about the movement and no opportunity for anybody to stand out spectacularly," Martin wrote, although he commended the principals for their performance.[35]

Audiences at subsequent performances were impressed but did not really warm to the ballet the way they did to more traditionally classical works like *Symphony in C*: "Attendance borne on the inky wave of the press did little more than nod in chilly acknowledgement," Bolender wrote in 1955, and while the ballet had many aficionados, it wasn't performed very often.[36] *Orpheus* was revived for the 1972 Stravinsky Festival at Lincoln Center and it remains in City Ballet's repertory, but despite the spectacular melding of music, choreography, and design, it has never had wide popular appeal, and without the commitment of the original cast, it is nothing like as powerful as it was when it premiered.

Ballet Society as an organization didn't last long, but its significance for the development of American ballet was enormous. The lessons it taught the participants—including Kirstein, Balanchine, and Bolender—were profound. Bolender viewed it as a bridge between the Diaghilev era, as represented by the Denham Ballet Russe repertory of lavishly produced one-act story ballets (e.g., *Gâité Parisienne*), and the streamlined nonnarrative choreographies that would become the backbone of City Ballet's repertory under Balanchine. Additionally, the dominance of visual artists in Ballet Society, particularly Seligmann for *The Four Temperaments,* also led Balanchine, who Bolender called "the magic man of the moment," to reject the Diaghilev model of full collaboration of choreographer, artist, and composer and make the choreographer first among equals: "In a sense all George was saying is choreography is a great art in itself and it must be recognized. It doesn't need anything else, except dance. . . . Ballet Society was like that step that had to happen."[37]

In addition to performing with Ballet Society and supporting himself with teaching and various odd jobs, Bolender was also working as an independent choreographer, assembling his friends and associates, many of them dancers who were passing through SAB, into a pick-up company with shifting personnel that performed in various locales in and around New York from 1947 through 1949.

In 1948, he put together an "Evening of Ballet" in a fully equipped theater in a barn in Southbury, Connecticut. The barn was owned by Jack Quinn, a Broadway gypsy Bolender had met in 1944, when he danced briefly in *The Merry Widow* after *Rosalinda* closed. "I got John Colman as accompanist and I took *Comedia Balletica,* and *Ma Mere l'Oye,* which I redid completely[,] plus a Mozart ballet to the Sonata in A major for piano, [and] I used Maria Tallchief and Tanny Le Clercq, Marie-Jeanne, Ruthanna Boris and Mary Ellen Moylan in it. Frank Moncion was the Pasha. I had the women under veils. I did little variations for them, and they were quite charming." Frank Hobi and Herbert Bliss were also part of the group, as were some SAB students. Bolender also danced.

During rehearsals and performances (there were two), everyone stayed in the same house, and Balanchine, now married to Tallchief, was present as an active participant, playing the piano for rehearsals if Colman was absent, fixing costumes, and lending his expert hand to the proceedings. "It was there he saw the 'Mother Goose' ballet and liked it," Bolender recalled, "although he never said so directly. This second version of the ballet began to have a quality that I liked, too. Also, Marie-Jeanne was wonderful in it.

You never know, really, whether it's your choreography or the dancer."[38] Balanchine did indeed like the ballet, and he took it into City Ballet's repertoire in its first season, with Kai as the Bird. It was in this version that the Bird's long hair entraps Hop O' My Thumb because of Kai's "very good hair." A year later, after she joined City Ballet, Reed received high praise in the role of the Young Girl.

The reviewer for the *New York Herald Tribune* called Bolender "one of the most gifted choreographers of the younger set" and wondered "how he managed to form such a company for two appearances" but speculated "that the time [off-season], the place [near New York] and the great esteem in which [Bolender] is held by his dancing colleagues turned the trick," adding that "with such a roster of artists it was a foregone conclusion that the Bolender ballets, a tiny stage to the contrary, would be accorded superlative performances."[39] Of the three works on the program, the reviewer liked the Mozart best.

Much of this program was repeated at the 92nd Street YMHA Dance Center a few months later, with a new ballet, *Image in the Heart,* substituted for *Mother Goose* and Reed and Una Kai in the cast. Lillian Lanese and Jerome Robbins also performed in what was the YMHA's first concert series devoted to ballet. The Mozart had been sufficiently reworked to qualify as a premiere, and, once again a critic, in this case Rosalyn Krokover, emphasized the high caliber of the dancers. She wrote, "Rarely does one encounter such quality in a small chamber group."[40]

The second of the three scenes in *Image in the Heart* takes place in a ballroom, and Krokover found it reminiscent of Tudor's *Dim Lustre.* Like *Mother Goose,* which Krokover compared it to unfavorably, the ballet, set to a score by John Colman, is based on reverie and metaphor; like *Zodiac,* it carries a message. A game of cards provides a metaphor for life; the male protagonist "is shown in conflict with his fellow players (men and women), who demand that he follow the rules of the game, which consist in his abandoning all that is most precious to him—his sensibilities, imagination and creative thoughts. Since he cannot do this he loses the game."[41] The organization of the ballet is cinematic; the first and third card-player scenes are interrupted by a flashback in which the protagonist, performed by Moncion, remembers the ballroom where he met his friends. Only he can see the beautiful woman who, portrayed by Le Clercq, in what Hastings called "the finest role she has yet had," represents his nonconformist creative ambitions.[42] He fails to distinguish between the real woman who loves him and the symbolic one, which means that he loses the game. Choreographically, in the ballroom scene, the friends, who represent society and the barriers it often erects against the artist as represented by Moncion, keep coming between him and Le Clercq, "the symbol of the attributes he must discard if he is to fit into society's pattern. . . . His companions freeze into immobility and come to life only when she is gone." The ballet ends with Moncion, who has lost the game and has been deserted by his friends, being watched over by Le Clercq, the "Image" in his heart.[43]

Miles White's costumes, particularly for the ballroom scene, turned out to be integral to the execution of Bolender's choreography. White had designed the costumes for *Oklahoma!* in 1943 and would become extremely successful on Broadway and in Hollywood, known for his ability to create costumes that enhanced movement instead of hampering it. For *Image,* White cut the fabric to pattern and the dancers had to make their own costumes. The fabric was jewel-toned, heavy satin, which weighted the full skirts. "The best part of all," Kai said, "was that I was really not a good dancer, at that point in my life, I really could hardly cope. . . . We had to do some double pirouettes on pointe. But I discovered that . . . if I got up on pointe the skirt held me up there . . . the centrifugal force of it going around. . . . I could do beautiful pirouettes in that skirt . . . I could do three!"[44]

In May, Bolender made another ballet for television. CBS had started a series of 30-minute live dance programs sponsored by Ford Motors titled *Through the Crystal Ball,* which aired on Monday nights, when theatrical dancers would be free to perform. Five programs were presented in two months. Berlanger, who had directed Bolender's *American in Paris,* produced the series, creating an opportunity for both experienced and inexperienced choreographers to work in the new medium, charged with making original works based on popular stories. Valerie Bettis and Pauline Koner participated, and Balanchine made a 30-minute version of *Cinderella* to music by Tchaikovsky. It starred Le Clercq and broadcast on April 25. Bolender titled his contribution *The Wild, Wild West* and cast Joan McCracken, who was dancing on Broadway, in the lead. Patricia McBride (the elder of two dancers with that name at New York City Ballet) and Le Clercq also performed, the latter getting a foretaste of the Western theme she would send up so brilliantly in 1955 in Balanchine's *Western Symphony.*

Bolender understood the broad appeal of stories from and about the American West, which is likely why he chose the "Wild West" as his subject. "If there is one section of the states that creates nostalgia for [most] people, it is certainly the far west accompanied by its sad and lilting frontier tunes," he wrote in a memoir of the making of Balanchine's *Western Symphony*.[45] According to Hastings, *Wild West* was the most successful of the ballets.[46]

Bolender as usual was occupied with many aspects of his professional and personal life in this period. He was performing in the sporadic seasons of Ballet Society and City Ballet (there was a nine-month hiatus in 1949, following New York City Ballet's second season[47]), developing his skills as a choreographer for the stage and the small screen, teaching, and, equally important, continuing his analysis. This took him to Provincetown for parts of several summers, where many New York psychoanalysts went to escape the city's heat, as many painters and writers had been doing since World War I, Eugene O'Neill the most famous among them. Painters Jared and Margaret French and Kirstein's brother-in-law Paul Cadmus were experimenting with photography outdoors on the dunes, photographing each other and their friends, including Bolender,[48] and, in 1947, Tennessee Williams was living in the Charles Webster Hawthorne residence, working on *A Streetcar Named Desire*.

In August 1947, Bolender wrote a letter to Yvonne Patterson that described a dinner party he gave that Williams attended at the "shack" Bolender had rented from the Hawthornes. It ended in disaster before it had really begun:

> My guests arrived at 7:30 to find me tossing together a clam chowder (which was magnificent). They drank themselves into an absolute frenzy and then before you could say anything of one syllable, bowls of clam chowder were being hurled around the room, screams, murderous threats, and in my stateliest manner, with chowder zooming past me, I chortled, "gentlemen, gentlemen." When the din and smoke of battle settled, the little affair was minus 3 gentlemen who had torn out spewing tempers. We all expected torsos to float up on the beach and other ghastly things, but later decided they all really wanted to sleep with each other and took this rather devious method. One sweet thing spent the rest of the evening picking clam chowder out of the wicker furniture with an ice pick.[49]

He ended the letter with the information that he owed a lot of money to his analyst and had stopped drinking. While he didn't mention Williams's name in the letter, it was he who started the stormy exodus; Bolender never knew exactly why.[50]

There were more-felicitous clam chowder episodes when, following the Southbury performances in the summer of 1948, Bolender went back to Provincetown with John Dunphy, who had been a close friend for some years. One fine day, Dunphy fell off his bicycle and Gloria Nardin Watts picked him up and gave him a ride home, to a "cabin on a dirt lane that was right behind my own, separated by a big hedge. We were friends immediately, made clam chowder together that day and spent all that lovely summer together," she recalled in an email in 2011, "and when the summer ended, we decided to rent a house together, at 300 1/2 East 65 St., where we lived [for] many years."[51] In this way, Bolender acquired a family of choice, serving as uncle to the Nardin children, one of whom was named Todd.

New York City Ballet's first season was announced that September. Bolender was on the roster of principal dancers, along with Maria Tallchief, Marie-Jeanne, Tanaquil Le Clercq, Beatrice Tompkins, Jocelyn Vollmar (who came from San Francisco Ballet), Nicholas Magallanes, Frank Moncion, and Herbert Bliss. They performed at City Center on Mondays and Tuesdays from October 11 to November 23, largely in the Ballet Society repertory, including *Symphony in C* and *Orpheus*. The only new productions were a revival of *Concerto Barocco,* using Eugene Berman's scenery and costumes, and Bolender's *Mother Goose Suite.*

The opening program was well reviewed by Martin. He had some caveats about the inexperience of the corps but otherwise praised the repertoire as "characterized by beautiful taste and a total disregard for war-horses."[52] What he had to say about *Symphony in C* is interesting in the context of American ballet, since its first version, *Le Palais de Cristal,* was originally made for the Paris Opéra Ballet: "The work itself is youthful in the extreme, a regular choreographic Fourth-of-July celebration: the fire-works themselves provide the interest, the choreography is all sky-rockets, Roman candles and pin-wheels which follow each other more or less in straight sequence against a definitely light-weight musical background and require no formal awareness from the performers."[53]

It would not be for several more years that Martin, who was basically a music critic, would fully grasp that for Balanchine music provided the impetus for choreography and that he cast dancers in his work at least in part for their understanding of the ways music and dancing worked together. Martin did find the speed and exuberance of the dancers who performed in the New York premiere of *Symphony in C*, Bolender among them, "not to be resisted," but wrote dismissively of the enthusiastic response from the audience.

About *Orpheus*, which closed the program, Martin had no caveats whatsoever. He called it "one of the most beautiful, the most completely satisfying, theatre experiences within memory. Against Stravinsky's serenely meditative score, Balanchine has conceived a profoundly touching action that is part gesture, part choreography, part theatre movement, and Noguchi has drawn the whole thing together texturally and visually, giving it accent and phrase by a motile décor of supreme eloquence. Here is a re-enactment of an ancient ritual in terms as remote as antiquity itself and as immediate as the mind and heart. The New York City Ballet," he concluded, "has certainly begun its career on a high level."[54]

The high level of that beginning can also be attributed to the dancers it attracted from other companies, Ballet Theatre among them. Janet Reed was one of Martin's favorites. In May 1949, not long before Balanchine invited Reed to join City Ballet, Martin hailed her return to Ballet Theatre, "after time out for matrimony, maternity and Broadway, an even more delightful artist than she used to be, and that was pretty delightful."[55] Martin cited an "increased security in her technique and maturity in her dancing, which apparently gives her greater freedom to be the admirable comedian that she is. She has an intuitive sense of supplying an unexpected other side to a character." He continued, "In 'Fancy Free' there is a wonderful tenderness about her night-roving, teen-age delinquent; in 'Pillar of Fire' the sweet little sister is a real viper; in 'Tally-Ho' the bored young wife's flirtation with the dissolute prince is an admixture of thrill and trepidation in deliberately playing with fire, and the whole performance is high comedy of rare substance. Here are three roles that are just about perfection."

Reed certainly wasn't perceived as delinquent by the servicemen she befriended during the war. A young naval officer she corresponded briefly with wrote her that he had her picture posted in his quarters and that he instructed sailors who came through his door not to swear in her presence.[56] She had worked hard to analyze her roles since performing with Loring's Dance Players, and once she joined Ballet Theatre, she was spurred on psychologically by Tudor, particularly for that less-than-sweet little sister in *Pillar of Fire*. If, in 1949, she was a completely convincing bored young wife in *Tally-Ho*, it was because of her talents as a dancer-actor, not because of her intuition or personal experience. In the three years since her marriage to Branson Erskine, she had scarcely had time to be bored.

The couple had been introduced by Muriel Bentley in June 1945, when much of the original cast of *Fancy Free* was dancing in the premiere of Robbins's *Interplay* at the Ziegfeld Theater. The concert version of Robbins's second ballet was part of a show that Billy Rose labeled "Concert Varieties," which included the Dunham company, Imogene Coca doing the Tamiment "PM of a Faun," and Zero Mostel, according to Jowitt, "imitating a politician, an opera singer, and a coffee percolator."[57]

Like *Fancy Free, Interplay* is, on one level, about the people who danced it; unlike *Fancy Free*, it is plotless. Choreographically and musically it is just as American, its mixture of classical steps and vernacular dance accompanied by Morton Gould's jazzy blues–shaded *American Concertette*. Martin reviewed the Ballet Theatre premiere in October, praising Robbins for proving that "not all American dance theatre works had to be storytelling, genre or period pieces, but that a purely formal approach could be made to composition in a strictly native vein and still be good."[58]

Native dancers like Reed, Bentley, and Robbins himself, reinforced its authenticity. Reed had what she called a "very personal feeling" about the central pas de deux, which Robbins had set on her and himself for the concert version (Kriza partnered her in the Ballet Theatre premiere). It was, to her, "the epitome of blues, and a certain low-down blues. That quality . . . that's the image I had in mind when I danced. It had an underneath drive, so that I went into the floor . . . with more, *weight*. [You aren't] skimming over the surface; you attack the steps with more weight. There's a wailing blues quality about it, and underneath throb."[59] That section of the ballet was referred to as "dirty" in rehearsals, but the mental image of a torch singer as she performed the role was one Reed said she found for herself.

Reed was twenty-nine when she danced in a ballet that was about dancers as teenagers, playing games, jitterbugging, engaging with each other and the music. According to Bolender, who saw a lot of her at the time socially as well as in performance, "Everybody used to think of Janet as being adorable, everybody loved to see [her] on stage because she was what everyone thought a dancer should be in those years, small, petite, very pretty, and a very good dancer." A form she filled out for Sol Hurok's booking agency in 1947 gives some interesting basic information about her at the time. On it, in clear handwriting, she revealed that she was five-feet-and-a-quarter-inch tall, weighed 103 pounds, and wore size 6C shoes. Elsewhere, she had given her height as five feet two inches, but here she only fudged her age, giving her birth date as 1920 rather than 1916. Asked about rituals she performed before going on stage, she said she wasn't superstitious and that she "put rosin on my shoes. Any rites I perform are practical." About any collecting she did, she responded, "I collect my reviews when I get them."

Branson Erskine, on the other hand, who had been wanting to meet Reed for some time, was a collector by profession. Tall, good-looking, and urbane, he was an interior designer and antiques dealer with a well-known shop on the Upper East Side of Manhattan called the Obelisk. The son of the founder of Sylvania Electric Products, he had grown up with a financial security that Reed had never known. However, because of acute physical illness diagnosed at a very early age, emotional security had eluded him for most of his life and would continue to do so. He was diagnosed with juvenile diabetes of the worst kind in 1922, not long before insulin was first used as a treatment for the disease. At that point, the nine-year-old began a lifetime of daily injections of the hormone, without which he would not have survived. To add to his problems, he had what was then called "brittle" diabetes, in which the levels of blood sugar in the body can fluctuate wildly. Too much insulin, according to his son, Reed Erskine, "often results in a violent hypoglycemia known as 'insulin shock,' [which] can cause hallucinations, and without an immediate dose of sugar to counteract it, coma and death." A nurse accompanied Branson to college to monitor those blood sugar levels, nothing like as easy to do in the twentieth century as it is in the twenty-first. People with this condition can also be susceptible to stress and depression, which, the younger Erskine, who was born in 1947, wrote, "made our family life very difficult."[60]

That being said, when Erskine finally met the all-American beautiful ballerina of his dreams, he was leading a lavish, highly social life style that was certainly bad for his health—alcohol flowed—and that he couldn't always afford. Reed probably knew about his precarious health before they were married, but possibly not, in the days before prenuptial agreements, his uncertain finances. In any case, after a courtship that—given Ballet Theatre's touring schedule—must have been sporadic, to say the least, they were married on May 23, 1946, less than a year after their first meeting, and twelve days after the close of Ballet Theatre's spring season at the Met. The wedding took place in the Roman Catholic Church of St. John the Baptist in Cliffside, New Jersey, in an effort to placate Erskine's mother, who was none too pleased that her son had married a ballerina. Dancers in the 1940s in the United States were not considered socially acceptable in some circles; that is one reason they dressed in suits and heels when on tour. Nora Kaye was Reed's attendant and Kaye's mother, to whom Reed was ever grateful for keeping herself and Kaye alive with hearty homemade soups when the two dancers shared an apartment, made Reed's hat. A reception, according to an announcement in *The New York Times,* followed at the St. Regis Hotel in New York.[61]

"Dancing is fun," Reed liked to tell her students, by which she meant performing on stage, not necessarily the hard work that goes on in class and the studio in preparation for it. By the time they were married, Erskine had been watching her having fun as Lise in Bronislava Nijinska's *La fille mal gardée;* the Girl in Pink in Michael Kidd's *On Stage;* the neglected wife in *Tally Ho;* Hera, also known as "the lascivious bride," in Tudor's *Undertow;* in soubrette roles in Balanchine's *Waltz Academy* and Lichine's *Graduation Ball;* and as the second girl in Robbins's *Fancy Free,* lacing her performances with energy, humor, and optimism. Small wonder, then, he wanted to meet her—if she made him laugh on stage, she would surely make him laugh off it. Moreover, because she was so beautiful, Erskine, the designer, wanted to decorate her, and once they were married he did just that. Reed Erskine remembered that his mother was always the best-dressed woman at the unemployment office when the ballet companies were on hiatus; Bolender recalled that her clothes and her jewelry were on all occasions "perfect."

The courtship was sporadic, since Reed was more often out of town than not, touring with Ballet Theatre, performing in the company's exhausting "ham and eggs" repertory, and originating new roles. One was the Girl in Pink in Michael Kidd's first major ballet, *On Stage,* which premiered in Boston on October 4, 1945. The work, to music composed by Norman Dello Joio, is about a ballet company, its focus a young girl who wants to be a ballerina but is afraid to audition. She is befriended by the theater handyman, as in Reed's life experience dancers often were. (In the 1930s, the doorman at the San Francisco Opera House provided the unpaid company members with pastries before morning rehearsals; it was often the only breakfast they had.)[62]

After the Boston premiere, Reed and the choreographer received a glowing review from Margaret Lloyd, who, writing for the *Christian Science Monitor,* described the ballet as "fun" and "Janet Reed, [as] the shy girl who is afraid of auditions, and Michael Kidd, [as] the Handyman, who capture the audience heart on."[63] Denby, reviewing it after the New York premiere, didn't much like the work itself, calling it "lowbrow in sentiment" and acknowledging its debt to silent film as a Chaplinade, although he praised Kidd and Reed's performances as "subtle."[64]

The premiere initiated Ballet Theatre's 1945–1946 season and it was a particularly grueling one; touring in the last year of the war was especially arduous. Reed performed in many ballets on the road in the roles that called for her talents as a soubrette and a comedian. But she also performed in the repertory program that included *Aurora's Wedding,* for which she frequently danced the Bluebird pas de deux, a classical tour de force that demanded precise, rapid footwork. Reed, who garnered many reviews in comic and soubrette roles but was seldom written up in such classical set pieces as this one, nevertheless took her classical abilities extremely seriously, so seriously, in fact, that Bolender, who partnered her in the third movement of *Symphony in C* after she joined City Ballet, said that her whole personality changed when she danced "classical things."

In Portland, where the company appeared at the public auditorium in the spring of 1946, Hilmar Grondahl, who had been reviewing music and dance for *The Oregonian* since the early 1930s and had followed Reed's career from the time she was a student in the Christensen school, was proud of the hometown girl and made her the focus of his review of a program that included *Waltz Academy, Tally-Ho, Graduation Ball,* and *Fancy Free.* "Where a characterization asks, in addition to the expected technical expertness, a free and natural expressiveness of spirit, a feeling of spontaneity and an inner urgency, there is the place for Janet Reed. [Her] dancing reflected a zest for life and warmth of being. . . . [It was] fresh and unstudied."[65] In another review, Grondahl put his stamp of approval on Reed as an American-born ballet dancer and on the change from American ballet's Russophile climate, stating, "It's now all right to dance in the Petipa tradition without having to end your name in ova or ski. Janet Reed is an example of someone not born within 500 miles of the Dnieper."[66]

In the summer of 1946, Ballet Theatre terminated its association with impresario Sol Hurok, the company was reorganized, and the dancers were on the road again, this time via ship to England, the first American company to tour there after World War II. Reed, however, was not with them, although she remained on the company roster. After years of focusing single-mindedly on her career, she was paying attention to her personal life and establishing her own family. Her son, Reed Erskine, was born in January 1947, and by the time Robbins started rehearsals in mid-November for *Look Ma, I'm Dancin'*, the fourth show he choreographed for Broadway, Reed was back in shape to dance the ingénue lead. *Look Ma*, whose scenario was conceived by Robbins, was about a Russo-American ballet company on tour, one of the principal characters an ambitious young choreographer who bears more than a little resemblance to Robbins himself. The troupe is bankrolled by a wealthy woman who wants to be a ballerina, played by Nancy Walker, an old friend of Robbins's from Tamiment days, who Bolender had gotten to know in southern California during his brief stint with Ballet Theatre. Her character is widely believed to be a satirical portrait of Lucia Chase, and the show itself is pretty clearly based on Ballet Theatre. Just as Robbins had put things he had witnessed on tour into *Fancy Free* and *On the Town*, he inserted into *Look Ma* the sleeping-car hijinks and berth-switching that had taken place as Ballet Theatre's dancers crossed and recrossed the continent, in a number that demanded considerable bravura dancing from the men in the cast.

According to Jowitt, apart from this extravaganza danced in pajamas, "Robbins' most interesting choreography was reserved for a duet for Reed and Harold Lang, as Eddie the choreographer on the make." They had known each other a long time; Lang's career as a dancer had begun with San Francisco Ballet in 1938, when the compassionate opera-house doorman had permitted the impoverished dancer to sleep backstage. In this duet, "[Reed is] practicing in a Des Moines theater basement, while *Swan Lake* is being performed on the stage overhead. She begins to dance to music of the ACT II pas de deux and Eddie steps in to partner and encourage her: He: "Three turns? She: "Just two." He: "Try three." She does, and he praises her. She's surprised he knows *Swan Lake*. He retorts, 'I'm that clever Winkler boy.' They continue to dance and talk, becoming more involved in the ballet's love story, freezing when anyone walks through. By the last ten bars, they're about to kiss when he drops her; he's just had a great idea for a ballet. It'll feature talking and dancing."[67]

Reed enjoyed working in *Look Ma,* although she wasn't thrilled with yet another ingénue role. What she found most interesting was the requirement that she and Lang make up their dialogue in the basement scene in which they fall in love. "We improvised that completely," she said. "And Jerry had the writers put it in [the script]. It was a great way of working."[68] And not at all what Reed was accustomed to with ballet choreographers, including Robbins himself.

Look Ma, I'm Dancin' was neither a critical nor a box-office success; it had just 188 performances and ran slightly less than six months. A brief write-up in *The New York Daily News* was hostile to both ballet and the show itself. Walter Terry wrote, "Look Ma emerged as a comedy about dancing, rather than dancing comedy."[69] After it closed, Reed returned to Ballet Theatre on a limited basis, performing her roles in *Fancy Free* and the Ballerina in *Petrouchka* and alternating with Nana Gollner as Lisette in Nijinska's staging of *La fille mal gardée.* Lillian Moore compared the two in a review for *Dancing Times,* writing that "Gollner is the stronger technician and dances the role of Lisette with ease and assurance, while Janet Reed's interpretation has a particularly appealing freshness and charm."[70] Reed, who knew what it was to live on a farm, had been doing "freshness and charm" offstage as well as on for a good many years.

Balanchine's invitation to Reed to join New York City Ballet in 1949 came at a good time. Ballet Theatre was still basically a touring company with very short seasons in New York; City Ballet was getting established as the resident ballet company at City Center and had announced no plans to tour; and Reed now had a husband and child to keep her closer to home. However, she did not jump at the chance, telling Mr. B., who wanted her badly enough to take her and Erskine to dinner at the 21 Club one evening, that she wasn't a Balanchine dancer.[71] Possibly she was referring to her short stature and lack of SAB training, although she had taken classes there. As Denby defined Balanchine dancers, she certainly fit the bill: "dancing in their lovely young freshness onstage" which "comes from the fact that they understand completely the classic dancing they are asked to do, understand it in dancers' terms. . . . For Balanchine they need not understand a dance by rationalizing psychologically, they need not put it over by emoting their role or glamorizing their personality. When they get the physical feel of a dance sequence, the bodily rhythm of the movement (and this is a profoundly personal and instinctively emotional recognition) they know they are right and that nothing will fail to carry. The audience will love them."[72]

Audiences from coast to coast had certainly loved Reed for a good many years and Balanchine knew it. Moreover, he had created a role for her in *Waltz Academy* in 1945, and, from several encounters with her at Ballet Theatre he knew that she had an indefatigable work ethic and the willingness to try anything that he associated with American dancers generally. His response to her hesitation was characteristically laconic: "Is all right, we make something for you," he said.[73]

The "something" he made for her first was the role of the deliciously exuberant leader of the "Fête Polonaise," in the third movement of *Bourrée Fantasque,* set to several different pieces composed by Emanuel Chabrier, which she performed with Herbert Bliss at the premiere on December 1, 1949. *Bourrée Fantasque* is a sophisticated, chic, witty endeavor and was received as it was intended, as a grand entertainment. Karinska's stylish black tutus were accessorized with headdresses that, like the hats of the period, were trimmed with little veils, flowers and butterflies; the tutus and men's tunics accented in saffron (Reed's), turquoise, silver, and cerise, received critical praise from Martins, who wrote they served well the "vivacity" of the music.[74] A studio photograph of Reed, taken from the waist up, appears very "New Look," the bodice off the shoulder, the arms in long fingerless gloves, although the tutu skirts were very short, unlike the mid-calf hems with which Dior proclaimed the fabric shortages from WWII to be over.

Doris Hering thought *Bourrée's* second movement, danced by the usually dynamic duo of Tallchief and Magallanes, somewhat static, but found nothing of the kind about the "Fête Polonaise": "Reed was swung in wide, airy arcs by her partner. And the accumulated corps de ballet and soloists massed for a leaping finale that left the audience laughing and shouting bravo in a single breath." Summing up the ballet as a whole, she said, "It is a master stylist's amalgam of French flavor and Russian classic technique geared to the very special exuberance and speed of young American dancers."[75]

Barbara Walczak, one of those young American dancers, recalled that Balanchine had some trouble setting the finale: "Somehow he couldn't quite get it. He asked us would we waive the union rules and would we consider simply going on, so that he could finish it. [The rehearsal] ended at eleven or midnight or something, we refused money for it."[76] Elsewhere, in a lengthy oral history interview, Walczak spoke of the dedication of the company's dancers at the time. They would often be deployed to put up posters announcing performances in such culturally clued-in New York neighborhoods as Greenwich Village, where Martha Graham stalked the streets in her Calder jewelry.[77]

Reed had made her New York City Ballet debut a month earlier, as the Young Girl in Bolender's *Mother Goose Suite,* along with Robbins as Hop O' My Thumb. Just as Bolender wanted to work with Balanchine after seeing *Serenade,* Robbins, after watching Ballet Society perform *Symphony in C* in 1948, was so excited by the choreography, not to mention by Le Clercq's dancing in the second movement, that he wrote to offer Balanchine and Kirstein his services as "anything they wanted." They soon accepted and hired Robbins as the company's associate artistic director.[78]

Hop O' My Thumb was a role Bolender often performed himself (along with the Beast) and Balanchine would frequently alternate him and Robbins in roles in the seasons to come: the opening movement of *Bourrée Fantasque* and the title role in *Tyl Ulenspiegel,* which was made for Robbins, are examples. This casting was logical, since they had both modern and classical training.

Reviewing Reed as the Young Girl in *Mother Goose,* Chujoy wrote that she danced with a "wistful quality . . . which gave a feeling of magic and dreams."[79] In Lew Christensen's *Jinx,* she reprised the role of the wire-walking object of Jinx the clown's affections, which she had originated seven years earlier as a member of Loring's Dance Players. Moncion had the title role in the company premiere; Bolender was cast in later performances. Terry didn't much care for the ballet, but found Reed "wonderfully appealing."[80] Critics generally felt it needed more work.

If the costumes for *Bourrée,* the first at New York City Ballet for which Karinska, then in her early 60s, received credit for design as well as execution, served well the Gallic stylishness of Emmanuel Chabrier's score, those by Robert Stevenson for the second "something" Balanchine made specifically for Reed evidently turned a lighthearted demonstration of nineteenth-century bravura dancing into something the audience reacted to as if it were a vaudeville turn. *Pas de Deux Romantique* was set to Carl Maria von Weber's *Concertino for Clarinet and Orchestra,* music Bolender used the word "tweedly" to describe. Stevenson, who had designed the striking costumes for Dollar's best-known ballet, *The Combat,* in this instance created a velvet-bodiced, much-ruffled tutu for Reed and a matching tunic for Herbert Bliss, who partnered her, both so lavishly trimmed with rhinestones and metallic ribbon that even in black-and-white photos they look more suitable for a Las Vegas floor show than the proscenium stage. Reed's elaborate tiara resembles something a grand duke might have bestowed on Mathilde Kschessinska. Bolender speculated that Erskine had provided the tiara for his wife and had paid for and approved the design of the costumes.

Pas de Deux Romantique premiered on March 3, 1950, at City Center on a program that closed with *Bourrée Fantasque.* The audience laughed heartily at the premiere and loved it. The critics were mystified. Reed, who didn't think she was being funny, was visibly furious as she exited into the wings. Balanchine, who, under the best of circumstances, disliked talking about his ballets, added to the confusion. He told various people slightly different things about this one: that it was intended to be a balletic version of coloratura singing, a demonstration of Romantic ballet technique, a stylization of a romantic pas de deux. Presumably, it was also intended to demonstrate Reed's ability, as Bolender once put it, to "make the technique look good on stage" and, as Balanchine consistently did with dancers, to challenge her. In a memoir she worked on at the end of her life, Reed spoke of this as "fulfilling": "He challenges a dancer and makes them do things they didn't know they could do."[81]

"The ballet proved something of an enigma to audiences and critics,"[82] Reynolds says, and Martin titled a column "To Laugh or Not to Laugh."[83] Martin and Terry attempted to analyze it, not very well, and Chujoy found it "slight, boring, wrong," and confirmed Bolender's memory of the audience's giggling reaction. "As soon as Janet Reed in her garish costume began to stylize the romantic ballet, the audience began to titter, and as the pas de deux progressed the laughs became louder and more general. [If it] was meant to be a parody, it was not amusing enough."[84]

Bolender attributed the laughter to the costumes and a possible statement that Balanchine was making about having them thrust upon him by Erskine. The multiple glittering ruffles on the tutu and the matching arm bands could easily have shifted the viewer's eye from Reed's execution of Balanchine's choreography and made her look silly. Thus, the most likely explanation for her fury was her desire to be taken as seriously as a classical dancer as she was as a comedian-soubrette, particularly by the City Ballet audience.

If Reed actually felt insecure about her technique, according to Bolender, "she never mentioned it. Janet was very good at keeping things to herself. She was not the kind of person who would need someone to be her analyst. She could really do her own. . . . She was a very intelligent, well-balanced human being in that respect [with] a very strong sense of herself—which isn't always true of dancers."[85]

There is no doubt that Balanchine took her seriously as a classical dancer, or he wouldn't have cast her in principal roles in *Serenade, Concerto Barocco,* and *Symphony in C,* all of which she performed during her first season with City Ballet. Bolender partnered her in the third movement of the Bizet ballet, and, in spite of a deepening personal friendship and the pleasure he took in dancing with her in much of the Robbins's repertory, not to mention his own, he did not find it an agreeable experience. "Janet was like another person when she danced classical," he said. "It would all become terribly elegant. She was too demanding: hold me here, hold me there, do this, put your hands here. We really never danced together except in Jerry's things," he added. "And then we could dance like a bat out of hell together. I could partner her and it was absolutely no problem whatsoever. . . . Anything classical[,] forget it!" Part of their difficulty Bolender attributed to the difference in their heights; at five foot eight he was seven inches taller, although, in pointe shoes, she would have been roughly five foot seven.

It was in Robbins's ballets, "Jerry's jazzy things," as Bolender termed them, that he and Reed most frequently danced together. *Pied Piper* was a technically complex work that was included in the repertory for the 1952 tour of Europe, where it was a hit as an exemplar of American ballet. Set to Copland's *Concerto for Clarinet and String Orchestra, with Harp and Piano,* a work he had made for Benny Goodman in 1948, it previewed the onstage pianist in *The Concert,* with, in this case, a clarinetist setting up his chair and music stand to strains of the opening music and then luring the dancers from the wings with his first notes. Most musicians were willing to do this, but this was not the case in Paris, where the ballet was called *Le joueur de flûte.* According to Bolender, their own musician was ill and the Frenchman who substituted for him insisted on playing from the pit, so Balanchine, who enjoyed performing mightily, volunteered to mime playing the clarinet on stage. "Balanchine would ham it up," Bolender remembered, while he and Robbins, who was still dancing, performed side by side, with Robbins muttering, "'What the fuck does he think he's doing for Christ's sake?' Jerry was a tough number, a very tough man."

Pied Piper was a hit in New York and on the 1952 tour, and Reed was definitely its star. Barbara Walczak said she was "wonderful in [it], like a valentine, charming."[86] She was also, according to Jowitt, the quintessential American brat: "Reed is a little hellion, an instigator of jazzy movements when the tempo heats up. She leads one guy in a chase around a huddle of dancers. When he catches up with her, she slams him. He manhandles her into a lift. When another fellow turns from the clump and socks her aggressor, she draws out index-finger guns and shoots them both." Reed told Jowitt that while the ballet certainly had a structure, she thought of it "as close to improvisation: 'It seemed to me it was thrown together. We just got in the studio one day and the music played and I started to do a lot of crazy stuff and it just—that was it.'"[87]

Robbins also cast Bolender in the revival of *Interplay* in 1952, with Reed in the role she had originated. Neither, however, was featured in *The Guests,* a collaboration with Marc Blitzstein that was the first piece Robbins made specifically for City Ballet; it premiered in January 1949. It was a highly political ballet that basically didn't work but nevertheless an important step in Robbins's development as a choreographer of intellectual depth.

Even more important was *Age of Anxiety,* Robbins's second work for City Ballet and the first in which Bolender created a principal role. This ballet, according to Chujoy and others, "marked the beginning of a new period in [Robbins's] creative life" because, unlike such works as *Fancy Free* and *Interplay,* the choreographer took on a much bigger subject than sailors on leave or dancers evoking their own adolescence.[88]

"In *Age of Anxiety,*" Chujoy explained, "Robbins evoked the basic emotions of a whole generation, a generation that has not yet outlived the horrors of a world war, insecure under the conditions of an uneasy peace and the radical changes in a civilization that does not quite know where to look for something or someone offering a modicum of assurance that all is not going to be destroyed morally and physically."[89] This description is more than a little reminiscent of the idea behind Bolender's *Zodiac:* the lack of balance in postwar society, the feeling, in another poet's words, that "the centre cannot hold."[90]

Once again, Robbins was working with Bernstein's music, but in this case, it was an already existing score. *Symphony No. 2 for Piano and Or-*

chestra premiered in Boston in 1949 and was inspired by Auden's last long poem, *The Age of Anxiety*. As more than one critic pointed out, it has "that American sound."[91] Filled with jazzy, jittery rhythms juxtaposed with lyrical passages, the music is highly dramatic and far more conducive to dancing than Auden's talky poem, for which he won a Pulitzer Prize and much criticism from his native England. The poem is an eclogue, defined as "a pastoral convention in which a natural setting is contrasted with an artificial style of diction." Auden's "natural setting" is a bar on New York's Third Avenue that shifts to an apartment on the city's West Side. The time is an All-Souls' Night during World War II. Bolender was one of the four protagonists, which included two other men, danced by Roy Tobias and the choreographer, and one woman, portrayed by Le Clercq, who disliked the ballet intensely. She also found the poem useless as a guide to her performance, and in his review of the premiere, Martin recommended strongly that audience members avoid reading it before viewing the ballet, because it would add to their confusion.

Structurally, both Bernstein and Robbins followed the scheme of the 135-page poem, which the City Ballet program described thus: "The Prologue: four strangers meet and become acquainted; The Seven Ages: They discuss the life of man from birth to death in a set of seven variations; The Seven Stages: They embark on a dream journey to find happiness; The Dirge: They mourn for the figure of the All-Powerful Father who would have protected them from the vagaries of man and nature; The Masque: They attempt to become or to appear carefree; The Epilogue." But while Auden's four strangers are definite personalities with names, professions and occupations, ambitions, and desires (Rosetta, a department store buyer; Malin, a Canadian airman; Quant, a world-weary clerk; Emble, a young naval recruit), Robbins parted company with the poet here and turned them into abstractions, unindividualized urbanites with a generalized, Freudian angst that was so obvious to one audience member on opening night that it was suggested the ballet's title be changed to the *Age of Psychiatry*.

Robbins also changed the locations from New York interiors to the less-than-pastoral city streets, the mise-en-scène a photo montage created by Oliver Smith, with one backdrop featuring the magnificently Art Deco Flatiron Building. Irene Sharaff's costumes, which consisted of simple jersey tights, leotards, and tops, the dominant color red but differently styled and patterned (Bolender's tights had one dark-colored leg and one light, Robbins's top had a collar, Le Clercq's top was draped), added to a visual atmosphere that reflected the austerity of New York in the postwar period, the slashes of red serving to heighten the dreariness of the city's November weather. These were not costumes that expressed character; Robbins's choreography did that. "He's very good at giving sharp, clear characterizations of both movements and psychological states," Bolender told Reynolds in 1970. "Often by [analyzing] the movement you could get through to the character. There was an urgency about the movements always. It was sustained as though in a tension, then would burst out and move into something else. We always appeared to be on the move, about to break and go into another area. He incorporated ballet kind of steps rather beautifully and managed to use symbolism that didn't have heavy connotation. It was so light and beautifully done. He seemed to focus the very word *anxiety* in his movement—jagged, almost unrelated things, like tics sometimes throughout the body. Everyone would move in exactly the same way to the same degree. Since the ballet was dealing with the times we lived in, he used movement that one could associate with . . . the street, for instance, but then heightened it so that it came out quite a different color."[92]

Between Bolender's description of the movement in general terms, vivid writing by critics, some grainy film taken by the indefatigable Ann Barzel, and a fine collection of photographs, many by George Platt Lynes, it is possible to get a pretty good idea of what it was like to watch a piece that, for Martin (at this point still far more interested in modern dance than ballet), justified the existence of New York City Ballet. But for others, it was too opaque to engage them. A photograph of the four protagonists, for example, three of them with knees bent, a fourth crouched on the floor, all of them looking up in fear, puts the ballet firmly into the postwar context—they could be looking for German bombers over London or perhaps for Soviet planes, since, by 1950, Americans were living in fear of a nuclear attack.

For Bolender, who once again was dancing about an idea, as he had in *The Four Temperaments* (this time, one rooted in psychoanalysis and geopolitical angst), *Age of Anxiety* ultimately proved to be a harrowing ballet to perform, both emotionally and physically, so much so that, although he thought it was one of Robbins's best works, he blocked much of it from memory. His blocking was so successful that, when many years later, the choreographer asked for help in reviving it, Bolender did not even remember that he was the character who "died."[93]

Nevertheless, Bolender found the rehearsals interesting and exhilarating, remembering that he, Le Clercq, Moncion, and Robbins "worked together marvelously. [Robbins] gave me things that expanded me, I felt, and sometimes he'd fight with me about getting things. He'd say, 'Do it bigger, don't be so lazy. Get it into the air.' And so I did."[94] A photograph taken by Ed Carswell of a 36-year-old Bolender and 22-year-old Le Clercq jumping exuberantly high into the air, arms flung wide, proves his point.

Martin took notice of the principals in his review of the premiere. "The four leading figures are in a sense shadowy in that they are not minutely characterized, but each has his sharp and distinctive flavor, and between them they evolve an intangible but potent dramatic line through the unrelated episodes. They are all admirably danced."[95]

Of the ballet's conclusion, Martin cited the poem's "short peroration in which the poet seems to imply a return to mystical religion as the answer; in Mr. Bernstein's music comes the dawn in a kind of glorious Technicolor and Mr. Robbins' four figures simply bow to each other with a new peace, which has come from nowhere discernible and [they] separate." Rosenthal's lighting for this inconclusive ending replicated a glorious sunrise. Martin considered the work a major achievement and returned to see it many times, finding it tremendously moving.[96] It stayed in City Ballet's repertory for the next five years, and large cast notwithstanding (with the corps, there were thirty-eight dancers), the company took it to England on its first tour abroad in the summer of 1950. By 1954, however, Martin had ceased to be moved by it, questioning its content and calling it "old-fashioned" and speculating that the times had changed to "an age of different anxieties, less selfish and more universal."[97]

6

Reed was persuaded by Balanchine to join City Ballet in 1949 in part because she was worn out by Ballet Theatre's constant tours and Balanchine's company at this time was performing only in New York in their new home in the "people's theater," also known as New York City Center, on West 55th Street (fortuitously not far from the Erskine apartment on East 57th Street). Apart from the opportunity to work with a choreographer whose nonnarrative ballets had interested her for several years, she would be able to establish the family life that had been denied her in her own childhood and continue her professional life, too.

Or so she thought. In the period from 1950 to 1955, City Ballet was frequently on the road, both in the United States and abroad, starting with eight weeks in England in the summer of 1950. It was in Chicago for a month the following spring, it was in continental Europe for five months in 1952, and it had its first cross-continental American tour in 1953, when the company initiated the first of many summer seasons at the Greek Theatre in Los Angeles. The same year, City Ballet traveled extensively in Europe, and in 1954, it made its first appearance in Seattle. The following year, the same one in which Kirstein and Balanchine established three-month "winter" seasons at home in New York, the company danced in Monte Carlo, France, Italy, Switzerland, Holland, and Germany. Reed wasn't always along; Bolender was seldom if ever absent.

Kirstein did not like touring any better than Reed: after the grueling complications of American Ballet Caravan's travels in South America in 1941, he had vowed never to do it again. Nevertheless, after much negotiation with the director of Covent Garden and verbal support from Ninette de Valois, founder of the Sadler's Wells Ballet (later the Royal Ballet), he was persuaded to undertake a British tour for the fledgling company.

In July 1950, the company packed up its forty-two dancers and repertory of eighteen ballets and headed for London, where it would have a five-week run at the Royal Opera House at Covent Garden, followed by a three-week tour of Croydon, Manchester, and Liverpool. Covent Garden paid half the transportation costs, and for the duration of the London season, it paid City Ballet £2,000.

Despite the financial assistance from the British, Kirstein knew the tour was likely to be a money-losing proposition. But it was worth it for what it would do for the reputation of American ballet abroad and City Ballet at home. He also seized the opportunity to promote American visual artists by arranging for an exhibition titled *American Symbolist Painters* at the London Contemporary Art Institute that was on view at the same time as the Covent Garden performances. It included the work of Paul Cadmus and Andrew Wyeth.

For Balanchine, the Covent Garden performances were beneficial for two reasons. They gave him the opportunity to show the British audience what he had been doing in the sixteen years he had been in the United States, and (possibly even more important to him) the dancers enjoyed a much longer run than they had at City Center, where, at that time, the seasons lasted only a couple of weeks.

The repertory, a smorgasbord of narrative and nonnarrative ballets was dominated by Balanchine's work (too many of the latter to satisfy most of the British press). But it included works by five other choreographers, reflecting the company's range. The company performed Balanchine's *Firebird, Bourrée Fantasque, Concerto Barocco, Divertimento* (Haieff), *Four Temperaments, Orpheus, Pas de Deux Romantique, Prodigal Son, Serenade, Symphonie Concertante,* and *Symphony in C;* Bolender's *Mother Goose;* Robbins's *Age of Anxiety* and *The Guests,* plus *Jones Beach,* which he had choreographed jointly with Balanchine; Dollar's *The Duel;* Christensen's *Jinx,* and Frederick Ashton's *Illuminations.* There was plenty of stylistic variety and the repertory balanced the entertaining with the intellectual, the neoclassical with the classical.

Chujoy, who was in London to cover City Ballet's Covent Garden season for *Dance News* and was on special assignment for both the *Herald Tribune* and *Newsweek,* vividly described the audience attending the July 10 opening performance of *Serenade, Age of Anxiety,* and *Symphony in C:*

London's ballet world attended in force; the literary, music, and art worlds were well represented; with Ambassador Douglas away from London, the American Embassy sent its ranking personnel; all the London and Paris newspapers and magazines sent their first-string critics; Scandinavian newspapers sent their correspondents; all wire services were there as well as all photographic services. Americans who were in London and had been foresighted enough to get tickets in advance came to the premiere; nearly the entire Sadler's Wells company stayed over the weekend in London to attend. S. Hurok flew in for the premiere from Paris, as did Barbara Karinska and Anton Dolin. American dance critics in Europe at the time, among them John Martin and Edwin Denby, were on hand.[1]

One British reviewer stated, "The company were facing a British audience for the first time but after the first curtain they knew from their reception they had won the admiration of the 'gods' and the stalls alike."[2] Audiences continued to love the company throughout the run, although the house was far from full after Covent Garden extended the season for an extra week. The British critics, however, with a few exceptions, gave the Balanchine repertory in particular a cold shoulder. They were especially sniffy about his *Firebird*, despite the brilliance of Tallchief's performance in the title role and their thirst for ballets with clear narratives and emotional content. "Some of the very good works," Bolender told Deborah Jowitt, "I remember got acid reviews. And I remember the little thing that I had done, *Mother Goose*, got one of the best reviews."[3]

Age of Anxiety was also critically acclaimed, possibly because of the dancing by the principals, who gave so much of themselves that by closing night, according to Bolender, they "were almost hysterical" from the passions induced by performing it."

"The ballet fits its music and its theme (which is nightmarish enough to satisfy the gloomiest Central European) and has an obvious conformity with modern life," said Cyril Beaumont, the weekend critic for the *London Times*. Of the cast, Beaumont said, "The four strangers who seek escape from this un-American pessimism, were danced with powerful deliberation."[4] For another critic, who had had enough of what he called "a surfeit of abstract ballets in which the detailed pattern of the music is embodied in complicated movements," the two Robbins works came "as a welcome relief."[5]

As principal dancers, Reed and Bolender (who, unlike Reed, loved to travel) were paid $40 a week, having taken a $10 pay cut on the grounds that England's living costs were lower than New York's. This was partly because rationing was still in place. Even clothing was rationed at this time, which may have been pertinent to the negative critical reception of those portions of the repertory that were largely without scenery and had minimal costumes. The British longed for lavish productions, like *The Sleeping Beauty,* in which Margot Fonteyn had triumphed in New York the previous year, just as much as they yearned for unlimited butter and shirts that came in more than two or three colors.

Bolender and Reed danced together in quite a bit of the tour repertory, including *Symphony in C* and *Mother Goose Suite.* The *Guardian*'s critic judged the latter to be a pleasant work. Another critic was deeply appreciative of Una Kai's physical attributes: "To parts of the body which dance as well as the legs, Kai as the Bird added the wonderful tresses of her hair," adding that "there was more of a suggestion of fantasy in this slender and pleasing ballet than this company has hitherto shown to be within its emotional range."[6] And while Beaumont "did not find the ballet particularly moving," he did commend "Janet Reed as the Young Girl [who] adroitly linked each scene with her miming and danced with an engaging lightness." In general, however, Beaumont did not find that lightness pleasing, writing summarily that "[she] is technically a strong dancer with a particular facility for steps of elevation, witness her leaps in *Bourrée Fantasque,* and she can dance with an unusual lightness, as in *Mother Goose Suite.* But her high forehead detracts from her appearance and her general manner is ebullient and more suited to revue than to ballet."[7]

Writing of Reed's performance in *Serenade* on opening night, another *Times* critic pointed to "her individual style" and said of her dancing in *Symphony in C* that "she is so like a ball that her partner actually bounced her on the ground in the finale." It is doubtful that Reed took this as a compliment. Jacques d'Amboise, who was a very young corps member at this time, remembered her *Symphony in C* performance quite differently: "She was indelible as a performer. I don't know anyone who has danced the Third Movement of *Symphony in C* who could come near the incandescent light she made on her entrance, her grand jetés in a circle, you could almost hear in [them] the sound of whee, wheee."[8]

Although Beaumont applauded the vitality of the American dancers, he chided the male soloists for having "less personality" than the women. Of Bolender, who was 36 in 1950, Beaumont said, "[He] appears to be an older man who dances well but with very composed features; he has an unusual facility for the execution of développés."[9] Another critic, with the initials B. N., slammed *The Four Temperaments* in general, commenting that it "lacked excitement and design," but was sympathetic to the dancers, writing that "it was something of a triumph for Tod [*sic*] Bolender to make an impression in the Phlegmatic movement dressed in a costume which resembled a tired, slightly undercooked cabbage."

Bolender alternated with Moncion in *Jinx*, in which Reed continued to dance the wire-walker role she had originated in 1943 with Dance Players. Lew Christensen's tale of circus superstition was also better received by story-hungry British critics than much of Balanchine's work. One reviewer praised Bolender for making the clown an impressive figure. The same reviewer gave Christensen a special bouquet as choreographer, especially for his "attentiveness" to Britten's music.

Richard Buckle, who was to become a lifelong friend of Reed, was the exception among his British colleagues in his response to Balanchine's work. He liked *Pas de Deux Romantique* far better than did the ballerina for whom it was made, writing that "[it] has a special quality that is easily missed: it is neither a display of spectacular dancing in the grand manner, nor is it a skit. It is a classical duet with suggestions of demi-caractère."[10] Although Reed, decades later, blamed Balanchine for giving her steps that were too difficult for her,[11] what brought uneasy laughter in New York brought fan mail in London. One audience member loved her so much in the ballet that he asked for a signed photograph of her in costume that was better than the picture that had appeared in the magazine *Ballet* that month.

Despite the mixed reviews of his work, Balanchine was pleased with the Covent Garden season, writing that "I shall never forget the long engagement the New York City Ballet had at Covent Garden in 1950. It was the longest period up to that time that we had had to dance on any one stage, and when we came back to the City Center the autumn of that year, everyone knew, I believe, that there was no stopping the objectives Lincoln Kirstein and I had set out to accomplish."[12]

Kirstein wasn't so sure. While the British representative of Covent Garden had told him that the London season would be the making of the company in New York and New York City Ballet was offered a second series of performances in 1952, he had taken the criticism by British reviewers extremely personally and was also upset by injuries to the dancers caused by the splintery floor of the opera house stage. Moreover, while he had expected to lose $25,000 on the British tour, the company lost nearly twice that.

"London did however add a status which we had not enjoyed before," he later wrote, "especially with dancers who had not been schooled within our orbit. Janet Reed, a sprightly swift soubrette, came from Lew Christensen in San Francisco. She was that American who for me most recalled Lydia Lopokova."[13] Kirstein felt that she was among those who attracted other dancers to the company, such as Nora Kaye and Diana Adams.

And he was as amused by Buckle's "floral tribute of bomb-site weeds and . . . citation 'To those Americans who fell at Covent Garden'" as he was touched by "small handmade bouquets of red and white carnations bought early at Covent Garden's flower market and delivered to every girl in the corps de ballet." Each had a card attached reading: "In gratitude and admiration for your wonderful dancing throughout the season from your friends in the Gallery and Amphitheater at Covent Garden. Please come back."[14]

Between the end of the London season and the basically unsuccessful three-week tour of the British provinces, the company had a one-week layoff, during which some dancers went to Paris, Tallchief and Taras among them. By the third week in September, Reed was back in New York, returning to the open arms of her husband and young son and preparing for the coming three-week season at City Center. Bolender, however, traveled to St. Jean de Luz, where he stayed for six weeks, working with John Colman on a new ballet Balanchine had assigned. He returned to New York in November, just in time to dance in the company's fall season opener.

The ballet was *The Filly*, subtitled *A Stable Boy's Dream*. In a way, it was a balletic *National Velvet* in which the stable boy of the title gets to ride the filly he has raised from a foal after she rejects all the professional jockeys. (In the 1944 film, a young girl rode to victory in the Grand National.) *The Filly* was Balanchine's idea, which Bolender loved at first. "In particular, there was something quite theatrically wonderful in a tiny child (the Foal) suddenly turning into Maria Tallchief! But the composition of the music was delayed for several years, and during that time too many hands became involved."[15] In an interview in 2004, Bolender said that Colman was a superb improvisational rehearsal pianist, "but he didn't like writing anything down. So the idea was stale by the time the music was completed."[16] When he referred to "too many hands," Bolender was making a rare criticism of the man he unfailingly called his teacher. This time, Balanchine, whose help he usually welcomed, insisted that he include a scene in the beginning using imagery from his 1925 *Barabau,* the first original ballet he did for Diaghilev's Ballets Russes. The plot, which was based on an Italian nursery rhyme, had nothing whatever to do with horses or transformation. Bolender felt the insertion destroyed the point of the ballet and, moreover, that the Ballets Russes model of equal emphasis on choreography, music, set, and costumes was finished. The ballet didn't premiere until 1953, when the reception was, at best, lukewarm. *The Filly* was put out to pasture after only one or two performances. Bolender chalked up the work to experience.

Martin reviewed City Ballet's post-tour opening program of "three of Balanchine's best ballets"[17] (*Serenade, Firebird* and *Bourrée Fantasque*) with the enthusiasm of a religious convert, his "salvation" something both Kirstein and Balanchine had worked hard to achieve. According to Bolender, Balanchine and Kirstein invited Martin to accompany City Ballet on the flight to England, seating the skeptical critic between them on the British Overseas Airways Stratocruiser Kirstein had chartered for the company.

In his November 22 review, after mentioning the company's high morale, Martin gave high praise to the company's dancers. "Without any stars in the narrow sense of the term . . . it has a brilliant set of leading artists. . . . Here too is an ensemble of note; there was not one of them last night who did not dance as if she were herself a ballerina, yet with a feeling for the unity of the group and the framework of the composition. What more can one ask of any company it would be difficult to say."[18]

For Kirstein, this review was just as crucial to establishing the company's reputation as the London season had been. Because of his position at the *New York Times,* Martin was the most influential dance critic in the city and, arguably, also in the United States. Moreover, in these early days, the "unity of the group" was apparent both onstage and off. There was a shared commitment to the enterprise itself, not only by the directors and the principal dancers but also by corps members. That was not too surprising, since Balanchine's choreography for them was nearly as interesting and challenging to dance as anything he made for the soloists.

Martin gave particular praise to *Serenade* in his review of this concert, which Balanchine had reworked to create no fewer than five major roles for a company which now had on its roster Maria Tallchief, Reed, Melissa Hayden (who had joined at the same time as Reed), and Diana Adams, who had just come from Ballet Theatre. Reed, Patricia Wilde, Yvonne Mounsey, Hayden and Adams danced those roles in this performance.

Judging from the ballets he choreographed, revived, and programmed in the period 1950–1957, Balanchine, whose Russian temperament was well laced with American pragmatism, was loosely dividing the company's principals between those he could count on for virtuosic classical and neoclassical dancing and, for lack of a more precise term, demi-caractère performers, American style. Tallchief belonged to the former group, Reed and Bolender to the latter, although both were arguably more versatile dancers. Reed, who made her mark in this company as a brilliant ballet comedian, just as she had with Ballet Theatre, frequently danced one of the lead violins in *Concerto Barocco* and was often partnered by Bliss or Bolender in the third movement of *Symphony in C.* Bolender's skills as a classical dancer came into play in a number of ballets, including the Haieff *Divertimento; Symphonie Concertante,* in which he partnered Tallchief and Tanaquil Le Clercq; and *The Card Game,* in which the role of the Joker was so demanding—twenty minutes of nonstop virtuosic dancing—that, according to historian David Vaughan, Bolender would prepare for it by taking a hot shower, rubbing his body with liniment, and drinking a double brandy before he went on stage.[19] Reed, too, performed this role, both of them to critical acclaim. B. H. Haggin had not liked either the music or the ballet when it premiered in 1937 and when it was revived in 1941. But ten years later, the dancers made him change his mind: "the beautifully clear, precise and sharp dancing of the company, the charming performances of Janet Reed, Bliss and some of the other soloists, the outstanding performance of Todd Bolender as the Joker, which is in a class with his Phlegmatic Variation in *Four Temperaments.*"[20]

Two Balanchine ballets highlighted the differences between Reed and Tallchief. The first was *Bourrée Fantasque,* in which Tallchief danced the lyrical adagio of the second movement and the ebullient Reed led the sparkling finale. "Balanchine used me for my jump and my vitality," Reed said in 1978. "That third movement is very bombastic, percussive. I danced it with Herbert Bliss, and at the end I would do *sissonnes,* each one getting higher until, on the last he would throw me out and let me go."[21]

The second was *À la Françaix,* a hastily put together "balletic hors d'oeuvre," set to Jean Françaix's *Serenade for Small Orchestra*, the pun in the title absolutely intended: Balanchine loved puns. For the September 1951 season, Balanchine had intended to revive *Apollo*, in which Le Clercq would have performed Terpsichore for the first time. However, Le Clercq had sprained her ankle so severely that she was out for the season, and Balanchine replaced a masterpiece with a slight little ballet that was reminiscent of some of the work Reed had performed in when she was with San Francisco Ballet. Nevertheless, *À la Françaix* had a long-lasting effect on how audiences and critics would perceive her and Tallchief.

In it, Reed was cast as the same fresh-faced, all-American girl she was in Robbins's *Fancy Free*, with André Eglevsky, cast against type, in a role that transformed him from his usual prince in white tights to an all-American athlete in white trousers, plying a tennis racquet instead of a crossbow. It begins with Reed dancing with two young men, when, as Walter Terry tells it, Eglevsky makes a bounding entrance and dispatches the competition with "some well-aimed leg beats. But soon a winged ballerina (behaving for all the world like a fugitive from *Giselle*), in the person of Tallchief, floats in and lures the fickle youth away from his new love to her own misty world."[22] More shenanigans occur between Eglevsky and the young men and the ballet ends with Tallchief, bourréeing like one possessed throughout, shedding her sylph costume to reveal a "brilliant bathing-suit affair," or, in the advertising parlance of the day, wearing a smile and a Jantzen.[23] Of this ending, one wag wrote, "Never trust a sylph."

Reed had danced with Eglevsky while both were still with Ballet Theatre in a lightweight piece by Massine called *Mademoiselle Angot*. It was not a pleasant experience: "I remember in one part he had to throw me up in the air," Reed said in an interview shortly after Eglevsky's death. "Since I'm rather small and he was very strong he threw me very high and simply did not catch me, and I went plummeting past him and hit the floor and went into grand plié. I don't know what was bothering him but I really was furious. . . . However, I didn't hold it against him too long because André is someone you can't stay mad with."[24] Eglevsky had joined City Ballet in 1950, where he and Tallchief enjoyed a long dancing partnership, not only in the company but also as guest artists around the country and on television.

In his review of the company's first New York season after the London tour, Martin wrote that it had no stars "in the narrowest sense of the term."[25] In the minds of its two unacknowledged star ballerinas, this was quite incorrect. Tallchief's performance in the 1949 *Firebird* had, according to Reynolds, "established [her] reputation . . . as the 'first among equals' in the New York City Ballet, [and] the leading home-grown American trained ballerina, the first of international importance."[26] On company rosters Tallchief's name came first, Reed's second, a point of contention between them that constantly had to be mediated by Kirstein and company manager Betty Cage, who became a close friend of both Reed and Bolender. The press, not to mention Balanchine, who Tallchief was married to from 1946 to 1952, made much of Tallchief's Native American origins, both nationally and internationally, and she was the first American ballerina in more than a century to perform as guest artist with the Paris Opéra Ballet.

Should Reed have been resentful? She was older and more experienced and had been the founding prima ballerina of the San Francisco Ballet, but her body type and her training were completely different from Tallchief's, as was her affect on stage. (The only role they shared was in the *Harlequinade Pas de Deux,* a negligible *pièce d'occasion.*) But Tallchief had studied with Bronislava Nijinska for five years, was a protégée of Tatiana Riabouchinska, and, even more important, was meticulously trained by Balanchine once he spotted her as a teenager in the Ballets Russes de Monte Carlo. Reed had not studied with famous Russian teachers, and there was nothing exotic or mysterious about her. Direct, forthright in speech and on stage, Reed was the fabled American girl next door, even in her 30s. But, while the two women were very different artists, each in her way was the quintessential American dancer, fearless, determined, and with a work ethic that kept them in the studio for as many hours as it took to get something right. As dancers with City Ballet, the roles they originated defined them; *À la Françaix,* as slight as it was, is a sterling example of typecasting.

What Tallchief could conceivably have held against Reed is subject to speculation; there was no question of competing for roles, but she may have been envious of her personal life. Tallchief's marriage to Balanchine was annulled on the grounds that she wanted children and he did not. Reed's son was a toddler when Reed joined City Ballet. Balanchine knew full well that she had a family, although, even then, he had often expressed his view that any woman could have a baby but only a few could dance.

Combining those onstage and offstage roles remains a difficult task even for twenty-first-century dancers, and Reed certainly struggled with conflicting demands throughout her career. She was absent from the company's first Chicago tour in the spring of 1951 because her son was ill. In 1952, lacking child care (husbands didn't provide that in the 1950s), she took the five-year-old Reed Erskine along on the company's first European tour, a five-month journey, during which stagehands befriended him in such illustrious opera houses as the Liceo in Barcelona, where the company had their first encounter with a seriously raked stage; the Palais de Garnier in Paris; and Covent Garden in London.

Young Erskine was already an experienced backstage kid at this time, and he retains an early memory of visiting his mother in the "very narrow dressing room [she shared with Tallchief] in the cramped confines of the City Center Theater" that sheds some light on the relationship between the two ballerinas:

> Maria seemed incredibly exotic to my young eyes. Her father, an oil-rich Oklahoma Osage chief, would sometimes drop by for a visit, and looked every inch [the part]. . . . In the dressing room then they seemed quite convivial, but I realized later it was really just their professionalism that kept them from engaging in open warfare. Maria was always a very competitive person, and had a somewhat hard-edged personality. She was the big star. My mother was the hard worker, the little pioneer girl who had to borrow money from her San Francisco landlady for the train fare to New York. Maria was the Beverly Hills Indian Princess who became a star with Ballet Russe de Monte Carlo while still in her teens, and married George Balanchine the same year my mother married my father. Maria could be condescending to "little Janet" which set my mother's teeth on edge. My mother was sensitive to slights, real and imagined. Being petite was not something she particularly enjoyed, and she sometimes felt that people underestimated her because of her small stature.[27]

That small stature (which included long legs and a short torso) plus her red hair and movie-star good looks made Balanchine, Robbins, and many other choreographers, including Bolender, want to work with her and audiences line up to see her dance. Bolender always regretted that she had not been available to originate the Vamp in his 1955 *Souvenirs;* she was killingly funny in a version he later restaged for *The Bell Telephone Hour.* But he, too, viewed her as a brilliant comedian and therefore did not consider her suitable for the lead role in *The Miraculous Mandarin,* which, apart from *À la Françaix,* was the only new ballet on the September 1951 season.

Bolender's *Mandarin* was the first in a series of ballets that were infused with his early modern training. Between 1951 and 1956, when *The Still Point* (which Emily Frankel and Mark Ryder had commissioned in the early 1950s by for their modern dance company) was transferred to City Ballet, Bolender came into his own as a choreographer of considerable range. However, that fusion of the modern and the neoclassical, which Balanchine had arguably achieved a quarter of a century earlier with *Apollon Musagète,* led a number of critics to question whether or not these were really ballets, none more so than *The Miraculous Mandarin.*

One night when Balanchine was out of town, Kirstein, in full Ballet Society impresario mode, summoned Bolender to his apartment to listen to a piece of music. "He gave me the recording of Béla Bartók's *Miraculous Mandarin,* and I listened to it and thought, Oh my God! This is really a wild piece of music," Bolender later said. "And then I thought, I don't know, it sounds too complicated. And he said, 'Take your time, whatever you need . . . you have lots of time.'"

To fund the production, Kirstein borrowed $10,000 from the Bartók Foundation in order to commission Alvin Colt, who later received many awards for his costuming of Broadway musicals, to design the costumes, makeup, and a multilevel set that was as integral to the choreography as anything Noguchi did for Martha Graham. "The set was beautiful—like matchsticks put together to create a number of levels, with staircases leading up to them so there could be movement in all directions," Bolender later recalled.[28]

Bolender struggled with the score for several weeks before he realized he could make it choreographically workable with some changes to Melchior Lengyel's 1926 libretto. Lengyel tells a seamy, violent tale of three gangsters who use a prostitute as bait. Not satisfied with merely robbing her customers, they dispatch them to the next world. In his original story, the victims they kill are an old man and a student. Then, according to one summary, "the Mandarin appears, a strange creature who, at first unmoved by the girl's overtures, later develops a passionate love for her. He is stabbed, strangled, and hanged by the ruffians but survives until his love is requited."[29]

The violence in the story, which inspired Bartók to create his equally violent score, made no sense to Bolender. "All that killing for no reason," he told Reynolds.

Who was the Mandarin, finally? A figment of her imagination? A real situation? So I changed the emphasis. I made the Woman the central character, not the Mandarin, as he was in the libretto. I used the idea of a war and what war does to people, especially what happens to people in cities—planes, guns, bombs. The Woman was then a lost person, as were the Men, so that explains the violence—they're like animals trying to survive.[30]

"What war does to people" was something Bolender had been thinking about for some time. The desperate situation of the Eastern European refugees he had met on the South American tour had certainly increased his awareness, and what war can do to unbalance society was something he had explored in *Zodiac* in 1946, using astrology as the guiding principle. In *Mandarin,* Bartók's music; Colt's multileveled constructivist set, which indicates a tenement fire escape; psychoanalytic concepts; and German expressionist dance as Bolender had experienced it in New York in the 1930s all play integral roles in the choreography. The relationships among the Mandarin, the Woman, and the Blind Girl (a character Bolender added to Lengyel's cast) seem particularly psychoanalytically driven: "The Mandarin could be in her imagination," Bolender said. "I had him dressed in a way that gave him a kind of extraordinary beauty. It could be another side of herself—the side she could esteem. This of course only went through my mind. What comes out on stage is a Mandarin. I tried to make it a very realistic situation."[31]

Mandarin had been scheduled to premiere in June 1951, but because of a delay in funding, it was put off until the fall season. This was not a problem for Bolender, who felt he needed more time. Unless they are Balanchine, choreographers always feel they need more time. Bolender was notoriously slow throughout his life, earning the nickname Sarah Snail when he was arranging the dances for *Les Troyennes* at the Met in the mid-1970s.

Mandarin finally premiered in the season opener on September 6, which ended with the lighthearted *Bourrée Fantasque.* The excellent cast included Melissa Hayden as the Woman, Hugh Laing as the Mandarin, Beatrice Tompkins as the Blind Girl, Frank Hobi as the Old Man, Roy Tobias as the Young Man, and Jacques d'Amboise as one of the thugs. Laing, who originated many roles in Antony Tudor's ballets, including the psychopathic young man in *Undertow*, is considered one of the great dramatic dancers of the twentieth century. Hayden, also a highly expressive performer, possessed a fine technique. D'Amboise, at 17, was so thoroughly involved in his role as a thug that at one performance in which Bolender was performing the title role, he came close to knocking him out with an uppercut to the jaw.

Due to the popularity of Bartók's music in general and considerable advance publicity about a work that had been controversial since its inception, *Mandarin* was a box-office success before it hit the stage and several performances had to be added to the scheduled run. All the critics, even those with a negative response to the choreography, praised the cast. Kirstein, reporting in a letter to Robbins, who was out of town, wrote that "Melissa is in her seventh heaven; she is the Bette Davis of the dance and there is a bucket of guts for her to put her points in." In a second letter to Robbins, he described the scene backstage before the premiere:

> Hugh [Laing] tore off his clothes and LEFT. Todd wept and shrieked. Milly [Hayden] went crazy. BUT, they danced like angels and the boys, including Jacques (sex box) d'Amboise, exuded blood and gism from every pore; it was really coherent and afterwards Oliver Smith said it was better than the Turkish Baths. I do not however think that this means it is a repertory favorite.[32]

Elsewhere, in a letter to Cadmus, Kirstein slammed Bolender for his hysterical behavior, also reporting that "No One knew what he meant, except that fucking corpses is fun."[33]

Obviously, Bolender was under enormous pressure before the premiere: a great deal of money was at stake, expectations were high because of the advance publicity, and he had a lot to prove. And, while Kirstein threatened never to work with Bolender again, he continued throughout their lives to hold him in high regard as a professional, writing him a glowing letter of recommendation thirty years later when Bolender was being considered for the artistic directorship of Kansas City Ballet. What's more, he continued to validate him as a choreographer by authorizing the creation of a handful of his ballets for City Ballet. These included *Souvenirs* (which he adored), *The Still Point, Creation of the World, Serenade in A,* and *Piano-Rag-Music,* the last two for the 1972 Stravinsky Festival.

As far as Martin was concerned, *Mandarin* was a success for both the company and the choreographer and well worth the wait. In a review following the premiere, he praised it as "a brilliant achievement . . . of a supremely difficult undertaking." After summarizing the story as "unrelievedly violent," Martin went on to say that Hayden and Laing "in its central roles are asked to perform and undergo unbelievable physical ordeals including hanging."

He also gave Bolender far higher marks for the choreography than any other critic. "[He] has done a superb job of [it]. There is little opportunity for any sustained line of movement, for the piece is a pantomime rather than a ballet, but he has created remarkably intuitive phrases and gestures, and for all the excess of action over dancing, there is not a moment that is less than vibrantly tense and alive."[34]

Of Hayden's performance, he wrote: "[It] is sheer black magic. . . . Her alternations of rigid extensions and complete relaxations, the sharp clarity of her pointes, her kind of physical voracity, all stem from an inner compulsion that is overwhelming in its power." Of Laing, he said, "[He] meets [Hayden's] vehemence with that curiously potent stillness of his which has real dominion in it. Mr. Bolender has given him some admirably inventive passages of movement and he performs them with wonderful style and dramatic value." Martin also praised the minor cast members; Colt for the set, costumes, and all-important makeup designs; and Jean Rosenthal for the red-bathed lights. The orchestra, led by Léon Barzin, also received plaudits for playing the score "to the hilt."[35]

In a later, summary review of the season, Martin compared À la Françaix with Mandarin and predicted that while both ballets had merit, neither was likely to endure. Using culinary metaphors, he considered the first to be a soufflé in danger of collapse, and the second too difficult to digest, like cabbage and dumplings.

Mandarin, in fact, outlasted À la Françaix by decades, but not with City Ballet. Bolender revived it in the early 1960s at the Cologne Opera Ballet and again in Kansas City in 1985 and 1992. À la Françaix, which Reed called a very useful ballet, stayed in City Ballet's repertoire for several more seasons. Bolender, who had alternated with Eglevsky as the hunky tennis player, partnering Hayden as the ingénue, also found it useful and revived it for Kansas City Ballet in 1981, and Lew Christensen programmed it for San Francisco Ballet when he took over the artistic directorship there in 1952.

Martin thought *Mandarin* was a good work for City Ballet to have done, for it "destroys once and for all the theory that it is an exclusively Balanchinean company that can dance daintily tutued musical abstractions in strictly virtuosic vein." He also thought it "a bold stroke" to have asked Bolender to choreograph the piece, "for Mr. Bolender's compositions have previously been at a far remove from this field," calling the 1945 *Comédia Balletica* "a clever etude by an obviously devoted pupil of Balanchine" and *Mother Goose Suite* an "enchanting and enchanted bit of lyric introspection."[36]

What Martin either did not know about or chose to ignore were Bolender's studies with Holm and Franziska Boas and his admiration for Mary Wigman and Harald Kreutzberg, both of whom he had seen perform in New York shortly after he arrived there in the early 1930s. The Woman's final soundless scream is pure Wigman; the characterization of the Mandarin as performed by Laing and Bolender is reminiscent of Kreutzberg's solo dances. Moreover, Bolender originated the multicharacter role of Alias in Loring's *Billy the Kid* and the role of an impoverished New York tenement father in his *City Portrait.* In both ballets, gesture plays as important a role as dance. In a later era, *Miraculous Mandarin* might have been categorized as physical theater, not pantomime, which has a lighter implication than the work's dark drama deserves.

The response from Martin's colleagues was more reserved. Doris Hering, writing for *Dance Magazine,* found the choreography uneven and the first half better than the second. She wrote that Hayden "as the girl tossing in boredom on top of a high, stair-decorated platform, her bitter encounter with the old man, the young man, and the blind girl presents a sharp picture of a soul in furious and purposeless torment. . . . And the first appearance of the Mandarin [is] something to remember."[37] Beatrice Gottlieb, a young critic writing for the *Kenyon Review,* commented that because "Bartók's music forced Bolender's hand[;] for the first time, his choreography had strength and cohesion. Isolated sections are feeble, but the total impression is of tremendous suspense and passionate feeling."[38]

By the time Gottlieb's review appeared in the spring of 1952, Balanchine had pulled *Mandarin* from City Ballet's November season and was refusing to schedule any more extra performances, despite box-office demand. Balanchine loathed Bartók's music generally, and the story of the prostitute and the gang of thugs who ran her, not to mention the Mandarin who could not die until he was physically loved by the antiheroine, was antithetical to his often-stated belief that "ballet is woman"—an idealized, unobtainable woman. Few works in the Balanchine canon contain violence, although there are the Drinking Companions and the Siren in *Prodigal Son,* the Furies in *Orpheus,* the Monsters in *Firebird,* and the "Central Park in the Dark" section of *Ivesiana,* in which a rape occurs. It's difficult to think of Balanchine doing his own version of a ballet whose subject was so raw that it was deemed immoral in 1926 in libertine Weimar Germany, where Konrad Adenauer, the mayor of Cologne, banned it. It should also be noted that as devoted as he was to Stravinsky's music, Balanchine never choreographed *Rite of Spring.* That too has a violent libretto and dissonant music, and it had a strong influence on Bartók. Asked how Kirstein, ever mindful of company revenue, responded to Balanchine's withdrawal of a ballet that was filling the City Center at every performance, Bolender replied, "Lincoln had no choice. I might do one good ballet but Balanchine did a thousand."

Mandarin certainly attracted public attention. Moreover, it set off one of those ubiquitous discussions about how much control company directors and funders ought to have over what the choreographers they have commissioned put on stage. Chujoy is interesting on this point. "Some of the protests against [it] contained more than just a hint of the advisability of some form of censorship. Two or three people, for instance, who contributed modest sums to the New York City Ballet through the purchase of tickets to the dinner dance of Ballet Associates in America were all for specifying that the money thus contributed only be used toward productions a priori approved by Ballet Associates."[39] Since Kirstein, who surely knew the ballet's checkered history, had assigned it to Bolender in the first place, the issue of administrative control is moot. And neither Kirstein nor Balanchine ever feared controversy, as mindful as they had to be of the desires of financial supporters, not to mention Morton Baum, the director of New York City Center, who accepted *Mandarin* and the expense of Balanchine's *Tyl Ulenspiegel* in exchange for Balanchine doing a *Swan Lake* for the November 1951 season. Die-hard classicists did not like that, either; the "white" acts two and four, which were all Balanchine did, had black swans mixed in with the white ones, a characteristic Balanchinean twist of tradition, but it wasn't enough for those who viewed City Ballet as an experimental company. They, and this included some of the dancers, felt that Balanchine should not have done a *Swan Lake* at all. Nevertheless, Bolender, who was one of that group, programmed this version, and only this version, thirty years later for Kansas City Ballet.

Both Bolender and Reed danced in the opening-night program of the November 1951 season, the former in the title role in *Mandarin,* the latter in the roles of a Wallflower and Hortense, Queen of the Swamp Lilies in a shortened version of Ruthanna Boris's *Cakewalk,* which had premiered the previous June.

Kirstein had instigated *Cakewalk,* which neither Denby nor Chujoy thought much of. According to Boris, a former member of the American Ballet and Ballet Caravan, he was desperate for a ballet with costumes. "If we do one more ballet in leotards, they'll kill us," he told her.[40] Boris was the first woman to choreograph on City Ballet, although not the first to be asked. Kirstein, who expressed his negative views of women choreographers in *Ballet: Bias and Belief,* had invited Agnes de Mille to make a ballet in 1950, no doubt because of the enormous success she had had on Broadway with *Oklahoma!* and at Ballet Theatre with *Fall River Legend* and *Tally-Ho.*[41] De Mille accepted the commission, but other commitments prevented her from fulfilling it.

Budget concerns sent Boris to the company warehouse in search of costumes, where she unearthed the ones used for Lew Christensen's 1947 ballet *Blackface* as well as the showboat backdrop. These gave her the idea for a ballet based on a minstrel show in which no one performed in blackface, the men wore tailcoats, and the women wore pointe shoes. Hershy Kay, who was to orchestrate the scores for Balanchine's hugely successful "applause machines," *Western Symphony, Stars and Stripes,* and *Union Jack,* added three traditional minstrel songs to seven short pieces by nineteenth-century American composer Louis Moreau Gottschalk. All of them were based on the cakewalk rhythm.

Reed received critical plaudits as the Wallflower, particularly from Hering, for "achieving the perfect balance between satire and good old corn."[42] But it was as Hortense, Queen of the Swamp Lilies in the second half that she was most memorable. She entered on a garlanded swing and, according to d'Amboise, presented herself so joyously that she seemed once again to be saying "Wheeeee!"[43] In San Francisco, Reed had prepared to dance Swanhilda by looking at nineteenth-century lithographs of *Coppélia;* for Hortense, she told an interviewer, she conjured up an image of nineteenth-century American ballerina Augusta Maywood, who was extremely successful in Europe in the title role in *Giselle*. Reed infused her performance with "a touch of Lillian Gish," the silent screen star, who knew how to use the muscles of her face, an obvious requirement for silent screen actors. [44]

All those childhood hours Reed spent in Medford's movie theater, watching Gish and her favorite silent film comedians, Charlie Chaplin, Harold Lloyd, and Buster Keaton, paid off in the development of a number of roles she performed during her City Ballet career, none more so than in the 1953 revival of Christensen's *Filling Station,* in which she defined the drunken Rich Girl. In a 1957 review that marked her return to the company following a two-year absence, Terry wrote of her: "[She] of course practically walks off with the ballet as the inebriated lass who staggers through a pas de deux, nearly pitches herself into the orchestra pit and with a marvelous expression of happy resignation on her face, reels through a game of catch (and she's the catch) with the truck drivers, a robbery and a shooting to hilarious effect."[45]

Reed took great pleasure in the maneuver, she told Tobias. "I used to enjoy the sort of suspense of running up to the edge of the footlights and taking an arabesque and falling forward towards the pit and depending on the truck drivers to catch my back leg. . . . If you hit it just right you could really make the audience gasp."[46]

Reed's comic timing was developed over many years of connecting with the audiences that fed her performing soul. "Timing comes through working in front of an audience," she said in 1977. "I toured with Ballet Theatre and with the San Francisco company and appeared night after night before all kinds of audiences and you do learn timing by the audience's reaction. Also you play around with phrasing, with the music, so that you can make the movement amusing by the way you phrase it, or with a look, and your own sense of the ridiculous. That's one thing, I probably never have been afraid to be ridiculous. And that's marvelous because that frees you to do anything you feel like."[47] There was one exception: audience laughter at the premiere of *Pas de Deux Romantique* infuriated her, no doubt because it was not her intention to look ridiculous in choreography she felt was beyond her technically.

Apart from audience pleasers, such as *Bourrée Fantasque,* and speedily made program fillers like *À la Françaix* and *Mazurka from "A Life of the*

Tsar," Balanchine made a number of works in the early days of City Ballet that some critics dismissed as novelties and others viewed as important contributions to the repertory and the growing American ballet canon. Bolender and Reed frequently performed roles in both.

The first of these was *Tyl Ulenspiegel,* with backdrop and costumes by Esteban Francés. The juicy title role of the peasant rebel was made specifically for Robbins, although both Bolender and Laing performed it a number of times. Balanchine used Richard Strauss's eponymous tone poem but not the libretto; for that, he drew upon a nineteenth-century novel that chronicled the struggle between Tyl, a Flemish peasant, and Philip II of Spain, historically one of Belgium's many oppressors. A number of dance critics thought the brief score—Robbins timed it at fifteen or sixteen minutes—too short to allow Balanchine to fully develop the plot, not to mention the lead characters of Tyl, Philip II, and the Duchess of Alba, but Francés's backdrop and costumes, which he based largely on Hieronymus Bosch's *Garden of Earthly Delights,* received a rave review from Emily Genauer, the art critic for the *New York Herald Tribune.* She gave particularly high praise to the backdrop, which resembles in style the one Francés did for *Renard,* pointing out that Balanchine's choreography also echoed the painting: "When Robbins [as Tyl] dumps a Spanish nobleman into a barrel so a rear view of him is seen from the waist down, with legs kicking wildly, the audience is literally getting one of Bosch's pet images."[48] Those images were also reflected in the costumes, particularly the *papier-mâché* masks worn by the secondary characters, which resembled the faces of Bosch's frolicking Flemish. Those masks, however, as Robbins pointed out, had their down side in performance; they made it difficult for the corps members to see the many props they were supposed to be handing over to him as he changed character.[49]

Bolender loved *Tyl Ulenspiegel.* In 2000, when he had seen countless ballets, he told Jowitt that "Balanchine did the most exquisite beginning to that ballet" he had ever seen.[50] It starts with a long, menacing drum roll as the curtain rises to reveal a slanting ramp containing a table with toy ships of various sizes on it and two young boys, one dressed in rags, the other in aristocratic garb, at either end of it. As Bolender remembered it, the child Tyl battled the toy ships deployed by the young Philip with a loaf of bread and succeeded in pushing them back up the ramp until the Philip figure seized the loaf of bread and ran off with it. Balanchine later wrote that "they chase each other around the table and disappear for a moment. The drum roll ends."[51]

Both Robbins and a number of prominent critics felt that there wasn't much dancing in the spectacle, which was more dependent on props than on steps. He told Reynolds, "There were just a few moments where there was what you might call 'dance pattern choreography.' . . . The whole thing was a race. I timed it out once. . . . I had to handle twenty-three props or costume changes in [a short] time."[52]

Props and costume changes notwithstanding, the role of Tyl brought out Bolender's inner Douglas Fairbanks. "I adored it because I had to learn to fence. . . . That was one of the big parts of it. I got caught with the royalty and I started fencing the whole group and I think the king and queen are there and everything. And I think I won. . . . [Or] I fenced with one person specifically and I'm not sure whether another one entered in or not. But whatever it is, I remember flipping their swords out of their hands. And it had such a sense of conspiracy because when you appear, suddenly you would appear from someplace and you could sneak back and you could go around and you'd come out again as something else."[53] Bolender had had plenty of practice at "coming out again as something else" when he originated the role of Alias in *Billy the Kid*. And, in *Tyl*, just as he had in *Renard*, he had an opportunity to make fun of organized religion, for which he never had much use, when, dressed as a monk, he begs for alms from the Duchess of Alba (Beatrice Tompkins) and then tries to molest her by kissing her.

In her February 1953 column for *Dancing Times*, Lillian Moore assessed Bolender's dancing the previous season. "He has been dancing a wide variety of roles, revealing new facets of his talent, and sometimes his dancing has cast a new light on roles. [He] is one of the few in this company who knows how to build a strong characterization as well as execute dance steps. In parts [from] the tennis player in *À la Françaix*, the eloquent [illegible] of the first movement of *Bourrée Fantasque* and the beetle in *Metamorphoses* to the title role of *Tyl Ulenspiegel* he has demonstrated both versatility and technical proficiency."[54]

Metamorphoses, another lost Balanchine ballet from this period, premiered on November 25, 1952, on a program that included *Concerto Barocco*, *Four Temperaments*, and *Symphony in C*. Denby considered it a masterpiece, but it did not last long. A visual spectacle, partly inspired by the previous spring's visit of an enchanting group of Balinese dancers, it contained an extremely challenging role for Bolender and an exotically witty one for the ever-stylish Le Clercq.

The music, according to Reynolds "a boisterous and rousing affair, with sweeping rhythms and jazzy, colorful and exotic percussive effects," was Hindemith's *Metamorphoses on Themes of Carl Maria von Weber.*[55] That, not Franz Kafka's eponymous novel or New York's ubiquitous cockroaches, was what provided the impetus for the ballet. Nevertheless, as in Robbins's *The Cage*, which premiered the previous year, the world of entomology provided a metaphor, albeit a far more playful one, than the vicious ritual killing he devised for his ballet. For Bolender, who danced a floor-bound pas de deux with an airborne Le Clercq, the work contained more than a hint of modern dance. Balanchine was experimenting choreographically with the use of weight in a duet that had Le Clercq costumed as an extraordinarily chic dragonfly. Bolender wore kneepads and Karinska's version of a carapace. Bolender imagined himself to be a beetle or possibly a turtle. "Balanchine didn't say much about the role, but from the beginning I was on my knees. He showed me how, and then I realized that I was going to be on [them] all the time. . . . Tanny was the flying insect, and I was the earthbound one. This was part of Balanchine's fantasy[,] [a] wonderful comparison, the heavy and the light, and how they can never get together. They try, and the crawling one is after the light one and she loves it. . . . There seems to be great affinity between the two, but there's no possibility of [consummation]."[56]

Bolender told Reynolds that the movement was not that of "a fast-moving beetle, but something very slow. . . ." He remembered that "the feel of my hands as I would lift them was always as though I were pushing them against air, or even through something."[57]

Le Clercq recalled the duet as "a beautiful, beautiful adagio" and that the problem that Balanchine had set himself to solve was making a duet with a man never rising any higher than his knees. "He partnered, for instance, by giving me support around my knee (the *Serenade* supported-promenade-in-arabesque idea), and I would do arabesque, à la seconde, and then bend the knee and bring it front, then switch legs and he would hang onto the other knee."[58]

An eyewitness account of the ballet by poet and filmmaker Charles Boultenhouse puts the reader in the City Center audience with him and confirms Bolender's memory of being on his knees (and lower) for the length of the ballet:

> [He] crawls on stage on all fours, black and glittering, brilliantly costumed as a beetle. A sort of disgust seizes the dancers at the appearance of this monstrous insect, and they vanish from the stage. [Le Clercq] shudders and lifts her feet carefully from his yielding grasp, as if he were sticky. The beetle is left alone. Crawling magnificently, it pauses in the middle of the stage, raises its arms, straightens its back (though still on its knees) and with a magic gesture of transformation causes golden hieroglyphic banners to descend above the dance area. He crawls away. Then, four by four, the dancers return, fantastically transformed into insects, glittering with antennae and fragile wings. The choreography evokes oriental gesture, though restrained and ritualistic, it is all flutters, wriggles, shivers and undulations: the unselfconscious eroticism of insects in the summer heat.

Of the pas de deux, which Boultenhouse cites as one of Balanchine's finest, he writes:

> Tenderly the beetle places Miss Le Clercq's foot now this way, now that, manipulating, supporting, guiding her in one position, then another. Crawling crouching or stretching, he never stands. The dance ends as she sinks into his embrace, her hands fluttering, but they are interrupted.[59]

Other critics had a mixed response. Hering pretty much loathed it; Terry found it brilliantly theatrical; Martin called it "an idiotic, visually gorgeous, richly humorous extravaganza."[60] A warehouse fire in the mid-1950s destroyed the production (along with *Tyl Ulenspiegel, Renard,* and a number of others), and that put paid to its life onstage. Another possible reason *Metamorphoses* has not been performed since is that it was highly dancer-specific, particularly the roles for Le Clercq and Bolender.

What Balanchine achieved in *Metamorphoses* was at once a choreographically experimental work and a visual spectacle, even though he had no budget for scenery. Kirstein and Rosenthal approached the mise-en-scène in much the way Graham had been doing for decades. Inspired by the so-called Chinese melody in Hindemith's score, Kirstein bought 300 wire coat hangers in the garment district, where he knew he would get them for next to nothing, and "hung a ladder of them; on it, Jean Rosenthal threw gold light; [making] a spidery pagoda.[61] In the meantime, according to Barbara Milberg Fisher, Rosenthal acquired "a couple of hundred bedsprings of various sizes" from a mattress outlet, had the stage crew gild them, "artfully connected them and hung them like Calder mobiles from the flies."[62] Karinska made the costumes with what Le Clercq described as a new stretchy material that really fit, minimal tulle, and wire.[63] "In the three parts of the ballet," Kirstein wrote, "costumes entirely transformed. There was little suggestion of growth from egg to extinction, but only of continual mutation in a strange aura which was less oriental or exotic than insectile."[64] What Karinska and Rosenthal created in the mid-twentieth century with minimal materials and lights would be achieved four decades later with computer morphing programs.

The making of *Metamorphoses*, particularly the costumes and scenery, provides a vivid example of the kind of ingenuity, pragmatism, and improvisation that Balanchine found in America and the willingness of the dancers to try anything. In this instance, it was Bolender, performing, painfully, on his knees, using weight in the same way he had as a modern dancer, yet employing his ever-eloquent hands to partner in neoclassical style.

"This is our theater, we can do what we want," Balanchine once told Reed, when she asked if she could change a step to make it work better for her.[65] For box-office reasons, however, this was not always the case for Balanchine. In 1951, he was able to get away with an idiosyncratic one-act version of *Swan Lake*, beautifully designed by Cecil Beaton. Two years later, the Sadler's Wells Ballet, on tour in New York, was filling the Metropolitan Opera House with evening-length productions of *The Sleeping Beauty* and *Swan Lake*, while the Ballet Russe de Monte Carlo sold more seats at City Center with *Scheherazade* and a truncated two-act *Nutcracker* than the more experimental resident company did. (According to Chujoy, when mixed bills failed to sell tickets for these companies, the story ballets were hastily substituted.[66]) In 1953, Balanchine duly agreed to mount a complete, two-hour *The Nutcracker*. The production was ultimately so expensive that some of the costs were concealed from Baum.

This was not, however, the first full-evening American *Nutcracker*. William Christensen mounted one for San Francisco Ballet in 1944 with considerable help from Balanchine and Danilova, whose memories he culled in an all-night session when they were in town with the Ballet Russe de

Monte Carlo. Balanchine encouraged Christensen to put his own stamp on the Ivanov choreography, just as he did himself for his own company a decade later, adding to the Waltz of the Flowers a Dewdrop Fairy, one of his technically difficult ballerina roles, and for one television production giving the Sugar Plum Fairy not one but four cavaliers in the second act, in an echo of *The Sleeping Beauty.*

Possibly because of a limited budget, possibly because after living in the United States for two decades, he well understood the conformist, middle-class characteristics of the ticket-buying public in mid-century New York, Balanchine changed the visual tone of the party scene in the first act, giving the Stahlbaum family a solid, bourgeois, somewhat stodgy home instead of the lavishly decorated drawing room he remembered from the Maryinsky production he had danced in in St. Petersburg. The Stahlbaum parlor in his *Nutcracker* could have belonged to any comfortably well-off family in the "better" neighborhoods of the five boroughs. And the comportment of the children—naughty Fritz, well-behaved Marie, the boys winning the tug-of-war they have with the girls over the stick horse—certainly reflected the way gender roles were viewed in the 1950, before feminist activist Betty Friedan upset the domestic apple cart with *The Feminine Mystique.*

At a time when little fantasy was being published for either children or adults, Balanchine drew a sharp contrast between the reality of the family party and Marie's dream of bellicose mice and toy soldiers, followed by a magical journey to a dancing candy store where sugar poured forth like the wine at the marriage at Cana. He denied, however, that the second act was a dream. "Actually it's not a dream—it's the reality that Mother didn't believe. The story ["The Nutcracker and the Mouse King"] was written by Hoffmann against society. He said that society, the grown-ups, really have no imagination, and that they try to suppress the imagination of children," he told Reynolds.[67]

There were many elements of the Maryinsky production that Balanchine retained, none more important than the growing Christmas tree: "[The ballet] *is* the tree," he insisted when Kirstein and Baum questioned the cost of having a three-dimensional tree. It opened like an umbrella. Rosenthal worked her usual miracles at the lighting board, and the electric lights on the tree set off sparks from time to time the same way they did in New York apartments in those days, lending unintentional verisimilitude to the proceedings.

The Nutcracker Prince's mimed account of the battle of the mice and toy soldiers for the Sugar Plum Fairy remained intact, as well as the highly acrobatic Candy Cane divertissement, which Balanchine had relished performing himself. According to Bolender, Balanchine adored acrobatics, and his first *Nutcracker* was replete with them, from the wind-up toy soldier in Act 1 to the Candy Cane, Tea, and Coffee divertissements in Act 2.

Reed, who had appeared as an elfin Sugar Plum in Willam Christensen's naïve staging of *The Nutcracker Suite* in Portland in 1934, originated Balanchine's Marzipan Shepherdess by default. Patricia Wilde, for whom Balanchine intended the role, came down with mononucleosis after a number of grueling rehearsals. Balanchine changed the difficult choreography he had made for Wilde, who was twelve years younger than Reed and known for her rapid, accurate pointe work; it was her feet that went wickety-wack in the 1957 production of *Square Dance*. While some company members thought the *gargouillades* Balanchine substituted were technically beyond Reed at that point in her career, Martin used the word "delightful" to describe her dancing, and for d'Amboise, who found both the music and the choreography boring, her smile and the sparkle with which she danced represented marzipan at "its sweetest stage."[68]

Bolender alternated with Moncion in the role of the sinuously acrobatic Arabian prince, who was at the center of the first version of Coffee, performing on a carpet, surrounded by four little girls from the School dressed as parrots. Like Reed's dancing, Martin found this divertissement "delightful," although he pronounced the work basically a bore. While Bolender didn't remember specific choreography, he did have a vivid recollection of a series of backbends that injured his middle-aged body so badly he was forced to crawl up the four flights of stairs to his apartment on East 65th Street, assisted by the other tenants in the building. By 1958, when the ballet was telecast on CBS's *Playhouse 90* and Arthur Mitchell seamlessly danced the role, the backbends had been eliminated from the choreography. Mitchell had also performed Coffee in the first televised production, in 1957, the year that Governor Faubus of Arkansas blocked the schoolroom door in Little Rock. In an interview for the Library of Congress, Mitchell recalled that Balanchine changed the choreography for the Sugar Plum Fairy's adagio, replacing the traditional single Cavalier with four men: Chocolate, Candy Cane, Tea, Coffee; and it was he, as Coffee who won her hand. "I hope Governor Faubus was watching," Balanchine said to Mitchell when the latter came offstage.[69]

When the company moved in 1964 to what was then the New York State Theater, with new designs by Rouben Ter-Arutunian, Balanchine changed the Coffee choreography to the current "hootchy-kootchy" Orientalist solo, because, he said, he wanted to give the fathers in the audience something to watch. It is this solo, as well as the ever-so-cute and winsome Tea variation, that date Balanchine's *Nutcracker* for a twenty-first-century United States audience, when such stereotypes seem disrespectful at best—and the young dancer cast as Marie is quite likely to be of Asian descent.

The 1954 *Nutcracker* was a howling success at the box office; Denby said it was "Balanchine's *Oklahoma!*" Bolender and many others said it saved the company from financial ruin. Parents, grandparents, aunts, uncles, cousins came to see the many children in the cast perform with a naturalness of manner that Balanchine insisted on. He treated them with the same courtesy he did the adult dancers. Balletomanes came to see Le Clercq's Dewdrop, Tallchief's Sugar Plum Fairy, and Robert Barnett's Candy Cane. Although Martin, who was not charmed by child performers, felt that "except for Tchaikovsky's melodious score, which contains in two suites probably the most familiar ballet music in the world, there is nothing about 'The Nutcracker' to justify its presentation,"[70] most critical reception was considerably warmer than that. For Chujoy, Balanchine's *Nutcracker* represented "a great achievement for American ballet. That American dancers, stage designers, costume designers, and lighting experts could rise to a level upon which they can create and interpret classic ballet is a manifestation for which to be grateful.... Above all, of course, stands Balanchine himself, the master magician, who succeeded in presenting a modern version of a children's ballet that means so much to the adult. Without losing a thread of the past he has brought the present a shade closer to the future, when ballet in the United States will assume its proper and rightful place in the scheme of our cultural life."[71]

In the second decade of the twenty-first century, ballet still struggles to keep its "proper" place in much of the United States, but for just about every ballet company in the country, the *Nutcracker* has become its most reliable source of a steady income. Just why has many explanations. Jennifer Fisher, author of *Nutcracker Nation*, accounts for this "immigrant" ballet's popularity by citing its child-centered optimism, the middle-class setting of the first act, and a magic kingdom in the second where people of different ethnicities have a lovely, celebratory time together.[72] By the time

Reed and Bolender were establishing their own companies—Reed in Seattle in the early 1970s, Bolender in Kansas City starting in 1980—a ballet company without a *Nutcracker* was unthinkable. As founder of the Pacific Northwest Ballet School, Reed presented Lew Christensen's 1961 version in a new production in 1975; Bolender presented his Balanchine-based staging for Kansas City Ballet in 1981. He tinkered with and revised it until he retired in 1995; he was still coaching individual dancers in it in 2005.

In 1954, a conversation Reed had with Balanchine about choreographers seeing their dancers only one way and her desire to try something new led to radically different roles for her in ballets that represented the depth of the Russian-born choreographer's vision of his adopted country. *Western Symphony*, in which Reed was cast as "a sylph of the Western plains doing a gentle spoof of a romantic pas de deux to 'Red River Valley,'" takes its title from its score, Hershy Kay's symphonic arrangement in four movements (Allegro, Adagio, Scherzo, and Rondo) of a dozen folk and popular tunes.[73] Some, but not all, are associated with the American West. With its rousing, full-cast finale of pirouetting dancers in Western garb, the ballet remains the audience grabber the choreographer intended nearly sixty years after its premiere, and is arguably Balanchine's *Oklahoma!* just as much as is *The Nutcracker*.

Bolender retained strong memories of *Western*'s premiere. He wrote about it for a book titled *Backstage at the Ballet* that was never completed. The first performance of Balanchine's applause machine was given on September 7, 1954, "on a hot sticky night" to a sold-out house containing an "audience eager to be pleased." While attendance the second week into a four-week season had been "phenomenal," it wasn't enough to "offset the enormous losses the company had accrued on a transcontinental tour."[74] The ballet therefore premiered without the spectacular costumes Karinska created the following year, including a Lily Langtry hat that became part of the choreography when Le Clercq wore it, or Broadway designer John Boyt's obviously phony but stylish Western ghost town backdrop. According to Bolender, Rosenthal's lighting was, as usual, skillful enough that the set wasn't missed and the dancers performed in rehearsal clothes, corps women and soloists differentiated by the colors of their sweaters, the men in jeans and dark-blue cotton shirts. "Eglevsky," Bolender wrote, "who carried the classical end of the ballet, was dressed in bright yellow sweater and black tights."[75]

Bolender, who alternated with Eglevsky in the Scherzo, watched the premiere from the wings.

The curtain rose, revealing four couples in practice clothes on a bare stage. By the time Diana Adams, Herbert Bliss and the four couples finished the first movement the audience was eager for more. . . . The second movement presented Nicholas Magallanes, the lonely cowboy, in black trousers, boots from an old ballet of mine [*The Filly*], a cowboy shirt belonging to G. Balanchine and a ten gallon white hat that had been bought for the occasion. [Magallanes] was accompanied by four little corps de ballet girls, and tho each was dressed in practice clothes, they were supposed to be little horses. They were soon joined by the cowboy's dream girl, Janet Reed. [Although] this second movement seemed to be a play on all the nostalgia associated with horse opera, movies that Americans [and Balanchine] know very well, the choreography underplayed the humor that seems about to burst forth at any moment. The audience . . . forced themselves to laugh at situations that any audience except opening night would merely smile at. Magallanes strummed his hat as tho it were a guitar, sadly, as Reed left the stage in an attitude of sweetness like little Eva heaven-bent.[76]

Reed actually visualized Giselle and a prairie flower as she built her character, bourréeing into the wings, leaving the rejected cowboy to gather up the reins and drive his "ponies" across the rear of the stage in a mild echo of one section of Balanchine's *Apollo,* where the young god "drives" his three muses in a virtual chariot.

Bolender thought the scherzo was a failure. "In great contrast to the rest of the ballet is the third movement, which demands precision, neatness, elegance, all the things we associate with classical ballet. That it lacked content of a cohesive nature was perhaps its chief fault. In the final measures of the movement, the choreography seemed suddenly to pale against the raucous blasting of the orchestra of 'Hail Hail the Gang's All Here.'"[77] That particular tune, which was written by Arthur Sullivan, is neither Western nor American and may also have sounded a false note.

For Bolender and everyone fortunate enough to have seen them dance it, the Rondo, the fourth and last movement, performed by an exuberant d'Amboise and a witty Le Clercq, "within seconds sealed the fate of *West-*

ern Symphony. The vitality of the choreography in this final movement is certainly in the best Balanchine manner." And, in the best tradition of American musical comedy, phalanxes of corps members enter the stage, dancing in the kaleidoscopic patterns for which Balanchine (and, before him, Busby Berkeley) became famous, "with each group adding more to steadily mounting excitement. This culminated in the entire cast pirouetting, each in his [and her] place, for the last 32 measures of the ballet. The curtain fell with the dancers still turning and the audience shouting with enthusiasm."[78]

Other details also echo musical comedy of the period, Western movies, and television shows: the "aw shucks" facial expression of the cowboy in the Adagio and d'Amboise's swaggering walk between demonstrations of classical pyrotechnics, not to mention the exaggerated hitching up of his pants (a move that is prevalent in de Mille's *Rodeo*) before he dances, body language that evokes the unselfconscious inelegance of Roy Rogers, James Stewart, and John Wayne.

In Hering's review in *Dance Magazine,* she labeled it "a study in cumulative energy" and said that Reed's "infallible sense of the serious salted with the ridiculous" made her performance "priceless." Hering reviewed more than one cast, commenting that Bolender and Carolyn George danced in the Scherzo with "more suitable modesty" than Eglevsky and Patricia Wilde had.[79]

Margaret Lloyd found it "a delightful bundle of contradictions, a neoclassic ballet tinged with the folk spirit. The juxtaposition is an incongruity as typical as are the entrechats and tours en l'air to cowboy tunes, or hints of all-hands-around mingled with the balletic port de bras. Fishdives and fouettés are tossed off in a barn-dance milieu. Reed does practically everything, including a half-circle of petits tours, in the humorous Adagio. The score, which has more quotations than Hamlet, is of course infectious, and to see the rhythms of square dance and round applied to, or subjected to, the courtly elegance of ballet is to the aesthetic-sense something like what chocolate-coated pickles might be to the gustatory."[80]

The chocolate-coated pickles analogy applies to Martin's response. "A somewhat startling hodge-podge of hoe-down and square [dance] set sur les pointes and with elegant classic port de bras. Here are no truly characterized Western plainsmen but only a company of strictly classic dancers showing how they would behave if they were plainsmen. Naturally the contrast is enormous and the result incongruous beyond words. After you have got the hang of it however, it is also witty and fairly hilarious. At this juncture, one suspects that [after costuming] it will emerge as a lively choreographic joke."[81]

Having made a crowd pleaser, Balanchine apparently decided to please himself with a ballet set to contemporary music that was unfamiliar to the audience, extremely difficult to play, and impossible for the dancers to count. *Ivesiana* was performed to City Ballet's music director Léon Barzin's arrangement of six short compositions by Charles Ives. It premiered September 14, 1954, very soon after the composer's death.

The section titles were taken from Ives's music. Reed, in the last role Balanchine would make for her, was the pivotal figure in the curtain-raising "Central Park in the Dark." Generally speaking, according to Reed, Balanchine saw her as "a very vivacious, lively dancer," certainly not the vulnerable blind girl who is violently attacked in a city park at night. In an interview with Mindy Aloff, who describes *Ivesiana* as "a ballet that presses acrobatics and such 'minimal' steps as walks on the knees into the service of a shockingly beautiful allegory of America," Reed recalled working on the ballet when the company was on tour:

> There weren't any actual steps in my section. Balanchine used the corps in all kinds of ways, and I wandered through people on the floor until I came in contact with a young man [Moncion]. Then the dance began to boil. I remember being in a small studio in Hollywood when Balanchine worked out a lot of these things. It was a matter of finding the movement that would give the impression of great violence. At one point he said (to Moncion), "Turn her upside-down." And I said, "you mean go around and around?" And he worked on this until we could make it continuous; we tried to get the effect of a pinwheel.[82]

Barbara Walczak, one of the twenty women in the corps, also had a memory of a rehearsal during which Balanchine got stuck, as he occasionally did. "He paused," she said, "and asked the dancers, what should we do now? One of the girls said, 'let's be cats and let's claw the floor,' and he said that's very good[;] put it in."[83]

Denby, who loved cats, said nothing about floor-clawing felines in his succinct, vivid description of Balanchine's foray into modern territory, a curtain-raising section that set the uneasy, questing, nightmarish tone of most of the piece.

Bolender was in two sections of the ballet. In "The Unanswered Question," which most critics and historians consider the most artistically viable part of *Ivesiana,* dancing with a very young Allegra Kent and four other men, Balanchine made use of Bolender's modern training, his ability to infuse every muscle in his body with musicality, and, when called for, understated drama. (In a review that appeared in the *Times* on March 7, 1955, Martin, calling the ballet a "magnificent weirdie," singled out Bolender [and the rest of the cast] for "being remarkably sensitive to the music."[84]) Kent's role required the physical daring Balanchine loved in American dancers, sustained strength, and a pliable body with perfect classical line, all of which she possessed in spades.

In some ways, "The Unanswered Question" is as menacing as "Central Park in the Dark," although it contains no act of violence. The vulnerability of both soloists is emphasized by their costumes, or lack of them. Kent wore a simple white leotard. Bolender's black tights were cut off below the knee, and his chest and feet were bare. Kent, who was all of 17 at the time, enters the stage poised on the shoulders of four men, who function a little like Bunraku puppeteers as they manipulate her in various positions, while Bolender follows her, sometimes on his feet, sometimes crawling, somersaulting several times, and, at one point, executing a *tour en l'air,* in the only overt employment of ballet technique in his role. As in the pas de deux with Le Clercq in *Metamorphoses,* the two are never able to connect physically, although they come close. As Bolender is supine on the floor, the men pass a rigidly postured Kent over his body; close to the end, they dip her curled in fetal position into his arms and immediately lift her out of them. But as Kent said in a 2004 interview, they don't relate. In the same interview, Bolender said he was never aware of the men, only the girl.[85] That was partly because the stage was darkly lit, so much so that when Kent had to turn in arabesque, she had a hard time finding her balance because she had no way to spot. That frightened her much more than Balanchine's requirement that she fall backward into the waiting arms of the men, who are holding her upright. While Kent loved making the audience gasp with that backward fall, what was most difficult for her, she said, was staying in character, her face impassive, expressing the dreamlike state of the title character in Balanchine's *La Sonnambula,* the piece that originally made her want to dance ballet.

When Bolender was coaching American Ballet Theatre's Herman Cornejo in this ballet for the Interpreters Archive, he told the impeccably trained Argentinean to eliminate from his performance every suggestion of ballet. "It's an acting role," he told him. "You are searching for something. You're not sure what it is." While several critics have suggested that "The Unanswered Question" is about, among other things, sexual humiliation, Bolender denied that, both in the interview and in his instructions to Cornejo, saying that for him, it was much more about anxiety, "because she keeps disappearing. . . . you are reaching out constantly as though in a fog, almost blind."[86]

"At the Inn" had Bolender on his feet in the only section of *Ivesiana* that even approached lightheartedness. Denby described the music as a "jazz that is small, sour, meticulously insane" and painted a picture of Bolender and Le Clercq dancing "side by side—with an intoxicated abandon and a miraculous rhythmic edge—invent[ing] a dizzy fluctuation of tango, maxixe [Brazilian tango], Charleston, and mambo steps, wandering into a horrid combination and out of it, and approach[ing] a rough climax, but [they] stop, shake hands, leave each other."[87]

Bolender said nothing about this pas de deux, but Le Clercq enjoyed herself thoroughly. "My part was nice," she told Reynolds, "free and jazzy. The music also was fun. It was like a puzzle trying to get it on time—and the orchestra would goof, and you were never quite sure."[88]

Ivesiana closed mysteriously and succinctly with "In the Night." Critic Marcia B. Siegel, writing about a revival in the 1970s, said "This final image . . . is the most ambiguous of all. It's so powerful one hardly dares name it. There's more here than the idea of the faceless crowd, the dispassionate, alienated urban millions. The image somehow says that we are also crippled or maimed in our single-focused journeys. And no one's destination is any more important than anyone else's, no one's path takes him away from the impartial fate that is waiting for all. And each individual journey finally has no effect on the larger journey that everyone travels. Seldom has Balanchine shown his derivation from the Russian fatalists more openly than in *Ivesiana*—and seldom has he spoken more directly to our time and our society."[89]

Years afterward, Reed remembered watching a rehearsal of this section with Balanchine in 1954, when he said to her quietly, "This is how I see America."[90] For Denby, though, Balanchine saw America in several ways:

Western Symphony and *Ivesiana,* . . . are as far apart as possible from one another in the kind of theater appeal they offer. *Western* is likable and lively, with good-natured jokes and fireworks, and it develops a dance momentum that for stamina, speed, and climax is irresistible. *Ivesiana* develops no speed of momentum at all, no beat; it is carried onward as if way below the surface by a force more like that of a tide, and the sharp and quickly shifting rhythms that appear have no firm ground to hold against an uncanny, supernatural drift. *Ivesiana* is a somber suite, not of dances, but of dense and curious theater images. Its expression is as subjective as that of *Western* is objective. But both ballets take as their subject matter familiar aspects of American life. And both are set to scores by native composers.[91]

Those "familiar aspects of American life" Denby noted are an idealized, humorous vision of the myth of the American West, the West of Reed's Oregon childhood, and a much darker and more realistic vision of urban America, specifically New York, where Bolender and Reed reached their sophisticated peak as dancers. Is "In the Night," as Siegel states, an expression of Russian fatalism, or is it, as in Balanchine's aside to Reed, a statement about the culture's ongoing urban-rural conflict, in which cities represent sin and danger and rural communities, goodness and virtue? Arguably it's both.

Writing about Reed in the *New York Herald Tribune,* Terry said that "[she] is of course a ballerina. Since she is not a bravura dancer, not a virtuoso, this fact sometimes escapes the viewer. But she is the New York City Ballet's most polished artist and far and away its most accomplished dancer actress. Her mere presence upon the stage brings a glow to the proceedings and her absence from any of the large array of roles she has created and performed would be an occasion for mass moaning."

Shortly after this appeared, Reed, now 38, exhausted from all the years of performing and touring and bad nutrition and thinking of going in a new direction with her career, created that occasion for mass moaning and took a two-year leave of absence from dancing.

Janet Reed and Jerome Robbins in Robbins's *Fancy Free*, 1944, Ballet Theatre. Photo by Alfredo Valente. Jerome Robbins Dance Division, New York Public Library for the Performing Arts.

Janet Reed and Michael Kidd in Jerome Robbins's *Interplay*, 1945, Ballet Theatre. Photo by Fred Fehl © Jerome Robbins Dance Division, New York Public Library for the Performing Arts.

Todd Bolender, Eleanor Miller, and Tanaquil Le Clercq rehearsing Balanchine's *Symphonie Concertante* at Carnegie Hall, November 5, 1945. Courtesy Balanchine Trust. Photo by Ben Greenhaus.

Todd Bolender as the Beast and Janet Reed as the Young Girl in Bolender's *Mother Goose Suite*, New York City Ballet, fall 1948. Photo by George Platt Lynes. Jerome Robbins Dance Division, New York Public Library for the Performing Arts.

Left to right: Maria Tallchief, Janet Reed, and André Eglevsky in George Balanchine's *À la Françaix*, New York City Ballet, fall 1951. Jerome Robbins Dance Division, New York Public Library for the Performing Arts.

Janet Reed and others in Ruthanna Boris's *Cakewalk*, New York City Ballet, 1951. Photographer unknown. Jerome Robbins Dance Division, New York Public Library for the Performing Arts.

Todd Bolender in the title role of his *The Miraculous Mandarin*, New York City Ballet, fall 1951. Photo by Fred Melton. Jerome Robbins Dance Division, New York Public Library for the Performing Arts.

Todd Bolender as the Husband in Jerome Robbins's *The Concert*, 1958. Photographer unknown. Jerome Robbins Dance Division, New York Public Library for the Performing Arts.

7

In the spring of 1956, when he was on temporary leave from City Ballet to stage *Rosalinda* for the Los Angeles Light Opera Company, Bolender wrote Balanchine a threatening letter:

> Over the past ten years I have been able to prove myself as a dancer and as a choreographer and it is as a participating choreographer that I would like to speak. I should like to include in the coming European Tour a new ballet that can raise no problems financially for the company for there is no scenery and the costumes are of the simplest possible. This time and without a shadow of a doubt in my mind I wish to use Tanny.
>
> This and checking with you about performing dates for *Souvenirs* and *The Still Point* in the European Tour are my reasons for writing to you now. . . . and . . . my feelings concerning the future of my ballets with the Company will be a strong factor in determining the acceptance of present contracts offered me.[1]

Bolender had received a letter from company manager Betty Cage complimenting him on the reports she had heard of his success with *Rosalinda,* which had had a four-week run in Los Angeles followed by four weeks of performance in San Francisco. He had taken John Mandia and Jillana with him to be his lead dancers and had held auditions in Los Angeles for the rest of the cast. Cage's letter also informed him that there were no plans to include his most recent (and ultimately most successful) ballets on an ambitious ten-week tour that would take the company to Munich, Frankfurt, Brussels, Antwerp, Paris, Cologne, Berlin, Zurich, Salzburg, Vienna, and Copenhagen, with Stockholm as the last stop. Given the choreographic encouragement from Balanchine and the amount of support Kirstein had given Bolender in the lengthy period of time it had taken him to make the two ballets, the news that his work was to be excluded from the tour came as a shock. There can be little question that at 42, Bolender knew his dancing career was winding down and that he was looking to his future as a choreographer, with working internationally in mind. Bolender and Reed, children of the Great Depression, worried about financial stability all their lives, their anxiety informed by a past of economic struggle and extremely hard work.

Starting with the American Ballet Caravan tour of South America of 1941, Bolender had spent more than a decade proving himself to be a versatile, dependable dancer in both major and minor works, primarily by Balanchine and Robbins but also by Loring, Lew Christensen, and Dollar. In Balanchine's *Symphonie Concertante, Four Temperaments,* and *Bourrée Fantasque*; Robbins's *Age of Anxiety* and *The Concert*; Christensen's *Jinx* and *Filling Station*; Dollar's *Five Gifts*; and the title role of his own *Miraculous Mandarin,* he had made an indelible impression on critics and audiences, not only in New York but also on national and international tours. In *Metamorphoses* and "The Unanswered Question" section of *Ivesiana,* he had literally gone down on his knees for Balanchine and danced on them.

Balanchine had been informally nurturing him as a choreographer throughout the decade and even before (*Mother Goose Suite* premiered in 1943 with the short-lived American Concert Ballet, a project to which Balanchine lent his name and *Concerto Barocco*), passing on assignments he had no time for himself, and inviting Sergei Denham to have a look at the ballet that became *Comédia Balletica,* which led to a one-year contract with the Ballet Russe de Monte Carlo. Balanchine's seeming rejection of *The Still Point* and *Souvenirs,* both of which had been very well received by both the public and the press, clearly cut Bolender to the quick.

Both ballets premiered in 1955; Mark Ryder and Emily Frankel's Dance Drama Company performed the former in April at the 92nd Street YM-YWHA and City Ballet performed the latter in November. *The Still Point* had debuted to great acclaim at City Ballet in the middle of March, just a few weeks before Bolender left for California. Like several of Bolender's previous ballets, *The Still Point* was a choreographic assignment; in this instance, Frankel wrote the libretto and selected the music (Claude Debussy's *Quartet in G*).

The project began with a phone call to Bolender from Mark Ryder, who Frankel was married to at the time. They wanted him to make a work for their new touring ensemble, an expansion of their Dance Drama Duo. They were modern dancers, although Frankel had had classical ambitions—she had traveled alone at age 12 from her home in Harrisburg, Pennsylvania, to study on scholarship at the Metropolitan Opera Ballet School. A serious injury to her foot prevented her from having a career in ballet, so she did just the opposite of Bolender and shifted from classical to modern dance, first studying with Martha Graham and dancing with her company. She then joined Charles Weidman's Dance Theatre Company when she was still in her teens, for a while performing with both.

Ryder, whose complete lack of ballet training strongly influenced Bolender's choreography for *Still Point*'s male lead, had also danced with the Graham Dance Company, where he originated roles in *Errand into the Maze* (the Minotaur) and *Night Journey* (Tiresias, the blind seer), for which he received plaudits from Walter Terry. A terpsichorean ideologue at a time when many members of the modern dance and ballet worlds were at each other's throats, Ryder had his feet firmly planted in the modern camp. He detested *l'école de la danse* and didn't much care for Bolender either.

Bolender's inquiring mind and openness to new ideas and ways of moving had led him away from Hanya Holm and modern dance to Balanchine and ballet; he was about as far from being an ideologue as one can get. As passionate as he later became about Balanchine's way of teaching—and as much as he admired such disparate ballets as *The Four Temperaments, Concerto Barocco,* and *Renard*—if he thought a work by the master wasn't up to snuff, he said so, although not necessarily in public. (About *Who Cares?* he once said, "Who cares!") In short, Bolender's view of the world at large can best be characterized as *anti*-ideological: aesthetic, political, and religious. *The Still Point*, with its blend of modern and classical movement, reflects that eclectic world view, one Bolender shared, in dance terms, with Loring and Robbins.

When rehearsals for *The Still Point* began in the summer of 1950, Bolender, who had been dancing in ballets of varying quality since 1937, still loved modern dance "when it was beautiful."[2] Moreover, he also "loved" Ryder's lack of ballet training. "[He] didn't even know how to lift," he told Reynolds a quarter of a century later. "Out of that I had to make a whole different kind of relationship between a man and a woman. . . . It was just a *man* on stage who moved and didn't dance, that is, he had no variation, he didn't do technical things—but did have the sense of dance. It was all dance, really. I tried to evolve it the way I feel Balanchine handles stories—in *Serenade, Sonnambula, Midsummer*—these are not pantomime things, but the story is there."[3]

The story is Frankel's, who, when she was in school, "never quite fit in," although "[she] tried to,"[4] and also had a truly traumatic experience when first in the Weidman company, where she was given a solo role, which caused tremendous resentment among the older dancers.[5] From these experiences, Frankel fashioned a libretto that is as deceptively simple as Bolender's choreography: A young woman tries to make friends with two other women. They are more interested in two young men and vice versa. The heroine is rebuffed by all four, with movement by the men that verges on brutality and sneaky viciousness from the women. Stage rear, they mime whispering to each other while she dances stage front, facing the audience. The two girls exit and the heroine performs an incredible solo, beating her body with her fists with adolescent self-loathing, her frustration verging on a tantrum in a mixture of anger and grief. As Reynolds points out, Frankel's choice of music is "inspired . . . the frequent pizzicatti brilliantly evocative of the heroine's nervous tension and inner torment."[6] This is true throughout the ballet but particularly for this solo. At the end of it, a third young man, his self-possessed movement indicating that he is less impetuous than the other two and likely more mature, comes onstage. They dance a dialogue of bodies, an exchange between an ordinary man in street shoes and slacks and a conflicted young woman wearing a summer dress, completing their "conversation" with gentle, sensuous tenderness.

Frankel's story is deeply personal but can also be universalized as a metaphor for a wide range of outsiders in American society in the conformist 1950s—Jews, African Americans, homosexuals, intellectuals, artists—who, whether male or female, were *auslanders* beyond the major cities. In the twenty-first century, they still are, unless they qualify as wealthy "art stars." Bolender, who grew up in a sports-oriented small city in Ohio, knew from a young age what it felt like to be an outsider. Frankel's story is Bolender's story too.

They were very different people, but they understood each other; in many ways, they came from the same place. And in the heat of a New York summer, with no air-conditioning to cool them off, only chocolate ice cream topped with blueberries on breaks, a collaboration began that would continue, on and off, for more than twenty years.

"With Emily Frankel I had a wonderful instrument," Bolender said, "because she had a very flexible body. She could work easily in balletic vein when I would explain what I wanted her to do. She created a performance that was really very specific, because she tried very hard with her untrained modern body to do the movement. I think I worked as much trying to work in her style as she tried to work in mine. It was a kind of give and take."[7] When, over twenty years later, in 1972, they made *Elektra,* that "give and take," as Bolender described it, had become a true melding of two seemingly antithetical dance forms. Frankel recalled, "He generally indicated a ballet step. . . . I'd sort of improv on it, he'd grab the improv and heighten it, transform it into a more creative, freer step."[8]

Balanchine, too, was intrigued by Frankel as a dancer. She remembered him coming to the studio in the summer of 1950 and offering her a contract, probably for City Ballet's fall and winter seasons following the company's return from their first tour to England. "[He] and Kirstein came . . . and saw me dance *Still Point.* I was invited by Balanchine to be a guest artist, but it didn't happen. I was told [it was] because the wonderful ballerinas that Balanchine was promoting did not need, would not want, would resent an outsider being brought in."[9] That, given the amount of time Kirstein spent soothing Reed and Tallchief's ruffled feathers over the self-promotion of Nora Kaye in the same period, has the ring of truth.[10] But only partly. "Balanchine loved [Frankel], he thought she was wonderful," Bolender said. " Her energy, vitality, the way she moved. . . . He liked [her] sexuality and . . . very athletic body."[11] But the real obstacle to a contract, Bolender suggested, was Frankel's minimal classical training and self-described bad ballet feet. It is also likely that everyone involved realized that *The Still Point,* the work in which Frankel would have appeared as guest artist, would not be ready in time for City Ballet's fall season.

It was actually nearly five years before *The Still Point* went up on the stage of the 92nd Street YM-YWHA, during which time both the Dance Drama Company and City Ballet were constantly touring, which made the scheduling of rehearsals extremely difficult. In addition, Ryder and Frankel

were also making choreography for their company and Bolender was working on several pieces of his own, including *Souvenirs.* He was also keeping
himself going financially when City Ballet was on hiatus by teaching at the
Fokine School in the Carnegie Hall building, and he was beginning to work
with Broadway producer Albert Marre. Intermittently, he was also working on the manuscript of "Backstage at the Ballet," a project he abandoned
because he was so much on the move that there was never enough time to
sit still and write.

In his personal life, the relationship between him and John Mandia was
deepening into love. In the closeted 1950s, they were unable to live together
openly until Bolender began to work abroad, but their personal and professional partnership would continue until 1970, when Mandia died young,
and suddenly, of a heart attack. *The Still Point*'s reasonable, sympathetic
hero may have been informed by Mandia's calm, patient personality.

The Still Point premiered on April 14, 1955, on a program that included
Hadassah's *Fairy Tale,* Sophie Maslow's *Diamond Backs,* Charles Weidman's *Penelope Is Pursued* (later titled *Soap Opera*), and Frankel and Ryder's
Whirligig, a title Bolender would use later for a ballet of his own. Frankel
had written all the librettos and chosen all the music. Participating choreographers were paid the munificent sum of $5 per performance. In addition
to the two artistic directors, the concerts were danced by Marilyn Poudrier,
Yvonne Brenner, David Gold, and Howard White.

It was stylistically (and deliberately) an eclectic program, performed entirely to recorded music that was equally varied. *Fairy Tale* was set to a piece
composed by Alan Hovhaness, and a jazz medley was chosen for *Diamond
Backs.* The evening, which was intended to be educational as well as entertaining, did, to some degree, reflect the intellectual, social, and political
concerns of mid-century practitioners of modern dance and its "Oriental" influences. Hadassah, a member of a Hasidic rabbinical family, had
grown up in Palestine, where she developed an interest in the connections
between Jewish dance and many Asian forms, including classical Indian.
She came to the United States in 1926, studied with Ruth St. Denis and
La Meri, and was deeply involved with the New Dance Group, which had
been established in 1932 to make social and political statements through
dance. Maslow, whose best-known work is the 1947 *Dust Bowl Ballads,* was
a leader of this group, and, like Frankel and Ryder, had been trained by
Graham and danced in her company. *Diamond Backs,* which concerned

itself with New York City street gangs, ends, like *West Side Story* (which premiered two years later), with a fatal knifing.

While Weidman had performed with the Denishawn company, where he had been very much influenced by Japanese dance, like Loring, Robbins, Kirstein, and, to some degree, Bolender, his primary interest was in developing dances that were expressive of American history and society.

A number of critics over the years have called *The Still Point* a small American masterpiece; like *Fancy Free*, it is about ordinary young people, although the music is French. Reviewing the concert for *Dance Magazine*, Doris Hering concluded with her customary clarity that despite the variety of forms, the Ryder-Frankel company "does have a basic style of its own—one that is robust, straightforward, and literal." She found Maslow's "sturdy depiction of teen-agers dancing and fighting in an aura of loneliness" best suited to this style and Ryder's "role as the rebellious knife-toting boy, [his] most sympathetic." Of Ryder in Hadassah's *Fairy Tale*—evidently a cousin of the Western-Asian "fusion dance" done in the early twenty-first century by such choreographers as Akram Khan and Shen Wei—Hering wrote that the "delicacies of hand and foot and head gesture escape him."[12]

The Still Point, she wrote, was a "work that was obviously deeply felt by the choreographer and lovingly danced by the company." She found the pas de deux "especially radiant," but she considered the closing section, in which the heroine, having found love and acceptance, "returns to solitude" to be unsatisfactory emotionally, if not artistically.[13]

Ted Shawn may have agreed, because at Jacob's Pillow, where the ballet was performed a few months later, the last section was eliminated at his request. "Ted thought the ballet would be a hit if it ended with the pas de deux," Frankel said: "The 4th movement was wonderful . . . choreographically excellent, but ending with the duet was 'commercial.'" At the Pillow, Frankel shed the pointe shoes she had performed in at the Y and was delighted to do so. "[They] limited me, but off pointe I could fly," she said.[14] In a short film clip on the Jacob's Pillow website showing her and Ryder in the pas de deux, she not only flies, she soars.

For New York City Ballet, Bolender restored the pointe shoes, placing all three women on toe, but not the fourth movement of the music. Shawn was right; the ballet was a hit without it. Over the years, *The Still Point* would sometimes be danced on pointe and sometimes in slippers, but only once, in the early 1970s, was the fourth movement reinstated. That was for Atlanta Ballet. Robert Barnett, who was directing the company at the time, said it was very beautiful, and the company toured with it all over the southeastern United States.[15]

Bolender brought Melissa Hayden and Tanaquil Le Clercq to watch Frankel rehearsing, in preparation for taking over her role when it was transferred to City Ballet. "When Tanaquil came and worked with me, and Melissa, briefly," Frankel recalled, "they eyeballed my feet, and [then] glommed onto my arms, head, torso." Le Clercq never danced *The Still Point*. A photo spread published in the *Herald Tribune* on February 26, 1956, as an advance for the City Ballet premiere shows Bolender rehearsing Le Clercq, supporting her in arabesque on what appears to be a rooftop, which indicates that she was still preparing to do it just two weeks before the March 13th company premiere. In the end, Bolender said, "She didn't want to be in it, and I never knew exactly why."

Hayden didn't want to be in it, either. In her autobiography *Melissa Hayden: On Stage and Off*, she recalls her first impression when she saw Frankel in the lead role: "It seemed much too much the story of an emotional woman who was out of touch with the world about her. I can't dance that kind of role. I must be able to ground every action on stage to a reality of feeling somewhere in my own experience."[16] Nevertheless, as Hayden learned the steps she tried to ignore her initial impressions of the role, and once the choreography was in her muscles, she made up her own scenario, investing it with her own experiences as an adolescent misfit who listened to classical music in her native Toronto and was frightened of the male gender. In some respects, her version of the story is pretty close to Frankel's: "[It] is about "a young girl who is experiencing the first pain of entering the adult world. That way I could soften the harsh dramatic qualities I objected to when I saw the ballet, yet I could still say everything the choreographer intended."[17]

Given the descriptions of Hayden's performance as the Woman in Bolender's *The Miraculous Mandarin*, this is a rather disingenuous statement about the need to relate what she dances to some aspect of her own experience. Kirstein called her the Bette Davis of the ballet in that role, which certainly points toward the kind of over-the-top dramatic acting Hayden had thought Frankel was doing. And fifteen years after the publication of her book, she told Reynolds something quite different about *The Still Point* rehearsal period with Bolender.[18]

Working with Todd, we seemed to build one layer on top of the next; he fed me that way. He was very detailed, very subtle. My whole body was to express my feelings—if I was pained, it should be through my whole body in a physical sense, rather than just on my face. . . . He noticed shoulders, hands; he was very constructive. . . . I had been through a period of being very classical [in Balanchine's *Swan Lake* and *Symphony in C,* for example] and *Still Point* taught me a great deal, which I could also relate to other ballets.[19]

If Ryder was lacking in classical technique, Jacques d'Amboise possessed it in abundance, his tour jetés and entrechats six performed with a cocky, streetwise American accent in *Filling Station* and *Western Symphony.* Much of his dancing at this stage of his career was colored by youthful impetuousness. Bolender was decidedly casting him against type, challenging him to turn down the heat but to dance with the same clarity as he did in ballets that called for bravura flash and flair in a role that required a far more nuanced performance than any previous one he had danced. In his review of the City Ballet premiere, Martin commended Bolender for getting "from Jacques d'Amboise a simple and admirable performance as Miss Hayden's partner."[20]

Jillana, Irene Larsson, Mandia, and Roy Tobias, all of whom Bolender had worked with before in *Mandarin* and *Souvenirs,* were cast as the secondary characters for City Ballet's premiere. Those characters are important: *The Still Point's* pas de deux, like the oft-performed one from *Don Quixote* or the Black Swan pas de deux from *Swan Lake,* can stand alone, and the latter has probably been programmed far more frequently than the complete ballet. But it has far greater emotional impact when danced in the context of rejection that the secondary characters provide. Watching it without that context is like listening to the middle of a conversation without knowing how it started.

In setting the ballet, Bolender paid as much attention to those characters as he did the protagonists. Francia Russell was one of the cliquish girls in a 1957 performance (*Serenade, Agon,* and *Stars and Stripes* were also on the program) a year or so after Balanchine had plucked the long-legged nineteen-year-old redhead out of class at SAB and put her in City Ballet's corps. "Dancing in *Still Point* was a high point of my career," she said, in 2013, citing Bolender's "refreshing and stimulating explanations"

of what he wanted, in which he appealed to the intelligence of the dancers and used humor to drive home a point.[21] Russell, an intensely musical
dancer, loved the Debussy score and said that she felt she could dance
more freely in *The Still Point* than in anything else she danced at City
Ballet.

In its classical version, performed to live music, *The Still Point* received
many critical plaudits. In a Sunday essay for the *Herald Tribune,* published
five days after the premiere, Terry spoke favorably of the changes Bolender
had made to the original choreography for the Ryder-Frankel company.

> Some of them [were] designed to serve the special qualities of the New
> York City Ballet, as different from the modern dance group, and some of
> them by way of tightening his choreographic lines. In the new presenta-
> tion, *The Still Point* offers the viewer patterns of visual effectiveness and
> a concluding pas de deux which is a beautiful piece of craftsmanship,
> but mainly the appeal is on an emotional level, for Mr. Bolender has not
> only succeeded in relating the elusive, strangely haunting images of the
> Debussy score (the String Quartet expertly transcribed for orchestra by
> Frank Black) to the movements of the dancers, but he has also laid bare,
> but with delicacy and tenderness, the secret sorrows, the longings, the
> desperations, the discoveries of the human heart.[22]

Of Hayden's performance, he said, "Every movement, every gesture,
even sudden spurts of physically striking action were made to serve her
characterization and her portrayal, emotionally poignant and dramati-
cally powerful, reached the heart."[23] Writing for the *New York Post,* Frances Herridge described the work as different from anything else in the
company's repertory: "It is romantic and lyric rather than classic ballet
and it has the emotional impulse of modern dance."[24] Robert Coleman,
his colleague at the *Daily News,* liked it, "for it is simple, unpretentious
and evocative."[25]

For Charles McHarry, writing for one of New York's many dailies, whose
ignorance of the art form was matched only by more than a suggestion of
homophobia, the ballet afforded an opportunity to express the downside of
the mid-century American Zeitgeist:

> "Still Point," set to some syrupy Debussy, starts off with two dames
> engaged in a happy shindig with two boys. The two couples are much

in love, obviously, and then this mixed-up youngster danced by Melissa Hayden comes on stage. Melissa, it is plain for all to see, has a big thing going for the two goons [to be] out of the picture. The gals resist despite some adroit arm semaphores and wonderful footwork by Hayden. . . . The frustrated Melissa is about to go jump off the roof of the nearest ballet school when along comes Jacques d'Amboise, biggest, youngest and most promising of the City Ballet troupe's boy performers. He changes everything, including Melissa's genes. When the curtain drops, Melissa's misguided instincts are all straightened out and she and Jacques are ready to buy a TV set, a Murphy bed and an apartment in the Bronx.[26]

McHarry commended the cast and singled out Jean Rosenthal's lighting but concluded that "as a production, 'Still Point' is stillborn."[27]

While she had been lukewarm about *The Still Point* in its modern dance incarnation, Hering found the neoclassical version to be a high point of City Ballet's spring season, and as an experienced, knowledgeable viewer of dance in New York, she was able to put it into the context of Bolender's earlier work. She began her review in the May 1956 issue of *Dance Magazine* with a summary of the premieres, describing the batterie of Balanchine's *Allegro Brillante* as "coruscating" and noting the "antic play" of Robbins' *The Concert,* and the "dancing in the great tradition by Maria Tallchief, Diana Adams, and Melissa Hayden. "Yet," she continued:

Most memorable of the entire season was a single instant when a young man extended his hand toward a girl, and her hand rose in an arc to meet his. It was the culmination of *The Still Point.* Bolender has uncanny insight into the feelings of young women. His girl in *Mother Goose Suite,* his debutante in *Souvenirs,* and the tortured protagonist of *The Still Point* are all sisters under the skin—poignant sisters seeking fulfillment in romantic love. Of them all, the girl in *The Still Point* is the most touching because she is delineated with the most depth and at the same time, with the most simplicity. In fact, simplicity is the prime virtue of this little ballet. Bolender has had the courage and the care to let the dancing speak out honestly without any mimetic overlay.[28]

The Still Point was hardly "stillborn," as McHarry put it. The ballet is still alive and kicking in the second decade of the twenty-first century, and in the intervening sixty years it has been performed by ballet and modern companies all over the world, from Vienna to Istanbul, New York to Seattle. The Kansas City Ballet danced the pas de deux a few days after Bolender's death in 2006, and it danced the complete ballet at the first Ballet Across America Festival at the Kennedy Center for the Performing Arts in 2008. In 2014, it was still in active repertory in Kansas City.

Souvenirs, which Bolender choreographed in the same period as *The Still Point*, has also endured into the twenty-first century; a section of it was performed in New York in 2006 at the Dance Magazine Awards ceremony, Bolender's own choice to represent his choreography.[29] In 2012, Kansas City Ballet danced it at the end of their inaugural season in the Kauffman Center for the Performing Arts with Kimberly Cowen, the last dancer Bolender trained, in the delectable role of the Vamp.

Souvenirs, which premiered in November 1955, is packed with delicious roles for both men and women. In a 2002 interview, Bolender said "[It is] about a point of view. I wanted to convey the wonderful simplicity of silent film acting, to get the point across with movement."[30] Made in close collaboration with composer Samuel Barber, set and costume designer Rouben Ter-Arutunian, and City Ballet technical director Jean Rosenthal, the ballet is actually far from simple and gets many points across with a good deal more than movement.

Barber's score, witty, nostalgic, and with just enough dissonance to remind you that World War I was about to obliterate the way of life it celebrated, is based on the social dances gaining popularity at that time, including the two-step, the galop, the schottische, and the tango, the last considered very daring in those days. Ter-Arutunian's clever sets and period costumes, the latter designed to express character and facilitate the movement; Bolender's smart libretto and meticulously detailed choreography; and Rosenthal's lights and innovative solutions to technical problems all come together in a highly entertaining ballet that is lighthearted but not lightweight. With Bolender in charge, everyone involved worked hard and well together to create from the fabric of early twentieth-century popular culture, specifically social dances and silent film, an affectionate send-up of both a bygone era and ongoing human foibles, including the insecurities of the young.

Bolender's ideas for ballets were usually triggered by music, whether a score had been assigned to him or not. *Souvenirs* was a little different. According to a note in a handsomely produced City Ballet souvenir program (undated, but likely for the 1955–1956 season, the text probably written by Kirstein), Bolender had, independently from Barber, been mulling over a work that would "recapture the fragrance of our immediate past—the world of just before the first World War—of the epoch of the tango, early films and rag-time before it became jazz."[31] Sometime in 1952, Bolender's friends Arthur Gold and Robert Fizdale invited him to hear them play the original two-piano version in a concert at New York's Town Hall. The bon vivant piano duo were also friends of Barber and had told Bolender that he should hear *Souvenirs* because it was a "beautiful dance piece."

Bolender agreed. "I was always listening to music like mad, because the possibility of doing something was always so imminent," he told Reynolds. "I thought [*Souvenirs*] was the most dazzling piece of music, and I went to Lincoln and said, 'don't we own [it]?'" In fact, Nancy LaSalle had provided the funds to pay Barber to expand the score for orchestra, with a new work by Balanchine in mind. Composer and choreographer had been unable to come to a meeting of the minds for the terpsichorean treatment of the score, and, according to Bolender, Barber was "horrified . . . [by Balanchine's] wild, crazy story."[32] So Kirstein and Balanchine told Bolender to go ahead and see what he could do.[33]

Barber, who was born in 1910 in Pennsylvania, is best known in the dance world for his *Adagio for Strings*; many choreographers, including Kenneth MacMillan, have made dances to this lyrical score. *Medea* and *Souvenirs* are cataloged as ballets in one biographical entry, and in 1948, his *Capricorn Concerto*, a highly structured score some critics said was influenced by Stravinsky, provided the music for Bolender's ballet of the same name. Barber had imagined *Souvenirs* taking place in the Palm Court of New York's Plaza Hotel at a tea dance. Bolender, inspired by *Monsieur Hulot's Holiday*, a nearly silent film that came out in 1953, in which Jacques Tati in the title role succeeded in creating considerable mayhem at a seaside hotel in France, shifted the mise-en-scène from urban New York to a luxury beach hotel around 1910.

"Sam came to my flat frequently, two or three times a week," Bolender told Reynolds. "I got working on it, did the tango first, or the tea dance, not sure which, or both maybe, and showed them to Lincoln and George, one day between the matinee and evening performance. . . . Lincoln asked [me] to do it for the fall season." While it took a lot of time to coordinate the choreography, the music, Bolender's libretto, and the set and costume designs and solve some technical problems, Bolender "was ready to go when Lincoln tapped [him]."[34]

Writing the libretto was troublesome: Bolender worked hard on it for many weeks and ended up discarding a "long thing, which I hated, so I started all over again."[35] What he finally came up with was six short scenes (Hering referred to them as reels in her review for *Dance Magazine*), each containing at least one story, beginning with a waltz in the lobby of the Royal Palms Hotel, which introduces the cast of guests and staff. The second scene, danced to a lively schottische in the third-floor corridor of the hotel, resembles a bedroom farce, with a Man About Town interrupting a honeymoon couple, a hotel maid fending him off with a feather duster, and a trouserless Groom straddling the gun of the cigar-smoking Husband. The third scene shifts to the ballroom for what several critics considered the heart of the ballet, where the ballet's only classical pas de deux is danced on pointe by one of the three wallflowers with the man of her dreams. In the fourth scene, danced to a two-step, a woman taking tea in the Palm Court plays two men against each other, one of whom is her husband; it ends with a spectacular wordless marital row. Next, in a scene titled "A Bedroom Affair," a vamp resembling Theda Bara or Gloria Swanson (who Bolender had seen on the street in Hollywood when he was 10 years old) pins a gigolo to the floor with the heel of her shoe. Performed to a hesitation tango, much of it takes place on a fainting couch covered with a tiger skin. An ostrich-feather fan also plays a part in the choreography, and the vamp's costume, a slinky, strategically beaded dress, is reminiscent of the women's garb in such Rudolf Valentino films as *The Sheik*. The finale gathers the entire cast on an ersatz beach in a grand galop that includes a cameo appearance by a capering King Kong. According to Bolender, Balanchine particularly loved the tango but couldn't resist making a suggestion, namely that the gigolo become a jewel thief. Bolender gave it some thought, but, mindful of what he felt was Balanchine's ruinous meddling in *The Filly*, decided that crime played no part in his story and never changed it.

The libretto made considerable demands on a designer whose budget was less than lavish. A period hotel lobby, an upstairs corridor (with several bedroom doors to slam), a ballroom, and a bedroom were required to frame the action, plus an elevator that would appear to go up and down. For the finale, a bath house was also needed. Props included canes, a beaded handbag, at least one cigar, a rifle, the feather duster and ostrich fan, and a small pistol. Costumes included a bridal gown, floaty pastel party dresses for the wallflower debutantes, an elaborate evening coat, suits for the men, many hats for men and women, a uniform for the elevator attendant, a pert little black-and-white costume for the chambermaid, and a gorilla suit. For the finale, a number of period bathing suits for men and women were also required.

Ter-Arutunian, whose first designs for ballet in his adopted country these were, proved himself to be more than equal to the task. At 16, he had seen the Ballet Russe in Berlin and had fallen in love with such colorful productions as *La Boutique Fantasque* and *Gaîté Parisienne* and with Alexandra Danilova. He remembered returning home from performances and making up his own designs for *Afternoon of a Faun* and *Swan Lake,* inspired by Léon Bakst. In the early 1940s, Ter-Arutunian studied art and film music in Berlin, both of which he put to use in creating the production for *Souvenirs.* By the time he arrived in New York in January 1951 on the *Liberté* with his mother and her "small black cat," he had had considerable practice in theatrical design, having done sets for shows for the U.S. army in Czechoslovakia and Germany and costumes for the Berlin State Opera Ballet (in 1940). In 1947, he approached a choreographer at the Opéra-Comique and was commissioned to make the designs for a neoclassical plotless ballet, in the manner of Balanchine.[36]

Not long after his arrival in New York, Ter-Arutunian joined the scenic artists union. He worked for CBS television for several years, but what he really wanted was to design for ballet, specifically the New York City Ballet. Through Betty Cage, he obtained an interview with Kirstein and that led to designs, but for opera, not for ballet. Bartók's *Bluebeard's Castle* and Ravel's *L'Heure Espagnole* were the first, followed by an extremely successful *Cinderella* in 1953. Ter-Arutunian did not actually meet Balanchine until 1955, when he did the designs for *Souvenirs*; nine years later he made new designs for *Swan Lake,* when it was redone for the New York State Theater at Lincoln Center. A new production of *The Nutcracker* followed; those designs were still in use in 2020.

While Ter-Arutunian was extremely successful in the United States as a designer for theater, television, film, and opera, dance was always his passion. He had firm ideas about what the medium required that were completely in line with Bolender's point of view, including the belief that music was the starting point. Before beginning, Ter-Arutunian always listened to the score. Moreover, as far as he was concerned, the design "is there to serve the dance, not to obscure it. [It] needs to be clear so the movement stands out from it and can be perceived clearly. It should be interesting enough to trigger the imagination of the viewer . . . to establish a certain atmosphere, which does not interfere with the movement but adds to it."[37] Lighting was something Ter-Arutunian took into consideration throughout his process. Bolender, too, was extremely attentive to the details of the lighting of his ballets throughout his career.

Ter-Arutunian also felt that costumes should not divert the viewer's attention from the dance and that they should not turn a ballet into a fashion show, although he cited *Souvenirs* as something of an exception: "[That] is hard to visualize without the costumes. . . . The choreography makes a great deal of use of the costuming and the costuming contributes to the effect of the ballet a great deal."[38] Bolender had a strong hand in those designs; at the Weyhe Book Store and Gallery on Lexington Avenue, he was shown "some little French pamphlets issued monthly with color pictures of designs from various fashion houses," most of them drawn in the period 1911 to 1914. The designs included a bridal gown, hats for men and women, men's suits, a "Pagoda dress," and a spectacular evening coat made of cut velvet trimmed with gold silk brocade. Most of the costumes for *Souvenirs* were based on those drawings and were executed meticulously by Karinska; the evening coat is an exact copy of the original design. Worn by the Vamp, it is an integral part of her character and her movement when she makes her first entrance, taking very small steps, as she emerges from an elevator into the hotel lobby. After tossing her room key to the gigolo, she exits the same way, ostentatiously wiggling her derrière, which is cupped by the drape of the coat.

In rehearsals, Bolender was "very conscious of the costumes as I worked—the narrow skirts and shoes—and I wanted the movement to fit that. I made the kids do it in rehearsal; even though they were ballet dancers, they were to maintain the look and style of the period."[39]

Bolender was equally definite about the sets. "Even before I started to design, [he] had thought of an elevator," Ter-Arutunian said. "He asked for an elevator, a group of palms, and a kind of pouf or banquette. The elevator was to open and a number of characters would be making their entrance from [it]. There was an elevator boy [Bolender called him an attendant] who opened the doors and closed [them]. The elevator would go up, take people with it, and it would descend and unload a group of characters. The device for [it] was a rather simple one. It had double doors which were in back of frosted [glass] which was in back of a grillwork Art Nouveau in character. In back of that for technical purposes was placed the blind which, when it was pulled down, revealed the light and the elevator would give the appearance [of] descending. When the blind was raised, it looked as if the elevator was going up." In practical terms, the device wasn't as simple as all that: the elevator had two doors, which meant there were two blinds that had to be operated simultaneously, so the cord that made them both function had to be lined up precisely. "Whoever was operating the elevator had to know what he was doing," Ter-Arutunian remarked.[40] For the finale, Bolender "wanted a beach scene, but we couldn't afford *anything,* what we got was a string of flags attached to a pole, with a lifeguard standing there, and Jean [Rosenthal] got a fan to blow on the flags."[41] Ter-Arutunian devised a bathhouse from the third-scene bedroom doors, which were painted white on the inside and could be turned around with hinges that swung in both directions.

Like *Filling Station, Souvenirs* is a comic story ballet rooted in American popular culture. While it contains a fair amount of slapstick (for which it got slammed by critics such as John Martin and Hering), it is far more subtle than Lew Christensen's piece and demands the wordless acting of such stars of the silent screen as Theda Bara, John Barrymore, Janet Gaynor, and Clara Bow and the comic timing of Charlie Chaplin, the Marx Brothers, and Mary Pickford, all of whom were part of Bolender's youth. The ballet is as much an homage to them and their colleagues as it is a tribute to pre–World War I culture and the leisure class.

You can see this in the details of the movement—the prim vulnerability of the three wallflowers as they settle themselves on the pouf and demurely cross their ankles, reminiscent of the body language of Gaynor and Bow; the ham-flavored grimaces of the gigolo, John Barrymore at his worst; the shyly triumphant bride and awkward groom, stock characters in countless silents; the coarse Man about Town, who manages to clench a cigar in his teeth and leer at the same time, much like Groucho Marx (a schtick Bolender would repeat as the uncouth Husband in Robbins's *The Concert,* which premiered a few months later). All of the cast members had to know what they were doing with every muscle in their bodies, including facial ones. Bolender's choreography is as detailed as the costumes; every dancer he coached, and he staged that ballet for more than half a century, remembered how meticulous he was, "down to the last eyelash," original cast member Yvonne Mounsey told Reynolds.[42]

Souvenirs premiered on November 15, 1955, with Bolender himself performing the role of the dapper Man About Town, manipulating a cane in Chaplinesque fashion, bonelessly leaning into the tea-table to flirt with the Wife, and getting himself chased in and out of the third-scene bedrooms. Irene Larsson was the Vamp and Mandia the Gigolo (they were titled The Woman and The Man in the staid 1950s), and Arthur Mitchell, in his first featured role, was the elevator attendant. Hering commended all of the ballet's creators, writing in *Dance Magazine* that "with the exception of its rather loosely choreographed ending, *Souvenirs* was a bright, compact series of images whose atmosphere derived from Bolender's keen sense of timing and from Ter-Arutunian's drape and glitter costumes and his witty take-off on the curlicue décor of the period[.] Barber's lightly sentimental score also added immeasurably."[43]

Martin and Terry were less enthusiastic. Martin chose to speak of influences, citing Charles Weidman's *Flickers* and Robbins's Mack Sennett ballet in the Broadway musical *High Button Shoes*, neither of which had Bolender seen. The most obvious influences on Bolender's choreography for *Souvenirs* have little to do with the period in which it is set. Agnes de Mille paved the way for the debutante's dream in *Oklahoma*; Loring put Billy the Kid's Sweetheart in pointe shoes to signify that she was a figment of the outlaw's dreams.

Terry didn't think it was quite a ballet. "[It] is an extended treatment of an idea suitable for musical comedy. But if it is musical-comedy stuff, it may be noted that other ballets have invaded this area, among them Ashton's *Façade*. So if there are faults to be found, they lie not so much in its musical-comedy leanings as in choreographic declines. But when *Souvenirs* really moves, it is in its unpretentious but engaging way, almost a genuine ballet. Not a significant work but great good fun."[44]

It is still difficult, if not impossible, for American critics to accept humor as significant work in any of the classical arts. *The Concert*, Robbins's comic masterpiece, which premiered in March 1956, got the same lukewarm critical reception as *Souvenirs*. Audiences, however, adored it, and so did Balanchine, who would watch from the wings and was delighted on one occasion to substitute for Bolender, who had come down with the flu, in the role of the wife-dominated husband.

In a letter to Yvonne Patterson in 2004, Bolender described the ballet and the part he played in it: "At the moment the KCB is in the midst of rehearsing 'The Concert,' a fairly long ballet, with me in the role of the henpecked husband who was always trying to invent ways to kill his wife and dreaming of being with a beautiful butterfly girl or anyone else who came along who would give him the time of day. The music was a series of Chopin pieces that made a marvelous background for the zany story Jerry invented."[45]

Subtitled "The Perils of Everybody" (a nod to silent film serials), *The Concert* is much more than a "zany story" and the Chopin score provides far more than background for what at the end of the day amounts to hilarious social commentary and an affectionate send-up of the conventions of nineteenth-century ballet. Among them are the character dances Robbins viewed as un-American when he was performing them with Ballet Theatre; the uniform lyricism of the corps in such ballets as *Les Sylphides*; and some of Balanchine's choreographic quirks, particularly, as Jowitt describes them, "the complicated daisy chains and cat's cradles [he] often creates with his ensemble."[46]

Just as he had based much of *Fancy Free* on the behavior of ordinary people on the street—sailors on leave and the young women they encountered in bars—Robbins's observations of audience behavior at concerts of "long-haired" music underlie much of the dancing in *The Concert*, particularly by Bolender as the downtrodden husband of an exceedingly bossy wife and Le Clercq as a dreamily besotted young woman so absorbed in the music she doesn't notice when a chair is pulled out from under her and maintains her seated balance, unsupported by furniture or partner.

These would be the last roles that Robbins created on Bolender and Le Clercq, and they were memorably wonderful in them. "I mean they were really, really marvelous," Barbara Walczak recalled in an interview half a century later.[47] By all accounts, Bolender was brilliant as the henpecked, Walter Mitty–like character, infusing his performance with references to Groucho Marx, carrying a "mistaken ballerina" off stage like an addled Franz kidnapping Coppélia, chasing Le Clercq with a butterfly net in a possible spoof of their roles in *Metamorphosis*, in which she was a dragonfly and he a plodding, turtle-like creature.

For Le Clercq, it wasn't all fun and games and comic timing: Robbins made specifically for her a "lovely introspective" solo in which she danced to a mazurka, slowly and thoughtfully, with "folding extensions and soft pawings of the floor."[48] Robbins later viewed this solo as the seed for *Dances at a Gathering,* but it was so tailored to Le Clercq's idiosyncratic approach to dancing that he eliminated it from *The Concert* after polio put paid to her dancing career. Every role she danced, in his work, Balanchine's, and Bolender's, was marked by intelligence and musicality and, when called for, quirky wit, French chic, and a quality best described as fey. "It was a very beautiful dance," Robbins told Reynolds, "sort of a reverie. I took it out when Tanny no longer danced; it was so her."[49]

Martin pronounced both Le Clercq and Bolender to be "excellent" in their roles, although he thought the ballet an insult to Chopin and to pianist Nicholas Kopeikine, who participated in the action on stage. Photographs of Bolender in the "butterfly" section, his pale blue practice clothes accessorized with dark-rimmed glasses, bowler hat, socks and garters, vest, and necktie, a manic expression on his face as he does some exaggerated tiptoeing in one section, show that he was as attentive to the details of his own performance as he was to the dancers he cast in *Souvenirs.*

Patronizing references to musical comedy by Terry and Martin, who called *The Concert* "a kind of nightmarish revue" and felt that the "Sylphides" waltz section would have been more effective in a Broadway show, may have disturbed Robbins, who was hypersensitive about his practice of both classical and popular art, but they wouldn't have bothered Bolender. "Comedy is the most difficult thing to do," he told Elizabeth Zimmer in January 2006, when he had again been helping to fine-tune a revival of *The Concert* at Kansas City Ballet. "It takes a kind of Broadway knowledge to make it work, a very shrewd, clever use of timing. All dance is about timing, finally, but the sharp timing of Broadway movement is on a totally different beat. Really good humor is forever."[50]

In her review for *Dance Magazine,* Hering praised "Mr. Robbins' rare facility for kinetic humor" while damning the ballet for its [lack of] "polish and creative discipline." She did, however, very much enjoy the "Mistake Waltz," describing it as "funnier and funnier, as the out of step character infected others until one never knew where the next flaw would turn up," but she basically dismissed the work as mere "slapstick."[51] Francia Russell, who was standing in the wings to watch Bolender in one performance with

Ballets: U.S.A. in the late 1950s, recalled in 2011 that he was so funny that she laughed until it hurt, leaving no doubt that "really good humor" lasts forever in the minds of the audience, whatever serious critics might think.[52]

Bolender turned 42 in February of 1956, but it doesn't seem to have slowed down his dancing. Blessed with a flexible body, powerful legs, the ability to analyze roles in plotless ballets, and a talent he shared with Reed for inhabiting a character, Bolender continued throughout the decade to perform major roles in both Robbins's and Balanchine's work in repertory that ranged from the humor of *The Concert* to the technically demanding *Symphony in C.* Some roles were increasingly difficult for him to perform, such as Coffee's deep backbends in the original *Nutcracker.* Playbills reveal, however, that for much of the decade, Bolender was perfectly capable of dancing The Husband in *The Concert* and the Scherzo in *Western Symphony* on the same evening, the Man about Town in *Souvenirs,* and the first movement of *Bourrée Fantasque* at a matinee.

Bolender, who could do an unsupported grand battement on the beach at the age of 90, was certainly well aware by the time he reached his mid-30s that his body would not hold up for constant performing forever. Temperamentally, he was a very American combination of idealism and pragmatism, and starting in 1950, with the commission from Ryder and Frankel for *The Still Point,* he began preparing himself to earn a living offstage by accepting a wide range of choreographic assignments, many of which could be accomplished when City Ballet was on hiatus.

In 1951, in a program at Carnegie Hall that included a performance of Balanchine's *Mazurka from the Life of the Czar,* Bolender was represented by dances set to Lully's *Concerto for String Orchestra,* which Bea Tompkins and John Mandia performed, and an "Allemand" from Couperin's Louis XIV suite. Two years later, he was creating incidental dances for *Love's Labour's Lost* and *The Merchant of Venice* in City Center productions directed by Albert Marre, who Kirstein had hired to be City Center's first artistic director for theater. Marre became a Tony Award–winning Broadway director (for *Kismet* and *Man of La Mancha,* among other musicals). Bolender's dances for these productions marked the beginning of a working relationship for the two men that would continue well into the 1960s and beyond.

In the same period, Bolender, showing his acute musical range, choreographed *La Nuit* for a program performed at the Museum of Modern Art in April of 1953 to honor contemporary French composer Henri Sauguet's first visit to the United States. Sauguet had done the music for Balanchine's 1926 ballet *La Chatte,* which Serge Diaghilev had commissioned, and he was a disciple of Darius Milhaud and Erik Satie. The Juilliard String Quartet performed the music, and Tallchief and Magallanes led a cast of four couples consisting of Jillana, Michael Maule, Irene Larsson, Roy Tobias, Barbara Walczak, Robert Barnett, Barbara Bocher, and John Mandia.

While Bolender made some beautiful ballets to such melodic classical composers as Mozart, Chopin, and Beethoven (the latter two when he was artistic director of Kansas City Ballet in the 1980s and '90s) he had a real passion for twentieth-century composers, starting with Stravinsky, whose *Firebird* he heard for the first time when he was very young in Canton, Ohio. He loved the Poulenc score for *The Masquers* ("the kind of tinny, bangy sound of it—it had a kind of improvised sound as though it had been written right at the moment and a group of musicians were just playing it right off the tops of their heads"), another work for Ryder and Frankel's Dance Drama Company, which premiered in March 1956. Frankel was again responsible for the libretto, which, as Bolender perceived it in general terms, was about "the influence people have over each other and how deadly or beautiful it can be."[53] Bolender built his observations of tensions within the Ryder-Frankel company into his choreography. This worked far better for the modern dancers than it would for City Ballet's classically trained ones in 1957, when he transferred and expanded the work for the company after their return from a grueling three months in Europe.

A photograph in the October 1956 issue of *Dance Magazine* of a broadly smiling Bolender, about to leave for Salzburg, the first stop on the European tour, suggests that he was satisfied with the compromise he had reached with Balanchine. *Souvenirs* was part of the tour repertory (Francis Mason remembered seeing it in Venice), but there was no new Bolender work featuring Le Clercq and the company did not perform *The Still Point.* However, when they were dancing in Berlin, Bolender staged the work on the Staatsoper Ballet, the first American choreographer to be invited to do so, garnering a positive review from the extremely difficult-to-please Horst Koegler. Writing for *Die Welt* in September 1956, Koegler was full of praise: "Bolender succeeds with a psychologically finely differentiated chamber ballet about the growing up of a young girl, and fully justifies the audacity of using so sensitive a piece as Debussy's string quartet as framework."[54]

On the whole, City Ballet's fifth European tour was a critical and audience success. In a City Ballet program essay for the 1956 winter season, Danish critic Kelvin Lindenmann cited "the extraordinary variety of choreography, wealth of innovation, happy musicality, and the sheer joy in the dancing," concluding that American ballet "is gushing with creative genius."

The tour repertory, which included Balanchine's *Bourrée Fantasque, Western Symphony, Swan Lake, Divertimento No. 15, The Four Temperaments, Serenade,* and *La Valse*; and Robbins's *Afternoon of a Faun, The Cage, Interplay, Fanfare,* and *The Concert,* was indeed highly varied. Audiences, too, loved the high-spirited energy of the American dancers. They particularly loved Le Clercq, whose dancing in *Western Symphony* was "witty down to her fingertips," as Bolender described it, and was laced with impeccable comic timing in the first movement of *Bourrée Fantasque.*

A film clip of a performance of *Western Symphony* on the raked stage of the Palais Garnier in *Afternoon of a Faun,* the 2014 film about Le Clercq's life, shows the audience cheering so loudly as she and d'Amboise strut, pirouette, and jeté through the "Rondo" that Hershy Kay's not-exactly-pianissimo score becomes nearly inaudible. The audience had reason to cheer; as Bolender said, "When d'Amboise and Tanny got together, they were dynamite." Le Clercq and Robbins were also dynamite, but in a different way, especially in the first movement of *Bourrée,* in which they were the centerpiece of a send-up of both the choreographer's own work and such nineteenth-century warhorses as Petipa's *Don Quixote,* as evidenced in a photograph of the two of them grappling for Le Clercq's fan.[55]

Bolender had been watching Le Clercq dance since 1935, when she was five-and-a-half years old, longer than Balanchine, longer than Robbins. Le Clercq, who had arrived from Paris fairly recently when Bolender first saw her, was the daughter of an American debutante from St. Louis and a French poet and intellectual. She was a student at the arts-oriented King-Coit School in New York, where Bolender was teaching modern dance on Fridays and Saturdays. The first thing he noticed about her was her long-legged body "and the face and the sharpness of her ability to pick up whatever I'd do—port de bras, walking, sometimes little steps, simple stuff." For a school show, he made the first of many choreographies on her, a classical Indian-style solo in a piece based on the Hindu legend of Nala and Damayanti. John Anderson reviewed her performance in the *New York Evening Journal:* "Mistress Tanaquil Le Clercq, who seems no age at all, reduces my critical vocabulary to dust and ashes, as she plays an ethereal swan with entrancing effect, one eye sagely on the audience, which automatically makes her my favorite actress!"[56]

In 1945, Bolender encountered Le Clercq on a train bound for Jacob's Pillow, where he was developing the ballet that would become *Comédia Balletica* and Le Clercq, by that time a spirited SAB student, was performing in something else. Her mother, who Bolender would come to know well over the years, was with her. Edith Le Clercq reminded Bolender of many characters portrayed in the movies and on stage by Bette Davis and Tallulah Bankhead; she was tough and demanding and once, on tour in the early 1950s, when she was traveling with the company, she greeted Bolender at 7:30 in the morning when they had arrived at midnight the previous day with "Well, you look like a boiled owl."[57] Bolender was more amused than insulted.

Le Clercq, like Bolender, was a founding member of Ballet Society, where at 17 she originated Choleric in *The Four Temperaments,* tearing up the stage of the Needle Trades High School Auditorium with adolescent fury. In Balanchine's *Orpheus,* she was a different kind of fury and well on the road to becoming the choreographer's muse-in-chief.

Le Clercq's ability to absorb quickly what choreographers wanted her to do combined with her physical equipment (short waist; long, powerful legs)and her Gallic intelligence, musicality, wit, and daring meant she was a choreographer's dream come true. Small wonder that Bolender, who had used her in his first ballet for television, *The Wild, Wild West,* and made her the centerpiece of *Image in the Heart* in 1949, wanted to make a new work on her for the 1956 tour. The choreographic competition, however, was acute: by that time, she was married to Balanchine and was a principal muse as well as a principal dancer. Robbins, too, was deeply in love with her, if not sexually, then as a dancer and offstage playmate.

Bolender had begun dancing with Le Clercq a decade earlier, in 1945, when he partnered her and another SAB student in a school showcase performance of Balanchine's *Symphonie Concertante* at Carnegie Hall. Two years later, he danced with her and Tallchief in the same ballet for Ballet Society, and throughout their careers with City Ballet, he was frequently paired with her in such Balanchine "novelties" as *Metamorphoses* and he often replaced Robbins in such ballets as *Bourrée Fantasque* when Robbins was working elsewhere. The pleasure both artists took in dancing together was manifest in the "In the Inn" section of *Ivesiana.* When he was asked what it was like to perform with her in *The Concert,* Bolender said, "That would take pages. She was such an inspiration to dance with."[58]

Le Clercq, as John Anderson had spotted in 1935, was a born performer; she instinctively knew how to hold an audience in the palm of her hand. Bolender said, "She didn't ever dance badly, because she had such a marvelous stage presence, she could cover up crappy performances."[59] In 1956, he recalled, they were the last ones on stage one night in Venice. "We had done *Bourrée Fantasque* and we were taking our bows at the end and the audience simply would not stop applauding. Tanny made a lovely little bow and said, 'Too-de-loo, we'll be back.' I don't think anyone understood a word she said. . . . She was great fun to dance with. . . . She'd make mistakes and say, 'Don't tell George.'"[60]

Like American Ballet Caravan's 1941 tour of South America, City Ballet's 1956 European journey was government funded, this time by the United States Information Agency. It was nothing like as grueling—for one thing, transportation was infinitely more reliable—but a look at both the programming and the schedule reveals an extremely demanding repertory with few opportunities for rest, let alone sightseeing.

While they spent enough time in Berlin for Barbara Milberg to get in trouble by crossing into East Berlin for a few hours, their longest stays were in Vienna (seven days) and Stockholm (eight days); the rest ranged from one night to four or five. Bolender, no longer in the first flush of youth, was dancing in *The Four Temperaments, Bourrée Fantasque, Fanfare, Pied Piper, Souvenirs, Interplay,* and *Western Symphony.* Le Clercq, who, according to one friend, had not wanted to go on the tour at all because she was feeling tired and run down, was performing, often with Bolender, in *Bourrée, Pied Piper, The Four Temperaments, Interplay,* and *Western Symphony* and in *Faun, Swan Lake,* and *La Valse.* And, just as in South America, there were many embassy and consulate receptions for the company, where making an appearance was not optional.

By the time they reached Copenhagen the last week in October, Le Clercq was feeling extremely ill. As Bolender remembered it, "Just before we went on stage [one] night, Tanny was standing in the wings and she was in agony, she was cramping, and she said she didn't think she could dance. I said to her come on, let's pretend we're on a beautiful beach, we'll have a wonderful time, and she went on stage and did wonderfully, and it was [one of] the last times she danced."[61]

It took a while for her to be diagnosed, during which time Balanchine and her mother, who, fortunately, had come along on the tour, barely left her side. She was replaced in *Swan Lake* and other roles; Bolender taught company class. Initially she was thought to have spinal meningitis, a death sentence in those days, but by the time the company left for Stockholm, the equally dire diagnosis of polio had been made and that most fully alive dancer was fighting for her life.

In stunned silence, the dancers checked out of their hotel and quietly got on the ferry for Malmö, taking the train from there for Stockholm. Each received a letter from the army informing them they could be vaccinated in Hamburg before flying home; Bolender remembered them being vaccinated in Sweden. According to *Dance Magazine,* the Salk vaccine was sent by air to Stockholm from the United States embassy in Berlin.[62] Many of the dancers had been vaccinated in New York before departing on tour, but Le Clercq had declined, fearing a reaction that would interfere with her dancing.

There was much speculation as to how Le Clercq contracted polio, including several accounts of her recklessness in Venice, where, on a gondola ride, she is said to have dipped her fingers in the filthy Grand Canal and then licked them to see if the water was salt or fresh. A local guest at one of the embassy parties came down with the disease shortly after the festivities; some thought Le Clercq had contracted it there. Balanchine blamed himself for casting her as a polio victim in a little ballet to raise money for the March of Dimes several years before; *Dance Magazine* took the opportunity to publish a reading list headed "What You Need to Know About Polio" in the same issue in which they announced Le Clercq's illness.

The valiant City Ballet dancers continued their performances in Stockholm and returned to the United States in mid-November without their director, who stayed by Le Clercq's side in Copenhagen for several months.

Her flashing legs trapped in an iron lung, unable to use her right hand to hold a book or write a letter, Le Clercq acknowledged gifts from her friends and family by dictating thank-you notes to her mother. Bolender received one of the earliest, shortly after the company returned to New York:

Blegdanes Hospitalet
Nov. 15 [1956]

Dear TootlesiePoodlesie—alias Puce, Pussy Piston
and a Snapping Garter, also one hell of a lousy S.P.

Edith is writing this for me as I can't use my hand—After the
opening salutation, she is looking very odd.

I want to thank you and John for the basket of roses—It was
one of the first that arrived and I had it right next to my bed and I
cried when I read who sent them—Today the butterfly came—It is a
beautiful butterfly and I can always paint on [it] a Derby and horrid
rimmed spectacles.

Everybody says I'm doing very well so I suppose I am. But it's
one of those things the patient never notices—The way I look at
it: I'm still flat on my back so my skin kills me and I've got a thing
pumping air—I'm lucky as I have full use of my left hand, so I can
read books—small ones—Guess that's about it.

Love to you both
Tansy

P.S. [from Edith Le Clercq] There's nothing I can add to this note
except to say she is the bravest human I've ever seen.[63]

The salutation can be read as a summary of Le Clercq and Bolender's relationship, onstage and off: Bolender's nickname in the company for many
years was Toddles; Le Clercq's was Tanny but perhaps Tansy for special
friends like Bolender. Puce was the made-up name that Robbins gave Bolender when setting *Age of Anxiety,* and the Snapping Garter has to refer to
Bourrée Fantasque and possibly *Western Symphony* and "one hell of a lousy
S.P." to the terrible *Still Point* she had reached, where, T. S. Eliot notwithstanding, there was no dance.

8

Balanchine did not return to City Ballet for nearly a year. Had it not been for the roll-up-your-sleeves-and-get-to-work-attitude of Kirstein, who did not expect him to come back, and the devastated dancers, who were willing to do whatever it took to keep their company alive without him, City Ballet might have closed its doors for good.

Bolender and Reed were two of those dancers. Bolender performed less and helped run the company, scheduling rehearsals, casting ballets, helping with programming, choreographing and teaching. He was an integral part of a dedicated group of people, headed by Kirstein, that included ballet master Vida Brown and Edward Bigelow. In June 1957, he took on an additional assignment in connection with celebrations of Stravinsky's 75th birthday. At Balanchine's request, he restaged *Renard* for the Boston Arts Festival, dancing the title role himself, with Francisco Moncion as the Rooster, Herbert Bliss as the Cat, and John Mandia as the Ram. Stravinsky acolyte Robert Craft conducted the Boston Symphony Orchestra.

When Reed came out of what she later called the first of her retirements, the New York press met her return to the stage with many verbal fanfares. "A Joyful Comeback" proclaimed the headline on Walter Terry's column in the *New York Herald Tribune* on February 3, 1957. "Sunbeam of Ballet Back to Shine on City Center," staff writer Carol Taylor announced in the *New York World Telegram* ten days later. Above the headline was a photograph of Reed, her smile wide, her eyes crinkled at the corners, holding up a pair of pointe shoes with ribbons dangling, ready to go.

The fanfares were a bit after the fact. The "sunbeam" had actually performed in the company's winter season as guest artist in *Serenade*, *Pied Piper*, and other ballets she had long been associated with. In Le Clercq's absence, she was very much needed to fill out the roster of principal dancers. Technically and physically, Reed was a very different dancer from Le Clercq. There was no question of replacing Le Clercq, but throughout Reed's career she had been a box-office draw. Critics, Terry among them, loved her, as did audiences all across the continent, from the smallest towns in her native Oregon to the country's largest cities.

Reed had taken an indefinite leave of absence from the company at the end of 1954 for a number of reasons. She was 38, several years beyond the customary age in those days for a ballet dancer to stop performing, and the twenty years she had been dancing professionally had taken their physical toll. Not only did her feet hurt from the brutal treatment all feet receive from pointe shoes (Bolender once referred to them as "that agony men don't have to go through"[1]), she was in a persistent state of exhaustion and engaged in an ongoing fight with anemia, caused in part by inadequate nutrition during her Depression-era childhood, not to mention the bad food (sometimes no food) she consumed while on tour with Ballet Theatre during World War II. At some point, her son, Reed Erskine, remembered, she was diagnosed with Addison's disease, whose symptoms include body aches, fatigue, low blood sugar, and depression, and he also recalled his father giving her injections of Vitamin B-12. Erskine had strong childhood memories, too, of having to tiptoe around their elegantly appointed apartment on East 57th Street when City Ballet was in season because his beautiful, sparkling mother "would spend the day before an evening performance resting up."[2]

Summing it up for Taylor, Reed said her career had ceased to give her "[any] of three compensations—artistic satisfaction, money, or fame. I was just not well enough to derive artistic satisfaction from my work."[3] And while she had certainly achieved more fame than she thought she had, City Ballet salaries, even for principals, had to be supplemented: in Bolender's case by teaching and choreographing and in Reed's by teaching and by her husband's unreliable earnings from the sale of antiques and his services as an interior designer. Spending more money on maintaining her body than she made as a dancer (or nearly as much) offended her thrifty principles and provided further impetus to leave the stage. Not that she ever abandoned the task: she was a follower of Joe Pilates, who her son described as "a cigar chomping Greek with weird contraptions. She was very much into that."[4] Pilates's last name was indeed Greek, but the German-born kinesthesiologist had emigrated to the United States in the mid-1920s and opened a studio on the Upper West Side of Manhattan. There, many dancers, including Balanchine, had become dedicated to an exercise program that can most easily be described as a combination of ballet and yoga, emphasizing the body alignment of the former and the breath of the latter. Reed continued this practice for the rest of her life.

Personal matters had also led to her departure from City Ballet: like any working mother of the period, Reed was pulled constantly between family demands and professional activities, touring among them. Sometimes she took her young son along, but even then she had no time to help him with his homework, read him to sleep at night, or correct his table manners: by dinnertime, she was in the theater, making up her face and warming up her muscles. Dancing disrupted the family life she had craved since childhood, and she felt deprived.

During her two years off stage, Reed took acting lessons and continued to hunt for antiques for the Obelisk, her husband's shop on Manhattan's Upper East Side. She also taught ballet in summer programs at SAB and at her old school in Portland, Oregon, while visiting her mother in the summer of 1956. It wasn't all work and no play: she and her husband hosted many parties in their beautiful apartment overlooking the East River. But it was an expensive life style, and the Erskine family ultimately needed her City Ballet salary to maintain it.

As for the lack of artistic satisfaction, after *Western Symphony* and *Ivesiana*, both of which premiered in 1954, Balanchine had showed no signs of making any more "somethings" for the intellectually curious Reed, who had told an interviewer in San Francisco that she had moved from Ballet Theatre to City Ballet in the latter's second season because she got bored when she wasn't learning new things. The role of the Countess in John Butler's ballet *The Unicorn, the Gorgon and the Manticore*, which had its City Ballet premiere on January 15, 1957, at City Center, provided an aesthetic incentive for her to return, in part because it gave her an opportunity to learn a new way of dancing, since Butler's movement vocabulary was infused with José Limón's traditional modern style and Doris Humphrey's technique. In developing the character, she would also contribute her considerable—and rare—talent as a ballet comedian.

There was considerable negotiation with Butler before the ballet could be programmed. *Unicorn* had premiered at the Library of Congress the previous year, with the choreographer's own company dancing it. Butler had infuriated Balanchine by demanding that one of his own dancers perform in the work. (Reed, Arthur Mitchell, Roy Tobias, Nicholas Magallanes, and Eugene Tanner ultimately were cast in the lead roles.) Writing from Copenhagen to Betty Cage, Balanchine pungently expressed his displeasure with Butler's arrogance. "Now about Butler: he should be very grateful to do this choreography for us without dictating his terms. If he is not satisfied with our dancers then we don't want him either. (Who the Hell he thinks he is?)"[5]

Even so, in Balanchine's view, *Unicorn* would be better than Edward Caton's ballet *Sebastian,* a highly melodramatic work also set to a score by Menotti, also under consideration for the company's first season with no new work by its director. "Please no 'Sebastian,'" Balanchine wrote. "It is the most dreadful ballet, lousy music, stinking story—better nothing than that. I don't like Cranko idea either. Don't spend money on that junk. Let Todd do his Poulenc ballet."[6]

On the whole, the critics had a lukewarm reaction to Butler's tale of a spoiled countess; a poet dreaming of a unicorn, representing youth; a gorgon standing in for manhood; and a manticore symbolizing old age. It ends with the poet's death. Their assessment of Reed's performance, however, was nothing of the kind, especially Terry's.

> As the Countess in the new "The Unicorn, the Gorgon and the Manticore," [Reed's] comedy timing is nothing short of masterful, her phrasing of a sequence of gesture is as clear as speech and more eloquent than words and the varied colorings she brings to movements designed to mirror fury or pettishness or greed or coquetry are as hypnotic as the prisms in a kaleidoscope.[7]

Bolender's Poulenc ballet, *The Masquers,* premiered a week later and was even less successful, despite a cast that included d'Amboise and Hayden, dancers the choreographer had been working with consistently since *The Miraculous Mandarin.* Like *The Still Point* (in which d'Amboise and Hayden continue to shine in a film of the concluding pas de deux), *The Masquers* was originally made for the Ryder-Frankel company, but unlike the earlier work it did not transfer easily or successfully to a classically trained company.

Poulenc's *Sextet for Wind Instruments and Piano Sextet for Wind Instruments and Piano,* much as Bolender loved the "tinny, bangy sound of it," turned out to be the wrong music for Frankel's complicated scenario, with its shifts from puppetry to real people. It looked much more melodramatic as a ballet than it had as a modern piece, and that, both for Bolender and the critics, spoiled it. Francia Russell, who was in the cast, recalled that Bolender got frustrated with both the dancers and his own failure to make the choreography gel with the music. "[He] lost his sense of humor, it was an unhappy time for him," she said.[8] Bolender admitted as much to Reynolds: with Balanchine gone, his administrative duties plus the work he had committed himself to making for other companies (not only the Ryder-Frankel organization, but also the Metropolitan Opera, for which he staged *L'Elisir d'Amore*'s incidental dances in 1956) meant that he had too much on his mind to solve *The Masquers'* many problems. "It wasn't the right time [for me] to be doing a ballet," he said. "I didn't have Balanchine's energy."[9] Or his speed. There are countless descriptions from dancers of Bolender's slow process in the studio. Edward Villella reports in his autobiography that when Bolender was choreographing *Creation of the World*, the dancers, particularly Villella's girlfriend, got bored while Bolender was figuring out the next step and started chatting among themselves. "Anyone who doesn't want to be in this ballet can leave," Bolender said, and out the door Villella's girlfriend went.[10] Moreover, while he had begun to wind down his career as a dancer, he was still very much needed to perform his roles in *Pied Piper, The Four Temperaments, Western Symphony, Symphony in C, The Concert, Fanfare,* and *Souvenirs:* rehearsals and performances undoubtedly diminished his time and focus as a choreographer.

One critic so disliked *The Masquers* that he ended his review with a plea for Balanchine's return. Martin, however, thought the ballet's beginning was some of the best work Bolender had done to date, writing in the *Times* that "[his] notable achievement lies in its having retained much of the expressiveness of its modern dance origins in its translation into ballet terms. Its first section, indeed, is by all odds the most interesting and creative thing Mr. Bolender has yet done, and may well point the way to his true métier as a choreographer."[11]

Hering weighed in on both new ballets in the March issue of *Dance Magazine*, citing Bolender as the only dramatic choreographer developed by City Ballet in its ten-year history. "Although he is a man of deep sensitivity," she wrote, "the quality of his work varies more widely than necessary. The fact that he occasionally becomes mired in sentimentality could probably be tempered by a more consistently interested management. Certainly a choreographer who is capable of a fine spun ballet like *The Still Point* could have found a similar discipline in his new work. As it was, the *Masquers* turned out to be a ballet tabloid. Its story of a girl who lost her life through fidelity to a cad and the cad's regeneration then guilt did not elicit compassion."[12]

Bolender agreed: "I got sucked away with the tear-jerker," he told Reynolds.[13] Given his experience with Balanchine's interference with *The Filly*, however, it is doubtful that he would have welcomed suggestions from Balanchine had he been present. By that time, he was perfectly capable of saying no to something he didn't think would work, and he had actually done so when Balanchine suggested that a jewel theft be part of *Souvenirs*.

While Hering found the opening, in which d'Amboise's "cad" kicks Hayden's "girl," disturbingly literal, she thought it the most effective part of the ballet. And she commended Bolender's "rare capacity to evoke emotionally open performances from his dancers. Hayden was touching in her impalpable role. Jacques d'Amboise added a new dimension of strength to his acting range." In a pointed comparison between *The Masquers* and *Unicorn*, she added, "Mr. Bolender's sentimentality was marred by literalness. Gian Carlo Menotti's was inflated by pretense." She blamed the composer and not the choreographer for the work's failures: "Menotti doesn't understand the expressive potential of dance. Butler contributed movement rather than having it grow from a central creative point."[14]

Hering did not fault the dancing in either work; she had high praise for Reed and Tobias in *Unicorn*, who were "good as crass society members." And, in the same review, she cited Reed's return to *Filling Station* as "the inebriated debutante alternately sagging into her partner's arms and flying blithely about the stage."[15]

The Rich Girl in *Filling Station* didn't bear much resemblance to the temperamental Countess in Butler's *Unicorn*, but it's no surprise that Reed gave masterful, fine-tuned performances as both. In 1978, the dancer who had originated roles in American stagings of *Swan Lake* and *Coppélia*, in Robbins's *Fancy Free*, and in Balanchine's postwar *Ivesiana* told Tobi Tobias she had done *Unicorn* as an "offbeat thing" and that no matter what she was dancing, she "was always very aware of the audience. I was *there* to amuse, entertain, amaze also not forgetting that I was enjoying the process, but I was thinking of my audience too."[16]

It took a lot of work and a good deal of thought to appear as freely spontaneous as Reed succeeded in doing on stage, especially in comic roles. The acting lessons she took with Wynn Handman during her leave of absence probably helped her develop the character of the Countess in Butler's ballet, although she had had some experience in playing bored aristocrats in Agnes de Mille's *Tally-Ho* when she was dancing with Ballet Theatre. Arguably, Hortense, the Queen of the Swamp Lilies in Ruthanna Boris's *Cakewalk* also satirized a certain kind of parvenu aristocratic snootiness.

"Janet never forgot her schtick," Russell said of her performance in *Western Symphony*, which ended with Reed winking broadly at the audience from a fish-dive position.[17] In *Souvenirs*, in which she made her debut as the Woman in April 1957 in Chicago, she used her face and body so effectively, in the same way as the beloved silent film stars of her youth had, that Bolender felt she was the best of them all. That was saying something, given the rave reviews Irene Larsson, who originated the role, had garnered. Jillana, Yvonne Mounsey, and Marian Horosko also slinked and stalked their seductive ways through the part, each of them approaching it from a different point of view. Horosko, who left City Ballet when the company moved to the New York State Theater at Lincoln Center because she felt the ethos of the company would change, interpreted the Woman as seriously seductive and somewhat vulnerable, differing with Reed's send-up of a combination of Gloria Swanson and Theda Bara.

The Chicago program also included *The Still Point*, giving the *Chicago American*'s dance critic Ann Barzel an opportunity to put both ballets in the context of Bolender's body of work to date. "This young choreographer's talents encompass a diversity of interests," she wrote.

> His past accomplishments include *Comédia Balletica*, an exercise in classical movement, and *Miraculous Mandarin*, a horror ballet with psychopathic undertones.
>
> His two current works are just as unlike. *Still Point* is a portrayal of inner despair; *Souvenirs* is a comic strip in motion. . . . The most enticing portrait is of a vamp, played to the hilt by Janet Reed.
>
> This was Miss Reed's first performance of the role, but the little charmer had the ballet going her way as soon as she was on stage. Her big scene was an outragious [sic] parody of Theda Bara.[18]

Balanchine returned to City Ballet the following fall and tackled *Agon*, making a role for Bolender in which he capitalized on every ounce of Bolender's training (in both ballet and modern dance), musical intelligence, and frank, open American attitude toward dancing and everything else.

The jazzy, wit-laced work premiered at the end of November, and was a success with both audiences and critics, much to Kirstein's surprise. Edward Villella, who understudied Bolender, wrote of the event, "I have never, *ever* heard such screams and shouts of approval before or after. It was truly unbelievable."[19] City Ballet's audience, by the end of 1957, was accustomed to seeing such nonnarrative, stripped-down works as *The Four Temperaments* and hearing such unmelodic music as Charles Ives's songs for *Ivesiana,* but neither of those ballets had elicited that kind of applause. Like them, *Agon* has no perceptible narrative; the costumes are City Ballet's black-and-white practice-clothes "uniform," the set is the standard blue cyclorama, and the music is difficult to follow for everyone concerned. But Balanchine and Stravinsky, who had begun working together on the project several years earlier, produced a masterpiece of American ballet, and urban American ballet at that. Into the work they packed much of what had attracted them to the United States in the first place: speed, energy, fearlessness, casual wit, jazzy rhythms, and urban edge, with music and choreography that were both laced with devil-may-care humor. The City Center audience recognized it immediately as an expression of their time and place, albeit a timeless one, and cheered the kinetic, competitive energy that makes it the quintessential New York City ballet.

For Villella, who had just returned to the company following a four-year absence and felt considerable dismay when he learned he would understudy Bolender in the musically complex work (he found the score difficult to adjust to and some of the choreography awkward to perform), "one factor worked in [his] favor, almost subconsciously. *Agon* was a wholly American work, a representation of the new classicism, and as an American the style of the movements readily, almost instinctively suited me."[20]

The style suited Bolender, too, although he was a very different kind of American from the New York–born, machismo-driven Villella. "Todd Bolender's easy wit and charm in the first pas de trois in *Agon* seem unrecapturable," Robert Garis wrote in his entry on the company in the *International Encyclopedia of the Dance.*[21] A performance filmed in Montreal in 1960, when Bolender had been dancing the role for several years, supports

Edwin Denby's opening-night description of him as "walk[ing] a Sarabande, elaborately coiled and circumspect. It recalls court dance as much as a cubist still life recalls a pipe or guitar. The boy's timing looks like that of a New York Latin in a leather jacket. And the cool lift of his wrong-way-round steps and rhythms gives the nonsense so apt a turn people begin to giggle."[22]

The "easy wit" was part of Bolender's persona, on stage and off. The timing took a lot more work, not only for Bolender but for all concerned, consuming many hours of rehearsal for everyone to get it right. The making of *Agon* has been well documented by a number of people, among them Villella, who describes in his autobiography how the atmosphere in the studio changed with Stravinsky's presence at rehearsals; Bernard Taper, a biographer of Balanchine; Bolender in countless interviews; and Barbara Milberg Fisher, who danced the first trio with him; and Barbara Walczak. Fisher recalled:

> On this November day, Balanchine has been rehearsing the First Pas de Trois for Todd, Basia, and me. The Gailliard for the two women follows Todd's solo, a kooky Sarabande that exploits Bolender's personal idiom as effectively as did the "Phlegmatic" variation in Hindemith's *Four Temperaments*. But this dance is exquisitely tailored to suit a cocky postmodern attitude, not a medieval humour.[23]

That "cocky postmodern" attitude, according to Bolender, was expressed in movement that was angular throughout, not just in the pas de trois. The three dancers were to rehearse it multiple times, long after the ballet had been completed, Bolender told Francis Mason in 1989. "Balanchine seemed never to tire of rehearsing [it] and often up to curtain time would have us repeat it many times, nor did I ever get weary of dancing it. Learning this[,] however[,] took a long time. But then once I learned to dance a role in one of Balanchine's ballets, it was forever a pleasure."[24]

That's not particularly consistent with what Bolender had to say about *Agon* over the years in a number of interviews with different people. In a 2003 interview in Kansas City, he said "I loved the ballet but hated dancing it." One reason was that it gave him "terrible stage fright," an ailment he didn't mention very often. "[The Sarabande] was a most peculiar variation and also the pas de trois involved with it, which I never really liked, was choreographed poorly. It seems to me that it suddenly comes to a halt."[25] It's possible that

Balanchine was also dissatisfied with the pas de trois, or there wouldn't have been all those last-minute rehearsals. What seems to have caused Bolender the most anxiety, however, was the finale, in which the eight women and four men are all on stage, dancing like mad to music that is rhythmically so complicated that Russell told an interviewer they should have been carrying metronomes while they danced. As it was, each dancer counted the music differently and they were almost never together. Bolender particularly blamed Hayden for this:

> [She] used to drive me nuts. . . . I just said well here goes . . . whatever Milly would do I did, exactly. . . . She was like a steam-engine. . . . Once we all came on stage . . . it was just like hell bent for whatever. . . . When [she] and I finally came together just toward the end we do a little pas de deux . . . and Diana and Arthur were opposite us and we . . . the four of us came together at the center and every time we would do it she was always either one count later or one count earlier. . . . I had to go ta-dum with her. I had no choice . . . we almost never ended exactly together. If we did it was an accident.[26]

Bolender also laid some blame for the chaos at Balanchine's door. In a 1974 interview with Nancy Reynolds for *Repertory in Review,* in response to a question about the score, Bolender replied, "You know, I must say that I've always felt that one of the things a choreographer could do for [the dancers] is either sit them down with the score for example or give counts which are not necessarily for the music, but which work for the dancer's ear—he never, ever has done this—his counts would always be some peculiar kind of thing. [With *Agon*] . . . We'd get lost so often he'd finally go to the piano and say 'Why don't you start counting from here' and he'd figure out some kind of counts. . . . It never meant anything to me, those counts. If I didn't get the music in my ear, his counts were of no help. . . . It was agony for me sometimes, even in *Four Temperaments,* which was a fairly simple score, he gave some kind of counting that always screwed me up."[27]

Critical response was guardedly enthusiastic. In an article titled "*Agon:* Its Future Importance," Christina Brundage called it a novelty unified by intellectual form. "It does not take itself overly seriously," she wrote. "An undercurrent of sly gaiety underlies it. The style is sharp and biting, yet it has broad strength." But she wasn't sure it would last: "It makes ballet an aesthetic experience for the mind [as opposed to the frivolities of traditional classical works]. Perhaps it will be a turning point."[28]

Martin, reviewing the premiere for the *Times,* spoke of the difficulties of the music and commended the magnificent dancing. "The chief soloists are Melissa Hayden, Diana Adams, Todd Bolender and Arthur Mitchell, and they all deserve some kind of Congressional Medal," he wrote, adding that the rest of the cast was equally deserving.[29] Hering described "the designs grow[ing] the way a vine grows with an exploring grace of its own" and, Bolender's opinion notwithstanding, admired the first pas de trois, especially "the aware way in which Mr. Bolender modified his naturally loose-jointed style to match that of the girls." She also liked the way Bolender "mingled wit and quiet authority" in the Sarabande.[30]

Bolender was less impressed with his own performance than the critics. He said he never really had the time he needed to develop his role because it came so late in his career as a dancer. By the end of 1957, when *Agon* premiered, he was already well embarked on a post-performing career as teacher, choreographer, and director that would take him all over the world. Between 1958 and 1962, when he left City Ballet, Bolender was a whirling dervish of activity, not dancing much but on the move in other ways he hoped would sustain him both practically and aesthetically when he could no longer bend that supple body to his or Balanchine's or any other choreographer's will.

In March, when City Ballet embarked for Tokyo, the first stop on an extensive tour of Asia and Australia, Bolender, according to a news item in *Dance Magazine,* stayed behind to work on an unnamed Broadway musical. That was *Time Remembered,* directed by Albert Marre, with whom Bolender began forging a long-term relationship after Kirstein appointed the latter director of the City Center theater program. *Time Remembered* was the musical version of a lighthearted period piece by Jean Anouilh that starred Helen Hayes and Richard Burton. *New York Times* critic Brooks Atkinson commended Marre for "[ingeniously combining] loveliness and drollery, piling magnificence so high it becomes funny,"[31] words that could just as easily have been written about *Souvenirs,* suggesting that Bolender wielded some influence on the production. The play was nominated for five Tonys; Hayes received one for Best Actress.

In the same period, Bolender also provided choreography for Marre's *At the Grand* (a musical based on the film *Grand Hotel*), which premiered in Los Angeles, had a brief run in San Francisco, and never made it to New York. The film's ballerina character was transformed into an opera diva, in part because Joan Diener, who Marre had recently married, was more comfortable singing than dancing. Evidently this was not considered an improvement on the original story, and Bolender did not have much to do.

He had other compelling reasons not to go on City Ballet's first tour of Asia and Australia. In January, Robbins, also on leave from City Ballet, began auditions for Ballets: U.S.A., a new company he would launch in Spoleto, Italy, in June, at the first Festival of Two Worlds, which Menotti founded. These became de facto rehearsals and continued throughout the spring. Bolender's involvement took two forms: he appeared as guest artist in *The Concert*, wielding his butterfly net and chomping on his cigar as the Husband, and he reworked his 1945 *Comédia Balletica*, renamed *Games*, a far less pretentious and more accurate title than the one Denham had bestowed on the ballet when he took it into the Ballet Russe repertory. Of Bolender's participation, columnist Leo Lerman wrote in *Mademoiselle* magazine, "In order to give festival goers a more comprehensive view of American dance Robbins has invited Todd Bolender."[32] The feature was illustrated with a collage of photographs of festival artists, most of which are head shots. A performance shot of Bolender in *Western Symphony* forms the centerpiece, however, a clever reminder that throughout most of the twentieth century, there was no more compelling symbol of the United States abroad than the cowboy of popular culture.

Robbins needed a classical piece as a curtain raiser to "represent ballet," Bolender told Deborah Jowitt, and while *Comédia Balletica* had received mixed reviews from various critics when the Ballet Russe did it, audiences had loved it, in part because the dancers, including the choreographer, had performed it with the playful commitment it required. The Ballets: U.S.A. dancers may have had the commitment, but what they didn't have was the training. "In order to represent ballet you have to have everything there that's right, including the dancers. [These] were not ballet dancers," Bolender told Jowitt, "and consequently there was no elegance to what they were doing."[33] That was not entirely true: while many of the dancers were not primarily ballet dancers, John Mandia and Barbara Milberg, both City Ballet dancers whose classical training was unimpeachable, were part of the *Games* cast. They also danced in Robbins's ballets, which included *After-*

noon of a Faun and the tour's hands-down hit, *NY Export: Opus Jazz*, which premiered in Spoleto and has endured into the twenty-first century. Arguably, *NY Export* is to the Robbins repertory what *Agon* is to Balanchine's, a less refined, tough-minded expression of Manhattan's exuberant grit. It was so successful that it got Ballets: U.S.A. a Broadway season that fall, followed by a national tour that was cut short by skimpy ticket sales.

Games was dropped from the repertory after the European tour (the company also performed in Florence and other Italian cities and at the Brussels World's Fair) and Bolender did not revive it for Kansas City Ballet. Ever the realist, Bolender felt strongly that the piece should have been pulled from the festival repertory after opening night, when it was especially badly danced, in part because Sondra Lee, who had performed prominent roles in Robbins's musicals, was injured.

Offstage, Bolender and everyone else had a very good time in Spoleto. The accommodations were less than luxurious, but the city is charming and the food and drink were wonderful. Photographs Bolender and Milberg took of an outré costume party Robbins himself threw indicate a festival atmosphere whether they were working or not.

For Bolender, who danced in every performance of *The Concert* and at least part of the time in *NY Export*, this wasn't exactly a holiday, but it was certainly a break from an extremely hardworking period in New York. Not only had he been preparing for the Ballets: U.S.A. appearances and assisting Marre with two musicals, he had also been choreographing for Robert Joffrey's fledgling company and continuing his collaboration with Emily Frankel, who, he said decades later, was extremely supportive in what was a transitional period of his professional life.

Like Robbins, Joffrey needed a ballet that would help set the company's classical tone and round out the repertory for a national tour that began in January. Set to Mozart's Sonata for Two Pianos in D Major, *Whirligig* premiered in New York at the Brooklyn Academy of Music in March. Sasha Anawalt has characterized it as "a straightforward let's-show-off-the-company piece, with the dancers in Greek tunics or sweatpants playfully jiving to Mozart."[34] Hering, however, reviewing for *Dance Magazine*, found it marred by "conventionality. It is to Mr. Bolender's credit," she continued, "that despite his longtime contact with Balanchine he was willing to attempt an abstract dance to Mozart. But its brisk patterns seemed rather unrelated to Mozart's inherent courtliness."[35] This was not Bolender's first attempt to choreograph to Mozart: in 1946, he had used a small part of another two-piano sonata to make a pointe piece for Katherine Dunham, and in 1948, he had devised a piece he called *Sonata in A* for a program he put together for an evening of dance performed in a barn in Southbury, Connecticut, which he later revived for a repertory evening at the 92nd Street YMHA with a new title, *Seraglio.*

A few days before Bolender departed for Italy, the Ryder/Frankel Dance Drama Company opened a six-week season at the 92nd Street YMHA, giving his *Romeo and Juliet* its New York premiere. The company had been touring since the first of the year with Frankel and Ryder, whose marriage was coming apart, telling the story of Shakespeare's star-crossed lovers in an extended pas de deux in which Bolender said, with some pride, he "had gone from A to Z" and back again in less than twenty minutes, the length of the overture of Tchaikovsky's work by the same title.

Both Lillian Moore and Hering reviewed it in separate issues of *Dance Magazine.* The former, who must have seen it on tour, found the story much too compressed. In addition, despite a narration by actor John Cullum, she complained that viewers who were unfamiliar with the story would not have known what was going on. Hering, writing after the New York premiere, had no complaints, calling the duet "an exquisite piece, moving tenderly and tempestuously through the Tchaikovsky music; depicting the lovers as if they were ensnared in a vast dream."[36] While she was dismissive of Ryder's performance as Romeo, mentioning only his fencing skills, Frankel received high praise for her "strong and fragile" interpretation of Juliet. Those qualities were equally apparent in her performance in *The Still Point,* which was also on the program; they were part of the reason she was effectively Bolender's muse for twenty years. He made his last piece for her in 1970, a gut-wrenching solo titled *Elektra,* set to part of Hans Werner's *Fifth Symphony,* which she first performed at the Hong Kong Festival in 1972.

Bolender was still absent from the company roster, performing with Ballets: U.S.A. on Broadway, when Reed returned to City Ballet, in September 1958, to replace Vida Brown as ballet master. Brown, who Russell dubbed "that genius ballet master," was leaving her post to get married, although she would stay involved for several more years to stage Balanchine's ballets on other companies. Russell's first experience with Brown came right after she joined the company, in January 1956, when, "in the three weeks before the season started, [Brown] taught [her], Richard Rapp, and Joan van Orden virtually the entire rep for the spring season—just the four of us for hours and hours every day."[37] That would have been more than twenty ballets, some of them, such as *Symphony in C,* technically demanding; others, such as *Bourrée Fantasque,* requiring comedic skills as well.

It was Reed's potential to transfer her own comedic (and theatrical) skills to City Ballet's dancers that made Hering welcome her appointment: "[She is] an incomparable dancer actress. Given time Miss Reed will certainly do much to restore dramatic verity to [*Orpheus, Firebird, Swan Lake*] and other works."[38] In Hering's view, the first two, plus *Con Amore,* had deteriorated the most in the past few years. "And," she added, "she will form a colorful contrast to Balanchine's preoccupation with the more abstract elements of classic ballet." Reed, who had danced very well in such plotless ballets as *Serenade, Concerto Barocco,* and *Symphony in C,* didn't believe in labeling any ballet as abstract. "Dancers are people and people aren't abstract," she told Tobi Tobias in 1978.[39]

D'Amboise agreed with Hering's prediction in slightly different terms, commenting that Reed would supplement Balanchine's direction. "No one can project personality as a dancer like Janet," he said. "She already approaches people after a ballet and offers suggestions to improve their performances, maybe by holding their head differently during a jump or something like that."[40]

A photograph of Reed in *Dance Magazine,* her gaze intent on something the reader can't see, an unnamed dancer standing next to her, is captioned "previously a distinguished member of the company, this year [she] has become its ballet master. Among her duties is the very important one of directing and coaching dancers who are learning new roles."[41]

Casting is often cited as the most difficult duty ballet masters perform, but along with directing and coaching, they are responsible for a great deal more than that. They teach company class, schedule rehearsals, support choreographers in the studio, supervise photo shoots, and act as intermediaries between dancers and choreographers, all tasks that have implicit complications. All require a meticulous eye for detail, monumental patience, the organizational skills of the mother of seven children, a voracious appetite for hard work, and the ability to keep one's opinions to oneself when they conflict with the artistic director's. Reed possessed some of these qualities, but not all.

City Ballet was already a large organization when it celebrated its tenth anniversary with an active repertory of roughly two dozen ballets (and a dozen more that could have been remounted at any time) and a company of fifty dancers, give or take. That's a lot of ballets and performers for a ballet master to care for, and Reed didn't do it alone. Una Kai, who had been dancing with the company since Ballet Society and had assisted Brown on the tour to Asia and Australia, continued to be associate ballet master and to perform in a number of ballets, although not as many as she wished. (She suspected that Reed did not cast her in some performances because she needed her more as associate ballet master.)[42] John Taras, who, according to one witness, made sure the office was nicely decorated and didn't do much else, was also a ballet master. The three met weekly with Balanchine and Betty Cage, principally for the purpose of making casting decisions. Reed was also responsible for scheduling rehearsals in several studios, a time-consuming, complex task for which many twenty-first-century ballet masters use computer software.

Some ballet masters are holy terrors. Reed, by some accounts, was one of them. There are a number of horror stories about her candor in giving corrections, her failure to work in the studio on a technical problem a particular dancer was having before she went on stage, and a general lack of tact in dealing with individual sensitivities. A very young Suzanne Farrell made her debut with the company as a corps member on a bill that included Bolender's *Creation of the World* and Balanchine's *Stars and Stripes*. When she came off stage from the latter, Reed was waiting to pounce. According to Farrell, Reed told her that if she couldn't learn to do piqué turns better her days in the company would be numbered.[43] Farrell was stricken, but later on, when Diana Adams could not dance a role Balanchine had made on her (Adams was in the early, precarious stages of pregnancy), Reed, joined by d'Amboise and "everyone around [Balanchine] at that time," persuaded him to "give [Farrell] a chance, let her do it."[44] The role was in *Movements for Piano and Orchestra*, and Adams, confined to her apartment, coached Farrell while lying on her living-room sofa.

There is no more hair-raising account of Reed as ballet master than Russell's recollection of being instructed to go bang her feet on a cement floor when she was in agonizing pain from numerous infected corns. "The idea was to get up on pointe and march around with vigor until my toes were numb" and she could no longer feel the pain. Russell was in rehearsal for a filming of *Apollo*, which the Canadian Broadcasting Company aired in 1960. She had been cast as Polyhymnia, her variation a vivid example of Balanchinean speed and reach. Russell danced it as one possessed, and as a result, was promoted to soloist, which in the long run made the agony worth it. "Janet *cared*," she said fiercely, "and that made it okay."[45]

It is unlikely that Reed intended to be cruel. She was herself extremely tough and driven, dancing when she didn't really feel up to it in order to hang on to her roles in her years with Ballet Theatre, performing when exhausted from anemia to keep her position with City Ballet, getting on with the job in the same way her ancestors had done when they settled the Oregon Territory. Psychically, if not physically, she was so strong, her daughter said, that it didn't even occur to her that others were not equally so.[46] Banging her feet against a cement floor is exactly what she would have done in similar circumstances, and throughout her career she squeezed her painfully bunioned toes into pointe shoes for performance after performance. Once she got onstage, she told an interviewer, "you sort of forget it and you don't really feel [the pain] until you get off."[47]

What she did recognize was ambition. Janice Cohen Adelson was dancing in the corps in 1956 when Balanchine made *Allegro Brillante*, one of his most technically difficult ballets. It had a cast of one principal couple and four others, and, he said, "contains everything I know about the classical ballet—in thirteen minutes."[48] Cohen, as she was then, longed, obsessively, to be cast in the joyous work, and on her own she learned every female corps role, and Reed knew that. One night, she was standing in the wings watching Balanchine and Reed doing some last-minute fine-tuning when one of the dancers tripped on a cable and injured her ankle. After a brief consultation with Balanchine, Reed came over to her and, once she confirmed that Cohen felt prepared to perform, told her to get into the costume. Sometimes, a ballet master can make a dancer's dream come true.

Since 1954, when Balanchine premiered his *Nutcracker*, auditioning and casting the children for their many roles in the ballet has been a major part of the ballet master's job in just about every classical company in the United States. For City Ballet in the late 1950s, Reed and Kai did this not only in New York for the home season but also in Washington, DC, and on annual summer visits to Los Angeles, where the company performed the cold-weather classic in addition to a mixed repertory in Hollywood's Greek Theater. This part of the job Reed enjoyed; she loved children and, according to Bolender, worked especially well with young boys. "She was a specific and clear teacher," he said, "and she made them feel important."

Her son was never a dancer, but a story he told about his first paying job, manipulating the bed that takes Clara and the Nutcracker Prince to the Kingdom of the Snow, illustrates Bolender's point about how well she worked with boys. Erskine was in his early teens when he made his debut with the bed.

I . . . vividly remember the first time under the bed as the Christmas tree grew and the tiny Nutcracker bed was whisked away and replaced by the big bed with me under it, waiting for my music cue to start the slow, magical tour of the stage with Clara aboard, and the cold sweat when I couldn't quite reconcile the counts, and then, from the wings, my mother's calm voice cuing me to start my stately crawl on padded knees, keeping an eye out for leftover wooden swords, dropped in the melee of the "mouse war," a clean-up essential before the "Snow-flakes" corps had to dance with those hazards underfoot.[49]

In 1959, *Dance Magazine* devoted a four-page spread to *Nutcracker* auditions in the Greek Theater's rehearsal hall, showing Reed in her element, demonstrating steps, smiling her stellar smile as she congratulated the chosen few (60 out of 500 children from local ballet schools), one of whom was John Clifford, who received the plum part of the Nutcracker Prince. While still in his teens, Clifford was taken into City Ballet as a corps member; he very soon became a principal and choreographic apprentice to Balanchine, much more formally identified as such than Bolender had been. Both men were among the choreographers who made work for the 1972 Stravinsky Festival, and Clifford danced in Bolender's *Piano-Rag-Music*.

Reed's approach to adult, professional dancers was rather different. With them, she was forthright and direct, and as someone who had been a star attraction throughout her dancing career, she definitely did not have the self-effacing personality that many successful ballet masters possess. Moreover, possibly because she had never danced in the corps—not in San Francisco or with Ballet Theatre or City Ballet—she wasn't particularly good at coaching its members. Bolender thought crowds of people flustered her, but he considered her an excellent coach of individual dancers. On one of her curriculum vitae, she took credit for coaching, among others, d'Amboise, Villella, Allegra Kent, and Patricia McBride.

Balanchine would make many wonderful roles on McBride, but when she was first in City Ballet, he was more focused on another dancer who entered the company at the same time, singling her out to demonstrate when he taught, giving her much more attention. Reed, however, was extremely interested in McBride, who was young and vulnerable, just as she had been when she started her training with Willam Christensen in Portland, and she kept a protective eye on her. She was aware of Balanchine's irritation with McBride for an error she had made in one of the first things she danced, although Balanchine never, by McBride's account, said anything to her about it. Reed advised her to do some outside performing when the company was on layoff, and, as it turned out, the additional experience on stage paid off. According to Reed, when she came back, "everything was fine. She could hold her own very nicely, but Balanchine [still didn't pay] much attention to her."[50] Reed kept "plugging" for her, as she put it, and she taught McBride her own roles in *Interplay* and the third movement of *Symphony in C*. One day she found her protégée standing in the wings, feeling very discouraged that Balanchine seemed to be ignoring her, and Reed had had enough. She went directly to her boss and told him he needed to talk to McBride, which she said he did right away, and shortly thereafter he made a solo role for the 17-year-old dancer in *Figure in the Carpet,* a "lost" Balanchine ballet that some of the original cast members still remember nostalgically. McBride danced with such clarity and speed that the ballerinas in the company were impressed, and her performance led to many more featured and principal roles, from Hermia in *A Midsummer Night's Dream* to Swanhilda in *Coppélia,* a ballet Balanchine and Danilova remounted in part for her in 1974 and with which she was identified for many years. She was frequently paired with Villella, starting with *Tarantella,* and with Mikhail Baryshnikov when he danced with City Ballet for one season. Robbins also created a number of roles for her. At a tribute to Robbins's ballerinas in 2011, McBride told Reed's daughter Jane Erskine that it was her mother who had made her career. Bolender cast her as Eve in 1960 in his *Creation of the World*.

Reed was ballet master at a time when Balanchine was making some extremely large-cast ballets. *Figure in the Carpet* was one of them, a none-too-subtle hint that the company was outgrowing its quarters at City Center. Moreover, the performance seasons were getting longer, which meant more paid work for the dancers, but the situation was also extremely tiring for the top tier. "One season, we were so up against it for ballerinas, because . . . the company wasn't big enough yet to have parts covered [and] dancers were injuring themselves," she said. "Balanchine became almost desperate to hire outside dancers, because good dancers from the School hadn't had time to develop into good soloists. I remember his wanting to hire some dancers from Europe and I was against it. It might have been easier for him to hire experienced dancers from other companies but it wouldn't have been as good for the company."[51] She cited McBride and Allegra Kent as examples of dancers Balanchine developed and, as an exception, her friend Violette Verdy as someone he took from outside, who "was already an established dancer and a wonderful addition to the company."

In her capacities as both dancer and ballet master, Reed understood Balanchine in very different ways from many of his muses and acolytes. She liked him and respected him, but she neither adored him nor followed him blindly. She was grateful indeed for the help he had given her when she was struggling to learn roles by herself at Ballet Theatre, especially the tricky footwork of the Ballerina in *Petrouchka*. She enjoyed dancing the parts she originated at City Ballet in *Bourrée Fantasque, Western Symphony,* and *À la Française* and the rather different role in the "Central Park in the Dark" section of *Ivesiana. Pas de Deux Romantique* was the exception, a humiliation for which she never really forgave him.

Reed was correct when she told Balanchine that she wasn't a "Balanchine ballerina" when he invited her into the company. The better part of her training was not at SAB, although she started taking class there virtually the minute she got to New York in 1942. She was 33, married, and had a child when she made the shift from Ballet Theatre to City Ballet, and she could not and would not give him the kind of wholehearted commitment he needed from the dancers who fed his creative soul. Her dedication to the art and her loyalty to him and the company were unquestionable, but his refusal to admit that he had been wrong to make technical demands on her she could not meet in *Pas de Deux Romantique* was probably the beginning of the contentiousness that characterized their relationship once she became ballet master.

"Balanchine never admitted a mistake," Reed said, remembering a time when a teenaged boy who had been appearing in City Ballet's productions in Los Angeles wanted to audition for the company. Balanchine agreed to have a look at him. "Before a performance, we went downstairs underneath the stage where there was a platform that we rehearsed on. The boy was scared to death and had not warmed up. Balanchine came up to him and said, 'Do a double air pirouette.' And the boy just jumped up in the air to do a double pirouette and came down with such a severe sprain I can't tell you. And Balanchine muttered [under his breath] something like 'I shouldn't have let him do that. He should have warmed up.'" The boy was still collapsed on the floor as Balanchine walked away without saying anything to him directly, leaving Reed to get ice and "put him back together again."[52]

Balanchine's inability to delegate also made it difficult for Reed to do her job as ballet master. Occasionally, Balanchine would ask her to do something he felt he couldn't handle, and she would happily agree. "But before I could even turn around, he was doing it himself. He would not let anybody take over. He would say to me, 'Oh, I'm too tired. You rehearse it.' I would start, and he'd be there like a shot. He wouldn't let me . . . [or] anybody . . . do something that he thought was his job—he wouldn't permit it. He wanted to be the only influence on his dancers." And he hated disagreements. Reed, however, was as uncompromising in her standards as she was in her work ethic. If she thought Balanchine was wrong about something she considered important, she considered it her duty to say so.

Reed left her post as ballet master in 1961 with no farewells from Balanchine, forced to make a choice, as so many women of her generation were, between family responsibilities and work that she loved, the difficulties of her relationship with Balanchine notwithstanding. "I couldn't carry on a double life, so I left. It was just one of those things. No good-bye, no nothing. Just, you're not there. But Kirstein thanked me. He said, 'I'm surprised you stayed as long as you did.'"[53]

Perhaps in part because Reed reminded Kirstein of Lydia Lopokova, a ballerina he had adored, he was deeply fond of her. He presented her with a beautiful Japanese print as a farewell gift, was instrumental in getting her a job in Seattle as founder of the Pacific Northwest Ballet School, and kept in touch with her until the end of his life.

· · ·

His Ballets: U.S.A. duties ended, Bolender returned to City Ballet for the winter season, a long one that ran from the end of November to the first of February 1959, and danced his usual roles in Balanchine's and Robbins's work. He performed very little in January, possibly because of an injury caused by the deep backbends Balanchine had choreographed for the Coffee variation in the 1954 *Nutcracker,* and the first part of the month was devoted to readying *Souvenirs* for a January 12 appearance on *The Bell Telephone Hour*'s "Adventures in Music" program.

Like *The Ed Sullivan Show, The Bell Telephone Hour* was a variety show, but its focus was on the arts. This particular broadcast included folksinger Harry Belafonte and a version of Camille Saint-Saëns's *Carnival of the Animals* performed by the Baird puppets and narrated by Shakespearean actor Maurice Evans. For *Souvenirs,* Gold and Fizdale played the two-piano version of Barber's score, and Bolender, who had been choreographing for the television camera since the early 1940s, compressed the ballet in several ways to make it suitable for the small screen and the omnibus format. The biggest change, though, arguably cut the heart from the work. The three wallflowers were reduced to one and the pas de deux with the dream lover—and the work's only classical dancing—was eliminated entirely. He also cut out the beach-scene finale and ended it with Reed, partnered by Roland Vasquez as the Gigolo, lying on the fainting couch, her seductive snarl matching the one on the tiger's head that was part of the period decor. An account of a rehearsal in a City Center studio published in the *New York Times* gives a vivid picture of the work that went into the transfer of *Souvenirs* from a fairly large proscenium space to the confines of a television sound stage. The writer focused his attention on Reed and Vasquez (both of whom he wrongly referred to as members of the corps de ballet) rehearsing the hesitation tango: "As Miss Reed continued to play the role of the seductress with Mr. Vasquez, they were being observed closely by choreographer Todd Bolender and Bill Colleran, director of the show. Bolender would interrupt the dancers. Once he advised Miss Reed just how to roll her eyes in the direction in which the camera would be standing when the show went on the air." Everyone, he reported, was having a good time. "Miss Reed and Mr. Vasquez, under the guidance of Mr. Bolender, were offering a comic caricature of a tango, Miss Reed was wriggling provocatively across the floor when she paused, the two dancers and the choreographer were laughing, they appeared to be enjoying the rehearsal."[54]

The company had a long layoff between February and May, when they had a four-week New York season, by which time Bolender was in London working on another Albert Marre show titled *The Love Doctor.* An engagement book in which he kept careful track of expenses and appointments, sometimes writing down brief opinions of performances he was seeing, tells the story of a frugal man who suddenly has enough money to buy some things he covets and some he needs in order to practice his profession as dancer and choreographer.

With a portion of the money he earned from *The Bell Telephone Hour* ($3,000, a fortune in those days and six times what he had received for *Comédia Balletica* sixteen years earlier), Bolender bought three drawings by James Rutledge, a Canton, Ohio, friend, for $30 on January 9, and a couple of weeks later made an $18 deposit on framing them. He was very much interested in visual art and in supporting his artist friends by collecting their work. Joan McCracken became a painter when she had to stop dancing because of diabetes, and a piece of hers remained a part of a personal collection that by the time Bolender died included a drawing by Paul Cadmus, some excellent Japanese prints, and several lovely Turkish mixed-media "cloud" paintings. His collaborations in Kansas City with visual artist Dale Eldred are some of the best ballets he ever made.

The *Souvenirs* fee also paid for a television set and hi-fi player, for a total of around $300, and $15 worth of vinyl recordings of percussion music and compositions by Burkhardt, Beethoven, and Milhaud, the last in preparation for *Creation of the World,* Bolender's last piece for City Ballet (at least until the 1972 Stravinsky Festival, for which he made two works), which premiered at City Center the following year. He also bought a piano on the installment plan, recording in his datebook that he paid ahead for several months because he was going to be out of the country. He did the same with his rent. On May 9, he departed for London on a British Overseas Airways Corporation flight at 11 p.m. He arrived at 1:30 p.m. (London time) the next day and checked in at an apartment hotel. That evening he had dinner with Marre, who had hired him to choreograph the dances for *The Love Doctor,* another of his musical costume dramas, this one based on Molière's medically oriented plays. (There were many, including *The Imaginary Invalid* and *The Doctor in Spite of Himself.*)

In early June, the research-oriented dance maker purchased medical catalogs in preparation for choreographing the play, and the following day he conducted auditions at London's Apollo Theater. In the evening, he went to a Ballet Rambert performance, judging Norman Morrice, who had a work on the program, to be a promising choreographer. Morrice was influenced by the "angry young men" in English theater who sought to dramatize ordinary lives. Like many American choreographers, including Bolender, Morrice approached choreography from that point of view. Sir Frederick Ashton, who Bolender counted among his friends and much of whose choreography he admired, disappointed him mightily a couple of days later with *Ondine,* a ballet based on a fairy tale. In a letter to Leo Lerman dated June 19, in which he was highly dismissive of British dance training, Bolender brought the columnist up to date on his activities, complaining that the *The Love Doctor* production was already behind schedule and describing his reactions to various performances he had seen. Of *Ondine,* he wrote, "Three long grisly acts . . . [and] not even the undulations of [Margot] Fonteyn as a fish could relieve the intolerable boredom." He assessed British theater in general as being "30 years behind the U.S." and found their "musical theater amateurish. I broke out in hives during the London production of *Irma la Douce*," he added. The only thing he liked, he told Lerman, who reported on theater for *Dance Magazine* throughout the 1950s, was a revival he saw of the "Purcell d'Avenant Shakespeare *Tempest.*"[55]

Bolender found considerably more joy in his purchase of an Austin Healey Sprite for £200 (on the installment plan)and transportation for the many sight-seeing trips he and Mandia took in it during their four-month stay in England.

The rehearsal process, which began on June 23, was fraught, as it often can be, but on June 30, Bolender received a check for $1,000 or, he noted, precisely, "three hundred forty seven point seventeen pounds," in compensation for the work and, implicitly, the grief involved. On the same day, he worked with the play's star, Ian Carmichael, at the New Theater, and that evening he attended a preview of *Once More with Feeling,* directed by Robert Morley, which he left after the first act. Ten days later, his own rehearsals were postponed for two weeks because Carmichael was ill.

The costumes, designed by Bernard Daydé, weren't ready until the middle of August, when Bolender saw them for the first time at Nathan's Costume Company on the evening of the 17th. "A hot session over the dancers' costumes," he noted. "Left Nathan's 10:30 pm."[56] After his experience with the Phlegmatic costume for *The Four Temperaments* in 1946, Bolender was insistent that costumes neither impede movement nor conceal the choreography. He had, after all, been a full participant in designing the costumes for *Souvenirs.*

The Love Doctor opened at the Piccadilly Theatre on October 12 and closed after sixteen performances on the 24th, by which time Bolender had returned to New York. "Beat from trip, stayed in bed," he wrote.[57] A week or so later he was back in class at SAB, getting in shape to dance in City Ballet's fall season, preparing to make *Creation of the World,* seeing movies and theater performances as he had in London, and looking after his burgeoning career as an itinerant choreographer.

In November, he went to see *Boys against Girls* and deemed the stars, Nancy Walker and Bert Lahr, "excellent, some material all right, dances bad." The next day he received a call from the Canadian Broadcasting Corporation asking him to stage *The Still Point* in early December. A few days later, the *Still Point* commission fell through, but Bolender noted "an attempt to get me there for *Pulcinella* March 10th." Meanwhile, he was rehearsing *Souvenirs* at City Ballet. At the end of the month, he received a call from Sarah Caldwell, who had founded the Opera Company of Boston the previous year, asking him to redo Robert Joffrey's choreography for *Voyage to the Moon* for a thirteen-week tour beginning January 1, for which he would receive a flat fee of $800, plus $50-a-week royalty, for a total of $1,450.

Bolender welcomed the assignment. The money was good and Caldwell was just the kind of driven, talented, strong-minded woman he liked to work with. He also enjoyed working with singers (many choreographers do not) because of their understanding of rhythm and breath. Two major dance interludes and movement for the chorus gave him plenty of scope for what could be regarded as part of a series of outer space ballets he worked on throughout his career. The first was *Zodiac,* made in 1946 for Ballet Society; the last was *Voyager,* made four decades later, for Kansas City Ballet, which Bolender considered his best work.

The American premiere of Offenbach's 1875 opera had been a shrewd choice on Caldwell's part. In 1959, John Kennedy was running for president on a platform that included planting an American flag on the moon in an escalation of the space race with the Soviet Union. In 1960, the fledgling opera company performed *Voyage to the Moon* on the White House lawn in a Kennedy administration validation of American art and American goals, just as the Roosevelt administration had done, rather differently, with its sponsorship of American Ballet Caravan's 1941 tour of South America.

Creation of the World, Bolender's last major piece for City Ballet, possibly his most ambitious to that point and at seventeen minutes one of his shortest, began as an assignment from management. "George asked me to do it," Bolender told Reynolds, who had danced in it shortly before she left the company. "It was one of those package deals they were doing, like *Panamerica*,"[58] referring to an evening-long program of short pieces with Latin American themes by different choreographers that had premiered in January 1960 and was, according to Reynolds, "a great big flop." *Jazz* was the title of the "package deal" in question, half an evening of four ballets set to music by Milhaud, Stravinsky, and Poulenc, European composers whose work had been influenced by American jazz, assigned to four different choreographers. Bolender "got Milhaud," as he put it, which, like Poulenc's *Les Biches*, which was assigned to Francisco Moncion, was already a ballet score. Balanchine kept Stravinsky's *Ragtime* for himself and delegated the same composer's *Ebony Concerto* to John Taras.

In 1923, Les Ballets Suédois had commissioned Milhaud to write *Creation* and Fernand Léger to design the sets. Jean Börlin, the company's principal dancer, did the choreography, and writer Blaise Cendrars, who, like many of his contemporaries, was fascinated by what they perceived as African culture, wrote the libretto. According to one reference, this *Creation*, subtitled *A Negro-Jazz Ballet*, "[was] a marriage of African creation myths and American jazz."[59] Léger's sets, some of them three-dimensional, featured jungle animals and tribal gods, and Milhaud's score was for the same instruments as a jazz band he had heard play in a Harlem nightclub a few years earlier.

Bolender's ballet could not conceivably have been more different or more American in its point of view. In his libretto, the African jungle becomes the Garden of Eden; Adam and Eve are not so much expelled as propelled directly through the centuries to the urban jungle of 1920s New York, where the city dwellers celebrate greed with cocktail parties, fall on their knees before a graph of the rising stock market, and are punished by its 1929 crash. But it doesn't end there; as it does in so many of Bolender's ballets, redemption is found in love and the curtain falls on the lead couple, backs to the audience, walking upstage center into a future in which they have each other, if little else.

Like *Souvenirs*, *Creation* was an exception to Bolender's usual practice of taking impetus from music, but for a different reason: he didn't think much of any of the scores for the *Jazz* program, because they had all been composed by Europeans. "Obviously [they] were inspired by the syncopation inherent in real American jazz," he told Reynolds, "but the basic beat and the results were a thin and arid derivation of the true essentials of our native-born Negro-inspired jazz."[60] Not finding Milhaud's score jazzy enough, Bolender turned to the Roaring Twenties, the era in which it was composed, to make a ballet that was as stylistically eclectic as Loring's *Billy the Kid* and, like it, a story with a moral point.

It was a large-cast ballet. For Peaches, the innocent country girl who gets in trouble in the big city, Bolender lured Reed back on stage. Villella was cast as Sweep, the street cleaner who falls in love with her; loses her to Snake, danced by Mitchell (the only cast member who knew how to do jazz dance); then finds her again, stripped of her jewels and, by implication, her virtue; and leads her into the sunset, as it were, at the end. Conrad Ludlow and Patricia McBride were cast as Adam and Eve and Lois Bewley was Bangles, the wicked woman, or Lilith.

The ensemble included ten men and ten women; Reynolds was a guest at a cocktail party. The technical demands on the cast were many: Bolender made use of his early training in modern dance for Adam and Eve, particularly the fashioning of Eve from Adam's rib, something Balanchine, by Bolender's account, adored. In the transition from the Garden of Eden to the city, the dancers move in somewhat apelike fashion, just for a few subtle seconds. There is "a parade of the ages" that serves as a form of time travel from the beginning of the world to New York in 1923. Social dances, specifically the Black Bottom and the Charleston, get performed in the city, and there are quite a lot of classical steps, particularly for Reed and Bewley, who danced on pointe, and Villella, who was given ample opportunity to show off his bravura technique with triple air turns. Rolling bodies after the stock market crash; a bit in which three dancers are shown sitting on the floor playing cards (a scene straight out of *Billy the Kid*); such character-revealing details as Eve, clad in a raincoat, taking out a compact and powdering her nose; and many other movement vignettes amount to choreographic comments on the theory of evolution, the urban-rural conflict that always has and always will drive American politics, class differences in American society, the excesses of the Roaring Twenties, and the American idolization of Mammon, a biblical symbol for greed. The cast falls on its knees to worship a graph of a rising stock market and rolls over dead when the market plummets. Balanchine had addressed all seven deadly sins in his eponymous ballet two years earlier; Bolender focused on only two, lust and greed, using the light touch so carefully honed in *Souvenirs* to tell a cautionary tale that amuses as it teaches.

Jazz premiered on December 8, 1960, as the first half of a program that included *La Sonnambula* and *Symphony in C.* Martin assessed *Jazz* as "an amusing idea to work on, but the result was one good piece [Balanchine's] and three good tries." Bolender's contribution was one of the good tries. Martin refers to the Ballets Suédois version as "fairly solemn" and says, "Mr. Bolender with a nice sense of mischief has shifted esthetics . . . to the Copacabana, and given us an ingenious and generally gay bit of tongue in cheek night clubbery." He concludes that "for all that he reminisces freely over the works of Balanchine and Robbins in the repertory, he manages at the same time to come up with some original bits of comedy." Martin also commends Bolender for "using his people well," particularly Reed, and backhandedly compliments Villella, who "performs winningly for him, and so do Arthur Mitchell, Conrad Ludlow, Patricia McBride, Lois Bewley (who is a very funny girl) and a dozen excellent bit players." Nevertheless, he found the ballet "little more than a gag."[61]

If Martin was going to emphasize influences on Bolender's choreography, he might have mentioned Loring's *City Portrait,* and *Billy the Kid.* Moreover, silent film, particularly Charlie Chaplin's *Modern Times* and *City Lights* with their vulnerable heroines, was as important an influence on *Creation* as it was on *Souvenirs.*

In a review of the "jazz evening" that appeared in the *Herald Tribune* on December 9, Terry considered Bolender's ballet to be the most entertaining on the program, describing it as "filled with chuckles and laughs along with flashes of virtuosity and touches of poignancy." As all critics did, he adored Reed, "who . . . has emerged from retirement to give a marvelous performance as Peaches. Hilarity, irony and lovely hints of tenderness were all present in her delicious characterization. [It] is a light ballet distinguished by the choreographer's mastery of antic humor, satiric gesture, and inventive gamboling."[62] As a critic, Terry paid Bolender the highest compliment someone in that position can when he said he would like to see *Creation* again.

Hering, however, was less than enthusiastic, writing in *Dance Magazine* that Bolender had "tried to prove all was not lost when Eve lost her innocence" and chastising him for being "unable to differentiate between satire and sentiment." She also felt that in general the corps seemed under-rehearsed, which it may well have been. It's not easy for a ballet master, in this case Reed, to keep her eagle eye on the dancers when she is herself performing.

For his part, Bolender, who had been told by Balanchine that *Creation of the World* was the best thing he had ever done, seems to have been satisfied with his accomplishment, telling Reynolds that "it takes a long time to learn how to do choreography, or to know what you're doing [and] not stumbling around."[63] *Creation* stayed in City Ballet's repertory for several seasons and Bolender restaged it on four more companies: the Turkish National Ballet in Ankara, the Washington National Ballet, the Cologne Opera Ballet, and Kansas City Ballet. For each company, he made adjustments in the libretto, the choreography, and even the costumes to fit the dancers and the circumstances of the places where the ballet was performed. Reed's luxurious ermine furs in the City Ballet version, for example, became a fluffy feather boa in Kansas City, presumably because the company was on a shoestring budget at the time.

For the next couple of years, Bolender continued to dance less and less, and he took on an increasing number of choreographic assignments, several of which took him out of New York. In 1961, an opera assignment took him to Fort Worth, Texas, to arrange the dances for a Franco Zeffirelli production of Massenet's *Thaïs,* for which, despite the inclusion of Jacques d'Amboise and Violette Verdy in the cast, he was given frustratingly little stage space. In the fall of that year, he went to Montreal to direct three plays for the Canadian National Theater, including Edna St. Vincent Millay's antiwar *Aria da Capo,* persuading actors to project with their bodies as well as their voices. Closer to home, he choreographed a new Metropolitan Opera production of *Die Meistersinger* (Terry liked what he did; Trude Rittmann thought his dances were clumsy and awful). He also worked on an off-Broadway play called *The Killers,* by Ionesco. In fact, Bolender seems to have accepted every offer he received. The projects weren't always successful, but just as he had as a dancer and young choreographer, he would try anything, and if it failed (as with *The Filly*), he would learn from the experience.

Marre commissioned him for several projects, including supervisor of dances for *Hail the Conquering Hero* (replacing Bob Fosse), for which Bolender received no credit, and to make the dances for a musical comedy version of Offenbach's *La Belle Hélène,* called simply *La Belle.* The most important project, however, was a job as choreographic coordinator of *America Dances,* a panorama of American dance from 1900 to 1961. While the emphasis was on popular culture (musical comedy from several eras, ballroom dance, jazz, and tap dancing), historical modern dance was well represented and there were two classical pas de deux on this first program, in addition to Valerie Bettis's *A Streetcar Named Desire,* a ballet that fused modern and classical technique. The star-studded extravaganza premiered on June 12 on the Public Garden stage, the centerpiece of the tenth anniversary of the Boston Festival of the Arts. From his staging of *Renard* for the same Festival of the Arts a few years earlier, Bolender knew well the space and the size of the audience, which was large.

Bolender's principal function was to create dance interludes that would connect these examples of American dance and seamlessly show their evolution. He did quite a lot more than that. The program was Marre's idea, but Bolender and Terry played strong roles in selecting choreography, the performers, and the format: a basically chronological presentation with a narration written by Terry, which, for the first season, was delivered by Ruth St. Denis, winner that year of the Capezio Lifetime Achievement Award. She also closed the show with performances of *Incense,* the ritualistic solo that she had first danced in 1906 in which her extremely flexible arms replicated the wafting of smoke. "She was wonderful," Bolender remembered. "She was in a gown that was made of silver beads. They weren't in rows . . . it had a kind of a shimmer to it. And she did a dance . . . and finally she was jumping into the air, like a flame."[64] St. Denis was eighty-four.

Other stars included Mia Slavenska, who danced the *Don Quixote* pas de deux, partnered by Villella, whose exuberant jetés elicited cheers from the audience and many plaudits from the critics. Later in the program, modern dancer Norman Walker and City Ballet's Suki Schorer joined them in a performance of *A Streetcar Named Desire,* which the Slavenska-Franklin company had premiered in Montreal six years earlier. No program titled *America Dances* could have been complete at that time without Maria Tallchief, who, partnered by Francisco Moncion, gave a powerhouse performance in a pas de deux from Balanchine's *Firebird,* arguably her greatest role, certainly the one for which she was best known. This was thought to represent contemporary ballet.

The show started with a spoof of Irene and Vernon Castle doing the turkey trot, the tango, and the hesitation waltz, danced by Maria Karnilova, Bolender's partner in crime in Ballets: U.S.A.'s production of *The Concert,* and Donald Saddler, who also did the choreography. An homage to George M. Cohan and vaudeville tap dancing by Don Liberto followed (and was found wanting by *Boston Herald* theater critic Eliot Norton), and the Pearl Lang company concluded the first half with a new work titled *Shire* with music by Alan Hovhaness.

Jazz, real American jazz, as opposed to Milhaud's European interpretation, was represented in the second half by Alvin Ailey and Carmen de Lavallade—neither of them yet the stars they shortly thereafter became—who performed Ailey's *Roots of the Blues,* a four-part work accompanied by singer Brother John Sellers, who the young choreographer had first encountered at Gerde's Folk City in Greenwich Village. According to Ailey biographer Jennifer Dunning, he incorporated material from the 1958 *Blues Suite,* which, like Bolender's early choreography, had premiered at the 92nd Street YMHA. The audience was so enthusiastic about their performance (evidently they tore up the stage) that Sellers kept right on singing after the dance had ended, "forcing Alvin and de Lavallade to keep moving until he and his musicians wound to a halt."[65] This undoubtedly threw off the program timing considerably, but it doesn't seem to have bothered Bolender. He and Ailey became lifelong friends and colleagues. The Ailey Company performed *The Still Point* in 1980, when Bolender also taught in The Ailey School, and the two men worked together a great deal in Kansas City in the 1980s, when the Ailey company was in residence there and Bolender was directing the Kansas City Ballet.

The Still Point took the place of *Streetcar Named Desire* the following year in what Bolender came to call "The Walter Terry Show," but other than transitions between numbers, Bolender's only choreography for the first performance was "The Glow Worm," also called "Ballet Girl," a solo in the style of 1920s musicals that was danced by Schorer and was described by one writer as "a fluttery [piece]." The costume was definitely part of the dance: battery-powered lights in the skirt lit up from time to time like fireflies. Another writer found the solo "clever, . . . with the hand-kissings, and mechanical doll twirling and pirouettes familiar to musical comedies of that era" and commended Bolender for his "interesting choreographic 'bridges' between the different styles of dancing."[66]

America Dances did an extensive tour of the eastern half of the country in the spring of 1962, going as far south as Georgia, performing before huge audiences. Rochelle Zide danced "Ballet Girl" and the lead role in *The Still Point,* and Natalie Krassovska, like Zide a Ballet Russe de Monte Carlo dancer (though unlike Zide a leading ballerina there), performed Anna Pavlova's signature solo, *The Dying Swan,* because, as Terry noted in the introduction in the program, Pavlova's tours, starting in 1910, "awakened America's interest in ballet." Ailey's *Blues* piece wasn't performed, but Saddler's send up of Jerome Robbins's and Agnes de Mille's musical comedy numbers was and St. Denis was a consistent participant, making a huge impact in Philadelphia on a very young Mindy Aloff. She "most of all [remembered her], in black leotard and cut-off tights, in her 80s, doing amazing Chinese splits. Her cloud of white hair also memorable."[67]

On Labor Day 1963, St. Denis celebrated seven decades of professional dancing with her performance of *Incense* at the Delacorte Theater in Central Park. The Rebekah Harkness Foundation underwrote the free concert. Several thousand people were in the audience, and 3,000 were turned away for lack of room. Lillian Moore, filling in for Terry at the *Herald Tribune,* dubbed it "the perfect entertainment for a typical American holiday" and loved Alexandra Danilova as narrator, reporting that she "brought the house down before she said a word."[68] St. Denis, she said, contributed genuine authenticity, and Terry's script neatly tied together all the diverse elements of the program. Ballet was again represented by Krassovska dancing *The Dying Swan* and an excerpt from *Swan Lake,* partnered by Ron Sequoio, who later preceded Bolender, briefly, as artistic director of the Kansas City Ballet. Moore gave high marks to Zide in *The Still Point* and to Norman Walker for his *Passage of Angels* and had little to complain about generally.

America Dances ended that year. Bolender had taken over the artistic directorship of the Cologne Opera Ballet, and Terry, generally as indefatigable in his promotion of American dance both at home and abroad as Bolender, had had a personal loss. There is little doubt, however, that Bolender's involvement in the historically oriented entertainment proved to be a major step in establishing his post-dancing career. It may well have gotten him his initial assignment from the U.S. State Department to work in Turkey, which he did off and on for close to twenty years, and it almost certainly influenced his programming in Kansas City, where, at least in the early years, mixed bills reflected the history of ballet in America.

Bolender also left City Ballet, the company that had nurtured his performing and dance-making career for nearly two decades, with as little fanfare as Reed had two years earlier, and headed for Germany to assume the directorship of the Cologne Opera Ballet.

9

In June 1963, a few months before Bolender headed for Germany, Janet Reed was on the road again, this time with her husband and two children, sixteen-year-old Reed Erskine and five-year-old-Jane, in a secondhand Nash Rambler station wagon, headed for a new life in the Hudson River Valley and a new role as a stay-at-home mother and housewife.

"The car broke down halfway there," Reed Erskine recalled. "But my parents wanted their kids to breathe fresh air and we all idealized 'country' living."[1] And, he remembered, his father was itching to get his highly skilled interior designer's fingers on a nineteenth-century house in Dutchess County.

Since Reed had left City Ballet in 1961, she had been augmenting her husband's shrinking income by teaching part-time at both Bard and Vassar Colleges, where she was visiting professor of dance. Two years later, both Erskines were ready to make significant changes in their lives. Branson, 50, was not in good health either physically or financially and needed to get away from city life; Janet at 47 would at long last be able to create the family life she had craved since childhood, and she would do so with the same "flinty determination" (her son's phrase) she had applied to her career as dancer, teacher, and ballet master.

After Jane Erskine was born in 1958, and in need of cash (Erskine's inheritance from his father, the founder of the Sylvania Corporation, was dwindling and Reed, on leave from City Ballet, was not earning any money), they sold their elegant co-op apartment on 57th Street, which had beautiful views of the East River, and moved to a rental down the street. A new high-rise building that blocked those views and replaced them with a brick wall did make it less painful to part with the beautifully furnished home that was, in the words of Erskine the younger, a "calling card" for his father's work as an interior designer and antiques dealer and the setting for many elaborate cocktail and dinner parties. Their guests were primarily old friends of his father's, but it is likely that some ballet people attended those parties. Edward Bigelow recalled many pleasant evenings spent with the Erskines when he was married to Una Kai, and it's possible that Kirstein was an occasional guest as well. In any case, excellent food prepared by Reed, who had become an accomplished cook, and plenty of very good cocktails and wine were consumed at those parties, both of which were extremely bad for Branson Erskine's health. Even with the daily injections of insulin he gave himself, alcohol, even in small quantities, was definitely contraindicated.

The search for a home began immediately, and it was through the social connections of Reed Erskine, who was attending Millbrook School, a private co-educational boarding school located in Dutchess County, that they found a house to rent (they thought temporarily) while they searched for Branson Erskine's dream house.

The house turned out to be a seventeenth-century Dutch stone dwelling on the Leila Delano estate; the Erskines lived in it until the end of the decade. "It was happy times all around," Reed Erskine remembered of the first few years. His father, he wrote, "bonded with the old lady, and fixed up the house and garden, making both look extremely attractive."[2] Reed kept her toe in the ballet world in various ways, continuing to teach adult ballet classes at Bard and Vassar, participating in a program the Ford Foundation funded in 1961 that set up scholarships for students from ballet schools all over the United States to attend SAB tuition-free, and taking her daughter into the city with her to see City Ballet performances.[3] Jane Erskine remembered the dancers emerging from their dressing rooms at the State Theater when her mother took her backstage, calling "Janet's here, come see Janet," and later wondered just how she had made the adjustment from her old life as an artist to her new one as (her words) "a suburban housewife."[4]

One way was to get away from time to time and put her professional experience to use as a consultant. In 1966, Reed began several years of service on the Dance Panel for the U.S. Department of State's Cultural Exchange Program, which President Eisenhower had established in 1954 as a peaceful way to counter Soviet propaganda during the Cold War. It was under its auspices that City Ballet toured Russia for the first time in 1962. Reed, according to her daughter, didn't much care for the bureaucratic aspects of serving on those panels, but she was proud of her role in selecting which companies and artists would best represent American dance abroad. As a reward for her efforts, she received a nice plaque from the State Department.

At home, Reed kept a well-run house (a perfectionist in everything she did; nothing was worth doing unless you did it well, she told her children frequently) and played the role of hostess as often as she did housewife. This part of the Hudson River Valley had attracted prominent and not-so-prominent writers and artists to the area, particularly in the summer, and the Erskines soon became friends with a number of them who lived close by. Among them were Gore Vidal, who lived in an enormous mansion down the road; Alice and Martin Provensen, early animators and children's book authors and illustrators whose *Fireside Book of Folk Songs* could be found on the music shelves in many households in the 1940s and 50s; novelist Mary Lee Settle, who was teaching at Bard; Richard Rovere, who for many years wrote the *New Yorker*'s politically insightful "Letter from Washington"; and playwright Lawrence Osgood. The parties resumed and the alcohol flowed. Reed Erskine well remembered the ease with which his mother transferred her talents as a performer from the stage to the social scene, entertaining her guests with impeccable comedic timing and an off-beat sense of humor "that was somewhere between Charlie Chaplin and Lucille Ball."[5] She did not speak much of her stellar career as a dancer, except when the Provensens brought a young Robert Gottlieb to a party at the Erskine house. Gottlieb later became editor of the *New Yorker* and before that an extremely important and influential book editor and publisher. His New York City childhood included visits to Ballet Theatre, where he saw Reed dance in *Fancy Free* in its first season, and to City Ballet, where he saw her perform in *Symphony in C* and *Cakewalk*, captivated by her, he said, in every role. By his own account of their first meeting, Reed was "as startled to find in Clinton Corners an obsessed young ballet lover who knew her work as [he] was to find there a ballerina [he] loved."[6] The ballerina and the bookworm bonded on this occasion, and, in a 1978 interview with Tobi Tobias, Reed spoke of Gottlieb's contributions to dance literature—he published many dance writers and the memoirs of Paul Taylor and Allegra Kent, among others—and to City Ballet, on whose board of directors he served for some years. "I know she could be rigorous as a ballet master," Gottlieb commented in 2017, "but in 'real life' she was just so much fun."[7]

Indications are that toward the end of the decade, "real life" was becoming a lot less fun for the Erskines than it had been. They were again running out of money, having pretty much used up the proceeds of the sale of their co-op; their social life with hard-drinking writers was once again taking its toll on Branson's health; and, while Reed Erskine after a couple of years at Cornell had, in 1967, joined the Peace Corps, and was on his own financially, Jane would soon need to be prepared for college. The Emma Willard School in nearby Troy, New York, was the logical but expensive place to send her. To achieve this, Miss Reed, as she was known professionally, would have to return to work. Whether it was for this reason or because Reed missed the culture of the professional ballet studio that she had known for most of her life, or a combination of the two, in August 1968, an advertisement appeared in the *Kingston Daily Freeman* announcing that Janet Reed, formerly a soloist with San Francisco Opera Ballet, American Ballet Theatre, and New York City Ballet, would be teaching one ballet class for children ages 7 to 14 on Saturday afternoons in Kingston's Young Men's Christian Association. This was the beginning of the Kingston School of Ballet, which opened in its own space six months later, in February 1969. One newspaper article identified it as the area's first school of professional ballet training. It was not exclusively so, however: an adult beginning ballet class was offered in the evening. Reed had had plenty of practice teaching these; from the time the family moved to Dutchess County, she had taught such classes at Bard and Vassar, and she continued to do so until they departed for Seattle a few years later.

By June of that year, it was announced in the *Freeman* that a number of Miss Reed's students had been selected to perform in Balanchine's *A Midsummer Night's Dream* during New York City Ballet's summer season in Saratoga. With provincial pride, the author of the article pointed out that from a pool of 250 children from many area schools who had auditioned, five out of the twenty-five who were chosen were from the Kingston School. Children from Reed's school also performed in Balanchine's *The Nutcracker* when it was programmed in Saratoga the following year, auditioned by Una Kai. After her years as ballet master, during which she and Kai conducted *Nutcracker* auditions in Washington, DC, and Los Angeles and at SAB, Reed well knew how to train students for the auditions and for the roles they would perform as Marie, Fritz, and the little Nutcracker Prince (if they were very talented), but more likely as the party children, mice, soldiers, little angels, and the polichinelles who emerge from under Mother Ginger's skirt. Reed, with Melissa Hayden, also taught in the summer at the Saratoga Ballet School.

Moreover, in the same period, she was also traveling the country as an adjudicator for the Ford Foundation National Evaluation of Ballet Instruction in the United States. This was an outgrowth of the Ford Foundation's grant to give scholarships to promising young dancers to study in New York at SAB. That program started in 1960, and the following year, Balanchine taught free seminars in New York for teachers from all over the United States. Jacqueline Martin Schumacher, Reed's old friend from Portland and San Francisco Opera Ballet days, attended at least one of them. By 1963, the program was in full swing, including substantial grants to seven ballet companies: New York City Ballet, American Ballet Theatre, the Pennsylvania Ballet, Ballet West (then called Utah Ballet), the Houston Ballet, the San Francisco Ballet, and the Washington National Ballet, which was founded in 1962 with Ford Foundation money. All but the last, which folded in 1974, the year Reed left New York State for Seattle, are major American companies in the twenty-first century. It is possible that the tuition-free scholarships the Kingston School offered to boys over 12 were funded by the same Ford Foundation grant; one newspaper article stated that SAB had approved the school's curriculum.

Reed relinquished her position as the Kingston School's only artistic director in March 1970 and began sharing the job with Fred de Mayo, a former principal dancer with the Metropolitan Opera Ballet who had studied with Balanchine and was teaching at New Paltz State College. By September he was in sole charge and Reed was artistic advisor and was teaching part time. In a newspaper interview, Reed accounted for the change in her involvement by citing her responsibilities to the State Department's Panel on Dance, but it was probably more complicated than that. She was also involved in the National Association of Regional Ballet's Choreographers Craft Conference touring program, which was established to support young choreographers and prepare dancers in ballet companies all over the country to work with a variety of dance makers, something that in the twenty-first century is taken for granted. The National Association of Regional Ballet was headed at this time by former *Dance Magazine* editor and critic Doris Hering, who later credited the organization with decentralizing American ballet. She hired both Reed and Bolender as consultants. "I was adjudicating, Janet was teaching, and Doris was the boss," Bolender said in a 2003 interview.[8]

In due course, Mrs. Delano, who was quite elderly when the Erskine family moved into their home on her estate, died and her property was sold. In 1970, the Erskines were compelled to move and they relocated to another rental, owned by decorator friends in nearby Germantown. The rent was reduced with the understanding that Branson would refurbish it as meticulously as he had the house on the Delano estate. Unfortunately, Branson's health was so poor at this point that he wasn't able to do the work, and Reed was increasingly needed at home. Yet again, like so many women of her generation, she was torn between her professional obligations, her need to earn money, and her family—indeed, there may never have been a time since her marriage in 1946 when she *wasn't* feeling the conflicting pull between home, stage, and studio.

In 1972, Branson underwent bypass surgery, the same year that Jane entered the Emma Willard School. Two years later, in January, Miss Reed taught a ballet class at the school. Jane A. Bennett, a sharp-eyed, interested reporter for the *Times Record*, Troy's daily paper, who observed her class, described Miss Reed's short red hair, blue practice clothes, and intensely blue eyes and her instructions to her young pupils to "Get the feet right and everything else will come, arms, head, shoulders relaxed." "It's important," she later pointed out, "in any of the performing arts to have life in the body."[9] This observation led Bennett to note that Reed, who was in her late 50s, had plenty of life in her own.

"No one who doesn't love dancing should try it," Reed told Bennett in an after-class interview, when speaking of the hardships of combining marriage and motherhood with a career as a ballerina. And while she had willingly stopped dancing at age 44, that hadn't been easy, either. "It was hard to give up performing and the idea of concentrating on myself," she said. "As a ballet mistress and later a teacher I couldn't think of myself again. I had to concentrate completely on the students or dancers I was working with."[10]

The article concludes with Reed's response to a question about missing the bright lights of Manhattan. She had no desire to return, she said, although country living had made her "fat." She liked living in the area, she was consulting for the Ford Foundation, she was still teaching two days a week at the Kingston School, and at the end of the month, in addition to adult ballet, would begin teaching body movement to some very lucky drama students at Vassar College. Life in the Hudson River Valley appeared to be treating both Miss Reed and Mrs. Erskine well.

Six months later, Janet Reed Erskine signed a contract with Pacific Northwest Dance in Seattle that would return her to the part of the country that had shaped her character and to urban life in a city that was very different from the Big Apple—much younger, slower-paced—but whose residents were far less interested in the arts and were therefore far less supportive. In 1974, Seattle had no resident ballet company separate from the Seattle Opera, and only a few of the city's movers and shakers had much interest in getting one off the ground. There were, of course, exceptions. One of them was Sheffield Phelps, who had been president of the Seattle Opera board and who, in 1974, became president of the board of Pacific Northwest Dance, which had been primarily a presenting organization and training program that supplied apprentice dancers for opera ballets.

The terms of Reed's contract, which was issued in the form of a letter from Phelps, were deceptively simple. In exchange for a salary of $18,000 a year; moving expenses from Germantown, New York, to Seattle; and one-way jet economy air fare from New York City to Seattle for the family (minus Reed Erskine, who by that time was married and living in Washington, DC), Reed signed on to direct the Pacific Northwest Dance Company School, teach the company, and "act as Ballet Mistress in aiding development and establishing the style of the Pacific Northwest Dance Company." She was to start work July 8. The contract was for two calendar years, extending through July 7, 1976. Once again, just as she had when she took a cross-continental train from San Francisco to New York in January 1942 with only the offer of a contract from Eugene Loring to be a principal dancer with Dance Players (a job that lasted a few months), Reed was taking an enormous risk, not only with her own future but with her family's as well. It was the family's "straitened circumstances," as Reed Erskine put it many years later, that "inspired my mother's move to Seattle and another demanding job."[11]

This time, however, Reed was not starting all over again as she had in 1942, and she wasn't traveling to an unfamiliar part of the country, where she herself was unknown to all but a small group of dancers and choreographers. Moreover, in the course of over forty years, she had contributed to the establishment of two major American ballet companies, the San Francisco Ballet and New York City Ballet, three if you count American Ballet

Theatre, which was only two years old when she joined as a guest artist in the spring of 1943. In all three companies she had worked with a wide variety of choreographers, and her teaching career had begun in Portland at Willam Christensen's school before she became a professional dancer. As ballet master at City Ballet, she had been responsible for casting and staging ballets by Balanchine, Robbins, Lew Christensen, Bolender, and Boris, and she had coached and developed such dancers as Allegra Kent, Edward Villella, Anthony Blum, Arthur Mitchell, and Patricia McBride. In Miss Reed, the Pacific Northwest Dance Company (PND) was getting a gifted, experienced, capable, dedicated, hard-working ballet master, coach, and school director, and at least one dance writer in Seattle knew that they were lucky to have her and said so. Maxine Cushing-Gray, one of Seattle's most knowledgeable classical-arts writers, enthusiastically hailed her appointment, which PND's executive director Leon Kalimos announced two months before she signed the contract. Like Phelps and other arts supporters, Cushing-Gray was eager for the city to have a resident professional ballet company.

She wrote in her newsletter *Northwest Arts* on April 26, 1974, that "what we may have, finally in Pacific Northwest Dance's long delayed announcement that Janet Reed has been engaged as ballet-mistress of this tiny appendage of Seattle Opera, is hope that within a year or two Seattle can enjoy the work of a resident group of trained dancers who are paid to perform, as Seattle now compensates its best musicians and actors for the many ways they enhance our life in this soberly beautiful place." After summarizing Reed's dancing career, she wrote of Reed's qualifications: "Her later work as ballet mistress of New York City Ballet gives Miss Reed a cachet of teaching and rehearsal competence that should add to the discipline, tradition and distinction already influential on the Northwest scene." Of Reed's new boss, who had managed the San Francisco Ballet for twelve years and then served as the executive director of the Marin Veterans' Memorial Building, a 2,000-seat house in Marin County, Cushing-Gray wrote, "[Leon Kalimos] the canny executive director of PND knows the dance world and now in Ms. Reed has artistic leadership to offer those who have hesitated to invest their hopes and money in Pacific NW Dance." And, most compellingly, she urged, "Let them all play fair with the dancers: provide decent rehearsal space and safe floors to work on, avoid exploitation through the overlong use of unpaid 'apprentices' and give an honored place in this community to the world's oldest art."

Both Kalimos and Reed were well equipped to meet the requirements of their new jobs. During his tenure as manager of the San Francisco Ballet, Kalimos had been at least in part responsible for putting the company in which Reed's career began on the national and international map. His association with the company had begun in the mid-1950s, when he was a late beginner in ballet and took a night class at the school paid for by the GI Bill. Willam Christensen started putting him in small roles. Kalimos got his foot in the management door by offering to find the company some tour bookings in California, and from there he went to handling all the finances and finding theaters to perform in when the San Francisco Opera was in season in the War Memorial Opera House. He helped locate and finance the purchase and remodeling of a new building when the one the company was renting on Washington Street became unavailable. In 1961, he was responsible for initiating the company's first season subscriptions—in twenty-first-century ballet companies, subscriptions are taken for granted as a means of ensuring some financial stability. Two years later, when dancers started leaving the company for better-paying jobs, Kalimos and Lew Christensen started issuing 40-week contracts, something that sixty years later remains out of reach for many dancers in American ballet companies.

Not only was Kalimos extremely good at arranging and managing tours, he was popular with the dancers because he made sure they had everything they needed while on the road, particularly when, in 1957, San Francisco Ballet went on an eleven-nation tour of Asia (the first American ballet company to do so) under the auspices of the United States State Department. Kalimos handled the many complicated logistics of that tour with considerable skill, dealing with contracts written in multiple languages, ordering specially built wicker baskets for costumes (curved, coffin-shaped to fit in the holds of airplanes), acquiring such practical equipment as lightweight electrical cables, and, no small thing, making sure the dancers had opportunities to see the sights in each country when they weren't on stage.[12]

The Asian tour was wildly successful on many levels. Audiences and critics loved the dancers and the repertory they performed, which included works by Lew Christensen and Balanchine. Equally successful international tours to South America and the Middle East followed. Lew Christensen, who was by then the sole artistic director of the company his brother had founded,[13] and Kalimos, as company manager, worked well together until Christensen began preparing for a run in Lincoln Center's New York State

Theater (renamed the David H. Koch Theater in 2008). Christensen's choreography was hardly unknown in New York—his *Jinx, Filling Station,* and *Con Amore* had all been audience-pleasing parts of the City Ballet repertory—but he needed the validation of critical and audience success in the city that for decades had been considered the dance capital of the United States.

Unfortunately, due to bad programming advice from Kalimos, who urged Christensen to open with an evening of his own choreography that included two new pieces, one of them based on pop art (which was all the rage in New York in the 1960s), the hard-to-please New York critics had a field day. Reviewers were particularly irritated by the pop art–inspired *Life: A Do It Yourself Desire,* which was the choreographer's quite cynical take on Lyndon Johnson's Great Society. In addition, Christensen's choice of the same music by Charles Ives that Balanchine had used for *Ivesiana* likely made some critics think him arrogant, especially since the company was performing in a theater that continues to be regarded as "Balanchine's house." Audiences were more receptive than the critics, not only to *Life* but also to the elaborately produced *Lucifer,* based on Milton's vision of the fallen angel in *Paradise Lost.* Reviewers, however, accustomed to the streamlined productions of Balanchine's and Robbins's ballets that were the usual fare at the New York State Theater, were unimpressed by the elaborate decor and costumes for these ballets and those for Christensen's *Beauty and the Beast,* suggesting that they were a cover for mediocre choreography and overwhelmed the dancing.

This was not by any means entirely Kalimos's fault. Christensen should have known better after his many years of close association with City Ballet what the critical establishment would or would not accept. Nevertheless, Kalimos had crossed the line into artistic direction, and while he and Christensen patched it up and seem to have worked well together until 1969, when Kalimos resigned because of difficulties with the company's board, it's likely that any artistic advice he offered was politely ignored. In his new position in Seattle, Kalimos was executive director; he did not hold the title of artistic director and neither did Reed. However, the lack of title did not keep him from exerting, or trying to exert, artistic control, and that plus a sexist attitude toward women made working with him difficult, first for Reed and later for Melissa Hayden, who briefly held the title in 1977.

Reed and Kalimos ought to have been able to work well together. They had quite a lot in common beyond their association with San Francisco Ballet and the Christensen brothers, albeit in very different eras. Both were native Oregonians, both had a passionate commitment to the art of the ballet, and both were extremely hard-working, practical people, dedicated to the task at hand. Neither, however, particularly liked being subordinate to anyone else. Kalimos had been an equal partner at San Francisco Ballet with the Christensen brothers until the company was reorganized as a 501(c)3 nonprofit and everyone became accountable to the board of directors, and Reed often disagreed with Balanchine when she was ballet master at City Ballet and didn't always keep her opinion to herself.

They evidently began well. Reed started her new job two months before she actually signed the contract by combining attendance at the Pacific Regional Ballet Association Festival, which was meeting in Seattle the week of April 22,[14] with a search for promising students for the first summer session of PND's professional development program. In early May, 150 advanced ballet students from the area's existing schools and studios auditioned formally at the Madrona Center, a municipal bathhouse that had been converted into a primitive dance studio. Reed was familiar with some of their teachers, particularly Ruthanna Boris, in whose *Cakewalk* she had been a hit as the Queen of the Swamp Lilies. Boris was teaching at the University of Washington, and Irene Larsson, who had originated the role of the Vamp in *Souvenirs,* was teaching in a Seattle studio. Reed was also well aware of the ballet department at the Cornish School of the Arts, which Mary Ann Wells had founded in 1916 at the request of Nellie Cornish. Wells and Reed had met when San Francisco Ballet was in Seattle in 1939. The Cornish program was (and still is) highly prestigious. Following these auditions, forty-two students that both Reed and Kalimos deemed promising were awarded scholarships to the professional development program.

One of them was Vivian Little from Bellingham, 48 miles north of Seattle, who was just about to finish high school. The dark-eyed, dark-haired, tall 17-year-old had been training since her early teens with, she said, "a woman named Lana McGinnis, who traveled from Edmonds, Washington to Bellingham once or twice a week to teach her students there." When Little was 15, McGinnis encouraged her to spend her weekends traveling between Bellingham and Edmonds to study with her own teacher, Dorothy Fisher, who directed the Dorothy Fisher School. When school let out on Fridays, Little would get on a Greyhound bus to make the 90-minute-or-so trip north and then would spend two days taking classes and rehearsing for concerts, returning home on Sunday afternoons. McGinnis took her to the PND audition, where Little felt so insecure about her own abilities (mortified is the word she used) that she didn't remember much about it, except that both Kalimos and Reed were present.[15] She needn't have felt that way. While she didn't make the cut for the group's first public performance in the Seattle Opera's production of *Aïda* at Expo '74 in Spokane, two years later she had the lead role in Reed's version in Seattle.[16]

The rigorous, six-day-a-week training program began quite soon after the auditions, under the direction of Lew Christensen, who by then was the co-director of San Francisco Ballet with Michael Smuin. He also created the professional development program that Reed had been contracted to implement and taught the first group until Reed's official arrival the first week in July.

Little had clear memories of Christensen's classes at the Madrona Center before Reed took over. "Lew scared me," she wrote. "I thought he didn't like me because he was giving me so many corrections! In my naiveté I decided to leave and get a job at the Bon Marché [a Seattle department store]." She didn't bother to tell anyone she had left, and when the company manager called her to ask why she wasn't in class, she told him why: she'd gotten another job. He explained that "Mr. Christensen very much liked me and was only trying to help me become a stronger dancer, and to get right back into class!"[17]

Encouraged, Little returned to class and was still there when Reed took Christensen's place. From Little's recollections, Reed's approach was harsher than Christensen's: "[Reed] was tough and demanding, always asking us to push harder, but she used humor and high levels of energy and encouragement while assisting us in technical challenges. Her corrections tended to be focused on issues of effort and expressivity versus mechanical [technical]. I will never forget [one day] while working on the adagio exercise in the center when there was a break between groups she stopped the class. She told us we would be better dancers (artists) if we read literature, went to see opera, theater, musicals and visited exhibits in art galleries or museums. I think she was trying to say that it was crucial for us to get out of the dance studio (where we mostly focused on technique) and that would help us to be more interesting, diverse dancers and have more to offer as performing artists."[18]

Reed's approach to training well-rounded artists came from several sources. First from her own initiative—when preparing to dance *Coppélia* in Willam Christensen's first version in Portland, in 1930, she looked at nineteenth-century engravings of ballerinas to see the style. In the early days of the San Francisco Ballet, she learned a great deal about opera from performing in the San Francisco Opera's productions. According to Michael Kidd, she and everyone else in Eugene Loring's newly constituted Dance Players "learned something about music, literature and acting in addition to rehearsing new ballets" at a performing arts workshop in New Hope, Pennsylvania, that Loring directed in the summer of 1942.[19]

Balanchine also encouraged dancers to get a cultural education, no doubt influenced by Diaghilev, who made sure that he and his Ballets Russes colleagues visited museums and sometimes personally escorted them to them. Bolender, who not only went to museums all over the world but also collected art whenever he could afford it, would tell Kansas City Ballet dancers not to go to the zoo when they toured to a new city. "Go to the museum."[20] There were certainly opportunities in Seattle in the 1970s for a cultural education. When Little and her classmates had the time, they could visit the Seattle Art Museum and a few art galleries. Their work with the Seattle Opera and the Seattle Symphony, which they did very soon, also helped them become well-rounded dancers.

The first PND classes took place at the Madrona studio, but once Reed was in place, Phelps lost little time in finding much better accommodations at the unlikely Home of the Good Shepherd, which had been both a convent and a home for "wayward girls." It was located on beautiful grounds some distance away from downtown Seattle in the north-central Wallingford district. The city of Seattle bought the property and the Seattle Opera leased it from the city until 1977, when PND became a separate organization from the opera, a clever way of giving the city fathers a sense of ownership in what would indeed become their resident ballet company.

Converting the center to studios and offices took a lot of physical work, and everyone was pressed into service. Little recalled "some of the men in the company helping to get the studios ready . . . sanding down the hardwood floors with electric sanders, laying down the marley floors and painting. There was still graffiti on the walls in the girls' dressing room [evidently a former dormitory room] '320 more days to go,' etc."[21] Reed contributed her own labor to ensuring that the studio floors would be as safe as possible for the young dancers, keeping them from injuries that could haunt them later in life. By November, one studio was ready for the apprentice dancers (a second was added the following year), as was office space for the administration, and the Good Shepherd Center remained home to the company that became Pacific Northwest Ballet until January 1993, when The Phelps Center, one of the most elegant and functional ballet buildings in the United States, opened next door to the Seattle Opera House. In 2003, the venue was remodeled and renamed McCaw Hall.

Lecture demonstrations soon began, a time-honored tradition in the establishment of American ballet companies: Reed had participated in them in Portland for Willam Christensen's school and company in the 1930s, when he charged 25 cents for tickets. PND's lecture demonstrations were held around the Seattle area and were open to all with no charge for admission. Their purpose was twofold: to introduce the apprentice company to a broad public and to give the students performing experience. Little remembered thinking at the time that it was odd that Kalimos rather than Reed made introductory remarks and took questions at the end, since Reed had done the choreography and planning for them. She particularly remembered Kalimos speaking about ballet technique, using one of the dancers to demonstrate external rotation from the hip, and showing "how essential it was for the dancer to turn their legs out in order to achieve high extensions." Little also recalled that Reed had choreographed a ballet she titled *Rodeo* for these lecture demonstrations, using music from Aaron Copland's *Appalachian Spring*.[22]

Choreography was no more part of Reed's contract than manual labor had been, but it wasn't in her nature to do less than what was required to get the job—any job—done. While she was not an experienced professional choreographer—very few women in ballet were in the twentieth century—she had choreographed for student groups at Vassar and Bard Colleges and for her Kingston school. Equally important, she had worked with a wide variety of dance makers in the course of her long career and could draw on that experience to make pieces both her students and the Seattle public would learn from.

"No one can teach you to choreograph," she wrote in an unpublished memoir toward the end of her life. "There is no way to learn except to 'do.' Every choreographer has found his own way of working. First you should be a dancer and it helps if you can read music, if you can't then you work closely with an accompanist. You have to have space, dancers who are willing to give of themselves and time."[23]

During her two years as director of PND's school, Reed definitely learned choreography by doing. She made a number of dances for the Seattle Opera and she choreographed the company's first story ballet, an abbreviated version of *Pulcinella* to Stravinsky's score of the same name, after Pergolesi. "Janet was very quick to produce choreography," Little said. "It seemed to flow easily from her. She'd observe us execute her movement phrase, sometimes it was clear she didn't like it and she moved on to another option. Sometimes she would work on the original phrase until we executed it the way she wanted it to be. All the while, she'd be coaching us about the mood or the characterization of the role(s). She would often do the movement herself and it was then that we could see what an amazing actress she was."[24]

Reed choreographed several opera interludes in this period. The first one was for Italian composer and librettist Arrigo Boito's *Mefistofele*, which opened the Seattle Opera's 1974–1975 season in September, several weeks before the young company was installed in its new quarters. Little remembered Reed taking considerable pleasure in arranging dances for this operatic version of Goethe's *Faust:* "We portrayed creatures from hell and in paradise. Her choreography was . . . not too balletic with the exception of the very subtle movements and poses in the paradise scene. In Hades, with Mefistofele, there was much writhing, rolling and reactive movement to the principal singers. I could see from Janet's energy that she was enjoying this process and work, [with which she conveyed] her [own] strength as a character dancer and actress."[25]

The next opera Reed worked on was *Manon*, which ran in March 1975 and required only the kind of interlude Reed had danced in decades earlier, when San Francisco Ballet was still part of the San Francisco Opera. In 1937, for example, she was listed in the cast of *La Traviata, The Masked Ball,* and *Faust* with choreography by Serge Oukrainsky.[26]

All Little remembered about *Manon* was waltzing in beautiful costumes. She had much stronger memories of working with Reed on *Aïda* in 1976, the last opera Reed did the choreography for before resigning later that year. In a possible echo of "The Unanswered Question" in Balanchine's *Ivesiana,* in which Allegra Kent was carried around by several men who she was required to trust not to drop her, Little, facing the audience with one leg extended and toes pointed straight at the opera house ceiling, is carried high over their heads by two male dancers. "I have many fond and funny memories of Janet and the cast of dancers while we were in the process of creating and performing [Aïda]," Little said. "[Her] sense of humor was witty and sarcastic, but there were times when she'd be rehearsing us and she would snap out a comment to the male dancers and I couldn't help but laugh and lose control of my role in the air."[27] It is telling, as well, that Reed incorporated children into her choreography for Aïda, ever mindful that young ballet students need opportunities to perform and realize exactly what they are training for.

On the whole, Reed's opera choreography was well received by Seattle's reviewers from the very beginning. Seattle Post-Intelligencer jazz and theater critic Maggie Hawthorn gave her high marks for her staging of Manon's first act ballet, calling the young company's participation in a dance interlude that is frequently omitted from the opera a "significant cultural event." She took note of the progress they had made under Reed's tutelage and their "grace and professional bearing."[28] However, in the same piece she slammed what she described as "the faked-up orgy scene" in Mefistofele, which, she said, "was an embarrassing paste up of writhing and amateur bumps and grinds which appeared to have been choreographed over the telephone."

"The charming little ballet in Manon was altogether another story," she added. "Ballet mistress Janet Reed has choreographed the interlude to suit the capabilities of her young dancers and she has captured the simple style of the early French setting. Actually, Manon is set in the 18th century and what Miss Reed has crafted is a sweetly winning but anachronistic recreation after the fashion of the romantic Marie Taglioni, who revolutionized European ballet in the 19th century by floating delicately on her tiptoes, bringing 'sur les pointes' into the permanent technique of the dance." Like Little, she admired "the "bell-shaped" costumes the corps members wore and found their dancing "generally quite ept."

In the same column, Hawthorn pointed out that PND, which had been going for only eight months at the time of her writing, still had a lot of work to do to become the professional resident ballet company that was Kalimos and Reed's goal. Nevertheless, she considered Reed's "school version" of Stravinsky's Pulcinella, which had had its first performances two weeks before Manon, and plans for a full-length Nutcracker to be presented at the Opera House during the holiday season to be reasons for optimism.[29]

Igor Stravinsky's witty, lighthearted, thoroughly danceable *Pulcinella Suite* (after Pergolesi) made a fine showcase for the young dancers in Reed's charge. The score provided many opportunities for expressing humor in dance—Reed as a performer was peerless at this—and for teaching both the apprentices and their audiences a thing or two about mime, ballet technique, and (no small thing), matching their movements with live music. And by setting movement for the musicians, which included three singers from the Seattle Opera, she created a thoroughly integrated entertainment of music and dance.

The music was not unknown to Reed. It's the same score Bolender used for his 1945 piece *Musical Chairs* and that Balanchine used, in a greatly expanded version, for the most elaborate production of New York City Ballet's 1972 Stravinsky Festival. Although Reed was not in the cast of Bolender's non-narrative take on the piece (it was a series of bravura solos by five dancers), she would certainly have seen it, if not when it premiered, then a year later when it was retitled *Comédia Balletica* for Denham's Ballet Russe and/or a decade later, when Bolender retooled it for Robbins's Ballets: U.S.A. and called it *Games*. Reed was still living on the East Coast in 1972 and in frequent attendance at City Ballet; it would be surprising if she did not see a work produced in part as a showcase for Edward Villella, a dancer she had nurtured when she was the company's ballet master.

According to Wayne Johnson, the arts and entertainment editor for the *Seattle Daily Times,* Reed's *Pulcinella* was responsible for introducing the music to the Pacific Northwest. The ballet premiered on March 4, 1975, at West Seattle High School in two free performances sponsored by the Washington State Cultural Enrichment Program. These concerts also marked the first time the Seattle Symphony, Seattle Opera, and Pacific Northwest Dance performed jointly. They would soon do ten more performances at area schools, including at a community college.

Johnson reviewed *Pulcinella* extremely positively as a "happy show" and a "delightful" entertainment, featuring excellent orchestral playing, good singing, and spritely dancing." But he didn't think much of the narrative content: "Ms. Reed's choreography told a silly little story about the amorous shenanigans of the rascal-clown Pulcinella," he wrote dismissively. "The story wasn't important. The way the dancers mimed and twirled and kicked up their heels with joy was important—and fun."[30]

Little didn't remember how many sections of the score Reed used, but she did remember that she, Charlotte Richards, and Tom Spanski were, respectively, Pimpinella, Rosetta, and Pulcinella. The plot involved Pimpinella and Rosetta competing for the attention of Pulcinella while dancing to a score that Little found challenging, despite Reed's helpful counts for the "odd" phrasing. What she most vividly remembered of Reed's directing was that while the steps were important, Reed emphasized artistic interpretation and the telling of the story.

Spanski was the only male in that first apprentice group, something Maria Tallchief noticed when she came west from Chicago to give master classes at the Good Shepherd Center studio a week or so following the first showing of *Pulcinella*. In a press conference she gave on behalf of PND on March 21, she issued high praise for the training her old City Ballet dressing-room roommate was giving young dancers. In the account by Carole Beers, Tallchief smiled at Reed as she spoke of the pleasure she took in "see[ing] the students being taught so well. It is good to see the students doing it properly, and not wasting their time." As for the lack of boys in that first class, she said, "You have the nucleus of a very good company here. But only one boy. I think boys give up when they see how hard a professional dancer must work. Besides, they have to make a living."

That characterization of male ballet students does not of course fit them all, and Reed enjoyed teaching them throughout her career, frequently citing her work with Villella in her program bios. Tallchief's remark about their scarcity in that first class must have stung a bit. In any case, Reed soon rectified the "only one boy" situation on a visit to the School of American Ballet, where she recruited Robert Sund, who had clear memories of her appearance in the studio where he was taking company class alongside City Ballet principal dancers Peter Martins and Helgi Tómasson. Sund, who was six feet two inches tall and was a scholarship student from Minnesota, recalled, this "midget red-headed woman" being escorted into class by the equally small school administrator, who told Reed who she could *not* recruit, presumably Martins and Tómasson, among others. Reed, Sund said, "lured me with the promise of pretty girls," although he had never done any partnering. After some negotiating, Kalimos offered him a job and flew him out to Seattle, evidently in time for the 1975 summer program, where he soon learned to partner a pretty girl named Vivian Little; he danced with her onstage and off for the next several years.

In a press release dated April 30, 1975, Kalimos announced that the company's summer school program of classes and choreography would begin on June 16 and run through August 22 and that the school would "officially" begin in September, when it would offer "the complete scope of training in classical ballet technique, from beginning through to the advanced scholarship level."[31] In a later press release, this was refined to a "graded curriculum of five divisions: threshold classes for 5 and 6 year olds, men's classes and advanced ballet technique, and adult classes at beginning, intermediate and advanced levels." The faculty included former Joffrey Ballet dancer Nancy Robinson and G. Hubbard Miller, who was the school's music director.[32]

A second studio opened at the Good Shepherd Center in time for the summer program, where Todd Bolender, Lew Christensen, and Willam Christensen had been contracted to teach technique to the professional students and apprentices and develop repertory. Reed had invited her old partner in dance and laughter to join her in her new endeavor, and after meeting with Kalimos in New York he was delighted to accept.

"I have been on the West Coast working with Janet Reed in Seattle," Bolender wrote to his protégé and friend Joel Schnee on August 25. "Janet's working her ass off and *she* asked for help so I went there."[33] Bolender was not the only one of Reed's East Coast associates she had asked for help; a letter from Lincoln Kirstein dated September 4, 1974, soon after her arrival in Seattle, urges her to be involved with "Ruthanna Boris's set up at the University of Washington,"[34] implying that she had asked him for advice. In a letter dated April 3, 1975, Kirstein wrote, "I think you have done a hell of a lot better than Ruthanna at the University; unquestionably you are more professional and capable [but] the University is not equipped to handle a professional situation."[35]

Reed must have said something about needing teaching help to Kirstein, because in the same letter he wrote that City Ballet dancer Frank Ohman was interested in teaching, as he was approaching retirement from the company and his dancing career was winding down. Earlier in the spring, Reed seems to have gotten in touch with Jerome Robbins, who responded with a brief note dated March 20, 1975, that said that he would try to work with her if he managed to get to Seattle, but he was "in Ravel up to our eyebrows and the Festival opens May 14th which is why I doubt I can get out there."[36] Robbins turned out to be right about that; there is no record of him working with PND dancers at any time, which is a shame, since his participation would certainly have bolstered Reed's standing with Kalimos and the board of directors.

Bolender's schedule was as busy as ever, but he adored working with Reed and in this period of his post-performance career, he was going pretty much anywhere he was given an opportunity to work. That peripatetic life began about the same time Reed left New York for Dutchess County and Bolender, without giving up the apartment on East 95th Street that he and John Mandia had begun sharing in the early 1960s, departed for Turkey, where he would continue to work off and on until 1979. From 1963 to 1969 he was directing opera-house ballet companies in Germany, first in Cologne, then in Frankfurt, and while he and Mandia had shared housing in both cities during their tenure with those companies (Mandia was Bolender's ballet master), New York remained their home.

When he arrived in Seattle in late June 1975, Bolender was impressed by the Good Shepherd Center's two "huge" studios and dressing-room space. He reported to Schnee that he was teaching the apprentice company's daily class and the beginning students. Sund, one of the apprentices, not only learned technique from Bolender, but, perhaps more important, how to work and how to teach. (Following his stint with PND, Sund became a principal dancer with San Francisco Ballet; after he retired from dancing he became a teacher of note.) Bolender's personal style in the studio was not like that of Sund's previous teachers, not even at SAB. He recalled that Bolender was extremely well organized and "eccentric and amusing."[37] From his description of Bolender's classes, it is clear that Bolender had been as inspired by Balanchine the teacher as he had been by Balanchine the choreographer; like Balanchine, Bolender compelled his students to dance the same steps over and over.

"We would do 16 glissades," Sund said, "and then repeat them." Bolender's careful lesson plans confirm that; in them he specified how many times to repeat each step. In notes labeled "About Teaching," Bolender instructs an unnamed teacher to structure a class for children with pliés, tendu battements, and then combinations of "a very simple but exacting nature—rond de jambe à terre with the sweep toward second, do not stop in 4th front."[38] Throughout a teaching career that began when he was a very young modern dancer, Bolender emphasized the need for professional dancers to go back to the basics from time to time and for all students to execute steps in class without holding anything back, just as Balanchine had. Like him, he would say, "What are you saving it for?" He also imposed a strict dress code, not only for students but also for faculty. When he was directing the Kansas City Ballet, according to James Jordan, his ballet master, he insisted that jeans were inappropriate garb for anyone working in a ballet studio, including visiting choreographers and stagers.

Little also recalled Bolender working them very hard indeed in company class, but with enormous patience. The 90-minute classes could run overtime by as much as half an hour, and the barre could last more than an hour. "I remember several variations of tendu combinations consisting of eight and sometimes 16 battements tendu en croix, [and] long and slow adagios with extensions held for an eternity," she said. As they did Sund, Bolender's methods affected her own teaching. "I have often referred to [their] benefits," she wrote. "His lengthy barre helped us to build strength and his attention to detail helped mold my work ethic. He might spend ten minutes on the detail of articulation of the elbow, wrist and fingers!"[39]

That first summer for Bolender (the second for Reed) was partly devoted to preparation for *The Nutcracker*, and while Bolender was indeed developing new repertory and in some cases Reed was coaching the dancers, as was stated in the press announcement, none of the repertory was intended to receive public performances until the following summer. One of the things they worked on was Lew Christensen's *Filling Station*, which was staged by San Francisco Ballet's ballet master Robert Gladstein, but Little well remembered being coached in the role of the tipsy Rich Girl by Reed, watching her "act out parts [at the same time] she was focusing on how to dance in a tipsy sophisticated way."[40] Both Reed and Bolender were involved in a week-long seminar for teachers, as was Kalimos. According to a write-up in the PND newsletter, the lectures, demonstrations, and class observations were free to the participating teachers and covered many subjects, including stagecraft, ballet technique, and a presentation on music in ballet by Henry Holt, conductor of the Pacific Northwest Wagner Festival. Kalimos lectured on school administration, company touring, public relations, advertising, marketing, and fund-raising, and Bolender did lecture demonstrations on choreography, using a work in progress. One teacher from Logan, Utah, whose two daughters were students in the summer program, sent a heartfelt note to Reed, thanking her for her kindness to her daughters and expressing her sincere appreciation for "having had the opportunity to watch your classes," adding that she was "taking home ideas which will help my students."[41]

While Lew Christensen didn't arrive in Seattle until September to stage his *Nutcracker,* there was certainly pressure in the summer to start training the apprentice company to perform it, since the new production was scheduled to premiere on December 19 at the Seattle Opera House. As is well known, *The Nutcracker* had been central to the financial survival of professional ballet companies (and civic ones) in the United States since 1954, when Balanchine, according to Bolender and many others, saved his groundbreaking New York City Ballet from financial ruin with his own magical version of the Tchaikovsky-Petipa-Ivanov classic. But as Kalimos well knew, San Francisco Ballet had done it first in 1944, with a production choreographed by Willam Christensen with some informal consultation with Balanchine and Danilova while the Ballet Russe was in the city on tour, and input from San Francisco's Russian émigré community. Lew Christensen had choreographed it again in 1954 and in 1967, when it was televised, bringing national attention to the West Coast company.

By 1975, *The Nutcracker* in multiple versions had become a dependable cash cow for ballet companies all over the country and Kalimos was both playing it safe and taking a risk with PND, making sure they had a full-blown, lavishly produced *Nutcracker* before they had an established school or professional company or even a company style. And he knew exactly how to do it. He had spent the better part of three years raising the $130,000 needed to fund San Francisco Ballet's 1967 re-choreographed and redesigned production, and in Seattle he approached the task in the same way, cajoling the executive board of the Seattle Opera to float the fledgling ballet company a loan and the city's monied citizens to supply the funds for the lavish production. Grant money from the state of Washington and the National Endowment for the Arts was also helpful (although it caused some resentment from other more established performing arts organizations). Arguably he was even more successful in Seattle than he had been in San Francisco, since in a shorter period of time he managed to raise almost twice what he had in the larger and wealthier city.

According to *Nutcracker* program notes, Kalimos started the process the day Reed arrived in Seattle, signing Robert O'Hearn to design the sets and costumes, as he had done for the 1967 San Francisco production, and Lew Christensen to restage his choreography. He also commissioned master lighting designer Tom Skelton to light the ballet. No expense was spared for a production Kalimos expected to be the new company's bread and butter for many years to come. Which it was: eight years later, in 1983, it was replaced with the very different—and charming—Maurice Sendak production, whose libretto was extremely close to E. T. A. Hoffmann's original story, wittily and whimsically translated into dance by choreographer Kent Stowell.

This first *Nutcracker* had a cast of 150 dancers, including children, and Reed, who was already extremely busy teaching that first group of apprentices, choreographing for Tchaikovsky's opera *Eugene Onegin*, and looking after her ailing husband, cast her net far to find them, alienating local ballet school administrators and teachers, who viewed this as a threat to their business. In a letter dated May 15, 1975, to the executive director of the Washington State Arts Commission, area teachers Dorothy Fisher, Gwenn Barker, Karen Irvin, Jan Collum, and Jo Emery attacked Reed's professionalism and integrity for attending an audition for SAB's summer program that had been held in Tacoma earlier in the month and "securing the names of certain dancers and since [approaching] them with offers of scholarships from her training program." In other words, the signers were accusing Reed of poaching their students and of violating PND recruitment policies, which had been presented at a meeting three years before she arrived in Seattle. As stated in the letter, those policies were that "dancers would be auditioned at special auditions; PNWD would only accept dancers graduating from high school and or those ready for a professional career; those dancers accepted would be of professional caliber and would be paid for performing."[42]

Reed had long been part of the SAB national scholarship audition process and therefore had every right to be present at this audition. Should she have invited the students she judged to be promising into her own program? Arguably what she ought to have done is ask them to audition and taken it from there, but she was not by nature patient and *The Nutcracker* loomed large on the horizon. She could be ruthless in her search for young dancers to train: a student of Jacqueline Martin Schumacher's, Reed's close friend since the 1930s, once overheard the two women arguing angrily about someone Reed, who was frequently a visiting faculty member at Schumacher's Portland studio, wanted to take back to Seattle to train for the apprentice company.

Ultimately, by hook or by crook and with students from the San Francisco Ballet School, such as Margaret Gray, who was hired to dance several different parts, roles were filled and the premiere took place in a gala performance on December 19. Thanks to rigorous rehearsals and meticulous coaching from Christensen, Gladstein, and Reed, who was given credit in every write-up for the excellence of her work with the children, *The Nutcracker* was a smashing success, giving six sold-out performances and receiving rave reviews from most Seattle-area critics.

"Everything was right," wrote Carole Beers in a review of the opening-night gala in the *Seattle Times*. "The lighting by New York designer Thomas Skelton; the scenic and costume design by another New York veteran Robert O'Hearn; the choreography by San Francisco Ballet's Lew Christensen; the Tchaikovsky music, played by Seattle Symphony orchestra musicians; and even the dancing." Of guest artists Cynthia Gregory and Ivan Nagy, Beers wrote, "[they] made the pas de deux truly grand in spite of a number of rather awkward lifts and carries." (Christensen was not responsible for those—with little rehearsal time available, Gregory and Nagy, both American Ballet Theatre stars, chose to dance the choreography they were accustomed to performing at galas and as guest artists all over the world.) After acknowledging the contributions by soloists from San Francisco Ballet in the Chinese and Ribbon Candy divertissements, Beers judged that PND's own soloists "looked quite respectable. After all, this was their first dance performance, other than in Seattle Opera productions." (Actually, it wasn't, if you count the many well-received performances of *Pulcinella* that preceded *Nutcracker*.) Beers deemed the corps de ballet's renditions of the Flowers and Snowflakes satisfactory, as were "the children who acted in the party scene: their madcap scampering delighted the capacity audience."[43]

Hawthorn, who claimed to have seen *Nutcrackers* performed all over the country, considered the $250,000 production "the most sumptuous" of them all and characterized the endeavor as a "make or break" situation for both Kalimos and Reed. Unlike Beers, she paid meticulous attention to the dancing, providing a record of the talents of the performers and some documentation of what Christensen's choreography actually was like.

Writing about the local talent, Hawthorn began with the youngest cast member and judged the Waltz of the Flowers "the loveliest dance segment, with the corps costumed in petals of true rose colors and led by an exquisite young member of PNWD, Charlotte Richards . . . [who] had a quickness and a grace which lifted her quite out of the ordinary." She also commended

Sund as a "feisty King of the Mice who dies with real flair, [and] Glen Hasstedt as an extremely acrobatic Chinese dancer."[44]

George Burley, arts and entertainment editor for the *Everett Herald,* chose to put Christensen's choreography in the context of other productions: "It is inescapable to conclude that this production is an eclectic packaging of the most appealing and workable elements of dozens of productions which have preceded it elsewhere."[45] It was actually the same choreography as for the 1967 San Francisco production, and from Little's description of Arabian Coffee, Christensen had definitely borrowed from Balanchine's first version of the divertissement, in which Bolender had been second cast, sitting in the center of a carpet "smoking" a hookah with four children from SAB costumed as parrots placed around the edges. Christensen put in more children than Balanchine had; the male soloist in this case was a magician who danced a pas de deux with an adult female dancer (Little danced the role in Seattle and in San Francisco), and in his version, carpets are part of the action.

One press release had stated that Bolender would dance Drosselmeyer at the opening gala, but there is no record either in the program or anywhere else that he actually did so or that he was even present in the audience. Bolender didn't mention that possibility in a letter he wrote to Schnee from Seattle on November 14, but he did say something about advising the guest teachers who were working with PND to prepare them for *Nutcracker.* What is clear from the correspondence is that Bolender had been in and out of Seattle for much of the second half of 1975 and the following year. In a letter he wrote from Seattle dated March 30, 1976, he reported, "The dancers here are coming along nicely and I should think in another year Janet should have a rather neat little company if she can take the pressures of the job. She teaches, runs the school, choreographs for the opera and hires dancers and tries to keep them on a budget that is almost laughable it is so small. . . . She seems to thrive on hard work."[46]

Six months later, Bolender wrote Schnee that Janet had resigned, Melissa Hayden had taken over, and he would be leaving for Vienna to stage *Souvenirs* and *The Still Point* five days later. Hayden, he added, wanted him to return the following summer.

It wasn't hard work that caused Reed to resign; Bolender was correct that she thrived on it and always had. It was a quarrel between Kalimos and Erskine over the telephone that placed her squarely in the middle that made her quit on the day before the 1976 summer intensive began. As Bolender remembered it, he had been slated to teach a class and develop some new repertoire for the fledgling company, and he was in his Seattle apartment, preparing his classes, when the phone rang at 9 a.m. It was Reed, almost hysterical, he said. "I couldn't believe it. Kalimos and Branson had fought. A terrible fight, she said, [and she] somehow got caught between them." Then she told Bolender he would have to take over for her. That meant he would have to teach all the classes in addition to doing some of the choreography and rehearsing the ballets, *Filling Station* among them, for the end of the session showcase. "I had to figure out how the hell to do it," Bolender said. "I was just there to teach a class a day or something like that and suddenly I had this whole stream of things I had to get done, everything had to change. I was the only teacher." There were about twenty-five students in the program that summer and some drop-in students, including Tommy Rall, star of 1950s film and Broadway musicals, who Bolender had first known during his brief stint with Ballet Theatre in 1944. In 1976, Rall was teaching at the University of Washington. "He and his wife (a former ballet dancer) came to take class every day," Bolender said. Since Rall had taught in the program the previous year, he would have liked to have hired him again, but he was told there was no money to pay him.[47]

In several printed interviews conducted some months after Reed's resignation and in some notes Reed possibly made in preparation for writing a memoir, it is clear that the combination of repeatedly being told there was no money for much-needed help of all kinds in the school; the quarrel between her husband and her boss; a lack of communication between her and Kalimos; and his refusal to involve her or anyone else on staff in artistic decisions made Reed, no quitter at any previous time in her life, resign so precipitously just as her contract was up for renewal on July 4, 1976. In undated notes, labeled "Why I Quit," Reed wrote that she was seriously overworked and that her new contract didn't indicate that anything was going to change. From the beginning of her tenure, she had been having trouble getting steady help because Kalimos "simply would not pay enough to teachers, pianists or office help."[48] Some of those jobs were being done by volunteers from the Seattle Opera, whose work she implied she found unsatisfactory. "The N.E.A. [National Endowment for the Arts] Boards," she concluded, "are happy if there is no red ink." While PND had a large board of directors and a track record in successful fund-raising for special projects such as *The Nutcracker*, Reed's notes imply that Kalimos did not inform them of the financial needs of the school, one reason money was in short supply for professional help. She hadn't gone directly to the board herself because she did not want to jeopardize the positions of people she had worked with from the beginning. It is interesting that she stated that it was she who suggested that Melissa Hayden replace her because she wanted the company to develop in the Balanchine tradition.

While Reed resisted taking her complaints of overwork and insufficient financial and staff support to PND's board, one can safely assume that she did not hold back at home about those issues and her disappointment that there was nothing in her new contract to rectify the situation. It is entirely possible that this caused Erskine to take matters into his own hands and telephone Kalimos directly. Once again, Reed was feeling the pull between work and family life. Under these overworked circumstances she couldn't have had much energy left for domestic issues, which, in some ways, the move across the country had not changed. Jane Erskine, who had graduated early from Emma Willard, was still an adolescent in the throes of rebelling against parental expectations that she would go on to college, and Erskine remained chronically ill with diabetes and basically had nothing to do once he had arranged their belongings in their apartment in Seattle's Magnolia district. It was a several-story walk-up, worth the climb for views of the city's beautiful setting between mountains and water and a perfect place for the parties that Reed was surely far too exhausted to host. They did get out and about to some degree; in 1975, Bolender wrote Schnee about going with the Erskines to see Valery and Galina Panov perform (and took the opportunity to rail against what he called Russian "defectives," in defense of American dancers) but it was hardly the active social life Erskine had enjoyed on the East Coast.

Bolender, with his customary can-do attitude, quickly pulled himself together after Reed's resignation and taught both the apprentices and the students in the summer program. And, despite being short-handed, with the help of the school's music director, G. Hubbard Miller, and former New York City Ballet principal Sara Leland, who staged two works by Balanchine and one by John Taras, Bolender produced and directed the promised showcase right on time. Titled *Ballet '77: A Summer Preview*, it opened on July 30 at Meany Hall on the University of Washington campus for a two-weekend run, with two different repertory shows. It was a great deal of work, but in the early 1940s, before Ballet Society or City Ballet had come into existence, Bolender had begun getting repertory programs on stage that included his own choreography and that of William Dollar, Mary Jane Shea, and Balanchine.

As he wrote to his friend Roy Tobias, the task was made easier because he had been working with the students "rather regularly for the past year and a half, and I was quite able to guide them very carefully thru [my] classes into the choreography that would be a test for them. Actually the choreography was not so demanding, mostly, but style always is and that is where I was a little afraid they might fall down but there were enough rehearsals and I was able to convey to them the quality of each of the works . . . sufficiently well to make them understand the immense range required of them. . . . They did well . . . Milly and Janet Reed giggled at certain attempts they made to be noble or serious or passionate but in the works that flowed easily or told a story, they did very well."[49]

The Seattle-area critics were certainly receptive to the showcase, which was also intended to be a preview of performances that would take place in the Opera House the following spring. In a review in the *Everett Herald*, George Burley was quick to credit "recently resigned ballet mistress Janet Reed with training her dancers well, pursuing with success much more than elementary stepping. For this first program, the 24 PND dancers (six of whom did not appear this first weekend) were trained in four divertissements and a short story ballet."[50]

The curtain raiser was Balanchine's *Pas de Dix,* which he first mounted in 1955, which Reynolds described in *Repertory in Review* as "a serviceable piece, intended to showcase the abilities of certain dancers."[51] In Seattle, those dancers were Sund and Little, among others, and Val Caniparoli, who had been dancing in the corps at San Francisco Ballet since 1973 and would soon become a soloist with the company and ultimately one of the most stylistically eclectic choreographers the United States has produced.

The short-story ballet was *Filling Station.* Burley gave top marks to Sund as Mac the service station attendant and to Little as the "stoned" debutante. "Both had appeared twice already during the evening, but here they could be seen in demanding solo work, which they fulfilled expertly and naturally."[52]

While Burley thought the strongest dancing of the evening was in a classical piece by John Taras titled *Designs with Strings,* Beers, reviewing for the

Seattle Times considered the work to be "the great bore of the program. The dancers must have thought so too," she added, "for they went through the poses and unimaginative combinations as if they wished they were elsewhere. Maybe in *Filling Station*." That she considered to be the hit of the evening; she described the 1938 ballet as Lew Christensen's most enduring work and a "masterpiece of Americana." She added, "The dancers, especially Robert Sund as Mac, mimed and danced brilliantly. Sund is Pacific Northwest Dance's ace, moving high, strong and handsome through leaps, difficult turns and entrechats six." Beers was equally delighted with Little and Caniparoli's performance as the drunken rich couple. "You knew they could really dance, but for their lolling heads and collapsing legs." Caniparoli had likely already danced the role with San Francisco Ballet, whose production Kalimos had borrowed for these concerts, and Reed's coaching of Little the previous summer in one of her signature roles had clearly paid off. Moreover, Beers gave Reed full credit for all the work she had done since her arrival in Seattle two years earlier: "Friday's concert made it abundantly clear that Janet Reed, who recently resigned as ballet mistress, has done a marvelous job of schooling the dancers." Kalimos, too, came in for praise, albeit barbed: Beers labeled him a champion of chutzpah while acknowledging that he had "work[ed] wonders securing some fine talent, teachers and choreographers."[53]

One of those teachers was former New York City Ballet member Marilee Stiles, who performed in both Balanchine works on the program. "She not only has a marvelously appealing long-limbed body, but is blessed with excellent technique," Beers wrote. Like her, Beers continued, company members "Rachel Westlake and Lisa McVeigh demonstrated a similar ease with Balanchine choreography, in *Valse* and in *Pas de Dix*. These pieces both are pleasant little abstract works, containing demanding dancing which requires a great degree of musicality. The adagio sections, ensemble dancing and feet do need work, however."[54]

While there was no Bolender choreography on the first program, for the second weekend he choreographed a new pas de deux titled *La Favorita* that Little and Sund danced. As Little recalled, Bolender had originally intended to choreograph a larger piece that would include more dancers, but he couldn't get it to come together. "He tried setting a piece on us to Mozart's *Turkish Rondo*. . . . What I remember vividly is the standing and waiting in his rehearsals. I was fascinated by what I thought was his perfectionism. He'd give us a phrase to show him, clearly he didn't like what he saw, started thinking in his head, marking out some movement, after a few minutes, would show us something different, have us try that version, etc. for hours, weeks. To me, he seemed to have been experiencing a choreographer's block and was only frustrated with himself, not the dancers. He was reflective and gentle. After several weeks, we were told that we would not be performing this new work but rather Robert Sund and I would perform his Donizetti pas de deux, *La Favorita!* After so much standing and waiting to finish his Mozart piece, it was such a relief to quickly rehearse and perform this bravura pas de deux. It was in the pas rehearsals that I came to know Todd's humor, dramatic side and his attention to detail."[55] According to a review Beers wrote of the summer performances in 1976, the pas de deux was "the smash hit of the Pacific Northwest Dance repertoire" for its "fast solos, languid adagio, breath-catching lifts." Her description of Little's "plunge" into Sund's arms in the concluding fish dive, which she performed with "such gusto that she nearly made the orchestra pit instead," is reminiscent of Reed's equally risk-taking performance in *Filling Station,* when she drunkenly leaned extremely close to the musicians playing in the pit at City Center in New York.[56]

Bolender said nothing in his correspondence about this episode of choreographer's block, if that's what it was. He had used Mozart's *Turkish Rondo* before, in the 1940s, and while he may well have wanted to re-choreograph it, it is also possible that he was restaging it and couldn't remember the steps. In any case, it's both compelling and commendable that he did not take out his frustrations on the young dancers in his charge.

On the face of it, Reed's precipitous declaration of independence from PND on the July 4th weekend was a highly irresponsible act, and Reed herself may well have perceived it as such. Not only did she immediately recommend Hayden as her replacement, she also wrote directly to her old comrade in pointe shoes—they had danced at the same time with City Ballet and they had overlapped at American Ballet Theatre and as teachers in the Saratoga Springs summer program.

Hayden summed up that history in a response dated July 28, 1976. "Just received your second lovely letter with the clippings and all and just last night I was talking to Don [Hayden's husband, Donald Coleman, who Kalimos had hired to direct the PND School] and saying kind of superstitiously how often your life and decisions have had a profound influence on my own ... and always for the good. The first with Jerry [Robbins] and *Interplay* far, far back. .... Then you were leaving NYCB coincidentally when I wanted to return and Balanchine only 'forgave' my leaving because he needed someone to fill the vacancy you left and now here in Seattle."[57] Evidently Balanchine's forgiveness stretched over the years, because in this letter Hayden reports that she had had a long talk with him and that he had "assured cooperation on every level."

Hayden went on to express some of her anxieties about moving across the country, far from her grown son and the area in which she had spent all of her adult life, and, reasonably, about her uncertainty about "the true level of administrative support, financial and otherwise once the going gets rough and the chips are down." And she regretted that Reed was planning to leave Seattle because she had been looking forward to working with her; she hoped she would reconsider. "Do you think," she asked, "one City could take the both of us?"[58]

A better question might have been, Do you think one city could take all three of us?—that is, including Bolender. Unquestionably, Seattle would have been extremely fortunate to have "taken" all three people and given them the money and the freedom to set the standards for training and hiring dancers and acquiring and creating repertoire, working with Kalimos and the board to establish a resident ballet company the city could be proud of.

While their family backgrounds were quite different, their professional experiences were somewhat different, and Hayden was a decade or so younger than Bolender and Reed, their work ethics were the same and their points of view on teaching and its relationship to performing were incontrovertibly shaped by Balanchine. In practical terms, all three were children of the Great Depression, which made them extremely frugal when it came to both their personal and their professional budgets, and they were as concerned about the salaries of any employees—dancers, teachers, accompanists and office workers—as they were about their own.

Additionally, Reed and Hayden's parallel lives as successful ballerinas who married and bore children while they were still dancing, hardly the norm in the middle of the last century, are worth noting, as is the fact that Bolender had enormous respect for them for it. Hayden and Reed's family backgrounds, however, had little similarity. Reed spent her early childhood in rural Oregon. Her training and early career in Portland were supported at least psychologically by her single mother and economically when her mother was able to manage it. Hayden, on the other hand, whose birth name was Melissa Herman, was first-generation Canadian. Her parents were Russian Jews who fled tsarist pogroms and landed in Toronto in the early part of the twentieth century. They spoke Russian at home, and while they were interested in the arts, they insisted that Hayden go to secretarial school so she would always be able to earn a living. They needn't have worried: because of her monumental talent and technical versatility, Hayden never needed those secretarial skills to put food on her table. Her performing career began in the corps of Radio City Music Hall's ballet company in the early 1940s and ended in 1973 at the New York State Theater with a gala performance of *Cortège Hongrois,* a ballet Balanchine made in her honor that remains in City Ballet's repertory five decades later. In between, she danced with Ballet Theatre and made countless television and stage appearances with various companies all over the world. Lincoln Kirstein dubbed her City Ballet's first real star in a company that didn't go in for stars, despite some historic battles for billing between Tallchief and Reed in the early 1950s.

After her retirement from dancing, Hayden moved from the city to upstate New York, where she taught at Skidmore College. She had just resigned from that position when she received the first letter from Reed. The timing was excellent: she needed a job and, like Reed, brought along her husband and teenaged daughter, leaving behind her adult son. They didn't stay long: for the next ten months, with Hayden as ballet master and teacher of advanced students and the apprentices, Coleman as school director, Bolender in and out of town teaching and choreographing, and Reed (who far from leaving the area, spent the rest of her life there) doing some teaching and informal advising), PNWB went through a period of adolescence that was hard in varying degrees on everyone involved.

Hayden began well. She was excited, she told Seattle journalists at a press conference, to be working in the place she called "the last frontier" for the establishment of a ballet company. "Of course," she told the assembled members of the press, "knowing Janet (Reed, former ballet mistress) and Todd (Bolender, resident choreographer) all contribute to my excitement in coming." She also spoke of her feeling for a city where she had performed many times on tour, citing City Ballet's appearances at the Seattle World's Fair in 1962 as being particularly memorable. One thing that contributed to

Hayden's optimism about PND's future was the experience the young dancers had been given in school shows, which "makes it look so professional in such a short time."[59]

While Hayden's contract had a starting date of September 7, she was already at work, teaching class and watching rehearsals for the upcoming Meany Hall showcase. And she had high hopes and great ambition for the future of the school. "What I'm interested in," she said, "is taking the talent of the area and allowing it to develop. There will always be a New York to go to . . . but the decentralization of dance, the regional ballet is on the rise. It has to be. I agree with the dance boom idea. It's real. It's not just Baryshnikov or the defectors from Russia. It's that ballet is an accepted discipline for girls and boys, like playing tennis." Even more compelling was her report of a conversation she'd had with Balanchine about recruiting dancers from SAB. In her account of their conversation, Balanchine had approved of the idea: "We produce too many dancers anyway. We can't use them all. They go other places, why not to Seattle?"[60]

Coleman arrived the following week to take up his new duties as school director, a role that had added considerably to Reed's workload, and start house-hunting with Hayden. And Bolender, satisfied, as he wrote to Tobias, who was living and teaching in Seoul, that he "was leaving Hayden with a well-trained, well-disciplined group of dancers," departed for Europe shortly after the Meany Hall performances. Hayden was impressed enough by the job he had done not only to ask him to return but also to offer to store his boxes of books in the very large house she and Coleman had leased for two years. "I had a good feeling about the whole situation," he told Tobias. "I somehow felt she would manage this and beautifully. I would come back from time to time and somehow a lovely company of dancers would suddenly surprise the dance world."[61]

That was not to be, at least not under her watch. According to an article in the *Bellevue-Kirkland Journal American* titled "The Immovable Object & the Irresistible Force," Hayden's first missteps involved the staging and rehearsing of *The Nutcracker* for its performances the previous December, when she played fast and loose with the choreography, transposing "bits" from Balanchine's 1964 version into Christensen's version. This did not go down well with Kalimos, who immediately removed them. From there, Hayden's tenure as a first-time ballet master who thought she was going to become the company's artistic director went speedily downhill. According to Bill Alpert, who wrote the article, the previous November Kalimos and Hayden had exchanged many memos in which Kalimos told Hayden she could not initiate any communications with the press office (and presumably not with the press itself) and was to confine her activities to rehearsing the dancers and, in her words, "leave administrative matters to 'the grownups.'" Also according to Alpert, she had been kept in the dark about budgetary matters, future performance dates, costumes, salaries, and even the school curriculum. What seems to have gone unacknowledged is her productive use of her relationship with Balanchine: thanks to his promise of assistance, Hayden had acquired the rights to six new Balanchine ballets, which, in soloist roles, had been performed by four guest artists from City Ballet, and she had been able to borrow their sets and costumes at no cost to the company's budget, which was no small thing.[62]

As had Reed, Hayden was feeling overworked (although with Coleman doing the school's administrative work she had been relieved of the bureaucratic burdens her predecessor had borne), but she did succeed in getting authorization to hire Ron Sequoio as a second ballet master, against Bolender's advice. Sequoio had had a small company in New York that had had modest success with some critics, but Bolender didn't think much of his teaching or his choreography. Of Sequoio's tenure with PND, Bolender wrote, "[He] loathed [Hayden] and me and spoke poisonously to the students about both of us but dedicated a ballet in Feb. to her."[63]

Despite Sequoio's help, Hayden's frustrations had reached the boiling point by March. When Phelps had dinner with her one night and scolded her about teaching class and rehearsing the dancers with a cigarette hanging out of her mouth and using bad language, behavior he said might be okay in New York but definitely not in Seattle, she resigned on the spot.[64] As chair of the board of directors, Phelps accepted her resignation with equal alacrity, although she stayed on through the spring in order to prepare the company to dance a new *Coppélia*.

The problems with Kalimos continued through the spring, when she and Reed called jointly for his resignation, providing red meat to the Seattle press, which had long expressed resentment of his constant press releases, and provoking a thoroughly misogynistic response from San Francisco Ballet's director, Michael Smuin. "I do not wish to say anything derogatory about Ms. Reed or Ms. Hayden," Smuin wrote to Beers, "but the direction and the administration of a ballet company is something about which neither of them have a great deal of experience but rather as being top interpretive artists, they spent their time and energy as dancers, and great dancers they were. However, one should not assume that because these two ladies were great dancers, that they will be teachers, ballet masters, choreographers or administrators. This of course is foolish; quite often the opposite is true. If we are to assume that one career leads naturally into another, why then did not Mr. Balanchine keep them on his staff at New York City Ballet?"[65] Smuin's own path, of course, had led directly from dancer with a number of companies, including San Francisco Ballet, to the directorship of the latter, so arguably his logic is as flawed as his knowledge of the facts: Reed had spent several years as ballet master at City Ballet and had taught throughout her career, and Hayden at this time was honing the teaching skills that ultimately landed her a job at North Carolina School of the Arts, where she taught until one month before she died of pancreatic cancer at the age of 83.

On May 17, Hayden, began an address at the Pacific Northwest Dance Ballet League's first annual luncheon by telling the assembled supporters of the ballet—including the PND board of directors and Kalimos—how much she regretted leaving Seattle, where she had arrived the previous summer with "great expectations to grow with Pacific Northwest Dance. I came here to serve dance as I have served it all my life. Even though I have a wonderful marriage and two marvelously adjusted children, dance has always come first."[66] She then proceeded to summarize her reasons for resigning (very much the same as Reed's) and scold the assembled company about priorities, essentially accusing Kalimos and the board (without naming them) of putting the financial cart ahead of the artistic horse. Her allusion to her happy marriage and "marvelously adjusted" children certainly reveals how conflicted the women of her generation were about what the feminist movement in those days called "having it all," although there is no evidence that she was criticized in Seattle for neglecting her ballet company duties in favor of her family life.

By the time Bolender returned in June, the Hayden-Coleman family had already returned to New York, leaving his boxes stacked in the studio. For the second time in two years, Bolender was compelled to deal with the fallout from conflicts between the artistic and management staffs at the young institution and a board that seemingly was attentive only to the executive director, and, as he wrote to Tobias, he wasn't happy about it. Nor did he support much of what Hayden had done: "[How,] I thought[,] could Milly Hayden do the destructive things she did last winter and then pack up and leave as tho it was a one sided issue, she playing the role of the 'Goods' and the management of Pacific North West Dance playing the 'Bads.'" By management, Bolender was referring to Kalimos, with whom he always conducted himself diplomatically, and, presumably, PND's board. In the letter, he alluded to what he considered Reed's "innate sense of propriety" without mentioning that she had joined Hayden in publicly calling for Kalimos's resignation. He wrote that "Janet said she hoped the Seattle Board would pick Milly because she could handle them. Well they did, and she did."[67]

Bolender got another workshop showcase up on August 12, 1977, at Meany Hall. The program included his own *Ma mere l'Oye; Summer Dances,* to a score by Tchaikovsky, choreographed on these students and young professionals, which he took to Turkey for the Turkish State Ballet; and a reprise of Tom Ruud's *Mobile.* As he remembered it, incoming Artistic Director Kent Stowell and incoming Associate Artistic Director Francia Russell were present at this showcase. Kalimos had wanted Stowell as artistic director all along, and according to Russell, he flew to Frankfurt where Stowell was the artistic director of the opera-house ballet to implore him to take the job. When Stowell and Russell arrived with their three small boys in tow (Russell recalled the Erskines' kindness to the children in particular), they found a shortage of personnel, including dancers and teachers; a larger performance venue than they had expected; and a hostile press. Nevertheless, at the end of their first season, the company was debt free and the budget for the following year had been doubled.

Like Reed, Bolender, and Hayden, Russell and Stowell had gotten to work with "only one purpose, and that was to make a good company, and in some ways our naiveté paid off, because we just put our nose to the grindstone and just did our job and tried to make things better year after year."[68] By the time they retired in 2005, Pacific Northwest Ballet was considered by organizations such as Dance U.S.A. to be one of the top five ballet companies in the United States.

Bolender returned to Europe in the fall of 1977, feeling that PND was potentially in good hands. He returned to Seattle a number of times, both to see his many friends in the city, including the Erskines, and to stage *Souvenirs* twice, the second time in 2002.

The 1972 Stravinsky Festival choreographers: George Balanchine, Jerome Robbins, Todd Bolender, John Clifford, Lorca Massine, John Taras, and Richard Tanner. Photo by Martha Swope © Jerome Robbins Dance Division, New York Public Library for the Performing Arts.

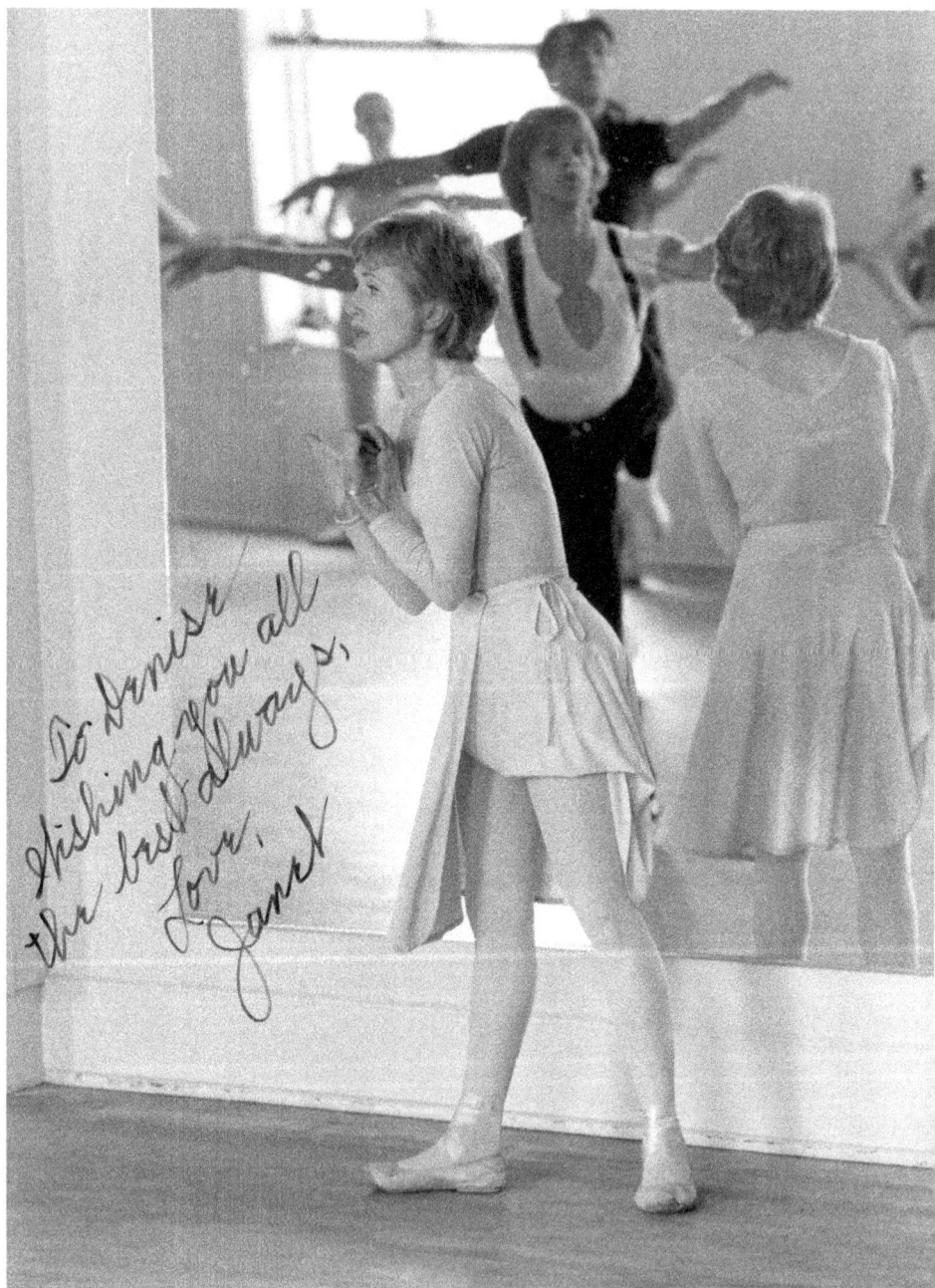

Janet Reed, ca. 1975, rehearsing Pacific Northwest Dance members at the Good Shepherd Center in Seattle. Photographer unknown. Pacific Northwest Ballet Archives.

Todd Bolender rehearsing Aydın Batur and members of the Turkish National Ballet in Istanbul in 1978. Photo by Ufuk Ülker.

Alvin Ailey, Donna Wood, Todd Bolender, rehearsing "The River" in State Ballet of Missouri Studios, 1986. Courtesy Kansas City Ballet.

Todd Bolender and Christopher Barksdale rehearse the title role in Balanchine's *Renard* in Kansas City, 2001. Courtesy Kansas City Ballet.

Francia Russell and Todd Bolender at Pacific Northwest Ballet's studios in Seattle, preparing a revival of *Souvenirs*, summer 2002. Photo © Matt Lawrence Photography. Pacific Northwest Ballet Archives.

Kimberly Cowen and Christopher Barksdale perform the Hesitation Tango from *Souvenirs* at the Todd Bolender memorial concert in Kansas City, December 2006. Photo by Steve Wilson. Courtesy Kansas City Ballet.

10

When a visitor asked Bolender what he considered his greatest achievement a few months before his death in October 2006, without a second's hesitation he said quietly, "The work I did abroad on behalf of American dance."[1]

That work had begun in 1941, with Bolender's participation as a dancer in American Ballet Caravan's U.S. government–sponsored tour of South America and continued with City Ballet's tours to England and the European continent in the 1950s. On the 1956 tour, he staged *The Still Point* on the Munich Staatsoper Ballet, thus introducing himself as a choreographer to German audiences. In 1958, Jerome Robbins programmed his *Games* for Ballets: U.S.A.'s tour to Spoleto, Italy, and the Brussels World's Fair.

In 1961, with over two decades of dancing and making dances under his belt, Bolender's business card might well have read "Have ballets, will travel"; between 1961 and 1980, he traveled to Turkey countless times; to Germany, where he ran opera-house ballet companies in Cologne and Frankfurt; to Switzerland, Austria, Canada, Israel, and many cities in the United States; and in 1974 back to Argentina. In each place, he was variously teaching, staging his ballets, choreographing new ones, or (particularly in Turkey but also in Geneva and Cologne) directing and choreographing American musicals. In Turkey, he did this under the auspices of the United States Information Service (USIS), for which he received an award from the State Department in 1971.

Bolender was still on New York City Ballet's roster when he headed to Ankara in the spring of 1961. That was the first year of the Second Turkish Republic, a time of considerable turmoil in the region, partly because Turkish politics historically have been tumultuous, and partly because of the Cold War. The Kennedy administration, through USIS and several other government agencies, was interested in keeping Turkey out of the Soviet sphere in the same way that the Roosevelt administration had sponsored American Ballet Caravan's tour of South American two decades earlier as a means of countering Nazi propaganda.

Turkey's geographical location—the Black Sea separates it from eastern Europe, the Mediterranean forms its southern border—made it strategically important to Europe and Great Britain, going back to World War I if not earlier, and, starting with the Cold War, particularly to the United States. Well aware of its pivotal role in world politics, Turkey joined the United Nations peacekeeping forces in the Korean War and in 1952 became part of NATO and thus an active participant in preventing Soviet expansion into the Mediterranean. As Bolender wrote to Schnee in 1995, because of this history, American money poured into Turkey during the nineteen-year period in which he was in and out of the country. "Plus," he said, with characteristic wit, "naiveté was running around dressed as freedom, everything red, white and blue."[2]

Bolender's first assignment in Turkey was to teach American technique to ballet students at the State Conservatory of the Arts and stage *Creation of the World* and *The Still Point* on the Turkish National Ballet, which at the time was under the direction of Molly Lake and Travis Kemp. Lake and Kemp were British, balletic heirs of Ninette de Valois, who, like her, had received their classical training from Enrico Cecchetti. Both the conservatory and the ballet company had been established with the help of de Valois at the invitation of the Turkish government, the first in 1947, the second in 1958. De Valois, the founder of the Royal Ballet and the Royal Academy of Dance, alluded from time to time to espionage activities during a relationship with Turkish ballet that lasted for nearly half a century, so she, too, was there at least in part representing her government. In a tribute published in *Dancing Times* in 1994, in honor of Dame Ninette's ninety-fifth birthday, Turkish poet, playwright, and translator Sevgi Sanli commended her for forty-seven years of advice and "dedicated work, years in which she both built the school and developed a professional dance company."[3]

In addition to her literary endeavors, Sanli was employed by the state-run opera houses in Ankara and Istanbul as a translator for visiting English speakers, and as such was one of the first people Bolender met when he arrived in the Turkish capitol. Hard-working, passionate about the theater (she was known internationally as a translator of both Shakespeare and contemporary playwrights), Sanli possessed a powerful intellect and a keen sense of humor. Like Reed, she loved to laugh, and she had the same tough-minded determination to succeed at whatever task was at hand. She was just the kind of woman Bolender most respected and enjoyed.

Sanli, in turn, liked Bolender immediately. "He had facility and charm when he taught the students,"[4] she said in 2008, in an interview at her daughter's home in England. As have many others, she described his low-key but firm approach to working with dancers in the studio, even when he was frustrated by what he viewed as a casual approach to their jobs—sloppy-looking practice clothes, arriving late to rehearsal, leaving before the rehearsal was over.[5]

On this first visit, Bolender spent his two-month stay trying to instill an American work ethic and Balanchine technique in dancers whose previous training was stylistically quite different from the latter, with Sanli acting as translator and, by her own account, as a diplomatic go-between. She was with him every step of the way, she said, including sitting in the wings when *Creation of the World* had its Turkish premiere: "I remember Meric [Sumen] in the lead role in *Creation*," Bolender wrote to Sanli from Kansas City in 1986. "And on opening night when she was to have a fox scarf thrown around her neck, the fox scarf couldn't be found until after the performance when it was found under your bottom on a chair in the wings."[6]

With or without the fox fur scarf, the performance was a success, according to Beatrice Appleyard, writing for the British publication *Dance and Dancers*:

> Todd Bolender's choreography is in what we have learned to call the "American idiom." It was a very courageous experiment on the part of the Director of the conservatoire to bring an American choreographer to work with the young Turkish dancers, who, until now, have worked only under British direction. It was . . . highly successful . . . and the dancers took to this new idiom like ducks to water and gave a performance of *Création du Monde* which astonished everyone with its understanding of the American way of life (and the American way of dancing).

The Bolender works were on the second program of performances commemorating the twenty-fifth anniversary of the conservatory. Of Gülcan

Tunççekiç, the lead girl in *The Still Point*, Appleyard wrote, "She is a dancer with great dramatic depths and can, with correct handling and production [*sic*; direction], become Turkey's Nora Kaye. She does to perfection that most difficult of all things in the theatre, to stand still, doing nothing. Downstage in the footlights, she lets us know every thought which passes through her mind while she stands immobile."[7]

When Bolender returned to Ankara to direct and choreograph a production of *Kiss Me Kate*, he cast the musical with a number of the dancers he had worked with on his first visit, including Tunççekiç, who went on to have a stellar international career. In the process, he learned a lot about state-supported opera-house politics, something he was to struggle with throughout his time in Turkey and even more so in Germany. Casting Bianca was particularly problematic, according to Sanli, because the person who wanted the role was flirting with the opera-house director, who then put considerable pressure on Bolender to give it to her. "There was nothing he could do about it," Sanli said.[8]

With 250 people in the cast and Bolender doing both the directing and the choreography, *Kiss Me Kate* was his biggest project to date. Nevertheless, his reworking of the Cole Porter musical, originally choreographed by Hanya Holm, his influential early teacher, was an enormous success, in spite of the limited amount of time (about six weeks) he was given to get it on stage. He could not have done it without Sanli, who not only translated Porter's highly textured, extremely sophisticated lyrics into Turkish but also acted as Bolender's personal translator, working with him from 8 a.m. until midnight, while, she said, "Todd taught actors to dance, dancers to sing," and much else.

"[He] was a perfectionist. . . . There was nothing he wouldn't do. . . . Everybody believed in him," Sanli recalled. Bolender didn't remember it quite that way; he wrote Schnee some years later that he had had considerable trouble in rehearsal with the actor who was performing the lead male role of Fred Graham, and at one point he walked out, informing USIS that he would return when he was taken seriously. "In the end," he wrote Schnee, "[the show] was a smash hit."[9] *Kiss Me Kate* was the first American musical to be performed by Turkish singers and dancers. According to Sanli, it was Bolender's choice to do Porter's most successful musical comedy (Bolender called it and other such shows "20th century operas") instead of the quintessentially American, groundbreaking *Oklahoma!* "He didn't care for it," she said in 2008, although she didn't say why.[10] Certainly he greatly respected Agnes de Mille's work as a choreographer, and when he assumed the artistic directorship of the Cologne Opera House Ballet the following year, he asked her to set *Rodeo* on the company. However, it's entirely possible that Bolender chose *Kate* because of his strong connection with Holm and the opportunities the book offers for physical comedy. Sanli particularly remembered translating for him when he choreographed the gangsters' tap dance, no doubt informing his choreography with memories of his own childhood training in acrobatic tap.

Kiss Me Kate played to full houses. "It's cold in Ankara at night," Sanli said. "People stood in line for tickets anyway, and the show warmed them up." It was equally successful in Istanbul the following year, not only with audiences but also with what Sanli referred to as the city's "old-fashioned critics."[11]

By that time, Bolender had assumed the artistic directorship of the Cologne Opera Ballet, where he stayed for the next three years, choreographing for opera ballets, staging his own work on the company for ballet-only evenings, running a summer ballet festival he created, and, when the company wasn't performing, continuing to work in the United States, Turkey, and elsewhere.

Bolender had several reasons for accepting the job in Cologne. Apart from his need for stable employment, his desire to promote the American way of dancing abroad was the most important, but he also wanted to learn to speak German and to know more, much more about German culture. During his time in Germany, he and Mandia, who acted as his ballet master, were as indefatigable in visiting museums and sightseeing as they had been during their London stay in 1959.

In many respects, he succeeded in accomplishing what he set out to do, but it certainly wasn't any easier for him to adjust to the opera-house system in Germany than it had been in Turkey, although in one letter to Schnee he commented that at least the Germans were efficient. In Germany, opera houses are run by an intendant and the ballet director, at least in the 1960s, was the lowest man (and they were all men then) in the artistic or administrative hierarchy. While Bolender knew well from choreographing for opera in the United States that the dance interludes were basically viewed as an opportunity for singers to catch their breath, he was not part of the opera-house staff when he created dances for a Franco Zeffirelli production of Massenet's *Thaïs* in Fort Worth in 1961 or for *Die Meistersinger* at the Metropolitan Opera in 1962. That meant, for better or worse, that he was treated as a guest artist and not part of the hierarchy.

In Cologne, Bolender's first order of business was to find a place to live, not only for himself and Mandia, but also for his friend Gloria Nardin and her two children. Nardin, who Bolender had first met in Provincetown in 1948 and had subsequently shared a house with in New York, had been recently and suddenly widowed. Bolender was extremely fond of her and her children (one son had been named for him) and he was glad to be able to offer her both refuge and a distraction from her grief. "We were a family in Germany," Nardin wrote in 2011 in response to an invitation to the ribbon-cutting ceremony for the Todd Bolender Center for Dance & Creativity in Kansas City. The house and garden Bolender found on Robert-Koch-Strasse in Cologne's Lindenthal district proved to be a refuge for him also—a comfortable home and a loving family to return to after a hard day at work.[12]

He had many such days during his three-year tenure in Cologne, particularly in the first few months, when he was learning German and German ways, including where the ballet company fit in the structure of the opera-house administration, protocols with regard to critics that would have been considered a conflict of interest by American newspaper and magazine editors, and how to deal with what he called the "exactness" of the German people. Actually, when it came to teaching and coaching, Bolender shared that "exactness"—every dancer who ever worked with him seems to have referred to him as a detail-oriented perfectionist. But as an American, he had as much tolerance for institutionalized hierarchies as Balanchine and Kirstein. Kirstein did not formally rank City Ballet's dancers until after the Australian tour in 1958 and Balanchine frequently cast corps members in the same roles as the company's principals.

Bolender's highest priority was retraining the dancers so they could perform what critic Wilfried Hofmann called his "four calling cards," but his first task was to rehearse them in those opera interludes others had choreographed. At the first stage rehearsal, he took one look at the carpet a previous ballet master had had placed on the floor in order to deaden the sound of the dancers' pointe shoes and blew his thinning top. "I cleared the stage of dancers and said get that rug the hell out of here! And I got them back on stage again."[13] By many accounts, Bolender was himself a bear on the subject of noisy pointe work, but his solution to the problem was to hold the dancers responsible for softening their toe shoes to make them an extension of the foot, as Pavlova had done. This instruction may have been one way that he failed to endear himself to some of Cologne's older dancers, who over the years had lost what openness to new ideas they may have had, and to be fair, had had to adjust to no fewer than three different ballet directors in the previous three years.

Corps member Beatrice Cordua, who well remembered her first impression of Bolender when he arrived in Cologne, "looking very American with sunglasses,"[14] had worked off and on with two of his predecessors there. The Hamburg native's training had been eclectic, to say the least. Initially, she had been schooled in Soviet ballet style mixed with some German Expressionist technique at the Palucca University of Dance in Dresden, after which she had spent some time at London's Royal Academy of Dance. Her first paid job was with the Hamburg Opera Ballet, and it was there that she was introduced to Balanchine technique. In 1962, the Hamburg Opera's intendant had invited the New York City Ballet to perform in honor of Stravinsky's eightieth birthday; during the run *Agon* was performed in Germany for the first time. Balanchine, Melissa Hayden, and Jacques d'Amboise all taught the Opera Ballet's company class, and Cordua had done so well that d'Amboise asked her to participate in a demonstration of the technique at the city's America House.

Cordua not only embraced the unembellished action of Balanchine technique, she developed a passion for neoclassicism and twentieth century music, and soon after the festival she left the Hamburg Ballet for the Cologne company to work with Aurel Milloss. Milloss was programming all-Bartók ballet evenings, including his version of *The Miraculous Mandarin*. Cordua didn't stay very long and neither did he. Milloss left mid-season to lead the Vienna Opera Ballet, and Maurice Béjart came in temporarily to choreograph the dance interludes for several operas. According to Cordua, he was sufficiently impressed by her work to ask her to return with him to Brussels to dance in Ballet du XX Siècle, the company he founded in 1960. She had only been there a short time, however, when she heard that an American who had danced with New York City Ballet was coming to Cologne, at which point she rapidly retraced her steps.

Cordua wasn't disappointed. Bolender's first company class excited her as much as the classes she'd taken in Hamburg, and Bolender immediately took note of the fact that she "did every bit of every step of every class."[15] This was not necessarily true of the rest of the company members, who did not impress Bolender with their previous training or their willingness to improve their technique. "They resented my trying to [prepare them to learn] Balanchine technique. Their training had been really miserable. They had no conception of how to use the feet, the legs and the hips."[16] Bolender nevertheless set to work readying the company to perform an all-Bolender program that was scheduled to open on December 22. The evening was highly ambitious and long. It consisted of four ballets: revivals of *The Still Point* and *Souvenirs* plus two new works, both of them plotless but musically very different. *Serenade in A, No. 9* was set to Mozart's Serenade for Orchestra no. 9 in D Major and *Theme and Variations* to twentieth-century German composer and librettist Boris Blacher's rhythmically complex *Orchestra Variations on a Theme by Paganini.* With this stylistically eclectic program, Bolender was challenging an already demoralized company to pull itself together and embrace new ways of moving and a more democratic approach to the art form than it was used to. Twenty-two years after American Ballet Caravan's 1941 tour of South America, Bolender was still on a mission to prove that American ballet could proudly take its place with anything being produced anywhere in the world. Few in Cologne, and even fewer in Frankfurt, were particularly interested in this message, perhaps because less than two decades after the end of World War II, it was coming from a citizen of a country some still viewed as a conqueror.

Bolender's violation of opera-house protocol certainly didn't help. It began with him giving Cordua the lead role in *The Still Point,* choosing a corps member instead of a company *artiste* for a principal part. For this transgression, he got into so much trouble with the highest-ranking women that he and Cordua had to rehearse in secret. He also managed to alienate Horst Koegler, a prominent—and powerful—German critic who wrote regularly for *Dance Magazine,* by refusing to allow critics to attend the dress rehearsal. Koegler and another critic appealed to the intendant, and Bolender was less than pleased to see them sitting there in the theater when the rehearsal began. Koegler never forgave him; the perceived slight colored much of what he wrote about Bolender's tenure in Cologne and (to a smaller degree) in Frankfurt.

In his correspondence with Rebecca Brownstein, his New York lawyer, who he relied on to take care of his business and personal affairs while he was out of the United States, Bolender wrote frequently of his difficulties in adjusting to a new country, a new language, and a new opera-house culture. He also wrote of his life with the Nardin family, which made all of that easier to deal with. For example, in a letter dated November 22, 1963, written before the news of President John F. Kennedy's assassination had reached Germany, he described his difficulties in communicating with a Deutsche Bank clerk whose English was no better than Bolender's German. After asking that Brownstein make sure that his request to transfer funds from his Deutsche Bank account to the Seamen's Bank in New York had been accomplished, Bolender concluded with: "Nothing else except a lot of work and aiming at Dec. 22nd. At the moment I'm in the finale of my 4th and last ballet for this season, now the big job really comes,—to get all those ballets into spick and span condition, plus scenry [sic], costumes, lights and orchestra and of course keep the weary dancers from knowing how weary they are."[17]

In an article that had appeared in the *New York Herald Tribune Magazine* six weeks earlier, Walter Terry poked gentle fun at Bolender's attempts to speak German to those weary dancers: "It is fractured German—'just do that with music,' *nein, nein, too klein* [no, no, too small] or *bleiben sie auf dem Boden auf sechs* counts [roughly, hold for six counts].[18]

Very shortly after writing to Brownstein, Bolender received the devastating news of President Kennedy's assassination, but as he wrote her on December 2, the sadness the Germans he encountered inside and outside the Opera House expressed did afford him some comfort, and—weary dancers and director notwithstanding—the ballet evening premiered as scheduled on December 22.

Two days later, Bolender wrote Brownstein again to thank her for sending a Christmas gift he pronounced "delicious" and to give her "the great news that my ballet evening was the biggest ballet success they have ever had here." Audience reception had been enthusiastic, with many bravos during the final curtain calls, and only Koegler, his anger still fresh at Bolender's attempt to bar him from the dress rehearsal, had responded negatively to the program, going so far as to write a "blistering" personal letter to Bolender "[saying] such discrimination had never before been practiced in Koln." Nevertheless, the Cologne papers, Bolender told Brownstein, had published rave reviews, and he was deeply relieved to have his debut program over with.

Hofmann confirmed Bolender's assessment of audience response on opening night:

Versatility, optimism and dynamics—these three—and other—important traits were responsible for an elegant Cologne first night audience being moved to applause unusual for this region. How genuine public enthusiasm was, can be judged if one realises that Bolender's first programme (on December 22) ran to three and a half hours, and after *Still Point* the audience had to spare its applause until (as required by the copyright owners) Debussy's Quartet was finished in its entirety in front of an empty stage.[19]

Hofmann went on to praise the stylistic variety of the program, commenting that it was hard to believe that the same choreographer was responsible for all four ballets. Of the two new works, Hofmann felt *Theme and Variations* was the more successful, writing that the Blacher ballet "genuinely belongs to the exciting genre of creation represented by Balanchine's *Agon.*" His description summarizes nicely Bolender's choreographic history and point of view:

[It] starts with a group of dancers (all dressed in grey rehearsal costumes) sitting on the floor facing the rear of the stage. Suddenly they jump to their feet and dash up-stage. With this—more exciting than it sounds—the mood is set and we are in for a swift permanently shifting scene of group dancing, employing—only for moments at a time—classical technique, jazz technique, modern technique . . . plus that weird vocabulary of ballet dancing made up of a perverted use of otherwise "normal" movements: an arabesque allongé with the extended arm supported on the partner's thigh; "normal" footwork and body carriage without any coordination or participation of the arms; a whipping attack; a brutal, coldhearted approach to the dance. This dance sequence, going over 15 variations, changes from exciting bravura dancing to sinister moods and weird moments, all culminating in a pas de deux for Carmen Panader and Riccardo Duse which one would like to see again and again for its suggestiveness that leaves us wondering if we understood what it was all about.[20]

Hofmann didn't find *Serenade in A, No. 9* nearly as interesting or effective and seemed to blame Mozart, Bolender, and the dancers for its failure to be Balanchine's *Symphony in C.* He acknowledged the use of the Balanchine idiom, but chided Bolender for failing to "fully exploit the impetus of the music." Of later performances, however, he wrote approvingly of the progress the men in particular had made under Bolender's "strict and relentless technical coaching," adding that his "pas de douze for men (5th movement) to trumpet music gives an idea how great male group dancing can be if set by somebody who[,] due to his own career as a dancer[,] has a special command of the male dance vocabulary."[21]

Cordua and Duse came in for considerable praise in *The Still Point,* a ballet that Hofmann reported moved some audience members to tears and that he considered to be one of the most important works of contemporary choreography. He wrote of Cordua's performance that she immediately established herself as an artist and commended Duse for his "assured presence on stage, radiating [his] understanding and love." Hofmann wrote less enthusiastically about *Souvenirs* and its cast, with the exception of Tilly Söffing as the Vamp. Hofmann, who had spent some years in the United States attending Harvard and many ballet performances, was knowledgeable about American dance in general and Bolender's work in particular, which meant he was able to contextualize this first ballet evening in ways other German critics could not.

The review concluded with the information that Bolender would arrange a "ballet festival week" in Cologne in July the following year and that negotiations were under way for the presentation of Balanchine's *The Nutcracker* in November. While the ballet festival took place as planned, the negotiations for the latter bogged down and the company didn't dance its first evening-length Balanchine work until October 1965.

Bolender's second ballet evening, which took place in July during the ballet festival week, consisted of *Danses Concertante* (his, not Balanchine's, whose first version Bolender had seen the Ballet Russe dance in the early 1940s), a reconfigured *Mother Goose Suite* he titled *Images, Creation of the World,* and *Kontraste,* set to music by contemporary Cologne composer Bernd Zimmermann, who became a friend. All four had costumes designed by American painter and designer Ed Wittstein, who was living in Europe at the time.

For *Mother Goose Suite,* Bolender made a new prologue in which the dancers performed in American Civil War uniforms, carrying red banners. This was intended to put the ballet in the context of American history, but in the context of recent German history it backfired. On opening night, as Hofmann described it in a review for *Ballet Today,* a hostile audience thought they represented World War II Russian soldiers carrying Communist flags and at once started to boo. Bolender immediately dropped the prologue, and according to Hofmann, the audience loved subsequent performances. Hofmann felt that the "fast changes of direction, swift footwork and incorporation of jazz elements" of *Danses Concertante* were too difficult for the corps de ballet. What he admired about it were the central pas de deux and several pas de trois.[22]

In his summary of Bolender's first Cologne season, Hofmann commended the American director for presenting a variety of well-rounded programs, adding that more than 600 dancers had signed up for the annual International Ballet Academy summer program. "Mr. Bolender it seems has brought ballet to town," he concluded.

The success of *Kontraste* led to Bolender arranging the dances for Zimmermann's twelve-tone antiwar opera *Die Soldaten,* which premiered in February 1965. Musically, Bolender and Zimmermann were highly compatible artists. Zimmermann had been very much influenced by Stravinsky, Milhaud, and Bartók, composers whose music had provided the impetus for quite a bit of Bolender's choreography. Visually, as well, the two artists were in tune with one another: *Soldaten*'s elaborate premiere production had a multilevel set similar to the one Bolender had used for *The Miraculous Mandarin* and featured film projections like the ones he would later employ for *Voyager* in Kansas City. That being said, *Soldaten* was not a critical success at its premiere (that came later), which may be one reason Bolender neither listed it in his curriculum vitae nor mentioned it in interviews.

In addition to Bolender's second ballet evening, the 1964 summer festival, or Ballet Week, as it was called, included two works by Béjart and an appearance by the Merce Cunningham Dance Company on July 12, during which they danced *Winterbranch*. This was the Cunningham company's first visit to Cologne, and Bolender's invitation to perform there earned the undying gratitude of David Vaughan, who was managing a company tour for the first time and hadn't realized there was a two-week gap between performance dates. Bolender was immensely helpful in many ways, Vaughan recalled, including making a studio available to Cunningham so he could make work and rehearse the dancers.[23]

According to several accounts, including Cordua's, the Cunningham company had a very mixed response from the audience. Many walked out; dancers, including herself, were unimpressed, but visual artists, including

Cordua's husband, loved *Winterbranch* in particular. Koegler was far more receptive to Cunningham's work than to Bolender's. In a report for *Dance Magazine* he not only was highly dismissive of Bolender's second program, which alternated with the first for the ballet week, he slammed the dancers, saying they were at their worst, "with no port de bras, the girls hysterical and the boys were badly disciplined."[24]

In the midst of his many tasks for the Cologne Opera Ballet and the summer festival, Bolender took on the job of directing a production of *Stop the World: I Want to Get Off* with book, music, and lyrics by Leslie Bricusse and Anthony Newley that opened in Cologne on October 10, 1964. While he didn't entirely love the circus-oriented piece about a clown who realizes at the end of his life that he hasn't been a particularly decent human being, he did want to continue to direct musical theater, an American art form to which he was arguably as committed as he was to ballet. The production was an enormous success with the opening night audience and he wrote to Brownstein that he thought "all of Cologne showed up at one time or another" at the party he threw at his house. "Everyone was so excited. Me too, because I've been used to such boos and ugliness lately that I was relaxed for the first time after a premiere." Press reception was mixed: a Dusseldorf critic, Bolender wrote, was "vicious," but that was more than mitigated by a Cologne critic writing that Bolender was "the only man in Germany who understands the musical style of this kind of entertainment." This was followed by a "wonderful" review in the Berlin paper *Die Welt*.[25]

Less than a week later, Agnes de Mille, who also understood a thing or two about musicals, arrived in Cologne, the first important American choreographer Bolender succeeded in bringing there to work with the company. (Balanchine had postponed *The Nutcracker* and Antony Tudor had refused his invitation.)[26] Bolender wanted de Mille to set *Rodeo*, still regarded as a masterpiece of American ballet, because of its blend of dance forms, its Copland score, its strong-minded tomboy heroine, and its setting on a Colorado ranch. The strong-minded de Mille, however, declined to do the work, because she doubted the Cologne Ballet contained a ballerina with a sense of humor and acting talent to play the Cowgirl or a male dancer who could tap dance to be the Champion Roper. Instead, she staged *The Bitter Weird*, a choice that greatly disappointed Bolender.

In a 2003 interview, Bolender could remember next to nothing about this "forgettable" ballet, not even the title. An earlier iteration of the ballet, titled *Ballade,* had been performed in 1953 by the Agnes de Mille Dance Theatre, her short-lived touring company, with music by Frederick Loewe and longtime de Mille musical collaborator Trude Rittmann, one of Bolender's traveling companions on the 1941 tour. The expanded version, a highly dramatic tale of a bride whose groom is murdered on their wedding day, had just premiered the previous fall at the Royal Winnipeg Ballet. The Cologne audience's response was as lukewarm as Bolender's. Koegler didn't like it either. Writing in *Dance Magazine* in December 1964, Koegler found the "Scottish" ballet to be a mixed blessing, but his critical assessment of Bolender's Copland dances, *Dance One* set to the American composer's *Danzón Cubano* and *Dance Two* to *El Salón México,* was unusually positive.

If Bolender found *The Bitter Weird* forgettable, what was completely *un*-forgettable was what de Mille chose to wear for her first rehearsal session with the dancers. She emerged from her dressing room costumed like a dance hall girl, or as a character, he said, in Tudor's *Judgment of Paris.* Her black satin cocktail dress had a backless bodice inadequately held up with two straps and she was wearing fishnet stockings and red high-heeled shoes. Bolender had been careful to educate the company about this important, influential American choreographer, so his heart sank when he first caught sight of her attire. "And I thought 'these dancers are going to faint. [But] they held themselves together pretty well," he said nearly forty years later in an interview in Kansas City.[27] This certainly wasn't de Mille's customary studio garb: photographs of her rehearsing dancers in musicals and in ballets do show her in high-heeled shoes but dressed in street wear, although seldom demonstrating movement. Which at least on that first day she didn't do in Cologne, either. "[All she did was talk]," Bolender said, "which she's wonderful at, but it was wasted on a group of dancers who [didn't] understand that much English. But of course I adored every minute [I spent] with her."[28]

Bolender had not intended for de Mille to be the first distinguished American choreographer he brought to Cologne. That was Balanchine, whose work the Cologne company had never performed. He started trying to get him there almost as soon as he arrived, wanting his *Nutcracker,* one might speculate, as a demonstration of American classicism and as a "teaching ballet," not only for the professional dancers in the company but also for students, including very young ones. However, Balanchine was extremely busy in 1963 preparing for City Ballet's move the following year from New York City Center to the New York State Theater, and there were many delays. After many negotiations, Balanchine finally said yes to a performance of *The Nutcracker* in Cologne, and a date in April 1965 was set for the premiere. The contracts were signed and the publicity had gone out all over Germany when Balanchine unexpectedly telephoned Bolender from Munich with the unwelcome news that he would have to postpone staging the *Nutcracker* for six months. "I reminded him," Bolender said, "that Germans are very exact people and to make a change such as this one might be incomprehensible to them. There was a moment's pause and Balanchine then said to me, 'The Germans are lousy at improvising—that's the reason they lost the war.'"[29]

For his second Ballet Week, in the summer of 1965, Bolender got from Balanchine the *Raymonda* "Pas de Dix." *The Bitter Weird* and Harold Lander's *Etudes,* which had been performed earlier in the season with American Ballet Theatre's Lupe Serrano as guest artist, were also on the program, as were the two Béjart works seen at the previous year's festival, which, according to Koegler, were "madly cheered." Koegler wrote of the technically demanding *Raymonda* "Pas de Dix" that the Cologne dancers were "dwarfed by Maria Tallchief and Jonathan Watts as guest stars."[30]

Bolender saved a clipping of a *Dance Magazine* review of a different program, performed on July 3, that was written by Rudolf Orthwine, who had been instrumental in organizing the Mordkin Ballet in New York in 1936 and then Ballet Theatre in 1940. Orthwine, who was *Dance Magazine*'s publisher, was particularly interested in Flemming Flindt's *The Lesson,* so much so that he went backstage to talk with Bolender about it. Bolender's suggestion that the ballet (Flindt's first) about a sadistic ballet teacher who causes the death of a student could be interpreted as "symbolizing the Nazi occupation of various European countries" is an interesting one. Orthwine also enjoyed *Le baiser de la fée* and *Etudes,* which were on the same program, as did the audience; "there were seven prolonged curtain calls,"[31] he reported. Orthwine also congratulated Bolender and Mandia for the "excellent" job they had done in building the company. This was not always easy for the calm and steady Mandia; at times Bolender would become so frustrated with opera-house politics and other difficulties that he would take it out on Mandia in rehearsal, making the dancers acutely uncomfortable. That didn't mean Bolender wasn't both grateful and respectful; in October 1964 he wrote Brownstein that "[Mandia] does the work of 20 men in this opera house and there are not too many people who appreciate his knowledge and know-how. Despite the German language which suits him not at all, he manages to make himself understood and to understand everything that is spoken to him."[32]

Preparations for *The Nutcracker* finally began in June of 1965, while the company was rehearsing for the summer festival. Balanchine sent Victoria Simon to teach the choreography and do the initial staging. It is well known that Balanchine had an extraordinary eye for spotting the dancers who could best fulfill his vision for a new ballet—Marie-Jeanne for *Ballet Imperial,* Le Clercq for Choleric in *Four Temperaments,* Arthur Mitchell for Puck in *A Midsummer Night's Dream,* and numerous others come immediately to mind. What's less known is his acuity in choosing the stagers of his repertoire. Simon was one of the earliest. "He knew what you knew," she said in *I Remember Balanchine.*[33] And because Balanchine knew what Simon knew about *The Nutcracker* (as a student at SAB and as a dancer with the company, she had danced nearly every children's and female role it contains), it was the first ballet she set, and Balanchine sent her to Cologne to do it.

Simon spent a total of eight weeks staging the two-act ballet, which she did in two separate four-week stints. What she found, when she arrived for the first one, in June, was a well-trained company with a thoroughly professional attitude toward their work, and, she said, "good principals." Bolender had accomplished much in quite a short period of time. The children, however, not only had to be taught the choreography, they had to be taught to dance.[34] That meant that Simon needed every bit of the eight weeks she'd been allotted to get the work up on stage.

Balanchine arrived in Cologne a week before the premiere to work with her to "clean" the ballet. He was greeted by Bolender, who immediately took him to the theater, thinking that it would be the perfect time for him "to get some decent lighting, because the lighting was of a sort of advanced modern starkness." It's unknown what Balanchine had to say about the lighting designer, who Bolender found difficult to work with to get what he wanted, but according to Simon, he was particularly pleased with the casting of Karin Jahnke as Coffee because she was "kind of sexy."[35] That quality was desirable for the 1962 revision of the divertissement, in which Balanchine replaced his original Coffee (made for a male dancer and four young students costumed as exotic birds) with the sinuous female solo.

The premiere took place as scheduled on October 16, and the audience response to the first evening-length Balanchine ballet to be presented anywhere in Germany was everything Bolender had hoped it would be. "[They] loved the *Nutcracker* but the German critics hated it. I think they didn't [like] old-fashioned ballet coming to Germany. They wanted everything to be avant-garde."[36]

That may well have been true of Koegler, who in response to questions about Bolender's time in Cologne slammed his *Baiser de la fée* and added "it was not a good idea of his of bringing Balanchine's *Nutcracker* ..., which we thought then and think even now as one of his worst ballets (much as we know that Americans held a different opinion)."[37]

On the other hand, British critic G. B. L. Wilson, writing in *Dancing Times*, considered the *Nutcracker* performances to be the culmination of what Bolender had accomplished in his two and a half years in Cologne and praised him for programming ballets by Cranko, de Mille, and Lander, as well as by Balanchine. While Wilson's preference was for the Beriozoff Lichine Petipa-based versions performed at that time by English companies, he nevertheless acknowledged the dancers for giving "full justice" to the work, particularly Jonathan Watts as the Cavalier. The children he dismissed as a failure for their lack of training, but he loved the Rouben Ter-Arutunian sets and costumes and, as did the audience, the growing Christmas tree.

Setbacks and criticisms notwithstanding, Bolender soldiered on, preparing for the next year's ballet festival week, doing some traveling, continuing his duties as director of the opera-house ballet, and preparing to leave Cologne at the end of his contract. Koegler's review of the 1965 festival did nothing to make him change his mind about staying. While Koegler designated *The Still Point, Souvenirs,* and *Contrasts* [sic] Bolender's best Cologne contributions, his assessment of the dancers was both odd and highly negative:

If [they] seemed technically and stylistically rather ill at ease in most of the ballets, the blame must be placed on the truly chaotic situation created by the public's dissatisfaction with the direction of the Cologne ballet. Another result of the chaos is the confusion of the audience in its standards of judgment. Most acclaimed dancers of the week were undoubtedly Tilly Söffing & Lothar Hoefgen, the 2 soloists who felt so deliberately humiliated by the management that both have now left Cologne—Söffing for the Dusseldorf co. of Erich Walter and Hoefgen for Béjart's Brussels troupe.[38]

By management, Koegler meant Bolender, and indications are that he was at least partly mistaken in blaming him for Walter's and Hoefgen's departures. From the reviews by Hoffman and others, it is clear that Hoefgen was far more comfortable with the Béjart repertoire than Bolender's, making his departure for Brussels a logical one. Söffing, moreover, kept her apartment in Cologne and offered it to Simon to rent while she staged the *Nutcracker*. From the tone of Bolender's correspondence with Simon about those arrangements, it is clear that they parted on good terms. Nevertheless, public attacks by other company members on his democratization of the company, his treatment by much of the German press, and his frustration with the upper management of the Opera House all reinforced his decision to leave the city by the Rhine. By the end of 1965, *The Nutcracker* had been mounted and the Nardins were back in the United States, which meant that he and Mandia were living in a gardenless apartment, and Cordua, his Cologne muse, was dancing (thanks to de Mille) with the Royal Winnipeg Ballet. Whatever pleasures living and working in Cologne had afforded had been lost. The Frankfurt Opera offered him a contract to run its ballet company at just the right time, and Bolender accepted it. Bolender said years later that he felt he had failed in Cologne, but if that were the case, it seems unlikely that Frankfurt would have offered him a job doing exactly the same things.

In 1965, while still under contract in Cologne, Bolender returned to New York to set *Kontraste* on American Ballet Theatre; de Mille had recommended the ballet to Lucia Chase. He also went to Winnipeg to stage *The Still Point* on the Royal Winnipeg Ballet, where Cordua could reprise her performance as the rejected young girl. Bolender asked her to return to Cologne for the rest of his tenure there, and she subsequently went with him to Frankfurt.

In Frankfurt, Bolender found the opera-house administration just as difficult to deal with as in Cologne, but he was able to remount *The Miraculous Mandarin*, which he hadn't wanted to do in Cologne since Aurel von Milloss had done his own there. He also made *Time Cycle* on this company. Both ballets were critically acclaimed by several people, including Koegler. Koegler began his review of Bolender's first Frankfurt program, which was published in the news columns of *Dance Magazine*, by saying that the program, for which *Donizettiana* was the curtain raiser, was artistically much more successful than anything Bolender had done in Cologne.

If [it] did not fully match the music's sparkle and the shadow of a certain "Mr. B." was too imminent for comfort, the company, almost completely reorganized, looked young, fresh and efficiently coached with steel-footed and well placed Heidrum [sic] Schwarz well on her way toward stardom. Next came Bolender's *Miraculous Mandarin*, set very cleverly on Hein Hekroth's labyrinthian revolving stage—an astonishingly convincing treatment of a notoriously difficult ballet full of tension, emotionally highly charged, with splendidly characterized roles (only the Blind Girl was a bit too much) and just the right sort of mystique. As the protagonists Beatrice Cordua and Paul Hebinger worked up a fiercely intense love-hate relationship, but Helmut Eisch was also impressive as the tottering Old Man.[39]

Bolender mounted *Mandarin* in Frankfurt in part because of that revolving stage, and in part because in Cordua he had a dancer to work with who had many of the same qualities that Melissa Hayden had brought to the role at the City Ballet premiere. "He coached me very well," Cordua remembered. "He was very subtle in his direction" and was extremely clear about the psychological motivation behind the movement.[40] *Time Cycle*, a new ballet set to music by the American composer Lukas Foss, rounded out what must have been an extremely long program. Koegler praised it to the skies, calling it Bolender's "greatest achievement."

[He] has choreographed a kind of meditation about time and transitoriness reminiscent of *Age of Anxiety* and *Ivesiana,* completely abstract, but with some strong emotional overtones—7 episodes of man's struggle against the uncontrollable powers of his inner and outer world. Using hardly any classic movements, drawing instead from modern dance vocabulary and integrating many influences of Far Eastern ritual theater, the choreography is full of plastique images of hallucinatory power. With no scenery at all, but ingeniously lit, the ballet keeps one's mind busy long after the final curtain has come down.[41]

Bolender's first season in Frankfurt ended with the making of the dance interludes for *The Bartered Bride* in a new production that premiered on July 9. "Once again," Bolender wrote to Brownstein, "[I] have come up against a non-ballet[-]understanding director and orchestra conductor."

While both professed to love ballet, Bolender wrote, neither had what he called "muscular awareness," i.e., the ability to judge "how much action one can do in a certain period of time or the reverse, how slow and sustained."[42] Plans to go to Turkey and Greece with Mandia the end of July, where Bolender would restage *My Fair Lady,* somewhat alleviated his frustration, especially since Mandia was making all the arrangements.

In addition, despite the negative reaction to Balanchine's *Nutcracker* in Cologne and what he perceived as a preference for contemporary ballet by the German critics, he was, he wrote Brownstein, programming *Giselle* for the Frankfurt company's 1967–1968 season. He had two reasons: he wanted to attract a "big ballet audience" and he wanted to "do a ballet that requires the skill of the girl dancers mostly. I have about 5 quite good lead girls who can alternate the several leads and 16 . . . adequate girls as corps. This ballet can act both as training and classical discipline for [them]." He admitted to being hard pressed for well-trained men in the company, which had only twenty-eight dancers, but was resigned to making do with what he had. "I would hope to get better men," he wrote to Brownstein. "But then one must always return to the agonizing point, no training—no dancers. Until training is taken seriously there will be no great development in the dance. Plus *Giselle* I shall do another ballet for the program but as yet have not made a choice."[43]

To stage *Giselle,* Bolender had persuaded Mary Skeaping, who he had met on a trip to London earlier in the summer, to come to Frankfurt for no fee, since the opera-house administration had given him no budget for visiting choreographers. Skeaping, who had been trained by Pavlova and danced in her company, had subsequently danced with the Royal Ballet and had also been a ballet master. In 1967, she was best known for her artistic directorship of the Royal Swedish Ballet, where she had mounted historically grounded productions of *Giselle,* earlier French court ballets, and *The Sleeping Beauty.*

Working with her turned out to be a profound pleasure for Bolender. On December 4, he wrote Brownstein that since Skeaping's arrival in Frankfurt on November 14, "[we] have been going a mile a minute," and that in just two weeks, a phenomenally short time, they'd had a full run-through of the stylistically and technically challenging ballet. "She is a very enthusiastic woman," he added, "and for her 65 years has a fantastic energy much greater I might add than mine." Better still, he wrote, "she is a mine of information, and I have learned so many things since her arrival, about dance, that I had never known before."[44]

In the same letter, Bolender wrote optimistically about the new opera-house management, specifically the general intendant, who he found to be open-minded about the making of new dance and, even better, cultivating a young audience for it. To those ends, he had provided Bolender with one of the smaller theaters, in addition to the Opera house itself. "Had he done nothing else than that," Bolender wrote, "I would have found this a most enticing offer, but he has arranged to have the company tour the suburbs of Frankfurt and the surrounding cities to create interest in the company, and the biggest relief is the new general music director has planned operas which have little if no ballet which has been and continues to be the beastly head-ache that I suffer at the moment." As a result, Bolender, who had been thinking of leaving before his three-year contract was up, had agreed to stay.[45]

Bolender settled on *Souvenirs* as the curtain raiser for the April program, and according to Koegler, *Giselle,* with Duse (who had come from Cologne with Bolender) as Albrecht, Heidrun Schwarz as Giselle, and Cordua as Myrtha, had garnered lukewarm response from the local press, while the reception for the "inevitable" *Souvenirs* was enthusiastic.[46] Cordua, who, like Bolender, had loved working with Skeaping, verified the tepid audience reception in a 2014 interview, speculating that it was because of Skeaping's insertion of unfamiliar music into the score and the restoration of the original choreography, which meant, Cordua said, that their expectations were not matched.[47]

In a subsequent column, Koegler announced that "the big ballet program in Frankfurt this fall will be Bolender's *Nutcracker.*"[48] Bolender wanted a new production for it, but the general manager of the opera house had no interest in spending the money. Bolender refused to use what he said were "the undanceable costumes for the Waltz of the Flowers" and was fired.[49] There wasn't much time left on his contract in any case, and while he didn't like being fired, he was ready to return home to his apartment on East 95th Street in New York and resume his career as an itinerant choreographer and teacher while he kept his eye out for a permanent job.

By the summer of 1970, Bolender was back in the routine of crisscrossing the North American continent and circumnavigating the globe, ballets and teaching notes in hand. Then tragedy struck, and struck hard. An obituary in *The New York Times* tells only part of the story:

BERKELEY, Calif., Aug 12—John Mandia, a former dancer with the New York City Ballet died of a heart attack here yesterday. He was 45 years old and lived at 176 East 95th Street in New York.

Mr. Mandia had just arrived here with Todd Bolender to assist with the final rehearsals of Mr. Bolender's The Still Point. The work is scheduled to be given a new production in New York this fall by the City Center Joffrey Ballet. Mr. Mandia had had a leading role in the original cast of its production by the City Ballet in 1956.

After leaving the City Ballet, he was a choreographer in Germany at the Cologne and Frankfurt Opera Houses, and had taught dramatics at the University of Washington.

Survivors include his mother, Mrs. Esther Mandia, and two sisters, Mrs. Pearl Rico and Mrs. Esther Pinto.[50]

Bolender wasn't with Mandia when he died. He was called out of rehearsal by someone at the hospital where Mandia had been taken, who told him that Mandia was in bad shape and said to hurry. By the time he got there, his companion of two decades had taken his last breath. When a shocked, devastated Bolender asked to see him, the request was denied; he was not a relative. The survivors list in the Times obituary ought to have included him; they had been living together on East 95th Street and in Germany since 1963; their relationship had begun in 1950 when Mandia joined City Ballet as a corps member.[51]

While it was Jacques d'Amboise who danced the role of the steady, mature young man who rescues the rejected young woman in the City Ballet premiere of The Still Point, and not Mandia, that character in the ballet, on which Bolender began work the year they met, was pretty clearly modeled on Mandia's personality. For two decades Mandia was a steady presence in Bolender's professional and personal life. During that time, Bolender did have other relationships, but to take a line from Kiss Me Kate, he was always true to Mandia in his fashion, and he never really recovered from his death.

Back in New York, Robbins asked Bolender to reprise his role as The Husband in The Concert, which City Ballet was reviving for the 1972 season in the 1958 iteration of the ballet, which Bolender had performed in while touring with Ballets: U.S.A. He initially declined, on the grounds that he was too old—he was 57—and out of shape. He reconsidered when Balanchine invited him to get back in performing trim by taking company class. On the first day, Bolender took a place at the barre, and Balanchine, before he began teaching, welcomed him back with a simple introduction: "This is Todd. He is one of us."[52]

Critic Don McDonagh, writing for the *New York Times*, also welcomed Bolender's return to his dancing home: "Of all the episodes in the work that reveal Mr. Bolender's humorous gifts, perhaps the tigerish butterfly gives him the most opportunity to display the artful double-take, the lusty clutch and finally slumped chagrin. It was a tour de force and it was delightful to see him again with the company if only for a visit."[53]

Shortly thereafter, Bolender applied his humorous gifts to one of two ballets he was asked to make for the first Stravinsky Festival, which took place that June in honor of the composer's eightieth birthday. *Piano-Rag-Music* was an extended pas de deux made specifically on the very tall Gloria Govrin and the much shorter John Clifford. The music may have reminded Bolender of the tall female Ballet Theatre dancer who had slung him over her shoulder and carried him out of a Montreal restaurant when he collapsed at dinner after fracturing his wrist in rehearsal. This is not mentioned in the handwritten notes in which Bolender outlined his plan:

> Girl enters 1st, smiles at pianist etc, then the male does a big en trance . . . brassy, jazzy. He defers to her and they decide to dance (a Castle one step) She takes off on her own and then he shows off— the rest of the number becomes a (illegible) competition with an occasional one-step thrown in. However she does a Johnny one note, which he tries to supersede, she keeps right on, they end dancing together and loosely acknowledging each other.[54]

What emerged from Bolender's preliminary notes, according to Clifford, was something rather different:

> Gloria and I were put through every conceivable comic contortion. At one point she picked me up by my shirt and threw me across the stage! At another I did a hand-spring over her shoulders while she was standing on toe. . . . This joke Pas de Deux went over extremely well both in New York and later on tour. I think the audience needed a little comic relief and we were glad to give it to them.[55]

The "day-glo" costumes as described by Clifford abetted the comic effect: Govrin wore orange tights and leotard with a practice skirt over them, with an enormous orange and white bow on her head. Clifford was all in purple, including a sweatshirt, his costume creating what he wrote was a "Dead End Kid."

Clive Barnes of *The New York Times* labeled the pas de deux "no shattering masterpiece but a joke with class," and Deborah Jowitt, writing in the *Village Voice*, called it "a romp made wholly out of . . . Clifford's brash, but likeable style, the serene and happy whorishness that Gloria Govrin can summon up, and the odd-couple look of these two together. The gags were, of course, predictable: the small, aggressive Clifford being effortlessly lifted out of the way by Big Gloria, and so on. What made the ballet worthwhile was that the jokes popped quickly and casually in and out of a texture of fast and intricate and friendly dancing."[56]

Serenade in A, a more serious work, premiered on June 21, and while Bolender, as always, found Stravinsky's music stimulating, he wasn't able to achieve the story he wanted to tell of couples shifting allegiances in "waves" of movement, and the critical response was lukewarm.[57]

The following year Bolender returned to twentieth-century German music, working again with Emily Frankel, at her request, to make a 70-minute solo based on Sophocles' *Elektra,* set to a score by Hans Werner Henze, who, like Zimmermann, was greatly influenced by Stravinsky.[58] The "blood and horror" solo, as Frankel described it, premiered in Hong Kong and in the spring of 1973 was performed at Alice Tully Hall in Lincoln Center to benefit the New York Public Library for the Performing Arts.[59] That year, Bolender returned to Buenos Aires for the first time since 1941 to make *Poème des Valses,* set to Ravel's lovely score, on the Ballet Estable del Teatro Colón.

New York remained home base for Bolender for the next six years, although he wasn't physically present in his East 95th Street apartment for much of them. He continued to travel to Turkey, staging and restaging musicals, including a very well-reviewed *Fiddler on the Roof,* for which he did new choreography. From 1974 to 1978 he spent many months in Seattle, helping Reed and then Hayden get the Pacific Northwest Ballet School off the ground. He also did a great deal of teaching, both nationally and internationally.

In the fall of 1976, he was particularly peripatetic. In September, he was in Vienna for five weeks staging *Souvenirs* and *The Still Point* ("what else?" he wrote to Schnee) on the Vienna Opera Ballet, during which time he was reunited with Georgia Hiden, who had been on the 1941 South American tour and had become a Balanchine stager. In early October, he flew to Tampa, Florida, where he reworked *El Salón México* to Copland's music for the students of Haydée Gutiérrez, who had received her own training in the Cuban National Ballet School in Havana and at the American Ballet Theatre school. The commission was funded by the National Endowment for the Arts as part of the country's bicentennial celebrations. While Bolender had high praise for Gutiérrez and for her dancing and teaching, the male students weren't quite up to scratch. "I got the cream of the crap," he wrote Schnee; nevertheless none of them was deemed adequate as a partner for Gutiérrez, who danced the lead role. For that task, Bolender recruited Miguel Campaneria from the Harkness Ballet and paid for his transportation, housing, and salary from his own pocket, a mark of how important it was to him that Gutiérrez have a capable partner in this ballet.[60]

In the same letter, sent from Vienna, Bolender wrote that he would be there until the end of the month and then go to Ankara to start working on a production of *A Little Night Music*. Correspondence with Sanli in this period indicates how much Bolender loved the Sondheim musical, which had premiered in New York two years before, and how committed he was to overseeing every detail of the production. He intended to ship photographs of period dress and furniture from Vienna to Ankara, writing not entirely in jest that he needed to prevent a minaret from being part of the set. Whether because of opera-house politics, Bolender's demands for complete control, a lack of funding, all of the above, or something else, the Sondheim project did not reach the stage. A rather different assignment took him back to Turkey in 1977, in a way bringing him full circle in his on-again, off-again love affair with that country, its landscape, and its people, but not necessarily with opera-house politics or their link to whoever was the Turkish premier of the moment.

This time, Bolender was asked to take on the reestablishment of the Turkish State Ballet, the same company on which he had staged *Creation of the World* and *The Still Point* during his first stint as a guest teacher and choreographer in 1961, when the company was based in Ankara. In 1977, the company was resident in Istanbul, and Aydın Gün, an opera singer and stage director Bolender had worked with when he was directing *Kiss Me Kate* and *My Fair Lady*, was the intendant of the Istanbul opera house. Given his past difficulties with opera-house management, his constant negotiations with U.S. State Department officials to get paid in dollars rather than Turkish lira, and his frequent frustration with a culture quite different from his own, Bolender was more than a little wary of accepting another assignment in Turkey.

After considerable correspondence with Sanli, Bolender decided to accept the position on offer and "try to make the ballet dance."[61] (He wrote her from Seattle on July 4 to thank her "deeply for [her] time, energy and enthusiasm in attempting to make a rosy path . . . in Istanbul."[62]) He arrived at the end of September, bringing with him two young American dancers; Gutierrez, as company teacher, who apparently didn't stay long; and a portmanteau of his ballets. Aydın Batur, Sanli's daughter, who had known Bolender since childhood, was a young member of the company and remembered vividly Bolender's thorough shake-up of the status quo right out of the starting gate. "He deleted everyone's memory," she said in an interview in 2008, "in order to give us a brand new start."[63]

Batur was right: to prepare for this seemingly Herculean task, Bolender gave the company a fresh start by cancelling the season, which had been planned by someone else, and starting to train the forty-two company members, twelve men and thirty women, to perform a program of his own work with one two-hour class a day for each gender. He also taught one pas de deux class a week. He described all this in a letter to Schnee not long after his arrival, in which he also declared the "ballet scene to be a mess. This winter the rebuilt opera house will open [a fire had destroyed much of it in 1970] and therefore the Intendant wants the ballet to come off smelling like roses, which is such a job to keep it from smelling like what you damned well know it smells."[64]

He planned, he said, to begin choreographing on January 1, 1978, and to present his first program on May 1. While his view of the theater and its "excellent" lighting equipment was positive, he intended to costume the dancers in black velour rather than Balanchine's practice clothes uniform, since there was no resident scenic or costume designer.[65]

In the February 1978 issue of *Dance News*, Hofmann, who had been in Istanbul with his Turkish wife, published an article titled "Bolender and Discipline in Turkey." In it he described Bolender and Gutierrez working with the 42-member company and credited Turkish ballet master Guloya Arlova with keeping the company alive through its previous few years of difficulty. While Bolender, he wrote, was a devoted master who was willing to teach the company, there was "incurable absenteeism."[66] Bolender evidently told him that the Turks worked hard but erratically, and as an example of this, Hofmann noted, the accompanist had failed to show up for a lecture demonstration. Nevertheless, Hofmann approved the dancers' ability to follow complicated rhythms and felt that at least in the studio, the female dancers projected well.

He still thought so when he returned to Istanbul in May and saw Bolender's show at the reopened Atatürk Cultural Center. In a report published in *Dance News* in September, Hofmann points out that due to terrorist activity from both the right and the left, the decision to reopen the opera house had to have been made personally by Prime Minister Bülent Ecevit, who saw to it that high security was provided when the theater opened officially on May 19. Bolender's program, which premiered on May 25, consisted of *Time Remembered* (originally titled *Mother Goose Suite,* the ballet that had so upset the Cologne audience in 1963), *The Miraculous Mandarin* (in a new production by Osman Sengezer, a prominent Turkish designer), *Tribute to Balanchine,* set to Tchaikovsky, which had premiered in Seattle as *Tchaikovsky Suite,* and a Copland piece, which may have been *A Summer's Day,* a ballet Bolender later revived for Kansas City Ballet. Two things stand out in this programming: the first is the statement Bolender was making about the influence of Balanchine on his own work; and the second is the absence of his best-known ballets, *The Still Point* and *Souvenirs.* In any case, Hofmann commended the dancers' technical prowess and dramatic abilities and quoted an anonymous "old observer" of theater life— probably Sanli—who said that she had not witnessed a similar evening in the past. Her daughter, who danced in the *Tribute to Balanchine,* thought what Bolender had achieved was "incredible."

Bolender returned to New York for the summer and from there continued his negotiations with his Turkish employers and his correspondence with Sanli. He wrote to her on August 10 about the renewed prospect of directing a production of *A Little Night Music* in Ankara, which he thought an excellent idea despite logistical worries. In the end he decided against it, because of the need "to get the ballet back to within shouting instance of where they were May 30th. I doubt seriously anyone has done more than 'think' of a ballet barre this entire summer, which means that preparations this coming season will be very demanding not only on the dancers but on me."[67]

That turned out to be a self-fulfilling prophecy, which meant working the dancers—and himself—extremely hard to repeat the previous spring's program for the season opener in October, after which rehearsals began for the last production Bolender would direct in Turkey. This was neither a ballet program nor an American musical but rather a revival of the Turkish *Deli Dolu*, a vaudeville-style operetta created by Turkey's answer to the Gershwin brothers, Cemal and Ekrem Reşit Rey, that had premiered in 1934.

As he had with *Kiss Me Kate* and *My Fair Lady* nearly twenty years earlier, Bolender worked in close collaboration with Sanli on every aspect of the production. A few months following the premiere, he wrote her that it was "only [her English translation of the musical] that made it possible for me to imagine what I was dealing with."[68] It was set in a hotel, and a seaside hotel at that. Bolender dealt with this production by inserting some details from his own work. A long cigarette holder like the one the Vamp had used in *Souvenirs* was carried by a young woman who announces her ambition to be a kept woman; he borrowed rolled stockings and a compact from *Creation of the World*. Directions for physical comedy abound in the script, and choreography furthers the plot in the same way it has done in American musical theater since the 1940s.

Once *Deli-Dolu* was up on stage at the Atatürk Cultural Center in March 1980, Bolender felt that his work and his time in Turkey were done, and he left immediately after the premiere. "Bone weary"[69] was the phrase he used in writing to Schnee, from dealing with opera-house politics, which were inextricably linked to government politics, and directing admittedly hard-working dancers whose notions of attendance and punctuality were far more flexible than his. Bolender left a country whose people and landscape he had come to love. He also loved their national dances, particularly one from the Black Sea area in which the men would leap like fish. American-style ballet left with him, and Batur and many of her colleagues were very sad to see them go. Bolender was replaced with a Turkish director whose focus was on making ballets based on Turkish themes.[70]

In a *New York Times* feature story on Bolender that Jennifer Dunning wrote while he was setting *The Still Point* on the Alvin Ailey American Dance Theater later that year, in which he described Turkish dancers as "good" and the Turks as "wonderful theater people," he again railed against "the civil service theater" he had found in Germany and Turkey, singling out the latter for being "fantastically disorganized."

"Finally," he told Dunning, "I got on a plane and came back to the States. I had had a feeling since I'd worked with Janet Reed and the Pacific Northwest Ballet in Seattle in 1975 that I really wanted to work with American dancers. There's something about them that's terribly special and very beautiful, a whole kind of energy and drive that I don't sense in any other dancers. And they're so conscious of line and of *working* in dance. If you get a good bunch of American dancers, there's really nothing like them."[71]

There could be no more American dancers than the Ailey company's, unless it was those in Martha Graham's company. Both leaders were pioneers in reflecting the diversity of the population of the United States in their company rosters, although Bolender may have been thinking primarily of ballet dancers when he spoke of line, which is not a term used much in modern dance. On the other hand, it was *The Still Point,* which Bolender originally made on a modern company, that he was setting on the Ailey dancers, and he told Dunning that when he made it he never thought of it as modern or ballet but as "*dance,* for God's sake."

The Ailey staging was Bolender's last as an itinerant choreographer. Shortly after the Ailey shows, he left for Kansas City to meet with the board of directors of the Kansas City Ballet, a barely professional company that was in considerable disarray. In January 1981, he officially took up his duties as the artistic director, a position he held until 1995, when he became artistic director emeritus. The prospects for success in getting a classical company on solid footing—artistically *and* financially—in a middle American city, where the symphony was also in trouble, were inauspicious, to say the least, but the appointment potentially gave Bolender the stable employment he needed and, equally important, the opportunity to work with dancers who were willing to give him their all in the studio and on stage.

11

The last twenty-five years of Bolender's life were extraordinarily productive. Between 1981 and 1995, when he became artistic director emeritus, he
was able to establish Kansas City Ballet (KCB, formerly Kansas City Civic
Ballet) as a major player in the city's cultural scene in Kansas City and in
the state of Missouri. Additionally, and of equal importance, he, with the
help of many friends and colleagues from New York City Ballet, established
a reputable school. Kansas City Ballet remains a highly respected regional
ballet company in the twenty-first century. His retirement, which officially
began when he was 81, was extremely active. He continued to choreograph
and coach the dancers in his own work, he gladly lent his presence to fund-
raising efforts as the company approached its fiftieth anniversary, he participated in many panel discussions about Balanchine and the impact the
Russian-born choreographer had on American dance and dancers, and he
was an active participant in the Balanchine Foundation's Interpreters Archive and Archive of Lost Choreography.

By the time Bolender died in October 2006, the company was well on
its way to having its own building, and shortly before his death, he participated in groundbreaking ceremonies for the Kauffman Center for the
Performing Arts.

Along the way, he built a company repertoire that is in itself a history of
American ballet, with Balanchine's work and his own at its foundation. He
also created a number of new ballets specifically for KCB's dancers, several
in collaboration with Kansas City artist Dale Eldred and, his last, *Arena,* in
1996, with two Kansas City artists, composer James Mobberley and visual
artist Russell Ferguson. Throughout his time in Kansas City Bolender not
only collaborated with the city's artists but also with the city's arts insti-
tutions. Mobberley, for example, was on the faculty of the University of

Missouri Kansas City's Conservatory of Music; Eldred and Ferguson were associated with the Nelson-Atkins Museum of Art, and musicians from the Kansas City Symphony played in the KCB orchestra.

Bolender also commissioned work for the company from novice choreographers, giving them the same opportunities that Balanchine had given him. Christopher d'Amboise was one of them, Thomas Ruud was another, and from within the ranks of the company itself, so was Daniel Catanach as the result of a choreography workshop Bolender taught one year in the summer program.

He accomplished none of this without practical assistance. In the early years, he had enormous support from Kirstein, who had written him a glowing letter of recommendation; from Balanchine, who gave Bolender his ballets for no licensing fee (as he did for many others); and from his many contacts in the dance world, including Reed, who taught several workshops and was present at a number of fund-raising galas. Paula Weber, a Kansas City choreographer and a member of the University of Missouri Kansas City faculty, said in 2011 that she still taught a combination she had learned from Reed in one of Bolender's summer programs.[1]

There were also a number of dedicated and very hardworking board members, and extraordinary financial support came from Muriel Kauffman, who loved going dancing with Bolender—she was good at it and he enjoyed partnering her and testing her ability to follow his steps. She referred to herself and Bolender as "Fred and Ginger." After one of those nights out on the town, she enclosed a check for $50,000 for the company in a note thanking Bolender for an evening of dancing. She was married to Ewing Kauffman, who had founded a pharmaceutical company that employed many residents of Kansas City and owned the Kansas City Royals, which she had urged him to establish when the Athletics moved to Oakland, California, on the grounds that Kansas City needed to have a major league baseball team for economic reasons. Her support of the company was steadfast, practical, and vital to its survival until she died, and Bolender very likely couldn't have gotten it so firmly established without her.

Like many regional ballet companies, the Kansas City Civic Ballet started on a shoestring and had its roots in the Ballets Russes. It was founded by Tatiana Dokoudovska, who had danced with de Basil's company and with Ballet Theatre in 1957, the same year that Bolender originated his last role for Balanchine, the Sarabande solo in *Agon*. Miss Tania, as she was called, started the company with a group of her students from the University of Missouri Kansas City Conservatory of Music and Dance with a program that was, to put it mildly, antithetical to what Balanchine was presenting in New York at the time. It consisted of Fokine's *Les Sylphides,* in which Dokoudovska had danced a major role at Ballet Theatre; *Ruse d'Amour,* her own adaptation of Fokine's *Russian Toys;* Léonide Massine's "Tarantella" from *La Boutique Fantasque;* the Silver Fairy variation from *The Sleeping Beauty;* and one other work in a "modern" vein.[2]

The company was organized professionally with nonprofit status, a board of directors, and a regular performance season that included an annual *Nutcracker,* which Dokoudovska choreographed, and spring repertory concerts.[3] By all reports, Miss Tania gave her life to this endeavor, as many others have done—and still do—in cities across America: teaching, rehearsing, choreographing, sewing costumes, and endlessly trying to raise money.

In 1971, the word "civic" was eliminated from the company's name, indicating full professionalism, and in 1976, Dokoudovska retired as artistic director to focus on teaching. In the four years between her departure and Bolender's arrival, the company was headed by two quite different directors, Eric Hyrst (1976–1978) and Ron Sequoio (1978–1980), who Bolender had known in New York and Seattle, respectively. Their tenures were sufficiently minor for both to be omitted from the text of the company's official fiftieth-anniversary history although they are represented by photographs of their choreography.[4]

When Bolender took over unofficially in the fall of 1980, he had two stipulations, both expensive: there would have to be live musical accompaniment for every performance, and even more essential, there would have to be a school. The board, which included Elizabeth Wilson (who, at the urging of Kirstein, had invited Bolender to apply for the job), agreed to his conditions and Wilson, joined by Sarah Rowland, who volunteered as company manager, and Wendy Powell, who was indefatigable in her advocacy and fund-raising, set to work with him to rebuild a nearly nonexistent company. Assets, such as they were, included a few dancers and an ill-equipped studio in a warehouse under a bridge that had a bad floor and a bare-bones office. Subscriptions had declined considerably (wealthy Kansas City balletomanes went to New York to see performances) and the company was heavily in debt.

"What Todd got when he came to Kansas City," Wilson said, "was absolutely nothing. He got a vestigial costume collection, I mean I wouldn't touch it with rubber gloves, one Codaphone, and an IBM typewriter we had to retrieve from the former general manager, who took them. [Todd's] salary was $25,000 a year. A board member gave him a check for the full amount."[5] Since Bolender did not yet have what he could call a company, namely a group of well-trained dancers to work with, he decided to cancel his first season's *Nutcracker* and wait until June to hold a performance. Funders did not like that idea at all, according to Wilson, and demanded to know why he wasn't mounting the company's only moneymaking endeavor. "Because Todd is coming in September," she told them. "He's going to audition dancers and train them as a company and then our first performance will be in June. It was a bit of a struggle to get some money to get started, we needed a better studio, barres in the studio, a floor, mirrors, shoes for the children, and so on."[6]

Studio space was found in the city's oldest district, at the Westport-Allen Center, which also housed the Kansas City chapter of the National Abortion Rights Action League and a branch of Alcoholics Anonymous. Carter Alexander, who danced with the company toward the end of Bolender's tenure as artistic director, remembers crossing right-to-life picket lines on an anniversary of *Roe v. Wade*, and on another occasion police shut down the building for a day because of a bomb threat from another anti-abortion organization.

After auditions, Bolender retained two of Dokoudovska's dancers. In October, Bolender traveled to the North Carolina School of the Arts in Winston-Salem to look for advanced students he could school as a company. James Jordan, who for many years was KCB ballet master and Bolender's assistant, was one of several he found there.

"He came and sat in front of the class," Jordan remembered. "No one knew who he was and some of us said rude things like 'Who's the old guy sitting in the front?' We didn't have a clue, but we found out later when he offered jobs to four of us and after we checked him out in the library. It sent a stir through the dance department, because he offered positions to unlikely people, not necessarily the stars of the class." The contract on offer was short term: "He wanted us approximately February 1, and it was for $200 a week through May 31, when a gala performance was planned, with no clue whether there would be a company or we would be offered anything beyond that," Jordan said.[7] Four North Carolina dancers accepted, as did fourteen others from elsewhere, including from Istanbul, Turkey, and the Lichine Ballet Academy in Beverly Hills. On May 31, Bolender presented a program that included *The Still Point* and *Souvenirs*. He also programmed Balanchine's *Pas de Dix* and two classical pas de deux, one from *Giselle* and the other from *Le Corsaire,* danced by City Ballet principal Patricia Mc-Bride and Alexander Godunov, who had defected from the Soviet Union two years before.

With his opening program, Bolender was signaling to the audience a shift in point of view: this would be a classical company that was attentive to ballet's French and Russian roots and to Balanchine's reinvention of the same tradition. *The Still Point* and *Souvenirs,* both mid-century pieces, represented a thoroughly American take on ballet, a melding of classical and modern technique in the former and the use of social dancing, comedy, and silent film acting techniques in the latter. One young viewer of this program, who went on to a performing and teaching career, said *Souvenirs* was what got him hooked on ballet forever.

Catanach, who danced with the company for a number of years and was featured in a good deal of Bolender's work (he danced the role of the Gigolo in the Brooklyn College performance of *Souvenirs* in 1987) was one of the founding company members who had not been trained by the teaching descendants of Balanchine. In a memoir published in *Dance Magazine* in January 2007, he recalled that Bolender had come to Beverly Hills and recruited him from the Lichine Ballet Academy. "[He] was a hard taskmaster. He told us to forget everything we knew about ballet, for we were about to learn a completely new approach. . . . I learned from Mr. Bolender how to dance, how to perform, how to have discipline and passion towards the art . . . Like Balanchine, [he] focused on finding the underlying music in the score that the naked ear doesn't hear. He passed on Balanchine's ideas of performing steps to the fullest and fastest potential." While this was certainly a new approach for Catanach and the other dancer Bolender auditioned and accepted from the Lichine School, that wasn't necessarily true for those who came from North Carolina, where former City Ballet dancer Mimi Paul taught.

At the end of 1981, Bolender summed up his first year in Kansas City in a letter to Geyvan and Paul McMillan, who he had become friends with in Turkey in the 1960s: "My schedule this year has been a little heavier than

I would like but in the situation of helping to form a new company I have little choice. I have to do a lot of work in order to make the whole project work, but really nothing that I find too much or revolting except occasionally the Ladies Guild drive me quite crazy with idiotic requests."[8]

The Ladies Guild was responsible for the Ballet Ball, an annual fundraiser put in place in the Dokoudovska years that continues to be one of the company's most profitable sources of income. In 1981, their "idiotic request" was for the dancers to perform an excerpt from *Swan Lake* on the hard, unyielding floor of a hotel ballroom. Apart from the physical and financial problems inherent in staging even a short excerpt under such conditions, Bolender had made known his feelings about this repertory staple in a 1975 letter containing programming advice for Schnee, who was directing a company in Kassel, Germany: "You must understand, that the public hears probably more than sees, and as long as the stage gyrations don't seriously interfere with the flow of lovely tunes—pretty maiden freaked out by a swan, a virile man undone by him, tricked by society to think black is white and a fadeout of unrequited love."[9] At Wilson's suggestion, Bolender came up with a waltz, which he set to Johann Strauss (not Tchaikovsky) for dancers costumed in inexpensive white dresses and tuxedos. And the guild satisfied its longings for *Swan Lake* with an ice sculpture and dessert pastries shaped like swans.

His first Ballet Ball provided an early lesson for Bolender in the art of balancing artistic integrity, audience education, and fund-raising in support of a specific artistic point of view. Little in his experience as a ballet director in government-funded state opera houses had prepared him for it. However, his personal charm, his many friends and colleagues in the dance world, his firsthand knowledge of the American heartland, and his longtime observation of what Kirstein and Balanchine had had to do to get New York City Ballet established as one of the world's major ballet companies combined to make him a formidable fundraiser in Kansas City.

"This has been a year that [I] hope shall never be repeated," Bolender wrote in his 1981 letter to the McMillans. "The amount of energy I have put toward is really more than I have, so in the past few months I have little setbacks that have allowed me a day of respite, but then I continue on as tho nothing had happened and maybe it hasn't and maybe it has. I don't wish to sound cryptic, etc. . . . I've had lots of trouble esp. on the administrative side. We are now looking for our 3rd G.M. in less than ONE year. I don't suppose this is unusual in the States but it certainly is in Turkey. Christmas is just next week, so is my opening of *Nutcracker*. It is a huge production and I need four arms, legs, heads as does everyone involved with producing it."[10]

What Bolender didn't explain to the McMillans is the amount of pressure he was under in making this new *Nutcracker*, since the conventional wisdom was—and continues to be—that in order to stay on their feet financially, all American ballet companies, for better or worse, need to program the holiday spectacle. Bolender's, which he frequently revised, put money in the bank for KCB until well into the twenty-first century with good reason: it is a highly theatrical version, with details that reveal the choreographer's understanding of what will appeal to children as well as a firm grasp on the classical tradition, freshened frequently by careful recalibration of such set pieces as the Waltz of the Flowers, a nearly psychedelic experience in this production.

Throughout his tenure, Bolender added many specifically American works to the repertoire, quite deliberately educating the Kansas City audience about the history of ballet in the United States and entertaining them in the process. Among them were Loring's *Billy the Kid*, Lew Christensen's *Filling Station* and *Jinx*, Robbins's *Afternoon of a Faun*, Ruthanna Boris's *Cakewalk*, and several works by Alvin Ailey, including *The River*. Originally made on American Ballet Theatre (much of it is on pointe) dancers from the Alvin Ailey American Dance Theater and KCB performed it on stage together for the first time in 1984. This was also the beginning of a residency by the Ailey Company in Kansas City; they spent several weeks there every year, performing, rehearsing, teaching dance classes in the public schools, and doing outreach performances in hospitals and senior centers. In effect, this was the pilot program for Ailey residencies and programs that by 2021 had expanded all over the United States, including AileyCamp for young people, spreading the word that American dance comes in many forms and is practiced—and cross-pollinated—by a highly diverse population.

In 1984, this wasn't news to Bolender, who had been choreographing on Black dancers since the 1940s. He cast SAB student Betty Nichols as Virgo in his *Zodiac* for Ballet Society and made a pointe piece on Katherine Dunham (at her request) when he was teaching ballet in her school. Moreover, he had known Ailey as a friend and a colleague since 1961, when he and Carmen de Lavallade were the hit of the first *America Dances* performances, for which Bolender coordinated the choreography, giving a show-stopping performance in Ailey's *Roots of the Blues*. They reconnected in 1980, when Bolender mounted *The Still Point* on the company and taught in the Ailey School. Both men considered dance to be dance; while Bolender was primarily a ballet choreographer and Ailey a modern one, each was eclectic in his own way. Ailey had been trained by Lester Horton, and like his teacher, he took from various forms—jazz, ballet, and social dances—whatever he needed to tell American stories in dance. And like Bolender, he was inevitably inspired by music. Putting the Ailey company members on stage with the Kansas City Ballet dancers to perform *The River* in a city where there was a substantial Black population was both a significant contribution to American dance history and good box office.

In the period 1981 to 1987, when he felt confident enough in the company to take it to New York, Bolender, whether his energy was low or not, worked tirelessly to establish the school and build a repertory that would reflect his point of view, his personal taste, and his experience as both a dancer and a choreographer and showcase the technique and talents of the dancers. Like most American ballet company artistic directors, he also programmed ballets that he might not find appealing himself but was reasonably sure would draw an audience. And while his correspondence in those years is filled with expressions of weariness and frustration caused by the less creative aspects of the job, there are also many indications that he was, with considerable enthusiasm, seizing the opportunity to revive and rework ballets he had created much earlier in his career, starting with Ballet Society and City Ballet, and works he had made more recently for other companies. Of the latter, *Tchaikovsky Suite* for Pacific Northwest Dance and for the Turkish State Ballet (for them titled *Tribute to Balanchine)*, several Copland ballets, and *Baiser de la fée* made for the Frankfurt Ballet and re-titled *Folk Tale* for KCB, come immediately to mind.

Just as important, Bolender's years in Kansas City freed him from Balanchine's shadow. While some critics did speak of Balanchine's influence in reviews, nobody compared him to one of the great artists of the twentieth century and found him wanting. Specifically for KCB's dancers, Bolender made over a dozen new ballets, including his own versions of such repertory staples as *Coppélia* and *The Firebird. Classical Symphony*, set to Prokofiev's Symphony no. 1; *Grand Tarantella*, set to Gottschalk; and the too specifically titled but gloriously musical *Tribute to Muriel*, set to Beethoven were all part of Bolender's programming menu, as Balanchine might have put it. All were not wonderful: *Galatea,* a pas de deux made in 1982 to the music of Franz von Suppé, a minor nineteenth-century Romantic composer, served its purpose early on in showcasing its two dancers, but it is uncharacteristically hokey.

Minor failures aside, Bolender certainly knew what he was doing and why. In a late-night conversation in 2004, he told a visitor that he was very glad that he had started his career when he did, that he had been able to choreograph on a fine group of dancers that included Le Clercq, Hayden (his principal muse at City Ballet), Reed, Marie-Jeanne, Moncion, Dollar, and Robbins and then had had the opportunity, thanks to Balanchine, to look at what he'd done onstage, changing and improving it without having to run a company. "By the time I got to Kansas City," he said, "I knew what I had to do choreographically, did it, and it all went very smoothly, bang!"[11]

Smoothly enough, at any rate, for Bolender, who never dreamed he would return to the Midwest except to visit family, to decide in 1982, much to the relief of the dancers he had hired on a "let's see if this works" basis, to give up the New York apartment that had been his home for a quarter of a century, signaling his commitment to staying in Kansas City.

"There are a billion things I am trying to do," he wrote Sanli that fall. "Listen to new music, read every and anything . . . see theater when it is possible and of course create new ballets, which I seem to be eager and interested in doing. At the moment I am in the preparation for a new autumn season which will begin Nov. 4. In the meantime I was asked by Saks Fifth Avenue, which has opened a large store here in K.C. in the most fashionable area, if I would along with other performing arts [organizations] do 'something' for their opening. I put together 5 beautiful Chopin pieces with 8 dancers—it was exciting for me, not to do something for Saks but to do something that required only a piano and a few dancers."[12]

Chopin Waltz, retitled *Chopin Piano Pieces* and expanded for ten dancers, was to become a permanent repertory item, and when Saks divided up the take among the participating organizations (tickets had sold for $50 each to an audience of 2,000), KCB received $16,000, a tidy sum in 1982.

A month later, Bolender wrote Sanli that he had hired Una Kai as ballet master and company teacher. "She is one of about three people that Balanchine trusts implicitly to stage his ballets, so we will have quite a few additions of Balanchine's works in the repertory over the next few years." Jonathan Watts, also a former City Ballet dancer who Bolender had worked with in Cologne and Frankfurt, was the head of the school. Bolender was pleased to report that "this means we all, the three of us, have had the same background which makes for a wonderful harmony in teaching."[13]

Kai stayed the longest. She and Bolender had known each other since the days of Ballet Society and were close friends. "I first met Todd in 1947 when Balanchine was choreographing *Symphony Concertante*. I danced directly behind him in *Four Temperaments* and the finale of *Symphony in C*," Kai recalled in a letter written after his death in the fall of 2006. "I tried to synchronize my movements to his because he was so wonderful—so limber and so musical. Best of all was working with Todd from 1981 to 1993 at Kansas City Ballet. It was an easy collaboration."[14] And a profoundly good thing for the company.

"The people of Kansas City are getting very interested in us," Bolender concluded optimistically in the letter to Sanli about his new staff. "And I believe barring [a] huge economic slump within the next few years[,] the KC Ballet will be a major national ballet company, or at least on its way. This would make me very happy, I've been trying to establish a good ballet co. in many places, maybe it will happen here. I am, as I was in Turkey, always hopeful."[15]

Watts didn't stay long at the school; Diana Adams replaced him in June 1983. Bolender was pleased to have her, as he wrote Sanli: "[She was] one of Balanchine's favorite ballerinas who after an injury to her foot stopped dancing but Balanchine made her Director of the School of American Ballet. She comes here as director of the Kansas City Ballet School and as a teacher for the ballet co. Then the three of us all Balanchine trained will be able to continue his training here but in earnest."[16]

Bolender wrote this letter two months following Balanchine's death, on April 30. In an interview with Francis Mason for *I Remember Balanchine* a year or so later, he spoke of the importance of SAB to the establishment of City Ballet and the strength of the influence of its training on ballet companies all over the United States. He was specific about the State Ballet of Missouri (which KCB became provisionally that year), himself, Kai, and Adams: "We are direct descendants of Balanchine, the teacher and the choreographer."[17]

While Reed didn't identify herself as a direct descendant of Balanchine the teacher, and Bolender didn't mention her in his interview with Mason, he did hire her to teach in summer programs in the early years in Kansas City with some frequency. Christopher Barksdale, who began his training with Bolender in Kansas City when he was 10 and retired as a principal dancer at 38 in 2009, certainly regarded her as a part of the Balanchine pedagogical lineage, saying in an interview that her classes in the summer program were just like Bolender's: "They taught the same way."[18] In Reed's interview for *I Remember Balanchine,* she spoke of her memories of dancing for him and working for him as ballet master without remarking on his teaching. She did, however, speak of his deep faith in the Russian Orthodox church, which led to an uncharacteristically mystical account of her experience of his death: "At the time Balanchine died, around midnight, I saw a ball of fire go across the sky and said, 'That means something, I don't know what,'" she told Mason. The next morning Reed learned from Francia Russell that Balanchine had died. "I wrote to Lincoln Kirstein and said I was in the Port of Angels [Port Angeles] on the Olympic Peninsula, home of the gods, and saw this flash of fire cross the sky, and I could only think that it was Balanchine's soul."[19]

Bolender was so busy with his KCB activities that he was unable to attend Balanchine's funeral in New York. By the following June, he was writing Sanli that the "company is now at 20 [with] 9 apprentices who are almost as good as the company dancers." He was taking them on tours of Missouri, Kansas, Arkansas, Nebraska, and Wyoming in the fall and spring, "and then at the end of May the final performances of the season will take place for which I will do a really big fancy new ballet with a wonderful sculptor, painter, designer who is very well-known in the U.S."[20]

The artist was Dale Eldred, who Bolender was to collaborate with on four ballets, *Danse Concertante, An American in Paris, Celebration,* and the first one, *Voyager,* which he told a friend years later he considered his best work. Set to Leonard Bernstein's lush and jazzy *Serenade after Plato's Symposium, Voyager* is profoundly autobiographical, paying homage to the choreographers Bolender had worked with—Balanchine, Robbins, Holm— and the dance he had observed in his travels (most notably in Turkey) in a multimedia expression of the human condition, which he said not long before he died was what all his ballets were about.

Voyager tells a heroic story, nothing less than humanity's journey to discover its place in the universe. In the five-section work's explosive opening, projections of a swirling, milky substance—projections from NASA's 1979 Voyager mission—form the background for seven men costumed in flesh-colored unitards to rise from the floor and travel in great space-eating jumps. The men are soon joined by the same number of women, who are similarly costumed.

In all five sections, Bolender keeps the dancers as constantly in motion as the planets themselves, even in quietly lyrical places, such as the central pas de deux. In a section for the men, in the 2006 revival, Barksdale danced a fluid solo backed by a film projection of himself performing slightly different choreography. Postmodern choreographer Lucinda Child had already done something like this in *Dance*. Both works are visually stunning, but where Child's imagery is psychologically distant, Bolender's packs a powerful emotional punch.

At the heart of *Voyager* is the fourth movement, where six dancers break into duets, then dance in a circle, each laying his or her head momentarily on the cupped hand of the next person. The gesture, reminiscent of Balanchine's *Apollo* when the young god rests his head on the extended hands of the three muses, expresses another theme of Bolender's work: the need for human beings to connect emotionally, physically, and intellectually.

A male duet, sensual, romantic, and completely unsentimental, predates by a couple of years the New York premiere of the one in Lar Lubovitch's *Concerto Six Twenty Two*, which seems pallid by comparison. Asked how the audience reacted to this duet, Bolender said they didn't seem to notice it particularly, and pointed out, with a small smile, that the ballet also contains one for two women.

In a New Year's Day 1985 letter to Sanli, Bolender summed up 1984 as a very busy one, in which he had created three new ballets from start to finish (*Voyager* among them) and that he "often felt disaster was hanging over me, but I also knew that no matter how difficult, this is the way it is always going to be, and finally do I really like or dislike what I'm doing and the answer always comes back, tho anguished at times to, yes I really do like what I do and I hope I can keep on doing it as long as there is breath in my body.

> The most important thing to have happened in this past year is the fact that St. Louis, really a major city in Missouri as well as in the U.S. has decided the KC Ballet is an excellent group . . . worthy to carry the name St. Louis as well as KC. . . . This is an ideal situation . . . as the resident ballet company of both cities and being in the same state, we can draw funds from the major art organizations [in each city supported] by the state.[21]

Bolender was especially pleased to be performing his *Nutcracker* in St. Louis at the end of the year, because it would be accompanied by the city's Symphony Orchestra, "one of the finest in America." The dual residency was to begin in 1986, with "each performance after that . . . the replica of the KC season. Finally this is exactly what I've been working toward since I arrived here four years ago THIS month. What would really please you is how wonderful the Co. has become. The girls are really good, the men are almost good, but then men are always the weakest link in a ballet co., until one has a school which is strong enough to be able to attract adolescent boys with talent but then that also depends on the strength of the Co., which makes it a reason to want to be trained at [its] school. That we must wait for and I hope my stresses and tensions can also wait."[22]

The Ballet Ball continued to be one of those "stresses," but in the fall of 1985 Alexandra Danilova was the guest of honor and received the key to the city from the mayor. "She was dressed," Bolender wrote, "in a dazzling red silk gown with long sleeves and a discreet and elegant collar and a huge scarf, red/orange of Thai silk flung about her shoulders. The best thing is that the Ballet *cleared* $92,500 for the one night—we were elated since fundraising is always with us and needs constant attention."[23]

In November, the agreement with St. Louis became official after a three-year trial, during which Bolender wrote that he "held out until I was absolutely certain of powerful financial support from St. Louis." He was pleased to write that the company was "scheduled to appear in Brooklyn in March 1987 and with an orchestra. If we get fairly decent reviews from that it will make life so much easier in terms of touring, although already our touring is picking up and the dancers are really progressing, esp. the girls but I do have a few very good boy dancers, who incidentally are very well disciplined."[24]

The company performed at Whitman Hall at the Brooklyn Center for the Performing Arts in an all-Bolender program consisting of *The Still Point* and *Souvenirs* plus two ballets created for the Missouri company, *Classical Symphony* and *Concerto in F* (to George Gershwin's score of the same name). The program received a glowing review from Francis Mason on WQXR radio and a dismal assessment from Anna Kisselgoff in the *New York Times*. Generally speaking, she slammed the dancers as "prone to affectation, unwitting caricatures of the Balanchine style. Extreme leg extensions uncoordinated with torsos that are rigid, tension in every limb, and above all, lack of turnout in the feet in the jumps, not to speak of weak toe work—these factors add up to an unrelenting harshness in style that looks more like below-standard dancing than a style with an aesthetic view-point."[25]

Nearly twenty years later, Kisselgoff's words still stung the man who in 1975 had commented that "critics are aphids" in a letter to Schnee. "If she had slammed me that would have been one thing," he said. "But the dancers had worked so hard and looked so beautiful, it was really terrible."[26]

Mason profoundly disagreed with Kisselgoff, reporting that Bolender's "young dancers from Kansas City have the quick classic Balanchine style. Watching them was a carry-back to the early days of the City Ballet, when Balanchine with Bolender and other gifted dancers accustomed us to per-formers who would go out on a limb. Like them, the Kansas City danc-ers have gusto and uplift in adagio as well as allegro in drama as well as comedy. They know above all that ballets don't die on the vine if they are presented with vigor and care."[27]

As Bolender knew might happen, once he and the company returned to Kansas City, he had some explaining to do to the board of directors. Kirst-ein knew this as well, and he wrote a letter supporting Bolender on SAB sta-tioneiy, addressed to Mrs. Robert W. Willits, who was the board chairman. The letter was signed by Danilova, Suki Schorer, SAB school director Na-thalie Gleboff, and Director Emeritus Natalie Molostwoff. It began, "Dear Pat, We are all extremely upset and angry concerning the review printed in the *New York Times* of the State Ballet of Missouri." After mentioning how impressed the SAB teachers were with the "liveliness" of the dancing, Kirstein slammed the *Times* for publishing invidious comparisons in recent days between the Dance Theatre of Harlem and New York City Ballet and informed Mrs. Willits that Pacific Northwest Ballet had also received a bad review from the same source the previous year. "Todd Bolender is a coura-geous and gifted ballet-master," Kirstein continued. "And he deserves the full support of your Board and audience."[28]

Dale Eldred, who had been present in the audience, also weighed in. He wrote to Bolender that he was proud of his "collaborative" association with you and the SBM [State Ballet of Missouri]." About Kisselgoff's review, he said, "Because I was there and know how the audience responded, and be-cause I have enough knowledge of ballet and ballet choreography to know good from mediocre, I was stunned and deeply angered by the frivolously vicious nature of [her] review in *The New York Times.* Not only was she wrong in what she chose to discuss, but she blithely ignored the SBM's key strengths—the liveliness, exuberance and strong theatricality of the dancers, and the powerhouse of fresh, inventive choreography."[29]

Bolender had had bad reviews before, but they hadn't threatened the livelihood of thirty or so people for whom he felt responsible. Kisselgoff's review seems to have strengthened his resolve rather than diminished it, and he continued to single-mindedly develop the company, the school, and the repertory, putting considerable thought into the last and how all three would work together.

In his first decade in Kansas City, Bolender remounted many works by Balanchine, his own work, and the work of other American choreographers, including Ruthanna Boris's *Cakewalk,* Lew Christensen's *Jinx* and *Filling Station,* and Antony Tudor's *Lilac Garden.* In 1981, presumably with Balanchine's approval, he began working with Francisco Moncion to reconstruct a "lost" Balanchine ballet, the *Haieff Divertimento,* which had been made on Moncion and Tallchief in 1947 for Ballet Society. When Balanchine died, he left the licensing rights to Tanaquil Le Clercq, who had danced in the corps, along with Bolender and Fred Danieli. Nancy Reynolds's description of the work in *Repertory in Review* bolsters the case that this was a good teaching ballet for a young company. She labeled it "a perfect chamber work for a leading couple and four supporting couples, with all the parts taken by soloists." In his 1947 review, Walter Terry had said that it was " a delicious piece of classical dance with undercurrents of contemporary rhythmics . . . [that] permits a lively group of Americans to pep up the danse d'école with their innate love of hoofing."[30] It took a while for Le Clercq to grant the licensing rights—she wanted it to look the same way it had in 1947—but the KCB premiere took place in 1985 and she was present in the audience, traveling with Moncion from her home in New York, something she did rarely, in support of Bolender, who she was friends with in one way or another from the age of 8 until she died at 71 on the last day of 2000.

Immediately after the company returned from New York, Bolender's latest addition to the repertory, *An American in Paris,* premiered to critical acclaim. Made in quarreling collaboration with Eldred and set in the 1920s, when Hemingway and other members of the Lost Generation were finding themselves in the City of Light, it premiered to critical acclaim. Bolender, who was revisiting a work he had first choreographed in the mid-1940s for a television production starring Gene Nelson and Marie-Jeanne, included some elements from the earlier production and also a gentle joke directed at Jordan, who he cast as a Cloud running back and forth since he was leaving the company. Dancing clouds had also been a feature of *Mother Goose,* Bolender's first ballet, which he had remounted for KCB early in his tenure there.

While Bolender certainly had plenty to do in connection with the ballet company, including counseling students, teaching company class, choreographing, rehearsing his ballets, attending production meetings, and making five-year plans for the board of directors, he was also extremely active elsewhere in the Kansas City world of the arts. In October 1988, he wrote to Schnee about the work he was doing with the Kansas City Opera. He was also choreographing for a UMKC Conservatory production of Eugene O'Neill's play *The Emperor Jones*: "Set 7th scene in Emperor Jones, using a black dancer from the company [Douglass Stewart] and a remarkable percussionist from St. Louis, the stage fairly smoldered. Then staged Venusberg scene from Tannhauser. . . . Opened fall season with Taras staging La Sylphide. Clark Tippett [restaging] his first ballet, 'Enough Said.' Music Geo Pcle [*sic;* George Perle]. Balanchine Valse Fantaisie and Ailey's The River. [A] gang buster program. . . . Ailey, 2 cos. Really burn up the stage."[31] This was the second time both companies had performed the ballet; the first time was in 1986, Jordan recalled.[32]

By the fall of 1990, the beginning of Bolender's tenth anniversary of directing the company, he was able to start the season with an all-Balanchine program that included *The Four Temperaments* (which he often said should only be performed by companies with very strong soloists), *Concerto Barocco,* and *The Firebird. The Nutcracker* followed, and in February, another repertory show consisting of Loring's *Billy the Kid,* Balanchine's *Apollo,* and Tudor's *Lilac Garden.* All programs were accompanied by live orchestra. The concluding program in May was advertised in the season brochure as an Anniversary Extravaganza to be created "especially for the company's talents" by the artistic director.

Increasing pain in his hips prevented Bolender from making a new work for the last program, and when the season was over he went to New York and had his right hip replaced, he wrote to Patterson, by the same surgeon who had done Suzanne Farrell's. He recuperated at Betty Cage's country home, driven there by John Taras once he was released from the hospital. Jordan visited him in the hospital before moving back to Kansas City; he would eventually take over the job of ballet master from Kai, who retired a couple of years later.

Back in Kansas City, Bolender, assisted by Jordan after Kai retired, continued to make his work the central focus of his life, with some time out for travel. He went to Turkey to visit his friends there, and on a trip to London he had a wonderful time shopping at Liberty's and going to the theater. He made frequent trips to New York, combining work with pleasure, seeing as much theater as he could, auditioning dancers at SAB, and taking side trips to Flourtown, outside Philadelphia, to visit Yvonne Patterson. These were multipurpose visits, mixing the pleasure of reminiscing about their years of living in the same building in New York and the 1941 tour of South America with the business of dance. Bolender wanted to look at Patterson's students—she taught until she was almost 100—with an eye toward giving them jobs in Kansas City and also to discuss the acquisition of William Dollar's *Five Gifts* for KCB. *Le Combat,* Dollar's best-known work, which Roland Petit had commissioned in 1949 for Ballets de Paris (Melissa Hayden brilliantly performed its leading role at City Ballet a year later), had joined KCB's repertoire in the early 1980s, when Dollar was still alive (he died in 1986). For various reasons, mostly involving production costs, the project was dropped, and Bolender continued to make new work for the company.

Bolender collaborated with Eldred again to make *Celebration,* commissioned to acknowledge the sesquicentennial of the University of Missouri. This was somewhat based on a ballet he had started for the Harkness Ballet before coming to Kansas City but for one reason or another had never completed. In it, he celebrates a lot more than the University of Missouri; he offers choreographic tributes to modern dance, neoclassical ballet, and such expressions of American popular culture as vaudeville, musical comedy, movies, and jazz. The music was mostly George Gershwin's, which was, it would seem, nearly as inspirational for Bolender as Stravinsky's was.

Box office was certainly on Bolender's mind when he mounted *Coppélia,* the 1870 comic ballet that Balanchine had staged on City Ballet with the help of Danilova in 1974, for the same reason. At the time, Bolender had written Schnee that "Balanchine was doing Coppelia and American ballet is over,"[33] but eighteen years later, he followed Balanchine's lead in staging story ballets with multiple roles for children. Such works fill the house with the child dancers' families and support the less family-friendly works in the repertory. In Bolender's version, Dr. Coppélius is not the broadly comic "mad scientist" he is in many productions; he's a failure and he knows it, which makes him a far more sympathetic character. For marketing reasons, Bolender intended to perform the role himself, but he worried that he lacked enough physical stamina at 79 to keep up the pace. Fairly late in the rehearsal process, he discovered that he was unable to lift the Coppélia doll. Nevertheless, the ballet was a financial success and helped the company "to keep the doors open" in Bolender's often-used phrase.

A year later, Muriel Kauffman and the Muriel McBrien Kauffman Foundation provided KCB with unprecedented financial stability. On July 30, Bolender wrote Patterson that he and a KCB board member had met with Mrs. Kauffman at the Marion Corporation offices, where she told Bolender that "she was presenting me and my co. the sum of $1 million to be used as endowment and security. I was floating on the plumpest cloud in the bluest heaven, finally after 13 years of sweat shop labor some one recognizes that perhaps we have not been wasting our time."[34]

The timing was excellent, since Bolender, now 80, was reluctantly approaching retirement. Work had been at the center of his life since he was in his teens. The KCB board began searching for and auditioning possible successors. Bart Cook, who had retired as a principal dancer with New York City Ballet in 1993 and had danced brilliantly in some of Bolender's roles in the Balanchine-Robbins repertoire, among them the Sarabande in *Agon* and The Husband in *The Concert,* was one of them. He came in as a ballet master in 1995 and left a few months later, when Bolender officially became artistic director emeritus on July 1. Initially, Bolender was delighted to be grooming Cook to take over, but by the summer their relationship had deteriorated badly. A video of an immensely comic Spanish-style trio the two men did with Cook's wife, Maria Calegari, for a gala ends with Cook and Bolender locked in a warm embrace that gives no indication that in fact they were at loggerheads. However, Cook was young, and by his own account less than diplomatic, and Bolender, according to Jordan and others, was having considerable difficulty letting go of the company he had worked so hard to build. The duet was created as a pièce d'occasion to thank Muriel Kauffman for the endowment; she died, suddenly, not long after that, and *Tribute to Muriel* was Bolender's choreographic eulogy for his friend and patron.

Later in July, Bolender took a three-week trip to New York, during which he had cataract surgery in both eyes that greatly improved his vision, and he spent time with many old friends, including Le Clercq and Betty Cage. "I haven't developed friends in Kansas City in the same way," he wrote Schnee, because of his workload. That load was lightened by his retirement, but he was doing a new ballet, which he envisioned with "lots of steps." The ballet was *Arena,* and Bolender, liberated from the daily routine of running the company, was doing a great deal of research for it and enjoying the process. In August, having returned to Kansas City, he wrote to Schnee that the first summer of his retirement was no different from the past forty or fifty and he had been consulting art books and "watching films I have either never seen before or searching out the old masterpieces of the 1950s and 60s. Bergman films—Seventh Seal, Virgin Spring." He described Bergman's direction of Liv Ullmann as "shattering." "I approach this new assignment [the new ballet] with considerable trepidation but then I also believe I have always approached everything in such a manner. I used to think life got easier as one got older—not so!![35]

In the fall the Ballet Ball was given in his honor, and in another letter to Schnee, Bolender noted that Jillana, Yvonne Mounsey, Robert Lindgren, Melissa Hayden, Janet Reed, and Una Kai were present and that "Jacques and Carrie d'Amboise sent a recorded message and Eddie Villella a 'darling letter.'" Bolender also told Schnee that "Jean-Pierre Bonnefoux and Patricia McBride are poised to take over" but that money was an issue.[36] Ultimately the board decided that William Whitener, who had danced with the Joffrey Ballet and Twyla Tharp's company and for some years had been the artistic director of the Royal Winnipeg Ballet, was the most qualified successor to Bolender. He took over in time to oversee the 1996–1997 season.

Arena premiered in October on a program that included Balanchine's *Scotch Symphony* and de Mille's *Rodeo.* In a review of the season opener that appeared in the *Kansas City Star* on October 12, Scott Cantrell, the paper's classical music editor, wrote dismissively of *Scotch Symphony,* calling it "not top drawer Balanchine," and found *Rodeo*'s Cowgirl heroine "frail." *Arena,* however, he thought well worth the wait and was struck by how "fresh and challenging" Bolender's "movements" were in a ballet in which he spotted the influence of Balanchine, Robbins, and Graham. Cantrell also described *Arena* as "bristling with invention" and listed its cast of characters—tarts, a politician, and an evangelist "compounded of Eva Peron and Tammy Faye

Bakker."[37] Bolender, who all his adult life was suspicious of institutionalized religion, had little use for evangelists and occasionally in this period expressed that low opinion in letters to his friends.

From Cantrell's account of the ballet and from the music (which had the "energies of Sacre" and contained "jazzy angularities"), it is clear that Bolender, in collaboration with Mobberley, was again revisiting some of his own work, specifically *Creation of the World*. The fall of Adam and Eve, the Roaring Twenties, and political corruption were all treated in one way or another in that 1960 ballet.

Arena was the last ballet Bolender made, but he continued to coach KCB's dancers in his work, supervising the mounting of the *Nutcracker* each year; fine tuning performances in *Chopin Waltzes, Danse Concertante* and *Voyager;* working well with Whitener on maintaining the existing KCB repertoire; and writing to Schnee positively about the direction in which his successor was taking the company. Whitener did take the company in new directions during his tenure (he retired in 2013), building the repertoire on his own professional experience, as Bolender had done and as most artistic directors still do. He added a number of works by Twyla Tharp and some by Robbins and increased the Balanchine holdings in the repertoire. He also choreographed on the company and for specific dancers: his *Carmen* was a vehicle for Kimberly Cowen, who Bolender had begun training when she was in her teens.

Whitener was innovative in his programming, drawing the attention of the national press when he decided to present a group of solo dances as the middle part of a repertory show in 2005. One of them was Mary Wigman's *Tottendanz* (Witch Dance), and Bolender had the pleasure of informing Cowen's thoroughly frightening performance of the role with his memories of seeing the choreographer do it in New York in the 1930s.

Whitener was not the first to make use of Bolender's prodigious memory for choreography. In 1997, Nancy Reynolds, founder of the Balanchine Foundation's Interpreters Archive, tapped him to recall on videotape a small part of the choreography for Phlegmatic in *Four Temperaments,* and to coach Albert Evans, who was dancing the role at New York City Ballet. In no way was the intention to have Evans interpret the role in the same way Bolender had; rather, it was to preserve what Balanchine had said to and shown the dancers on whom he had created the roles. The taping was done in City Ballet's studios and Bolender took Barksdale with him to demonstrate. He was now 84, but Reynolds remembered him going into a full plié, right down to the floor, when they were taking a break from filming.

Bolender felt that Evans was approaching the role from a very different place from what Balanchine had intended, or certainly from his own interpretation. "The way Todd redid the solo it was introverted, and Albert was doing it in an extroverted manner," Reynolds recalled in an interview with Nicole Dekle Collins for *The Dance Enthusiast*.[38] Bolender's coaching was gentle, his words precise as he guided Evans through the first minute or so of Phlegmatic's entrance: "It's as if you're being pulled by a string," he says at one point.

In 2004, Reynolds approached Bolender again, this time to coach Herman Cornejo, principal dancer at American Ballet Theatre, in his role in "The Unanswered Question," while Allegra Kent coached Janie Taylor of New York City Ballet in her role as the sole woman in that section of *Ivesiana*. Earlier that year, Bolender had coached City Ballet soloist Arch Higgins in the Phlegmatic entrance as part of a Guggenheim Museum Works & Process program. Always an unwilling public speaker, he issued very little information in the interview portion of the program.

Bolender's work with the Balanchine Foundation wasn't confined to the Interpreters Archive; he also was deeply involved with the Foundation's Archive of Lost Choreography. When Reynolds put out a call for suggestions for ballets long gone from the repertoire whose reconstruction could be filmed for the archive, Bolender was one of the first, if not the first, to respond, with Stravinsky's *Renard*, which Balanchine made for Ballet Society in close collaboration with the composer. Bolender had not only originated the title role, he had, a decade later, at Balanchine's request, reprised it and restaged the ballet for the Boston Common Festival in honor of Stravinsky's seventy-fifth birthday. When he began working on the reconstruction in 1999 for Kansas City Ballet, the "ballet burlesque" hadn't been produced for more than half a century, with the exception of a rechoreographed version by Lew Christensen (the original Rooster) in 1955.

"*Renard* requires dancers with a strong sense of theater, plus a knowledge of style, and how. . . . [it] relate[s] to various choreographies," Bolender wrote Schnee on August 6, 1999, early in a process that would take close to three years to complete. "This is not only a problem with students but many young people trained in various dance techniques are too often trained by teachers without a well enough developed sense of how 'style' is built into technique."[39] A few months later, he wrote Sanli from Destin, Florida, where he was on holiday, that he had a few sections left to "clarify" and needed to "pick a cast that I might think capable of helping me get an almost lost Balanchine ballet once again on stage." The plan was for the company to go into rehearsal in the spring for the filming and for the ballet to be performed live on a mixed bill the following February. "It is complicated tho short in running time," Bolender told Sanli; it also presented considerable difficulties for the dancers because of the costumes and the masks.[40]

Bolender was as meticulously obsessive about reconstructing the costumes as he was with the choreography, and he integrated both elements in the same way he had done with *Souvenirs* in 1955. Jordan, who was indispensable in the studio and everywhere else during the reconstruction process, remembered driving Bolender to virtually every hardware store in Kansas City to find exactly the right kind of spring to put in the Fox's tail.[41]

As recently as 2019, the dancers who performed the work at Symphony Space in 2004 have spoken of the detailed particularity of Bolender's coaching for a ballet that on the surface looks like a ballet for children but, like his own *Mother Goose,* is nothing of the kind. Matthew Donnell, who understudied another dancer in the role of the Cat when he joined KCB in 2000, remembered feeling pretty nervous about working with a man whose reputation as a stickler for detail and a strict disciplinarian in the studio preceded him. Donnell recalled Bolender's passion for *Renard* and thinking that while he didn't fully understand the ballet, "I sure as heck know I need to treasure this experience." Another experience with Bolender he treasured was being coached as Drosselmeyer and being told to swoop across the stage like a large bird before sprinkling fairy dust on the sleeping Clara.[42]

Donnell was right about Bolender's love for *Renard.* In an interview in Kansas City conducted sometime between the premiere in Kansas City and the Symphony Space performance in March 2004, part of a twelve-hour "Wall to Wall Balanchine" celebration of the choreographer's centennial in which Donnell danced the Cat, he said he thought the ballet burlesque should be restored to New York City Ballet's repertory and should be included in those of many other ballet companies. *Renard* was certainly well received by critics in Kansas City when it was performed there as part of a 2002 Stravinsky Festival, and in New York, Jennifer Dunning of the *New*

York Times and Deborah Jowitt of the *Village Voice* wrote glowing reviews. The Symphony Space audience applauded loudly and rhythmically when the dancers marched onto the stage, still in character, to take their bows.

The restoration of *Renard* gave Bolender a project in "retirement" that he could be thoroughly engaged with for more than three years, if you include putting on the finishing touches in the SAB studios for the 2004 performance. Those years also brought considerable sadness to Bolender's life, as it does to all who live a long time, as old friends and close colleagues died. The death of Janet Reed in February 2000 was extremely hard on him. She had been scheduled to join him in the Florida panhandle for a winter holiday, but because the weather was cold and gray when he got there, he had telephoned her suggesting she come another time when it might be warmer. They had had a number of reunions in Seattle since Bolender had taken the job in Kansas City. He would routinely take Reed; Irene Larsson, the original Vamp in *Souvenirs;* and Ruthanna Boris out to lunch. After Branson Erskine died in 1994, Bolender and Reed took some trips together, including one to Santa Fe, where they saw the sights and visited with d'Amboise and his wife, Carolyn George, who Bolender had partnered in *Western Symphony.*

Traveling together again was not to be. In early March, Bolender wrote Schnee about recent events in his life, stating that "the most drastic to me has been the death of Janet Reed who had a stroke a week ago and when offered life support . . . was still quite capable of saying 'no way,' but within days she no longer could talk or recognize anyone or anything. She died last Friday and this has been a severe emotional time for me coming so immediately upon the heels of Betty Cage's death." Of a memorial celebration of Cage's birthday, held at SAB, Bolender told Schnee she "would have hated such schmaltz," and that he was now feeling the need to see old friends since "time [was] running out."[43]

A telephone conversation he had had with Reed shortly after his return from Florida had been their last. They "had talked about everything," he told Schnee, just as they had been doing for the past fifty-eight years, by letter, by phone, and face to face.

Reed was living in a basement apartment in her daughter's house in Seattle and had the stroke while she was getting ready to go out for her daily walk. Jane Erskine and her partner had both gone to their jobs and their daughter had gone to school when it happened. Reed was fully conscious but completely unable to move, so she lay on the floor of her apartment for many hours, unable to call for help or reach the phone. She was taken to the hospital as soon as she was discovered, then to a nursing home, where she slipped into a coma and died of kidney failure a few days later.

Bolender was unable to attend Reed's memorial because of some health problems of his own. Had he done so, he would have told the story of the loss of his wig when they were dancing together in *Pied Piper* and spoken, too, of the laughter that was such an important part of their decades of friendship. The memorial took place in the studios at Pacific Northwest Ballet at the Seattle Center. Francia Russell and Kent Stowell attended, as did Reed Erskine, some PNB dancers, a few of Jane Erskine's friends, and the taxi driver who had taken her around town when she needed it and "adored her."

Michael Kidd, who had cast her as the lead in his first ballet, *On Stage*, also adored her. "Janet's ability to combine balletic skill with emotional qualities, whether dramatic or humorous, were extraordinary," he wrote in a condolence letter to her children, which Jane Erskine read aloud at her memorial. "She touched audiences as few performers can." He and Reed had been lifelong friends, in part, Kidd added, because of her ability to "connect with people, and her straightforward honesty."[44]

In a *New York Times* obituary, Anna Kisselgoff said many of the same things, and some years later in an essay about American ballet, she called Reed "the quintessential American ballerina."[45] There were tributes in several British publications as well; Reed was remembered there, half a century later, for her performances in *Symphony in C* and *Bourrée Fantasque* in 1950 when City Ballet had their first tour there.

Two thousand six was a big year for Bolender; he spent a good deal of time helping to raise money for Kansas City Ballet's fiftieth anniversary celebrations in 2007 and for a building for the company that would—finally—be a permanent home. It contains several studios, including a large one in which the professional company can rehearse for performances and can easily be converted into a theater for lecture demonstrations and informal performances of new choreography. A separate studio for the school, a place for parents to wait comfortably for their student children, dressing rooms, administrative offices, and a box office were all on the wish list, and did become a part of the building, a completely renovated power station located at 500 West Pershing Road. To Bolender's immense pleasure, the building was built in 1914, the year of his birth. It was announced at his ninetieth birthday celebrations in February 2004 that the building would be named the Todd Bolender Center for Dance and Creativity, and characteristically he commented that what happened in the building once it opened was infinitely more important than what it was called.

Bolender did not live to see that opening in the summer of 2011; nor did he live to accept his long overdue Dance Magazine Award in 2006, but he knew in May that he was going to receive it. He began preparing his acceptance speech (expressing some dread about giving it) and making decisions about which of his choreographies he wanted performed at the award ceremony in New York, which took place on November 13 at Florence Gould Hall. It is telling that he wanted the "Hesitation Tango" from *Souvenirs* to be performed and Christopher Barksdale and Kim Cowen, the last KCB dancers he trained, to dance it.

On October 10, Bolender suffered a stroke just as he was preparing to go to the tech rehearsal for KCB's season opener, which included a revival of his *Grand Tarantella*, a ballet close to his heart in part because he had linked it directly to the school by including children in the cast. It had been a busy week for him; a few days earlier he had been at the groundbreaking ceremony for the Kauffman Performing Arts Center. A newspaper photograph of him with Muriel Kauffman's daughter, Julia, captures his talent for making someone feel that they were the only person present and that he was delighted to be with them. The next day, the 92-year-old summoned the energy to attend a *Tarantella* rehearsal and, according to Barksdale, was both disappointed and angered by changes that had been made in the choreography. He spent the rest of the day "fixing it and he was not nice about it," Barksdale said.[46]

For a short while, it looked like Bolender might recover from the stroke sufficiently to attend the Dance Magazine Award ceremony a month later, but two days later he had a second stroke and died at two in the afternoon. He was surrounded by dancers he had trained and loved, including Barksdale and Cowen; Kevin Amey, who had worked with Bolender for many years in several capacities, including production manager; KCB executive director Jeffrey Bentley; and Jordan.

Lisa Thorn Vinzant, who by that time was company ballet master, was also in the room. She had to rush back to the theater to rehearse *Tarantella*, which she recalled was very hard. "Everyone had an idea of how you were supposed to act and react and it was heartbreaking. I was trying to keep myself composed and somehow people got mad at me for it. They had no idea, he was a huge part of my life—I was so young when he hired me at 18 and to spend all those years with him and then see him in his last moments, yet it was special to be there."[47]

For Cowen, who met Bolender in 1987 when she was a twelve-year-old ballet student in St. Louis and danced in his *Nutcracker* there, it was also extremely hard to be with him as he breathed his last. "I called Lisa Thorn to ask how he was doing," she remembered. "Kevin called a minute later, and said get down here if you want to say good-bye. [Bolender's] hands were still warm, I was talking to him, whispered in his ear, Chris started talking, [his] eyes opened for a second, knew that Chris was there. Hands started to get colder. [Someone said] 'he's gone.'"[48]

KCB's fall program opened that night. The company danced their hearts out in *Tarantella*. Cowen said she made herself stop crying by 4 p.m. so her eyes wouldn't be swollen and puffy for the performance. However, she was unable to smile during a ballet Bolender had designed to delight the audience with the dancers' execution of the rapid, buoyant, technically difficult steps. When Cowen really came apart, however, was at a hastily thrown together memorial for the company on Sunday, October 15, in which she danced the young girl's gut-wrenching solo in *The Still Point*. In that performance, she put every ounce of the grief for the man who had mentored her, nurtured her talent, and in many ways looked after her since her girlhood; every anguished movement came from the heart.

There were many newspaper obituaries for Bolender in cities all over the country; in one capacity or another, he had worked in all of them. Writing for the *New York Times*, Kisselgoff noted that he became part of ballet history through his memorable performance in *The Four Temperaments* in 1946. She called *The Still Point* his masterpiece and cited his "sure touch" in *Souvenirs*, "a City Ballet staple for years." She added that his version of *The Miraculous Mandarin* was "a darker ballet," and that "in 1960 his version of Darius Milhaud's *Creation of the World* equated the fall of man with the 1929 stock market crash."[49]

A month after Bolender's death, Cowen and Barksdale had the upbeat assignment of showing off Bolender's "sure touch" for the Dance Magazine Award ceremony, which took place on an extremely rainy evening in New York. Bolender was first on the program, and a video survey of his dancing career and choreography KCB had prepared for the occasion was screened before his award was presented by Suki Schorer, substituting for Jacques d'Amboise, who had a last-minute scheduling conflict. William Whitener accepted the award, after which Bolender's protégés amused the distinguished audience with their fine-tuned, detailed, every-eyelash-in-place performance as the Vamp and the Gigolo in the "Hesitation Tango."

D'Amboise did make it to Kansas City in December, when he was the master of ceremonies at Bolender's memorial at the Lyric Theater, in which spoken tributes were interlaced with film of Bolender in signature roles and performances by KCB's dancers of the *Tarantella* finale and the grand pas de deux from his *Nutcracker,* with former KCB dancer Louise Nadeau dancing Sugar Plum. There was live music for both dances, performed by members of the Kansas City Symphony. Robert Barnett, an old friend from City Ballet days, was one of the speakers; reunions at Barnett's place in Asheville that included Kai, Barbara Milberg Fisher, Hayden, and other members of Balanchine's company had been one of the pleasures of the last decade of Bolender's life. The memorial concluded with an eloquent tribute by Jordan and the playing of the "Round of the Princesses" from Stravinsky's *The Firebird Suite,* a fitting conclusion for the man who at age twelve heard this music for the first time in Canton, Ohio, and decided he wanted to make dances.

Afterword

"It is because of Todd Bolender, Janet Reed, and dancers like them that ballet in America is what it is today," the late Edward Bigelow told his lunch guest at a restaurant near Lincoln Center in 2008, after asserting that Bolender's greatest achievement had been the establishment of Kansas City Ballet as a major regional company.

Bigelow had dedicated his life to the Balanchine-Kirstein enterprise, starting in 1941 as an SAB student. He was a founding member of City Ballet, where, along with Bolender, he was cast in Robbins's *Age of Anxiety* and *Fanfare* and originated roles in Balanchine's first *Nutcracker.* But his principal role until Balanchine's death was as an assistant in several capacities to both Balanchine and Kirstein in the administration of the company. In the last years of his life, Bigelow worked to preserve the Balanchine-Kirstein legacy in several ways, among them curating two photo exhibitions at Lincoln Center's David H. Koch Theater that included images of Bolender and Reed.

In other words, he knew Janet Reed and Todd Bolender well. He had danced with them and worked with them and was well aware of what they were capable of as dancers, teachers, in Reed's case as a ballet master, and in Bolender's case as a choreographer and artistic director. At that lunch he spoke approvingly of ballet companies outside New York, not all of them by any means part of the so-called Balanchine diaspora, because those companies provided opportunities for dancers to work west and east of the Hudson, perform principal roles they might not otherwise be given in the major coastal companies, and, of equal significance, be able to live decently on their salaries.

In the second decade of the twenty-first century there are approximately 100 professional and semi-professional ballet companies in the United

States. They provide work for dancers and give a wide variety of choreographers opportunities to make ballets on dancers who, by and large, are hungry for new ways of dancing, are committed to technical versatility, and are willing to work hard. And while many American ballet companies are linked in one way or another to Balanchine (Pacific Northwest Ballet, Atlanta Ballet, Pittsburgh Ballet Theatre, Miami City Ballet, San Francisco Ballet, Kansas City Ballet, Charlotte Ballet, and Ballet Chicago are all examples), a number are not. Lew and Willam Christensen, Robert Joffrey, a number of former Ballet Russe dancers, and some from England can also be counted as "dancers like" Bolender and Reed who are responsible for the dissemination and establishment of classical, neoclassical, and contemporary ballet across the country. British-born Toni Pimble, who was trained at England's Elmhurst School, has been artistic director of the Eugene Ballet in Oregon, which she founded with Riley Grannan, since 1978. Paul Vasterling, a southerner, was a dancer, teacher, ballet master, and choreographer with the Nashville Ballet before he became the artistic director in 1998. Pimble and Vasterling are both working choreographers and their repertoire is not confined to the companies they lead—Vasterling's work is in the Eugene Ballet's repertoire; Pimble's is in the Nashville Ballet's and a number of others. Pimble was among the first New York City Ballet Diamond Project choreographers. Both tell American stories their audiences can relate to. Pimble has done several ballets based on Native American culture; the first was *Children of the Raven,* narrated by Shoshone-Bannock tribal member Ed Edmo at performances in Eugene and on extensive tours, including one that took the company to Taiwan and another to Syria. Vasterling, who has a history of collaborating with Nashville artists of every discipline, worked in 2019 with Nashville poet Caroline Randall Williams to make the evening-length *Lucy Negro Redux,* with Kayla Rowser in the title role. Rowser, who is Black, danced with Nashville Ballet for twelve years, performing many of the great ballerina roles—Aurora in *The Sleeping Beauty,* Odette/Odile in *Swan Lake,* and Juliet in *Romeo and Juliet* (in Vasterling's versions of those ballets); the Russian girl in Balanchine's *Serenade;* and in more contemporary work.

Rowser, who retired from the stage in 2020, was a technically versatile, intellectually curious dancer who analyzed roles. There are many supremely gifted dancers like her on the rosters of small and medium-sized companies in the United States who are dancing in repertoires that show both their range and the stylistic eclecticism that is the hallmark of twenty-first-century American ballet. In addition to the inevitable *Nutcracker,* these repertoires usually include a number of evening-length story ballets and shorter works by Balanchine, Robbins, William Forsythe, Nicolo Fonte, Trey McIntyre, Val Caniparoli, Julia Adam, Twyla Tharp, and Helen Pickett, to name a few.

Portland's resident ballet company, Oregon Ballet Theatre (OBT), is fairly typical of a small regional ballet company. Its repertoire reflects the training, professional experience, personal taste, and point of view of its three artistic directors. In its thirty years of existence, OBT's dancers have performed work by all of those choreographers and by James Canfield, Dennis Spaight, August Bournonville, Christopher Stowell, Nacho Duato, James Kudelka, and a number of others. Those ballets have given the dancers the chance to be, in Reed's words, "whatever [they] want to be,"[1] from a weary pioneer mother in McIntyre's *Robust American Love* to a joyous Aurora at her coming-of-age party in Stowell's staging of *The Sleeping Beauty* to the Waltz Girl in *Serenade,* the ballet that made Bolender shift from modern dance to ballet and in which Reed danced many performances. Reed, it should be remembered, was the star of Willam Christensen's first company, the Portland Ballet, which sowed the seeds from which OBT grew.

Canfield was the company's first artistic director. He trained with Mary Day at the Washington School of Ballet, and danced with the Joffrey Ballet when it was based in New York. He starred in John Cranko's *Romeo and Juliet,* originated roles in Gerald Arpino's ballets, and performed in revivals of *Petrouchka* and *The Green Table* and in Paul Taylor's *Cloven Kingdom.* In his fifteen years at the helm of OBT, Canfield made many short ballets that reflected American popular culture, both musically and choreographically, frequently collaborating with Portland's visual artists and musicians. He brought some Balanchine works into the repertoire, and perhaps his most innovative programming was an evening of *Giselles* that started with the traditional Romantic classic and concluded with Donald Byrd's hard-edged, urban, contemporary deconstruction, *Life Situations: Daydreams on Giselle.* However, the company's crown jewel in those years may well have been his *Nutcracker,* set in nineteenth-century St. Petersburg with a new libretto written by company historian Carol Shults, in which Marie is a student at the Imperial Ballet School, Fabergé replaces Drosselmeier, Kschessinska is a party guest, and dancers from the Maryinsky perform the second-act divertissements for Marie and the Nutcracker Prince, both roles danced by adult company members. At the end of the ballet, Kschessinska, who has become the Sugar Plum Fairy, takes the tiara from her head and places it on Marie's, passing on the role to the ballerina in training. Campbell Baird designed the production, in many respects after Fabergé; he also designed Vasterling's very different, Nashville-oriented version.

Canfield came from the Joffrey branch of the American ballet tree; his associate artistic director and resident choreographer Dennis Spaight, who also put an aesthetic stamp on the company, was related to the Balanchine-Christensen branch through his career as a dancer with the San Francisco Ballet and Pacific Northwest Ballet and, because he danced in his company, Maurice Béjart's Ballet of the Twentieth Century. Spaight began choreographing early in his short career (he died at 38 in 1993), winning an award from Baryshnikov for *Crayola,* a ballet danced in silence that was influenced by Robbins's *Moves.* For his *Scheherazade,* the first ballet he made on OBT's dancers, he collaborated with Portland artists—easel painter Henk Pander, lighting designer Peter West, and costume designer Ric Young.

Canfield left the company in 2002 and Christopher Stowell took over the directorship the next year. Stowell had the strongest ties to Balanchine and Lew Christensen by dint of his training from his parents, Kent Stowell and Francia Russell, Pacific Northwest Ballet's founding artistic directors; his studies at SAB; and his career as a dancer with the San Francisco Ballet. He added many Balanchine works to OBT's repertoire, including *The Nutcracker, Four Temperaments,* and *Apollo,* and the company's first works by Robbins, including *The Concert, In the Night,* and *The Cage.*

Stowell also made a number of short ballets for OBT's dancers. One was a half-evening-length *Carmen* that was quite different from one Canfield made; another was *The Second Front,* to a score by Shostakovich, a neo-classical work with considerable political relevance. (It premiered shortly before Stowell left.) Stowell was responsible for giving OBT's dancers the opportunity to perform in the company's first evening-length productions of *Swan Lake* and *The Sleeping Beauty.* These performances gave the Portland audience an opportunity to see, in live performance, the story ballets that are the backbone of classical ballet. Stowell's staging of *Sleeping Beauty,* which compressed the ballet into two long acts with one intermission and included a new "Jewels" pas de quatre, gave the children in the audience a magical version of Perrault's fairy tale, and in Stowell's words, "satisfied our adult hunger for a rich arts experience."[2] Without the dancers, particularly the principals and soloists who danced Aurora and the Prince, this could not have been accomplished.

Kevin Irving, OBT's third artistic director, programmed this *Sleeping Beauty* as part of the company's thirtieth-anniversary season, although his own background and interests lie squarely in neoclassical ballet, modern dance, and contemporary work, much of it classically based. Irving's early professional training was in modern dance at The Ailey School and his first job was with Elisa Monte Dance. With Les Grands Ballets Canadiens de Montréal, Irving danced in classical and neoclassical works, including the central pas de deux in Balanchine's *Agon,* and in many of James Kudelka's choreographies. Tharp was his next employer, and after her company disbanded he became ballet master and associate director of Nacho Duato's Compañia Nacional de Danza in Madrid. From there, he assumed the artistic directorship of Sweden's GöteborgsOperans Danskompani. In 2013, he became OBT's artistic director, bringing several pieces by Duato into the repertoire and such choreographers as Pickett and Darrell Grand Moultrie. Nicolo Fonte, who has frequently collaborated with Portland musician Thomas Lauderdale, the leader of the band Pink Martini, became resident choreographer in 2014.

For the company's thirtieth-anniversary season, Irving paid homage to the company's history and lineage by programming a new work by Canfield, Stowell's *Sleeping Beauty,* Spaight's *Scheherazade,* Balanchine's *Stravinsky Violin Concerto,* and de Mille's *Rodeo,* which Spaight acquired for Ballet Oregon, a precursor of OBT. Forsythe's *In the Middle, Somewhat Elevated,* Fonte's evening-length *Beautiful Decay,* and Tharp's *Baker's Dozen,* the last a company premiere, are as much expressions of Irving's point of view and experience as they are of Canfield and Stowell's choreography and programming. None of these artists are ballet ideologues, any more than Reed and Bolender were. Ballet in America in the twenty-first century is all about the eclecticism of American culture, the blending of high and low art, and the inclusion of many techniques and many points of view. And like Bolender and Reed, the dancers in this company give this art form, which is still perceived as foreign in many parts of the country, and the audiences everything they've got.

As this book goes to press, ballet companies all over the world have had to cancel their seasons due to the COVID-19 pandemic. It's impossible to predict who will survive and who will not or if live performance of any art—theater, opera, symphony—can be revived after a lengthy hiatus. Nevertheless, artistic directors and choreographers are already taking steps to keep their dancers employed and their companies in the public eye with streaming performances that have already been done and new choreography made for the camera. Ballet isn't going to die in the United States any more than it did in postrevolutionary Russia or in London during the World War II blitz or in occupied Paris. But what it will look like—and who will be watching—is impossible to say.

Acknowledgments

This book could not have been completed without the help of a great many people, from my nearest and dearest to some that I've never met but who were nevertheless willing to tell me, via telephone and e-mail, what they knew and what they felt about Todd Bolender and Janet Reed and what makes ballet American.

The generosity of my colleagues has been staggering. Deborah Jowitt, Betsy Cooper, and Nancy Reynolds sent me transcriptions of their interviews with Bolender; Deborah Hickenlooper Sowell sent the transcription of hers with Reed; Alastair Macaulay shared his memory of an interview he did with Reed in the late 1980s and connected me with Robert Glasstone, who gave me valuable insights into Turkish ballet, and with Robert Gottlieb, who described to me on the telephone his *coup de foudre* when, in 1944, he saw Reed dance in *Fancy Free*. Robert Greskovic has answered endless e-mail questions about both artists and given me the benefit of his wisdom about photographs, as has the late Marvin Hoshino. Lynn Garafola taught me how to "read" photographs, and I am grateful to Joanna Dee, whose dissertation on Katherine Dunham Lynn and Eric Foner directed, for sending me material on Bolender and Dunham's school. Rita Felciano has been an invaluable sounding board, as has Sandra Kurtz, who shared her knowledge of Seattle's ballet history and fact-checked the Seattle chapter.

I owe a very great deal to those who have edited me throughout my arts-writing career. In no particular order, Mindy Aloff has shepherded me patiently and skillfully through the writing of much of this book. The late Tobi Tobias conscripted me into this challenging, gratifying profession of dance writer when she was reviews editor at *Dance Magazine* and (too many years ago) suggested I write about Reed. The late Francis Mason, in addition to publishing one and a half chapters in *Ballet Review,* underwrote the transcription of my interviews with Bolender. I am also greatly indebted to George Dorris, who published part of chapter 1 in *Dance Chronicle* as "Janet Reed: The Early Years" and interviewed the late Horst Koegler via e-mail on my behalf, and to Jack Anderson, who at various dinner tables helped me obsess about titles and clarify my thinking about a number of issues. Heartfelt thanks go to Meredith Babb for accepting my proposal, for her patient extension of several deadlines, and for her own contribution to the preservation of dance history—she is responsible for the University Press of Florida's outstanding list of dance books. I must also thank, at the press, Rachel Welton, Marthe Walters, and Kate Babbitt, freelance copy editor par excellence.

Barry Johnson and Bob Hicks have been making me a better writer for about thirty years at *The Oregonian* and *Oregon Arts Watch.* When Alexander Kafka was editor of the *Chronicle of Higher Education Review,* he assigned me an essay on what makes American ballet American. I thank many editors at *Dance Magazine,* including Marilyn Hunt, K. C. Patrick, Wendy Perron, and the late Gary Parks.

There would be no book without the dedicated help of the staff at the Jerome Robbins Dance Division of the New York Public Library for the Performing Arts, particularly Charles Perrier, Phillip Karg, and the late Monica Moseley. Without the generous hospitality of my friend Lillian Kraemer, I could not have used the library except virtually from my home in Portland, Oregon. For two decades she has given me shelter, sustenance, and the use of her living room to conduct interviews with several sources, including Beatrice Cordua, Christopher Barksdale, Kimberly Cowen, and Bolender himself.

The late Una Kai, Joel Schnee, the late Sevgi Sanli, and Sanli's daughter Aydın Batur-Ord have been enormously helpful. No one has been more helpful than James Jordan, who has been deeply involved in this project since he picked me up at the Kansas City airport in 2001, my first trip to interview Bolender about Reed. That trip was funded with a grant from the Oregon Committee for the Humanities, and I am extremely grateful for it. In Kansas City, the following must be thanked: Jeffrey Bentley, William Whitener, Kevin Amey, Ramona Pansegrau, Elizabeth Wilson, Wendy Powell, Lisa Hickok, and too many others to name here, who gave me access to their memories as well as concrete materials. I must give additional thanks to Kansas City Ballet, to which Bolender left his ballets and his professional and personal papers for permission to quote from those materials, as well as those held by the Jerome Robbins Dance Division at the New York Public Library for the Performing Arts. Unfortunately, Sarah Rowland, Bolender's executor, denied me access to his appointment diaries, which would have made the task of figuring out the complicated chronology of his life both easier and faster.

Reed's children, the late Jane Erskine and her brother, Reed, have been extremely forthcoming with information and documentation of their mother's professional and private life, and the latter has also done considerable fact checking. Pacific Northwest Ballet archivist Sheila Dietrich provided indispensable materials. I thank Emily Frankel, Vivian Little, Barbara Walczak, Jacques d'Amboise, the late Barbara Milberg Fisher, and Janice Cohen Adelson for their insights and memories, too.

In Portland, thanks go to Blaine Truitt Covert for the gift of my jacket portrait and to my book preparation assistants Heather Wisner, Joshua Hicks, Kate Thompson, and Angie Jabine. Damien Jack was also of great help as a researcher, fact checker, and editor for the first half of the book. I really couldn't have done it without them.

All errors, needless to say, are mine.

I am not a trained academic historian and I was quite often overwhelmed by the task of organizing so much material into a cogent historical account. One night, about five years ago, I dreamed that I was in my study, working, and suddenly crashed my head down on the keyboard and yelled "Writing history is hard!" From the doorway I heard laughter. I turned around and saw the benevolent ghost of my husband, Franklin C. West, historian of twentieth-century Germany, who I was married to for nearly forty years, standing in the doorway. To him and our descendants I dedicate this book with love.

Notes

Chapter 1

1. Todd Bolender, interview with Deborah Jowitt, New York, New York, April 7, 2000.

2. Although *Pied Piper* was an extremely popular ballet on both sides of the Atlantic, it was in City Ballet's repertory for only a few years. It premiered there in 1950.

3. Todd Bolender, "Backstage at the Ballet," unpublished manuscript, box 15, folder 1, Todd Bolender Collection, Kansas City Ballet Archives, Tatiana Dokoudovska Library for Dance, Kansas City, Missouri (hereafter Todd Bolender Collection).

4. Bolender, "Backstage at the Ballet."

5. Francis Mason, *I Remember Balanchine* (New York: Doubleday, 1991), 178.

6. Quoted in Debra Hickenlooper Sowell, *The Christensen Brothers: An American Dance Epic* (Amsterdam: Harwood Academic Publishers, 1998), 122.

7. Lincoln Kirstein, *Ballet: Bias &Belief: Three Pamphlets Collected and Other Dance Writings of Lincoln Kirstein,* edited by Nancy Reynolds (New York: Dance Horizons, 1983), 72.

8. Kirstein, *Ballet: Bias and Belief,* 97.

9. Transcript of Yvonne Patterson, interview with the author, Flourtown, Pennsylvania, February 24, 2010, 3.

10. Undated newspaper clipping, Todd Bolender Collection.

11. Quoted in Nancy Reynolds, *Repertory in Review: 40 Years of the New York City Ballet* (New York: Dial Press, 1977), 39.

12. Kirstein, *Ballet: Bias & Belief,* 199.

13. Reynolds, *Repertory in Review,* 54.

14. Bolender, "Backstage at the Ballet."

15. Quoted in Reynolds, *Repertory in Review,* 54.

16. Newspaper clipping from Ballet Caravan 1937 tour, Todd Bolender Collection.

17. Todd Bolender, interview with Betsy Cooper, Seattle, Washington, July 2002.

18. Kirstein, *Ballet: Bias & Belief,* 202.

19. Kirstein, *Ballet: Bias & Belief,* 202.

20. Olga Maynard, *The American Ballet* (Philadelphia: Macrae Smith Company, 1959), 218.

21. Todd Bolender, interview with Betsy Cooper, 3.

22. Todd Bolender, notes for "Backstage at the Ballet," box 15, Todd Bolender Collection.

23. Loring was the most experienced choreographer in Ballet Caravan, which isn't saying much. He had arranged some dances for amateur theater performances in his native Milwaukee.

24. Cyril W. Beaumont, *Supplement to Complete Book of Ballets* (London: Putnam, 1952), 153.

25. Fred Danieli, interview with Peter Conway, 1979, Jerome Robbins Dance Division, New York Public Library.

26. Quoted in Kirstein, *Ballet: Bias &Belief,* 59.

27. Maynard, *The American Ballet,* 163.

28. Reynolds, *Repertory in Review,* 61.

29. Robert Pollack, "American Ballet Comes of Age," *Chicago Daily Times,* October 7, 1938, 15.

30. Gilbert Brown review, *Milwaukee News,* October 31, 1938, newspaper clipping, Todd Bolender Collection.

31. Brown review, *Seattle, Times,* October 31, 1938.

32. Newspaper clipping of review by Alfred Frankenstein, *San Francisco Chronicle,* November 8, 1938, Todd Bolender Collection.

33. Kirstein, *Ballet: Bias & Belief,* 62.

34. Kirstein, *Ballet: Bias & Belief,* 62.

35. Newspaper clipping, *Los Angeles Evening Herald,* November 17, 1938, Todd Bolender Collection.

36. Kirstein, *Ballet: Bias & Belief,* 63–64.

37. Newspaper clipping, *Tulsa Tribune,* December 7, 1938, Todd Bolender Collection.

38. Kirstein, *Ballet: Bias & Belief,* 67.

39. Transcript of Janet Reed, interview with Tobi Tobias, May 19 and 25, 1978, Dance Oral History Project, Jerome Robbins Dance Division, New York Public Library, New York, New York, 39.

40. Jacqueline Martin Schumacher, interview with the author, Portland, Oregon, 2001.

41. Janet Reed, unpublished memoir, copy in author's possession.

42. Janet Reed, unpublished memoir, copy in author's possession.

43. Reed interview with Tobias, 5.

44. Mary Metzer, telephone interview with the author, August 16, 2004.

45. Reed interview with Tobias, 5.

46. Janet Reed, filmed interview with Reed and Maren Erskine, 1997, in author's possession. My thanks to Reed Erskine for sharing this video with me.

47. Reed interview with Tobias.

48. Janet Reed, unpublished memoir, copy in author's possession.

49. Sowell, *The Christensen Brothers,* 92.

50. Mindy Aloff, "Lake, Prairie, Pillar, and Park: The Landscape of Janet Reed," *Encore Magazine of the Arts* (Portland, Oregon), November/December 1978, Reed's emphasis.

51. Sowell, *The Christensen Brothers,* 94.

52. Reed interview with Tobias, 7.

53. Janet Reed, unpublished memoir, copy in author's possession.

54. Janet Reed, unpublished memoir, copy in author's possession.

55. Reed interview with Tobias.

56. Transcript of Todd Bolender, interview with the author, Kansas City, Missouri, November 17, 2001, 10.

Chapter 2

1. Gil Brown, "Janet Reed Wildly Applauded in Ballet," *Seattle Star,* November 20, 1939.

2. Brown, "Janet Reed Wildly Applauded in Ballet."

3. Newspaper clipping, ca. November 1937, Hilmar Birger Grondahl Scrapbooks, 1929–1977 (hereafter Grondahl Scrapbooks), Oregon Historical Society Research Library, Portland, Oregon.

4. Frederick Lee Staver, "San Francisco's Ballet Goes Touring: Part Two," *Dance,* July 1940, 7.

5. Todd Bolender, conversation with the author.

6. Newspaper clipping, *Klamath Falls News and Herald,* ca. November 1939, in Janet Reed, Scrapbooks: Clippings, Programs, and Announcements, 1935–44, New York Public Library for the Performing Arts, New York, New York (hereafter Janet Reed Scrapbooks).

7. Newspaper clipping, ca. November 1939, Grondahl Scrapbooks.

8. Janet Reed to Esther Reed, [1939], Janet Reed Papers, Jerome Robbins Dance Division, New York Public Library for the Performing Arts, New York, New York (hereafter Janet Reed Papers), my italics. Christensen married Gisella Caccialanza in 1941, a month before American Ballet Caravan embarked on its South American tour.

9. Frederick Lee Staver, "San Francisco's Ballet Goes Touring: A Log Book of a Young Company's First Extensive Travels," *Deseret News,* June 1940, 14–15.

10. Janet Reed, unpublished memoir, in author's possession (hereafter Reed unpublished memoir).

11. Staver, "San Francisco's Ballet Goes Touring: Part Two," 7.

12. Staver review in *San Francisco News* quoted in Cobbett Steinberg, *San Francisco Ballet: The First Fifty Years* (San Francisco, CA: San Francisco Ballet Association; Chronicle Books, 1983), 38.

13. Newspaper clipping, *Arkansas Democrat,* February 2, [1940], in Janet Reed Scrapbooks.

14. Newspaper clipping, *Chicago Tribune,* [February 1940], in Janet Reed Scrapbooks.

15. Newspaper clipping, *Chicago Daily News,* [ca. February 1940], in Janet Reed Scrapbooks.

16. Newspaper clipping, *Chicago Herald-American,* [ca. February 1940], in Janet Reed Scrapbooks.

17. Staver, "San Francisco's Ballet Goes Touring: Part Two."

18. Quoted in Stephen Cobbett Steinberg, "America's First Swan: A Conversation with Willam Christensen and Janet Reed," in *Why a Swan? Essays, Interviews, & Conversations on "Swan Lake,"* compiled by Janice Ross and Stephen Cobbett Steinberg (San Francisco, CA: San Francisco Performing Arts Library and Museum, 1989), 66.

19. Transcript of Janet Reed, interview with Tobi Tobias, May 19 and 25, 1978, Dance

Oral History Project, Jerome Robbins Dance Division, New York Public Library, New York, New York, 7.

20. Janet Reed, filmed interview with Reed and Maren Erskine, 1997, in author's possession.

21. Quoted in Steinberg, "America's First Swan," 67.

22. Quoted in Steinberg, *San Francisco Ballet*, 42.

23. Richard Hays, *Seattle Times,* mid-December 1940, quoted in Janice Ross, *San Francisco Ballet at Seventy-Five* (San Francisco: Chronicle Books, 2007), 117.

24. Russell McLaughlin, "Debut of Ballet Company Delights a Big Audience." *Detroit News,* February 7, 1941.

25. *San Francisco News* quoted in Steinberg, *San Francisco Ballet,* 38.

26. John Martin, "Ballet Caravan in Seasonal Debut," *New York Times,* May 25, 1939.

27. John Martin, "Festival of Dance Has Its Opening," *New York Times,* December 27, 1939.

28. Anatole Chujoy, *The New York City Ballet* (New York: Knopf, 1953), 122.

29. "Music: Sleeping Beauty," *Time,* February 22, 1937.

30. Both Bolender and Reed performed in *Barn Dance,* Bolender when he was on the Littlefield Ballet's final tour in 1941 and Reed when it was taken into Ballet Theatre's repertory in 1944.

31. George Amberg, *Ballet in America: The Emergence of an American Art* (New York: Duell, Sloan and Pearce, 1949), 66–67.

32. "Music: Dancing Philadelphians," *Time,* July 19, 1937.

33. Needless to say, Bolender, a lifelong liberal Democrat who rebelled against his conservative Republican upbringing by casting his first presidential vote for Roosevelt in 1936, voted for him again.

34. Janet Reed, interview with Tobi Tobias, May 19 and 25, 1978, Dance Oral History Project, Jerome Robbins Dance Division, New York Public Library, New York, New York.

35. Reed unpublished memoir.

36. Reed unpublished memoir.

37. Reed unpublished memoir.

38. Reed unpublished memoir.

Chapter 3

1. Todd Bolender, interview with the author, Kansas City, Missouri, October 28, 2003, 10.

2. Todd Bolender, interview with Betsy Cooper, Seattle, Washington, July 2002, 4.

3. Bolender interview with the author, October 28, 2003.

4. Lincoln Kirstein to Nelson Rockefeller, June 12, 1941, New York City Ballet Records, 1934–1976 (hereafter New York City Ballet Records), Archives and Manuscripts, New York Public Library.

5. Bolender, unpublished memoir in author's possession.

6. Todd Bolender, interview with Nancy Reynolds, New York, New York, April 22, 1974.

7. Quoted in Nancy Reynolds, *Repertory in Review: 40 Years of the New York City Ballet* (New York: Dial Press, 1977), 70.

8. Lincoln Kirstein, *Ballet: Bias & Belief: Three Pamphlets Collected and Other Dance Writings of Lincoln Kirstein,* edited by Nancy Reynolds (New York: Dance Horizons, 1983), 80.

9. Kirstein, *Ballet: Bias & Belief,* 79.

10. Unsigned review, *Jornal do Brasil* (Rio de Janeiro) June 26,1941.

11. Unsigned review, *Diario Coriola* (Rio de Janeiro), June 26, 1941.

12. Unsigned review, *Jornal do Commercio* (Rio de Janeiro), June 26, 1941.

13. Unsigned review, *Correio da Notte* (Rio de Janeiro), June 28, 1941.

14. Kirstein, *Ballet: Bias & Belief,* 79–80.

15. Conversation with the author.

16. Bolender, unpublished memoir.

17. Bolender, unpublished memoir.

18. Many thanks to historian Frederick Nunn for sharing his knowledge of the White Sepulchre ships with me.

19. Bolender interview with Betsy Cooper.

20. Bolender interview with Nancy Reynolds.

21. Mordecai Paldiel, *Diplomat Heroes of the Holocaust* (Jersey City, NJ: KTAV Publishing House, 2007), 226.

22. Lincoln Kirstein, *Thirty Years: Lincoln Kirstein's The New York City Ballet: Expanded to Include the Years 1973–1978, in Celebration of the Company's Thirtieth Anniversary* (New York: Knopf Doubleday Publishing Group, 1978), 84.

23. Kirstein, *Thirty Years,* 84.

24. Kirstein, *Ballet: Bias & Belief,* 86.

25. Trude Rittman, interview with Nancy Reynolds, New York, December 9, 1976.

26. Kirstein, *Ballet: Bias & Belief,* 88.

27. Trude Rittman, interview with Nancy Reynolds, New York, December 9, 1976.

28. Kirstein, *Ballet: Bias & Belief,* 88.

29. Kirstein, *Ballet: Bias & Belief,* 88.

30. Silvio Salmena, unidentified newspaper clipping (Rio de Janeiro), June 29, 1941, box 1, folder, 10, New York City Ballet Archives, Ballet Society Collection.

31. Author unknown, unidentified newspaper clipping (Santiago de Chile), August 29, 1941.

32. Kirstein, *Ballet: Bias & Belief,* 90.

33. Kirstein's wife Fidelma stayed with the company. It may have been on this trip that Fidelma and Bolender formed their friendship; he was deeply fond of her.

34. Kirstein, *Ballet: Bias & Belief,* 91.

35. Lincoln Kirstein, telegram to Walter Prendergast, Lima, Peru, September 11, 1941, New York City Ballet Records, New York Public Library.

36. Aaron Copland and Vivian Perlis, *Copland: 1900 through 1942* (New York: St. Martin's Press, 1984), 325.

37. Beatrice Tompkins to Lincoln Kirstein, 1941, New York City Ballet Records.

38. Beatrice Tompkins to Lincoln Kirstein, 1941.

39. Unknown author, tour memoir, n.d., New York City Ballet Records.

40. Beatrice Tompkins to Lincoln Kirstein, 1941.

41. Michael Horowitz, Bogotá, to Franklyn Weinberg, October 9, 1941, New York City Ballet Records.

42. Michael Horowitz to Franklyn Weinberg.

43. John Taras quoted in tour memoir in New York City Ballet Archive.

44. Beatrice Tompkins to Lincoln Kirstein, 1941.

45. Bolender's photo album is in box 10 of the Todd Bolender Collection.

46. Bolender, interview with Reynolds.

47. Beatrice Tompkins to Lincoln Kirstein, 1941.

48. Caption in Bolender's photo album.

49. Todd Bolender, "Backstage at the Ballet," unpublished manuscript, box 15, folder 1, Todd Bolender Collection, Kansas City Ballet Archives, Tatiana Dokoudovska Library for Dance, Kansas City, Missouri.

50. Todd Bolender, conversation with the author, Kansas City, Missouri, June 2006.

Chapter 4

1. Eugene Loring, interview with Marilyn Hunt, New York, 1976.

2. Loring interview with Hunt.

3. Janet Reed, interview with Tobi Tobias, May 25, 1978, Oral History Archives Dance Collection, New York Public Library, New York, New York, 27.

4. George Amberg, *Ballet in America: The Emergence of an American Art* (New York: Duell, Sloan and Pearce, 1949), 167.

5. Quoted in Aloff, "Lake, Prairie, Pillar, and Park: The Landscape of Janet Reed," *Encore Magazine of the Arts* (Portland, Oregon), November/December 1978, 9.

6. Reed interview with Tobias, 11.

7. John Martin, "Premiere Is Seen of 'City Portrait'; New Ballet by Eugene Loring Presented by Dance Players at National Theatre[;] Music by Henry Brant[;] Settings Are After Reginald Marsh—'Billy the Kid' and 'Jinx' Also on Program," *New York Times,* April 29, 1942.

8. Quoted in Amberg, *Ballet in America,* 166.

9. Todd Bolender to Yvonne Patterson, March 1991, Series III, Yvonne Patterson and William Dollar Papers, 1925–2002 (hereafter Patterson and Dollar Papers), Jerome Robbins Dance Division, New York Public Library, New York, New York.

10. Todd Bolender to Yvonne Patterson, ca. May 1991, Series III, Patterson and Dollar Papers.

11. Yvonne Patterson, interview with the author, Flourtown, Pennsylvania, February 24, 2010.

12. Reed interview with Tobias; Joel Lobenthal, *Wilde Times: Patricia Wilde, George Balanchine, and the Rise of New York City Ballet* (Lebanon, NH: ForeEdge, 2016), 30.

13. Edwin Denby, *Dance Writings* (Gainesville: University Press of Florida, 1986), 175–76.

14. John Martin, "The Dance: New Projects; American Concert Ballet Gets under Way—Notes from the Field," *New York Times,* November 21, 1943.

15. Todd Bolender, conversation with the author, June 2006.

16. Todd Bolender and Una Kai, interview with the author, Kansas City, February 2014.

17. Martin, "The Dance: New Projects."

18. Baird Hastings, "Robbins, Bolender, Milloss; Three Choreographers," special issue, *Chrysalis* 3, nos. 5–6 (1950): 12

19. Walter Terry, review of *Mother Goose*, *New York Herald Tribune*, February 3, 1957.

20. Quoted in *George Balanchine, Balanchine's Complete Stories of the Great Ballets* (Garden City, New York: Doubleday, 1954), 240.

21. Martin, "The Dance: New Projects; American Concert Ballet Gets under Way."

22. Denby, *Dance Writings*, 175–176.

23. Denby, *Dance Writings*, 176; Reed interview with Tobi Tobias, 8.

24. Quoted in Francis Mason, *I Remember Balanchine: Recollections of the Ballet Master by Those Who Knew Him* (New York: Doubleday, 1991), 340.

25. Reed interview with Tobi Tobias, 38.

26. Reed interview with Tobi Tobias, 38.

27. Rosalyn Krokover, *The New Borzoi Book of Ballets* (New York: Knopf, 1956), 129.

28. Reed interview with Tobi Tobias.

29. Reed interview with Tobi Tobias, 29–30.

30. The material on Reed's work with Antony Tudor comes from her interview with Tobi Tobias, 15–20. *Bluebeard* was Michel Fokine's ballet about the wife-murdering potentate set to Offenbach's music. It premiered in 1941.

31. Reed interview with Tobi Tobias, 16. Tudor, who was dancing the kind, considerate Friend (casted against type), watched every one of them from the wings when he was not on stage.

32. Reed interview with Tobi Tobias, 17.

33. Reed interview with Tobi Tobias.

34. Quoted in Judith Chazin-Bennahum, *The Ballets of Antony Tudor: Studies in Psyche and Saire* (New York: Oxford University Press, 1994), 8.

35. Reed interview with Tobi Tobias, 18.

36. Newspaper clipping, Martin review of Ballet Theatre's 1943–1944 season, in Janet Reed, Scrapbooks: Clippings, Programs, and Announcements, 1935–44, New York Public Library for the Performing Arts, New York, New York (hereafter Janet Reed Scrapbooks).

37. Denby, *Dance Writings*, 218.

38. Smith had also created the quite different décor for de Mille's 1942 *Rodeo*.

39. Quoted in Tobi Tobias, "Bringing Back Robbins's 'Fancy,'" *Dance Magazine*, January 1980.

40. Nancy Reynolds and Malcolm McCormick, *No Fixed Points: Dance in the Twentieth Century* (New Haven, CT: Yale University Press, 2003), 283.

41. Quoted in Tobias, "Bringing Back Robbins's 'Fancy,'" 71.

42. Nancy Reynolds and Malcolm McCormick, *No Fixed Points: Dance in the Twentieth Century* (New Haven, CT: Yale University Press, 2003), 283.

43. Deborah Jowitt, *Jerome Robbins: His Life, His Theater, His Dance* (New York: Simon & Schuster, 2004), 79.

44. Tobias, "Bringing Back Robbins's 'Fancy,'" 71.

45. Reed interview with Tobi Tobias, 28.

46. Tobias, "Bringing Back Robbins's 'Fancy,'" 72.

47. Denby, *Dance Writings*, 221.

48. Denby, *Dance Writings*, 221.

49. Denby, *Dance Writings*, 221.

50. Denby, *Dance Writings*, 224. Although de Mille had created the role on Reed, she danced it herself at the premiere.

51. Quoted in Selma Jean Cohen, *The American Ballet Theatre, 1940–1960,* Dance Perspectives no. 6 ([Brooklyn, NY]: Dance Perspectives, 1960), 42.

52. Todd Bolender, interview with the author, Kansas City, Missouri, January 25, 2003, 4.

53. Robert A. Simon, "Musical Events: Young Groups," *New Yorker,* November 17, 1945.

54. Denby, *Dance Writings*, 340.

55. Ballet Russe souvenir program for 1946–1947 season, in author's possession.

56. Denby, *Dance Writings*, 322.

57. John Martin, "Bolender's Work Danced at City Center," *New York Times,* September 18, 1945.

58. Margaret Lloyd, review in *Christian Science Monitor,* September 18, 1945.

59. Remi Gassmann, review in *Chicago Times,* date unknown.

60. Eunice Brown, "An Experiment in Negro Modern Dance," *Dance Observer* 13, no. 1 (1946).

61. Todd Bolender to Eunice Brown, January 9, 1946, box 7, folder 3, Katherine Dunham Papers, Special Collections Research Center, Southern Illinois University, Carbondale, Illinois. The letter is impeccably typed on the letterhead of Dunham's school, which suggests that Dunham wrote the letter herself and asked Bolender to sign it. At this date, the word "Negro" was not a derogatory term.

Chapter 5

1. Anthropologist Margaret Mead abandoned a manuscript she had almost finished because she felt that "every sentence was out of date. We had entered a new age." Margaret Mead, *Blackberry Winter: My Earlier Years* (New York: Morrow, 1972), 271.

2. Todd Bolender, interview with Nancy Reynolds, New York, New York, April 22, 1974.

3. "The Best of the Century," *Time,* December 26, 1999.

4. Todd Bolender to Una Kai, 2004, box 19, folder 26, Todd Bolender Collection, Kansas City Ballet Archives, Tatiana Dokoudovska Library for Dance, Kansas City, Missouri (hereafter Todd Bolender Collection).

5. Bolender to Kai.

6. "Balanchine as Teacher: A Symposium Moderated by Francis Mason," *Ballet Review* (Winter 1991): 61–97.

7. Bolender, interview with Nancy Reynolds, New York, New York, April 22, 1974, 17–18.

8. Nancy Reynolds, *Repertory in Review: 40 Years of the New York City Ballet* (New York: Dial Press, 1977), 73.

9. Jacques d'Amboise, *I Was a Dancer* (New York: Knopf, 2011), 58.

10. Todd Bolender, interview with Nancy Reynolds, New York, New York, April 22, 1974.

11. Edwin Denby, *Dance Writings* (Gainesville: University Press of Florida, 1986), 415

12. D'Amboise, *I Was a Dancer,* 62.

13. Nijinska did *Renard* in 1922 with a bigger cast that included acrobats and in his first choreography, Serge Lifar did it in 1929.

14. Bolender's re-creation of *Renard* was filmed for the Balanchine Foundation's Archive of Lost Choreography; see "Listing of the Archive Videos," *The George Balanchine Foundation,* http://www.balanchine.org/balanchine/03/gbfvideoarchives.jsp.

15. John Martin, "The Dance: Progress; Ballet Society Adventure Starts Off Well," *New York Times,* February 16, 1947.

16. Lincoln Kirstein, *Thirty Years: Lincoln Kirstein's The New York City Ballet: Expanded to Include the Years 1973–1978, in Celebration of the Company's Thirtieth Anniversary* (New York: Knopf Doubleday Publishing Group, 1978), 94.

17. Lisa Jo Sagolla, *The Girl Who Fell Down: A Biography of Joan McCracken* (Boston: Northeastern University, 2003), 144.

18. Baird Hastings, "Todd Bolender," *Chrysalis: The Pocket Review of the Arts* 3, nos. 5–6 (1950): 13.

19. *The Ballet Society* 1 (1946–1947), box 24, Todd Bolender Collection.

20. Quoted in Andrea Harris, *Making Ballet American: Modernism Before and Beyond Balanchine* (New York: Oxford University Press, 2018), 87.

21. Quoted in Reynolds, *Repertory in Review,* 74.

22. Anna Kisselgoff, "Todd Bolender, a Dancer and Director, Is Dead at 92," *New York Times,* October 16, 2006.

23. Joel Lobenthal, "A Conversation with Betty Nichols," *Ballet Review* 41, no. 3 (2013): 56.

24. *Classic Black: The Experience of the Black Dancer in Choosing a School,* video resource, Jerome Robbins Dance Division, New York Public Library for the Performing Arts, New York, New York.

25. Lobenthal, "A Conversation with Betty Nichols," 57–58.

26. Quoted in Reynolds, *Repertory in Review,* 81.

27. Quoted in Reynolds, *Repertory in Review,* 81.

28. Quoted in Debra Hickenlooper Sowell, *The Christensen Brothers: An American Dance Epic* (Amsterdam: Harwood Academic Publishers, 1998), 237.

29. Quoted in Alan M. Kriegsman, "ABT, Back To Life," *Washington Post,* January 20. 1983.

30. Quoted in Martin Duberman, *The Worlds of Lincoln Kirstein* (New York: Knopf, 2007), 417, my italics.

31. Todd Bolender, "Backstage at the Ballet," unpublished manuscript, box 15, folder 1, Todd Bolender Collection, Kansas City Ballet Archives.

32. Reynolds, *Repertory in Review,* 87.

33. Quoted in Robert Tracy, *Spaces of the Mind: Isamu Noguchi's Dance Designs* (New York: Limelight Editions, 2000), 111.

34. Bolender, "Backstage at the Ballet."

35. John Martin, "Stravinsky Work in World Premiere; Ballet Society Features His 'Orpheus' at City Center to Balanchine Dance," *New York Times,* April 29, 1948.

36. Bolender, "Backstage at the Ballet."

37. Bolender, "Backstage at the Ballet."

38. Bolender, "Backstage at the Ballet."

39. "Barn Theater Features Dance Stars in Ballets by Bolender," *New York Herald Tribune,* 1948, box 12, folder 10, Todd Bolender Collection.

40. Rosalyn Krokover, review of *Image in the Heart,* box 11, folder 37, Todd Bolender Collection.

41. Krokover review of *Image in the Heart.*

42. Hastings, "Todd Bolender," 14.

43. Hastings, "Todd Bolender," 14–15.

44. Todd Bolender and Una Kai, interview with the author, Kansas City, February 2004.

45. Bolender, "Backstage at the Ballet."

46. Hastings, "Todd Bolender," 15.

47. Anatole Chujoy, *The New York City Ballet* (New York: Knopf, 1953), 216.

48. See Paul Cadmus, Jared French, and Margaret French, *Collaboration: The Photographs of Paul Cadmus, Jared French, and Margaret French* (Santa Fe, NM: Twelvetrees Press, 1992).

49. Todd Bolender to Yvonne Patterson, August 1947, Series I, Yvonne Patterson and William Dollar Papers, Jerome Robbins Dance Division, New York Public Library, New York, New York.

50. Todd Bolender, interview with the author, Kansas City, Missouri, January 25, 2003.

51. Gloria Nardin, email to author, August 2011.

52. John Martin, "The Dance: Newcomer; City Ballet Company Makes a Happy Bow," *New York Times,* October 17, 1948.

53. Martin, "The Dance: Newcomer; City Ballet Company Makes a Happy Bow."

54. Martin, "The Dance: Newcomer; City Ballet Company Makes a Happy Bow."

55. John Martin, "The Dance: Addenda; More Miscellanea about the Ballet Season," *New York Times,* May 8, 1949.

56. Jane Erskine, conversation with the author, Portland, Oregon.

57. Deborah Jowitt, *Jerome Robbins: His Life, His Theater, His Dance* (New York: Simon & Schuster, 2004), 103.

58. Jowitt, *Jerome Robbins,* 103.

59. Janet Reed, interview with Tobi Tobias, May 19 and 25, 1978, 34, Dance Oral History Project, New York Public Library, New York, New York.

60. Reed Erskine, interview with the author, New York, New York, March 14, 2018.

61. Reed-Erskine wedding announcement, May 1946, *New York Times,* in Janet Reed, Scrapbooks: Clippings, Programs, and Announcements, 1935–44, New York Public Library for the Performing Arts, New York, New York.

62. Jacqueline Martin Schumacher, interview with the author, Portland, Oregon, March 2007.

63. Quoted in Selma Jean Cohen, *The American Ballet Theatre: 1940–1960,* Dance Perspectives no. 6 ([Brooklyn, NY]: Dance Perspectives, 1960), 47.

64. Edwin Denby, *Dance Writings* (Gainesville: University Press of Florida, 1986), 326–327.

65. Newspaper clipping, Hilmar Birger Grondahl Scrapbooks, 1929–1977 (hereafter

Grondahl Scrapbooks), Oregon Historical Society Research Library, Portland, Oregon.

66. Hilmar Grondahl, undated clipping in the *Portland Oregonian* [probably 1944], in Grondahl Scrapbooks.

67. Quoted in Jowitt, *Jerome Robbins,* 140.

68. Quoted in Lawrence Greg, *Dance with Demons: The Life of Jerome Robbins* (New York: G. P. Putnam's Sons, 2001), 131.

69. Quoted in Jowitt, *Jerome Robbins,* 140.

70. Quoted in Cohen, *The American Ballet Theatre,* 60.

71. Francis Mason, *I Remember Balanchine: Recollections of the Ballet Master by Those Who Knew Him* (New York: Doubleday, 1991).

72. Denby, *Dance Writings,* 299.

73. Janet Reed, filmed interview with Reed Erskine and Maren Erskine, 1997, in author's possession.

74. Quoted in Reynolds, *Repertory in Review,* 101.

75. Quoted in Reynolds, *Repertory in Review,* 102.

76. Barbara Walczak, interview with Peter Conway, April 16 and 19, 1979, Dance Oral History Project, Jerome Robbins Dance Division, New York Public Library, New York, New York.

77. Barbara Walczak, interview with Peter Conway.

78. Jowitt, *Jerome Robbins,* 144.

79. Anatole Chujoy, *The New York City Ballet* (New York: Knopf, 1953), 225.

80. Quoted in Reynolds, *Repertory in Review,* 96.

81. Janet Reed, unpublished memoir in author's possession.

82. Reynolds, *Repertory in Review,* 114.

83. John Martin, "City Ballet Seen in Fifth New Work; George Balanchine 'Pas de Deux Romantique' Offered—Reed and Bliss Dance It," *New York Times,* March 4, 1950.

84. Chujoy, *The New York City Ballet,* 242.

85. Todd Bolender, interview with the author, Kansas City, Missouri, January 25, 2003.

86. Barbara Walczak, phone conversation with the author.

87. Quoted in Jowitt, *Jerome Robbins,* 207.

88. Chujoy, *The New York City Ballet,* 238.

89. Chujoy, *The New York City Ballet,* 239.

90. The line is from William Butler Yeats, "The Second Coming."

91. Rosalyn Krokover, *The New Borzoi Book of Ballets* (New York: Knopf, 1956), 26; Jowitt, *Jerome Robbins,* 164.

92. Quoted in Reynolds, *Repertory in Review,* 110.

93. Quoted in Reynolds, *Repertory in Review,* 109.

94. Todd Bolender, interview with Deborah Jowitt, New York, New York, April 7, 2000.

95. John Martin, "City Troupe Gives Ballet by Robbins; Presents World Premiere of His 'Age of Anxiety,' 'Inspired' by Bernstein and Auden," *New York Times,* February 27, 1950.

96. John Martin, "City Ballet Seen in Robbins' Work; Troupe Offers 'Age of Anxiety' for First Time This Season—Bolender Suite Given," *New York Times,* September 8, 1951.

97. Quoted in Reynolds, *Repertory in Review,* 110.

Chapter 6

1. Anatole Chujoy, *The New York City Ballet* (New York: Knopf, 1953), 251–252.

2. Quoted in Chujoy, *The New York City Ballet*, 254.

3. Todd Bolender, interview with Deborah Jowitt, New York, New York, April 7, 2000, 4.

4. Quoted in Nancy Reynolds, *Repertory in Review: 40 Years of the New York City Ballet* (New York: Dial Press, 1977), 110.

5. Quoted in Reynolds, *Repertory in Review*, 110.

6. Quoted in Reynolds, *Repertory in Review*, 93.

7. Cyril Beaumont, "Kirstein, Balanchine, and Others," *Tempo* 17 (1950): 15. Beaumont illustrated his staggering misunderstanding of Balanchine's musicality in this review of the London season.

8. Jacques d'Amboise, conversation with the author.

9. Beaumont, "Kirstein, Balanchine, and Others," 15.

10. Quoted in Reynolds, *Repertory in Review*, 114.

11. Francis Mason, *I Remember Balanchine: Recollections of the Ballet Master by Those Who Knew Him* (New York: Doubleday, 1991), 342.

12. George Balanchine, *Balanchine's Complete Stories of the Great Ballets*, revised and enlarged edition (Garden City, NY: Doubleday, 1977), 656.

13. Lincoln Kirstein, *Thirty Years: Lincoln Kirstein's The New York City Ballet: Expanded to Include the Years 1973–1978, in Celebration of the Company's Thirtieth Anniversary* (New York: Knopf Doubleday Publishing Group, 1978), 116–117. Reed actually came from Willam Christensen, not his younger brother.

14. Kirstein, *Thirty Years: Lincoln Kirstein's The New York City Ballet*, 116.

15. Reynolds, *Repertory in Review*, 149.

16. Todd Bolender, interview with the author, Kansas City, February 2004.

17. Quoted in Reynolds, *Repertory in Review*, 149.

18. Quoted in Kirstein, *Thirty Years: Lincoln Kirstein's The New York City Ballet*, 116–117.

19. Phone interview with David Vaughan.

20. B. H. Haggin, "Ballet and Opera Chronicle," *Hudson Review* 14, no. 1 (1961): 111–117.

21. Quoted in Mindy Aloff, "Lake, Prairie, Pillar, and Park: The Landscape of Janet Reed," *Encore Magazine of the Arts* (Portland, Oregon), November/December 1978, 8.

22. Quoted in Reynolds, *Repertory in Review*, 127.

23. Quoted in Reynolds, *Repertory in Review*, 127.

24. Janet Reed, interview with Tobi Tobias, May 19 and 25, 1978, 53, Dance Oral History Project, Jerome Robbins Dance Division, New York Public Library, New York, New York.

25. John Martin quoted in Kirstein, *Thirty Years: Lincoln Kirstein's The New York City Ballet*, 116.

26. Reynolds, *Repertory in Review*, 98.

27. Reed Erskine, email to author, March 3, 2013.

28. Quoted in Reynolds, *Repertory in Review*, 126.

29. Mary Clarke and David Vaughan, eds., *Encyclopedia of Dance and Ballet* (New York: Putnam, 1977), 236.

30. Quoted in Reynolds, *Repertory in Review*, 126.

31. Bolender quoted in Reynolds, *Repertory in Review*, 125.

32. Quoted in Deborah Jowitt, *Jerome Robbins: His Life, His Theater, His Dance* (New York: Simon & Schuster, 2004), 196.

33. Quoted in Martin Duberman, *The Worlds of Lincoln Kirstein* (New York: Alfred A. Knopf, 2007), 479.

34. John Martin, "Ballet by Bartok in Premiere Here; 'Miraculous Mandarin' Unveiled at City Center–Laing and Hayden in Chief Roles," *New York Times,* September 7, 1951.

35. John Martin, "The Dance: Novelties; Balanchine and Bolender Go in for Extremes," *New York Times,* September 16, 1951.

36. John Martin, "The Dance: Novelties; Balanchine and Bolender Go in for Extremes."

37. Quoted in Reynolds, *Repertory in Review,* 126.

38. Beatrice Gottlieb, "Dance Chronicle: Significance and Insignificance of Technique," *Kenyon Review* (Spring 1956).

39. Chujoy, *The New York City Ballet,* 301.

40. Quoted in Reynolds, *Repertory in Review,* 121.

41. Lincoln Kirstein, *Ballet: Bias & Belief: Three Pamphlets Collected and Other Dance Writings of Lincoln Kirstein,* edited by Nancy Reynolds (New York: Dance Horizons, 1983), 97–106.

42. Quoted in Reynolds, *Repertory in Review,* 121.

43. D'Amboise, phone interview with the author.

44. Aloff, "Lake, Prairie, Pillar, and Park," 9.

45. Walter Terry, "Dance: A Joyful Comeback," *New York Herald Tribune,* February 3, 1957.

46. Janet Reed, interview with Tobi Tobias, 23, May 19 and 25, 1978, Dance Oral History Project, Jerome Robbins Dance Division, New York Public Library, New York, New York.

47. Reed interview with Tobi Tobias, 22.

48. Quoted in Reynolds, *Repertory in Review,* 129.

49. Reynolds, *Repertory in Review,* 127–128.

50. Bolender interview with Deborah Jowitt, 14.

51. George Balanchine, *Balanchine's Complete Stories of the Great Ballets* (Garden City, NY: Doubleday, 1954), 411.

52. Quoted in Reynolds, *Repertory in Review,* 127.

53. Bolender interview with Deborah Jowitt, 14.

54. Lillian Moore, *Dancing Times,* February 1953.

55. Reynolds, *Repertory in Review,* 141.

56. Bolender unpublished memoir, 15. Perhaps Bolender meant "consummation" rather than "attraction."

57. Quoted in Reynolds, *Repertory in Review,* 143.

58. Quoted in Reynolds, *Repertory in Review,* 143.

59. Charles Boultenhouse, "New York, 1952: Metamorphoses," *Ballet Review* 23, no. 1 (1995), 29.

60. Quoted in Reynolds, *Repertory in Review,* 142.

61. Kirstein, *Thirty Years: Lincoln Kirstein's The New York City Ballet,* 130.

62. Barbara Milberg Fisher, *In Balanchine's Company: A Dancer's Memoir* (Middletown, CT: Wesleyan University Press, 2006), 113.

63. Reynolds, *Repertory in Review,* 142.

64. Kirstein, *Thirty Years: Lincoln Kirstein's The New York City Ballet,* 131.

65. Janet Reed, unpublished memoir, copy in author's possession.

66. Chujoy, *The New York City Ballet,* 295.

67. Quoted in Reynolds, *Repertory in Review,* 157.

68. Jacques d'Amboise, telephone interview with the author.

69. Arthur Mitchell oral history, 2004-08-26 : National Visionary Leadership Project / interview conducted by Renee Poussaint. [Washington, D.C.] : National Visionary Leadership Project, c2009, https://lccn.loc.gov/2010655540.

70. John Martin, "City Ballet Gives New Nutcracker," *New York Times,* February 3, 1954.

71. Chujoy quoted in Reynolds, *Repertory in Review,* 157.

72. Jennifer Fisher, *Nutcracker Nation: How an Old World Ballet Became a Christmas Tradition in the New World* (New Haven, CT: Yale University Press, 2004), 3.

73. Aloff, "Lake, Prairie, Pillar, and Park."

74. Bolender, "Backstage at the Ballet," unpublished manuscript, box 15, folder 1, Todd Bolender Collection, Kansas City Ballet Archives, Kansas City, Missouri.

75. Bolender, "Backstage at the Ballet."

76. Bolender, "Backstage at the Ballet."

77. Bolender, "Backstage at the Ballet."

78. Bolender, "Backstage at the Ballet."

79. Doris Hering, "New York City Ballet: First Half of Season Beginning August 31, 1954, New York City Center," *Dance Magazine,* October 1954, 9, 66.

80. Quoted in Reynolds, *Repertory in Review,* 163.

81. Quoted in Reynolds, *Repertory in Review,* 163.

82. Aloff, "Lake, Prairie, Pillar, and Park."

83. Barbara Walczak, interview with Peter Conway, April 16 and 19, 1979, page 172, Dance Oral History Project, Jerome Robbins Dance Division, New York Public Library, New York, New York.

84. John Martin, "Ballet: A Magnificent 'Weirdie'; Troupe at City Center Dances 'Ivesiana,'" *New York Times,* March 7, 1955.

85. "Allegra Kent and Todd Bolender Coaching The Unanswered Question (from Ivesiana)," Jerome Robbins Dance Division, New York Public Library Digital Collection.

86. "Allegra Kent and Todd Bolender Coaching The Unanswered Question."

87. Quoted in Reynolds, *Repertory in Review,* 164.

88. Quoted in Reynolds, *Repertory in Review,* 166.

89. Marcia B. Siegel, *The Shapes of Change: Images of American Dance* (Berkeley: University of California Press, 1985), 227.

90. Janet Reed, unpublished memoir, copy in author's possession.

91. Edwin Denby, *Dance Writings* (Gainesville: University Press of Florida, 1986), 450–451.

Chapter 7

1. Todd Bolender to George Balanchine, spring 1956, box 19, Todd Bolender Collection, Tatiana Dokoudovska Library for Dance, Kansas City Ballet Archives, Kansas City, Missouri (hereafter Todd Bolender Collection).

2. Todd Bolender, interview with the author, Kansas City, Missouri, October 28, 2003, 16.

3. Nancy Reynolds, *Repertory in Review* (New York: Dial Press, 1977), 175.

4. Emily Frankel, "Alone in a Crowd," *Em's Talkery,* September 18, 2009, http://emtalkery.blogspot.com/2009/09/alone-in-crowd.html.

5. Teague Jackson, *Encore: The Private and Professional Triumph of Emily Frankel* (Englewood Cliffs, NJ: Prentice-Hall, 1978), 61ff.

6. Reynolds, *Repertory in Review,* 174.

7. Todd Bolender, interview with the author, Kansas City, Missouri, October 23, 2003*, 16.

8. Emily Frankel, email to author, August 26, 2009.

9. Emily Frankel, email to author.

10. Martin Duberman, *The Worlds of Lincoln Kirstein* (New York: Alfred A. Knopf 2007), 471–493.

11. Todd Bolender, interview with the author, Kansas City, Missouri, January 25, 2003, 2.

12. Doris Hering, "Reviews," *Dance Magazine* 29, no. 6 (1955): 61.

13. Doris Hering, "Reviews," *Dance Magazine* 29, no. 6 (1955): 61.

14. Emily Frankel, email to author.

15. Todd Bolender, interview with the author, Kansas City, Missouri, January 25, 2003.

16. Melissa Hayden, *Melissa Hayden: On Stage and Off* (Garden City, New York: Doubleday, 1963), 93.

17. Hayden, *Melissa Hayden,*94.

18. Nancy Reynolds, *Repertory in Review,*175.

19. Reynolds, *Repertory in Review,*175.

20. John Martin, "The Dance: Summary," *New York Times,* March 18, 1956, box 13, Todd Bolender Collection.

21. Francia Russell, email to author, 2013.

22. Walter Terry, "'The Still Point,' A New Ballet Hit," *New York Herald Tribune,* April 15, 1955, box 13, Todd Bolender Collection.

23. Terry, "'The Still Point,' A New Ballet Hit."

24. Frances Herridge, "Hayden Superb in Bolender Ballet," *New York Post,* March 14, 1956, box 13, Todd Bolender Collection.

25. Robert Coleman, "City Ballet Presents Bolender's 'Still Point,'" *Daily News,* ca. March 14, 1956, newspaper clipping, box 13, folder 5, Todd Bolender Collection.

26. Charles McHarry, "Gal Gets Guy In New Ballet," *Daily News,* March 14, 1956, newspaper clipping, box 13, Todd Bolender Collection.

27. McHarry, "Gal Gets Guy in New Ballet."

28. Hering's review is quoted in Reynolds, *Repertory in Review,* 75.

29. Bolender is the only Dance Magazine Award recipient to receive the honor posthumously. He received it in 2006, just a few weeks after he died.

30. Todd Bolender, interview with the author, Seattle, July 2002.

31. Bolender interview with Nancy Reynolds, 2002.

32. Todd Bolender, interview with Betsy Cooper, Seattle, Washington, July 2002.

33. Reynolds, *Repertory in Review,* 169.

34. Bolender interview with Nancy Reynolds, 2002.

35. Todd Bolender, interview with Nancy Reynolds, New York, New York, April 22, 1974.

36. Rouben Ter-Arutunian, interview with Joan Kramer, August 26, 1976, 27, Dance Oral History Project, Jerome Robbins Dance Division, New York Public Library, New York, New York.

37. Ter-Arutunian interview with Joan Kramer, 93.

38. Ter-Arutunian interview with Joan Kramer, 93.

39. Bolender interview with Reynolds.

40. Ter-Arutunian interview with Joan Kramer, 93.

41. Quoted in Reynolds, *Repertory in Review,* 169.

42. Quoted in Reynolds, *Repertory in Review,* 169.

43. Doris Hering, "Reviews," *Dance Magazine* 29, no. 6 (1955): 61.

44. Quoted in Reynolds, *Repertory in Review,* 170.

45. Todd Bolender to Yvonne Patterson, 2004, box 19, folder 34, Todd Bolender Collection.

46. Deborah Jowitt, *Jerome Robbins: His Life, His Theater, His Dance* (New York: Simon & Schuster, 2004).

47. Barbara Walczak, telephone interview with the author, 2012.

48. Hering review for *Dance Magazine,* quoted in Reynolds, *Repertory in Review,* 173.

49. Quoted in Stephanie Jordan, "Celebrating the Composer's Voice: Perspectives on Robbins' Chopin Ballets," *News from the Jerome Robbins Foundation* 6, no. 3 (2019): 15.

50. Quoted in Elizabeth Zimmer, "Humor in Dance," *Dance Magazine,* January 22, 2007, https://www.dancemagazine.com/comedy-central-2306890416.html.

51. Doris Hering, review for *Dance Magazine,* 1956.

52. Francia Russell, interview with the author, Seattle, Washington, 2000.

53. Quoted in Reynolds, *Repertory in Review,* 178.

54. Quoted in Reynolds, *Repertory in Review,* 174.

55. Cover of *Dance Magazine,* February 1950.

56. Quoted in "LeClercq, Tanaquil," in *American National Biography: Supplement,* vol. 2, edited by Mark Christopher Carnes (Oxford: Oxford University Press, 2002), 340.

57. Bolender interview with the author, February 25, 2003, 8.

58. Bolender, interview with the author, February 25, 2003, 35–36.

59. Todd Bolender, interview with the author, Seaside, Florida, November 16, 2004, 35.

60. Bolender, interview with the author, November 16, 2004, 35.

61. Bolender, interview with the author, November 16, 2004, 35.

62. *Dance Magazine,* December 1957.

63. Tanaquil Le Clercq, Blegdanes Hospitalet, to Todd Bolender, November 15, 1956, box 19, folder 30, Todd Bolender Collection.

Chapter 8

1. Todd Bolender, interview with the author, Kansas City, Missouri, January 25, 2003, 10.

2. Reed Erskine, email to author, ca. 2018.

3. Quoted in Carol Taylor, "Sunbeam of Ballet Back to Shine on City Center," *New York World Telegram,* February 13, 1957.

4. Reed Erskine, email to author.

5. George Balanchine to Betty Cage, quoted in Richard Buckle, *George Balanchine, Ballet Master* (London: Penguin Group, 1988), 206.

6. Quoted in Buckle, *George Balanchine: Ballet Master,* 206.

7. Walter Terry, "Dance: A Joyful Comeback," *New York Herald Tribune,* February 3, 1957.

8. Francia Russell, interview with author, ca. 2014.

9. Quoted in Nancy Reynolds, *Repertory in Review: 40 Years of the New York City Ballet* (New York: Dial Press, 1977), 179

10. Edward Villella, *Prodigal Son: Dancing for Balanchine in a World of Pain and Magic* (New York: Simon & Schuster, 1992), 110.

11. John Martin, "Dance: Repertoire," *New York Times,* March 3, 1957.

12. Doris Hering, "Reviews," *Dance Magazine* 31, no. 3 (1957): 12.

13. Quoted in Nancy Reynolds, *Repertory in Review,* 179.

14. Doris Hering, "Reviews," *Dance Magazine* 31, no. 3 (1957): 65.

15. Doris Hering, "Reviews," *Dance Magazine* 31, no. 3 (1957): 66–67.

16. Janet Reed, oral history with Tobi Tobias, May 19 and 25, 1978, 23, Dance Oral History Project, Jerome Robbins Dance Division, New York Public Library, New York, New York.

17. Francia Russell, interview with the author, Seattle, Washington, 2000.

18. "Todd Bolender Acclaimed by Sell-Out Ballet Crowd," undated clipping, box 13, folder 9, Todd Bolender Collection, Kansas City Ballet Archive, Tatiana Dokoudovska Library for Dance, Kansas City, Missouri (hereafter Todd Bolender Collection).

19. Villella, *Prodigal Son,* 48.

20. Villella, *Prodigal Son,* 48.

21. Robert Garis, "Agon," in *International Encyclopedia of the Dance: A Project of Dance Perspectives Foundation,* vol. 4, edited by Selma Jeanne Cohen (New York, NY: Oxford University Press, 1998).

22. Edwin Denby, *Dance Writings* (Gainesville: University Press of Florida, 1986), 461.

23. Quoted in Barbara Milberg Fisher, *In Balanchine's Company: A Dancer's Memoir* (Middletown, CT: Wesleyan University Press, 2006), 159.

24. Quoted in Francis Mason, *I Remember Balanchine: Recollections of the Ballet Master by Those Who Knew Him* (New York: Double Day, 1991), 179.

25. Bolender interview with the author, January 25, 2003, 10.

26. Todd Bolender, conversation with the author.

27. Todd Bolender, interview with Nancy Reynolds, New York, New York, April 22, 1974.

28. Christina Brundage, "Agon: Its Future Importance," *Dance Magazine* 32, no. 9 (1958):32.

29. John Martin, "Ballet: World Premiere of 'Agon,'" *New York Times,* November 28, 1957.

30. Doris Hering, "Reviews," *Dance Magazine* 32, no. 1 (1958):24.

31. Brooks Atkinson, "At the Theater," *New York Times,* February 5, 1953.

32. Clipping of article by Leo Lerman in *Mademoiselle Magazine,* 1958, box 17, Todd Bolender Collection.

33. Todd Bolender, interview with Deborah Jowitt, New York, New York, April 7, 2000.

34. Sasha Anawalt, *The Joffrey Ballet: Robert Joffrey and the Making of an American Dance Company* (New York: Scribner, 1996), 116–117.

35. Doris Hering, "Reviews," *Dance Magazine* 32, no. 3 (1958):85.

36. Doris Hering, "Reviews," *Dance Magazine* 32, no. 3 (1958): 85.

37. Francia Russell, email to author, ca. 2015.

38. Doris Hering, "Reviews," *Dance Magazine* 33, no. 1 (1959).

39. Janet Reed, interview with Tobi Tobias, May 19 and 25, 1978, Dance Oral History Project, Jerome Robbins Dance Division, New York Public Library, New York, New York.

40. "Backstage at the New York City Ballet," *Dance Magazine* 33, no. 1 (1959).

41. "Backstage at the New York City Ballet," *Dance Magazine* 33, no. 1 (1959).

42. Todd Bolender and Una Kai, interview with the author, Kansas City, February 2014.

43. Suzanne Farrell, *Holding On to the Air: An Autobiography* (New York: Summit Books, 1990), 54.

44. Farrell, *Holding On to the Air,* 54.

45. Francia Russell, interview with author, Seattle, Washington, 2000.

46. Jane Erskine, interview with the author, Seattle, Washington, 2004.

47. Reed interview with Tobias, 24.

48. Quoted in Reynolds, *Repertory in Review,* 171.

49. Reed Erskine, email to author, 2019.

50. Reed interview with Tobias.

51. Reed interview with Tobias.

52. Quoted in Mason, *I Remember Balanchine,* 342.

53. Quoted in Mason, *I Remember Balanchine,* 345.

54. John Shanley, "Dancing Flirtation," *New York Times,* January 11, 1959.

55. Todd Bolender to Leo Lerman, June 19, 1959, box 2, Leo Lerman Papers, Rare Book & Manuscript Library, Columbia University, New York, New York.

56. Entry for August 17, 1959, Bolender's engagement diary, box 20, Todd Bolender Collection.

57. Entry for October 12, 1959, Bolender's engagement diary, box 20, Todd Bolender Collection.

58. Todd Bolender, interview with Nancy Reynolds, New York, New York, April 22, 1974.

59. Debra Craine and Judith Mackrell, *The Oxford Dictionary of Dance* (Oxford: Oxford University Press, 2000), 48.

60. Quoted in Reynolds, *Repertory in Review,* 210.

61. John Martin, "Ballet: High-Brow Fun," *New York Times,* December 8, 1960.

62. Walter Terry, review in *New York Herald Tribune,* March 16, 1961.

63. Bolender interview with Nancy Reynolds.

64. Bolender, interview with the author, January 25, 2003.

65. Jennifer Dunning, *"But First a School": The First Fifty Years of the School of American Ballet* (New York: Viking, 1985), 141.

66. Elinor Hughes, photocopy of unidentified newspaper clipping, Todd Bolender Collection.

67. Mindy Aloff, email to author, ca. 2018.

68. Lillian Moore, "'America Dances' Gaily in the Park," *New York Herald Tribune,* September 4, 1963.

Chapter 9

1. Reed Erskine, email to author, March 2, 2013.

2. Reed Erskine, email to author, September 21, 2017.

3. Reed Erskine, email to author, 2018.

4. Reed Erskine, interview with the author, New York, New York, March 14, 2018, 1.

5. Reed Erskine, email to author, September 21, 2017.

6. Robert Gottlieb, *Avid Reader: A Life* (New York: Farrar, Straus and Giroux, 2016), 263.

7. Robert Gottlieb, email to author, October 5, 2017.

8. Todd Bolender, interview with the author, Kansas City, Missouri, January 25, 2003, 17. The Ford Foundation also made a major contribution to decentralizing American ballet; at the same time, it reinforced SAB's position at the apex of American ballet pedagogy.

9. Jane Bennett, "Your Tummies, Girls, Get Your Tummies In," *Times Record,* January 18, 1974.

10. Bennett, "Your Tummies, Girls, Get Your Tummies In."

11. Reed Erskine, email to author, March 2, 2013.

12. Debra Hickenlooper Sowell, *The Christensen Brothers: An American Dance Epic* (Amsterdam: Harwood Academic Publishers; 1998), 336.

13. Willam Christensen had departed for Salt Lake City in 1963 to establish the ballet department at the University of Utah and the company that would become Ballet West.

14. Vivian Little, email to the author, February 16, 2018.

15. Vivian Little, email to the author.

16. John McFall both choreographed and danced in the production of *Aïda* at Expo '74.

17. Vivian Little, email to author, February 16, 2018.

18. Vivian Little, email to author, February 16, 2018.

19. Michael Kidd to Janet Reed's children, May 9, 2000, copy in author's possession.

20. James Jordan, conversation with the author.

21. Vivian Little, email to the author, February 22, 2018.

22. Vivian Little, email to the author, February 16, 2018.

23. Janet Reed, unpublished memoir, copy in author's possession.

24. Vivian Little, email to author, February 16, 2018.

25. Vivian Little, email to author, February 16, 2018.

26. Willam Christensen replaced Oukrainsky as the company's artistic director the following year.

27. Vivian Little, email to the author.

28. *Seattle Post-Intelligencer,* March 17, 1975.

29. *Seattle Post Intelligencer,* March 17, 1975.

30. Wayne Johnson quoted in *Pacific Northwest Dance News,* August 1975, Pacific Northwest Ballet Archive, Phelps Center, Seattle, Washington.

31. Robert Sund, telephone interview with author, 2018.

32. Leon Kalimos, Pacific Northwest Dance press release, April 30, 1975, Pacific Northwest Ballet Archive, Phelps Center, Seattle, Washington.

33. Todd Bolender to Joel Schnee, August 25, 1974, box 19, folder 39, Todd Bolender Letters to Joel Schnee, 1974–2000, Jerome Robbins Dance Division, New York Public Library, New York, New York.

34. Lincoln Kirstein to Janet Reed, September 4, 1974, copy in author's possession.

35. Lincoln Kirstein to Janet Reed April 3, 1975, Janet Reed Papers.

36. Jerome Robbins to Janet Reed, March 20, 1975, Janet Reed Papers.

37. Sund telephone interview with the author.

38. Bolender, "About Teaching" notes, box 15, Todd Bolender Collection, Kansas City Ballet Archive, Tatiana Dokoudovska Library for Dance, Kansas City, Missouri (hereafter Todd Bolender Collection).

39. Vivian Little, email to author, February 22, 2018.

40. Vivian Little, email to author, February 16, 2018.

41. *Pacific Northwest Dance News,* August 1975, Pacific Northwest Ballet Archive, Phelps Center, Seattle, Washington.

42. Dorothy Fisher, Gwenn Barker, Karen Irvin, Jan Collum, and Jo Emery to James Haseltine, Executive Director of the Washington State Arts Commission, May 15, 1975, Pacific Northwest Ballet Archive, Phelps Center, Seattle, Washington.

43. Carole Beers, "'Nutcracker' Gala Filled with Magic," *Seattle Times,* December 20, 1975.

44. Maggie Hawthorne, "Gala 'Nutcracker' Magnificent in Seattle Debut," *Seattle Post Intelligencer,* December 22, 1975.

45. George Burley, "PND's 'Nutcracker' Magnificent Staging," *Everett Herald,* December 20, 1975.

46. Bolender to Joel Schnee, March 30, 1976, Todd Bolender Letters to Joel Schnee, 1974–2000, Jerome Robbins Dance Division, New York Public Library, New York, New York.

47. Bolender interview with author, January 25, 2003, 10.

48. Janet Reed, "Why I Quit," n.d., unpublished document, copy in author's possession.

49. Todd Bolender to Roy Tobias, June 12, 1977, box 19, Todd Bolender Collection.

50. George Burley, "PND Does Well in 1st Solo Performance," *Everett Herald,* August 2, 1976.

51. Nancy Reynolds, *Repertory in Review* (New York: Dial Press 1977), 168.

52. Burley, "PND Does Well in 1st Solo Performance."

53. Carole Beers, "A Happy 'Preview' for N. W. Dance," *Seattle Times,* August 1, 1976.

54. Beers, "A Happy 'Preview' for N. W. Dance."

55. Vivian Little, email to author, February 22, 2018.

56. Carole Beers, "Dancers Delight Sold-Out House," *Seattle Times,* August 16, 1976.

57. Melissa Hayden to Janet Reed, July 28, 1976, Janet Reed Papers.

58. Melissa Hayden to Janet Reed, July 28, 1976.

59. Carole Beers, "Hayden Happy with New Role," *Seattle Times,* September 1976.

60. Beers, "Hayden Happy with New Role."

61. Bolender to Tobias, June 12, 1977.

62. Bill Alpert, "The Immovable Object & the Irresistible Force," *Daily Journal-American* (Bellevue, Washington), May 20, 1977.

63. Bolender to Tobias, June 12, 1977, copy in author's possession. Sequoio stayed in Seattle and opened a company called Festival Ballet with dancer/choreographer James DeBolt. They then went to Kansas City after Tatiana Dokoudovska retired from Kansas City Ballet. In 1980, Bolender succeeded Sequoio as company artistic director.

64. Bolender to Tobias, June 12, 1977.

65. Michael Smuin to Carole Beers, April 18, 1977, Pacific Northwest Ballet Archive, Phelps Center, Seattle, Washington.

66. Hayden's address at the PNW Dance Ballet League's first annual luncheon on May 17, 1977, was published in the *Daily Journal-American* (Bellevue, Washington) on May 20, 1977.

67. Bolender to Tobias, June 12, 1977.

68. Kent Stowell, interview with author, Seattle, ca. 2016.

Chapter 10

1. Todd Bolender, conversation with the author, June 2006.

2. Todd Bolender to Joel Schnee, January 27, 1995, Todd Bolender Letters to Joel Schnee, 1974–2000, Jerome Robbins Dance Division, New York Public Library, New York, New York (hereafter Bolender Letters to Schnee).

3. Sevgi Sanli, "Madame's Turkish Company," *Dancing Times*, April 1994, 715.

4. Sevgi Sanli, interview with the author, October 2008.

5. Sanli interview with the author.

6. Todd Bolender to Sevgi Sanli, 1986, in author's possession.

7. Beatrice Appleyard, "Britons Bring Ballet Back to Middle East," *Dance and Dancers*, July 1961, 24–25.

8. Sanli interview with author.

9. Bolender to Schnee, January 27, 1995.

10. Sanli interview with the author.

11. Sanli interview with the author.

12. Todd Bolender, interview with the author, Kansas City, Missouri, January 25, 2003.

13. Todd Bolender, interview with the author, Kansas City, Missouri, January 25, 2003.

14. Beatrice Cordua, interview with the author, New York, New York, January 10, 2014.

15. Cordua interview with the author.

16. Bolender interview with the author, Kansas City, Missouri, January 25, 2003.

17. Todd Bolender to Rebecca Brownstein, November 22, 1963, Todd Bolender Collection, Kansas City Ballet Archives, Tatiana Dokoudovska Library for Dance, Kansas City, Missouri (hereafter Todd Bolender Collection), copy in author's possession.

18. Walter Terry, "Nein, Nein, Too Klein," *New York Herald Tribune*, October 11, 1964.

19. Wilfried Hofmann, "Cologne: Todd Bolender's Cologne Debut," *Ballet Today*, March 1964, 26.

20. Hofmann, "Cologne: Todd Bolender's Cologne Debut."

21. Hofmann, "Cologne: Todd Bolender's Cologne Debut."

22. Wilfried Hofmann, "Cologne Ballet Week: New Bolender Ballets," *Ballet Today*, October 1964, 26.

23. David Vaughan and Melissa Harris, *Merce Cunningham: Fifty Years* (New York: Aperture Foundation, 1997), 139.

24. Horst Koegler, "Presstime News," *Dance Magazine*, September 1964, 81.

25. Todd Bolender to Rebecca Brownstein, October 19, 1964, Todd Bolender Collection.

26. Cordua interview with the author.

27. Bolender interview with the author, January 25, 2003.

28. Bolender interview with the author, January 25, 2003.

29. Transcript of Todd Bolender interview with Francis Mason for *I Remember Balanchine*, 1985, in author's possession.

30. Horst Koegler, "Presstime News," *Dance Magazine*, September 1965, 100.

31. Rudolf Orthwine, *Dance Magazine*, August 1965.

32. Bolender to Brownstein, October 19, 1964.

33. Mason, *I Remember Balanchine*, 406.

34. Victoria Simon, telephone interview with the author, 2019.

35. Simon interview with the author.

36. Bolender interview with the author, January 25, 2003, 8.

37. Horst Koegler, email to George Dorris, December 2006, copy in author's possession.

38. Horst Koegler, "Presstime News," *Dance Magazine*, September 1965, 100–101.

39. Horst Koegler, "Presstime News," *Dance Magazine*, ca. December 1966, 101

40. Cordua interview with the author.

41. Horst Koegler, *Dance Magazine*, June 1967, 77.

42. Todd Bolender to Rebecca Brownstein, ca. July 1967, Todd Bolender collection.

43. Todd Bolender to Rebecca Brownstein, ca. 1967.

44. Todd Bolender to Rebecca Brownstein, December 4, 1967.

45. Bolender to Brownstein, December 4, 1967.

46. Horst Koegler, "Report from Germany," *Dance Magazine*, ca. April 1968.

47. Cordua interview with author.

48. Horst Koegler, "Presstime News," *Dance Magazine*, October 1968, 105.

49. Todd Bolender, "Backstage at the Ballet," unpublished manuscript, box 15, folder 1, Todd Bolender Collection.

50. "John Mandia, an Ex-Dancer with City Ballet, Dies at 45," *New York Times*, August 13, 1970.

51. Mandia was never a choreographer; he was ballet master in Cologne and Frankfurt.

52. Todd Bolender, interview with the author, January 25, 2003.

53. Don McDonagh, "Witty Performance by Todd Bolender in a Robbins Ballet," *New York Times*, January 18, 1972.

54. Todd Bolender, notes on *Piano-Rag-Music*, box 15, Todd Bolender Collection.

55. John Clifford, *Balanchine's Apprentice: From Hollywood to New York and Back* (Gainesville: University Press of Florida, forthcoming).

56. Clive Barnes, "Ballet: Seconds at Stravinsky Feast," *New York Times,* 23, 1972; Deborah Jowitt, "Happy Birthday, Dear Igor," *Village Voice,* June 29, 1972.

57. Nancy Reynolds, *Repertory in Review: 40 Years of the New York City Ballet* (New York: Dial Press, 1977), 294.

58. Emily Frankel, email to author, August 26, 2009.

59. "Big Brag: Elektra," *Em's Talkery,* June 18, 2009, http://emtalkery.blogspot.com/2009/06/big-brag.html.

60. Todd Bolender to Joel Schnee, November 16, 1976, Bolender Letters to Schnee.

61. Todd Bolender to author, July 4, 1978, in author's possession.

62. Todd Bolender to Sevgi Sanli, July 4, 1977, in author's possession.

63. Aydın Batur, interview with the author, October 2008.

64. Todd Bolender to Joe Schnee, October 25, 1977, Bolender Letters to Schnee.

65. Todd Bolender to Joe Schnee, October 25, 1977.

66. Wilfried Hofmann, "Bolender and Discipline in Turkey," *Dance Magazine,* February 1978.

67. Todd Bolender to Sevgi Sanli, August 10, 1978, in author's possession.

68. Todd Bolender to Sevgi Sanli, ca. May 1980, in author's possession.

69. Todd Bolender to Joel Schnee, January 26, 1979, Bolender Letters to Schnee.

70. Aydın Batur, email to author, 2019.

71. Jennifer Dunning, "Todd Bolender and 'The Still Point,'" *New York Times,* November 30, 1980.

Chapter 11

1. Paula Weber, conversation with the author, August 27, 2011.

2. Wyatt Townley, *Kansas City Ballet: The First Fifty Years* (Kansas City, MO: Rockhill Books, 2007).

3. Bolender replaced the annual *Nutcracker* in his second season with choreography for the children that was meticulously calibrated to whatever level each one had reached in the school.

4. Townley, *Kansas City Ballet.*

5. Elizabeth Wilson, interview with the author, New York, New York, 2008.

6. Wilson interview with the author. The company actually gave its first performance on May 31.

7. James Jordan, interview with the author, March 10, 2008.

8. Todd Bolender to Geyvan and Paul McMillan, December 16, 1981, in author's possession.

9. Todd Bolender to Joel Schnee, November 14, 1975, Todd Bolender Letters to Joel Schnee, 1974–2000, Jerome Robbins Dance Division, New York Public Library, New York, New York (hereafter Bolender Letters to Schnee).

10. Bolender to Geyvan and Paul McMillan.

11. Todd Bolender, conversation with the author, February 2004.

12. Todd Bolender to Sevgi Sanli, September 1982.

13. Todd Bolender to Sevgi Sanli, October 22, 1982, in author's possession.

14. Una Kai to the author, November, 7, 2006.

15. Todd Bolender to Sevgi Sanli, June 30, 1983, in author's possession.

16. Bolender to Sanli, June 30, 1983.

17. Quoted in Frances Mason, *I Remember Balanchine: Recollections of the Ballet Master by Those Who Knew Him* (New York: Doubleday, 1991), 181.

18. Christopher Barksdale, interview with the author, New York, New York, 2007.

19. Quoted in Mason, *I Remember Balanchine,* 345.

20. Todd Bolender to Sevgi Sanli, June 1984, in author's possession.

21. Todd Bolender to Sevgi Sanli, January 1, 1985, in author's possession.

22. Bolender to Sanli, January 1, 1985.

23. Todd Bolender to Yvonne Patterson, November 1986, Bolender's italics, Series I, Yvonne Patterson and William Dollar Papers, Jerome Robbins Dance Division, New York Public Library, New York, New York (hereafter Patterson and Dollar Papers).

24. Todd Bolender to Sevgi Sanli, November 15, 1985, in author's possession.

25. Anna Kisselgoff, "Dance: "Missouri Ballet," *New York Times,* March 30, 1987.

26. Todd Bolender, interview with the author, Kansas City, Missouri, June 2006.

27. Broadcast of *The World of Dance with Francis Mason,* WQXR, April 5, 1987.

28. Lincoln Kirstein to Mrs. Robert W. Willits, December 1987, box 19, folder 29, Todd Bolender Collection.

29. Dale Eldred to Bolender, April 1, 1987, box 19, folder 19, Todd Bolender Collection.

30. Nancy Reynolds, *Repertory in Review: 40 Years of the New York City Ballet* (New York: Dial Press, 1977), 77.

31. Todd Bolender to Joel Schnee, October 25, 1988, Bolender Letters to Schnee.

32. James Jordan, email to author, 2019.

33. Todd Bolender to Joel Schnee, 1975, Bolender Letters to Schnee.

34. Todd Bolender to Yvonne Patterson, July 30, 1994, Patterson and Dollar Papers.

35. Todd Bolender to Joel Schnee, October 31, 1995, Bolender Letters to Schnee.

36. Bolender to Schnee, October 31, 1995.

37. Scott Cantrell, "'Arena' Was Worth the Wait," *Kansas City Star,* October 12, 1996.

38. Quoted in Nancy Reynolds, "TDE ASKS: Nancy Reynolds, George Balanchine Foundation Video Archives Director," *Dance Enthusiast,* June 14, 2016, https://www.dance-enthusiast.com/features/the-dance-enthusiast-asks/view/Nancy-Renolds.

39. Todd Bolender to Joel Schnee, August 6, 1999, Bolender Letters to Schnee.

40. Todd Bolender to Sevgi Sanli, January 29, 2000, in author's possession.

41. James Jordan, email to author, 2004.

42. Matthew Donnell, telephone interview with the author, December 18, 2018.

43. Todd Bolender to Joel Schnee, March 2004, Bolender Letters to Schnee.

44. Michael Kidd to Reed Erskine and Jane Erskine, May 9, 2000, in author's possession.

45. Anna Kisselgoff, "Golden Ages: Dance; 1930's to 1960's, When Dance Grew Strong," *New York Times,* May 15, 1994.

46. Christopher Barksdale, conversation with the author, 2019.

47. Lisa Thorn Vinzant, email to author, 2019.

48. Kimberly Cowen, interview with author, New York, New York, spring 2007.

49. Anna Kisselgoff, "Todd Bolender, a Dancer and Director, Is Dead at 92," *New York Times,* October 16, 2006.

Afterword

1. Francis Mason, *I Remember Balanchine: Recollections of the Ballet Master by Those Who Knew Him* (New York: Doubleday, 1991), 340.

2. "Keeping Beauty Timeless: Christopher Stowell on Balancing Tradition and Innovation," from program for *The Sleeping Beauty,* Oregon Ballet Theater, *issu.com,* https://issuu.com/artslandia/docs/sleepingbeauty/s/10202486.

Bibliography

Primary Sources

UNPUBLISHED INTERVIEWS

Barksdale, Christopher. Interview with the author, New York, 2007.
Bolender, Todd. Interview with the author, Kansas City, Missouri, January 25, 2003.
———. Interview with the author, Kansas City, Missouri, February 25, 2003.
———. Interview with the author, Kansas City, Missouri, October 28, 2003.
———. Interview with the author, Seaside, Florida, November 16, 2004.
———. Interview with Betsy Cooper, Seattle, Washington, July 2002.
———. Interview with Deborah Jowitt, New York, New York, April 7, 2000.
———. Interview with Nancy Reynolds, New York, New York, April 22, 1974.
Bolender, Todd, and Una Kai. Interview with the author, Kansas City, February 2004.
Cordua, Beatrice. Interview with the author, New York, New York, January 10, 2014.
Cowen, Kimberly. Interview with the author, New York, New York, Spring 2007.
Donnell, Matthew. Telephone interview with the author, December 18, 2018.
Erskine, Jane. Interview with the author, Seattle, Washington, 2004.
Erskine, Reed. Interview with the author, New York, New York, March 14, 2018.
Kirstein, Lincoln. Interview with Nancy Reynolds, 1974.
Loring, Eugene. Interview with Marilyn Hunt, New York, New York, 1976.
Metzer, Mary. Telephone interview with the author, August 16, 2004.
Patterson, Yvonne. Interview with the author, Flourtown, Pennsylvania, February 24, 2010.
Reed, Janet. Filmed interview with Reed and Maren Erskine, 1997. In author's possession.
———. Interview with Tobi Tobias, May 19 and 25, 1978. Dance Oral History Project, Jerome Robbins Dance Division, New York Public Library, New York, New York.
Rittman, Trude. Interview with Nancy Reynolds, New York, New York, December 9, 1976.
Russell, Francia. Interview with the author, Seattle, Washington, 2000.
Sanli, Sevgi. Interview with the author, October 2008.
Schumacher, Jacqueline Martin. Interview with the author, Portland, Oregon, March 2007.
Simon, Victoria. Telephone interview with the author, 2019.

Stowell, Kent. Interview with the author.

Sund, Robert. Telephone interview with the author, 2018.

Ter-Arutunian, Rouben. Interview with Joan Kramer, August 26, 1976, Dance Oral History Project, Jerome Robbins Dance Division, New York Public Library, New York, New York.

Walczak, Barbara. Telephone interview with the author, 2012.

———. Interview with Peter Conway, April 16 and 19, 1979, Dance Oral History Project, Jerome Robbins Dance Division, New York Public Library, New York, New York.

Weber, Paula. Interview with the author, 2011.

Wilson, Elizabeth. Interview with the author, New York, New York, 2008.

REVIEWS

Alpert, Bill. "The Immovable Object & the Irresistible Force." *Bellevue-Kirkland Journal American,* May 20, 1977.

Appleyard, Beatrice. "Britons Bring Ballet Back to Middle East." *Dance and Dancers,* July 1961, 24–25.

Atkinson, Brooks. "At the Theater." *New York Times,* February 5, 1953.

Barnes, Clive. "Ballet: Seconds at Stravinsky Feast." *The New York Times,* June 23, 1972.

Beers, Carole. "A Happy 'Preview' for N.W. Dance." *The Seattle Times,* August 1, 1976.

———. "Dancers Delight Sold-Out House." *The Seattle Times,* August 16, 1976.

———. "Hayden Happy with New Role." *The Seattle Times,* September 1976.

———. "'Nutcracker' Gala Filled with Magic." *The Seattle Times,* December 20, 1975.

Bennett, Jane. "Your Tummies, Girls, Get Your Tummies In." *Times Record,* January 18, 1974.

Beaumont, Cyril W. "Kirstein, Balanchine, and Others." *Tempo* 17 (1950): 9–15.

Boultenhouse, Charles. "New York, 1952: *Metamorphoses.*" *Ballet Review* 23, no. 1 (1995).

Brown, Gil. "Janet Reed Wildly Applauded in Ballet." *Seattle Star,* November 20, 1939.

Brundage, Christina. "Agon: Its Future Importance." *Dance Magazine* 32, no. 9 (1958).

Burley, George. "PND Does Well in 1st Solo Performance." *Everett Herald,* August 2, 1976.

———. "PND's 'Nutcracker' Magnificent Staging." *Everett Herald,* December 20, 1975.

Cantrell, Scott. "'Arena' Was Worth the Wait." *Kansas City Star,* October 12, 1996.

Dunning, Jennifer. "Todd Bolender and 'The Still Point.'" *New York Times,* November 30, 1980.

Hawthorne, Maggie. "Gala 'Nutcracker' Magnificent in Seattle Debut." *Seattle Post Intelligencer,* December 22, 1975.

Hering, Doris. "New York City Ballet: First Half of Season Beginning: August 31, 1954, New York City Center." *Dance Magazine,* October 1954.

———. "New York City Ballet, September 14 through 26, 1954, New York City Center." *Dance Magazine,* November 1954.

———. "Reviews." *Dance Magazine* 29, no. 6 (1955): 61.

———. "Reviews." *Dance Magazine* 31, no. 3 (1957): 12.

———. "Reviews." *Dance Magazine* 32, no. 1 (1958).

———. "Reviews." *Dance Magazine* 32, no. 3 (1958).

Herridge, Frances. "Hayden Superb in Bolender Ballet." *New York Post,* March 14, 1956.

Hofmann, Wilfried. "Bolender and Discipline in Turkey." *Dance Magazine,* February 1978.

———. "Cologne: Todd Bolender's Cologne Debut." *Ballet Today,* March 1964.

———. "Cologne Ballet Week: New Bolender Ballets." *Ballet Today,* October 1964.

Kisselgoff, Anna. "Dance: "Missouri Ballet." *New York Times,* March 30, 1987.

Koegler, Horst. "Presstime News." *Dance Magazine,* September 1964.

———. "Presstime News." *Dance Magazine,* September 1965.

———. "Presstime News." *Dance Magazine,* June 1967.

———. "Presstime News." *Dance Magazine,* October 1968.

Martin, John. "Ballet by Bartok in Premiere Here; 'Miraculous Mandarin' Unveiled at City Center—Laing and Hayden in Chief Roles." *New York Times,* September 7, 1951.

———. "Ballet Caravan in Seasonal Debut." *The New York Times,* May 25, 1939.

———. "Ballet: High-Brow Fun." *New York Times,* December 8, 1960.

———. "Ballet: World Premiere of 'Agon.'" *New York Times,* November 28, 1957.

———. "Bolender's Work Danced at City Center." *New York Times,* September 18, 1945.

———. "City Ballet Seen in Fifth New Work; George Balanchine 'Pas de Deux Romantique' Offered—Reed and Bliss Dance It." *New York Times,* March 4, 1950.

———. "City Ballet Seen in Robbins' Work; Troupe Offers 'Age of Anxiety' for First Time This Season—Bolender Suite Given." *New York Times,* September 8, 1951.

———. "City Troupe Gives Ballet by Robbins; Presents World Premiere of His 'Age of Anxiety,' 'Inspired' by Bernstein and Auden." *New York Times,* February 27, 1950.

———. "Dance: Repertoire." *New York Times,* March 3, 1957.

———. "The Dance: Addenda; More Miscellanea about the Ballet Season." *New York Times,* May 8, 1949.

———. "The Dance: Fall Season in Retrospect; Ballet Theatre Comes Through in Spite of Difficulties—Week's Programs." *New York Times,* November 7, 1943.

———. "The Dance: Newcomer; City Ballet Company Makes a Happy Bow." *New York Times,* October 17, 1948.

———. "The Dance: New Projects; American Concert Ballet Gets under Way—Notes from the Field." *New York Times,* November 21, 1943.

———. "The Dance: Novelties; Balanchine and Bolender Go in for Extremes." *New York Times,* September 16, 1951.

———. "The Dance: 'Orpheus'; Ballet Society Presents A Masterpiece." *New York Times,* May 16, 1948.

———. "The Dance: Progress; Ballet Society Adventure Starts Off Well." *New York Times* February 16, 1947.

———. "The Dance: Summary." *New York Times,* March 18, 1956.

———. "Festival of Dance Has Its Opening." *New York Times,* December 27, 1939.

———. "Premiere Is Seen of 'City Portrait'; New Ballet by Eugene Loring Presented by Dance Players at National Theatre Music by Henry Brant Settings Are After Reginald Marsh–'Billy the Kid' and 'Jinx' Also on Program." *New York Times,* April 29, 1942.

———. "Stravinsky Work in World Premiere; Ballet Society Features His 'Orpheus' at City Center to Balanchine Dance." *New York Times,* April 29, 1948.

Martin, John. "2d Season Opened by Ballet Society; Troupe Offers Danieli 'Punch and the Child' in Premiere at the City Center." *New York Times,* November 13, 1947.

McDonagh, Don. "Witty Performance by Todd Bolender in a Robbins Ballet." *New York Times,* January 18, 1972.

McHarry, Charles. "Gal Gets Guy in New Ballet." *Daily News* (New York), March 14, 1956.

McLaughlin, Russell. "Debut of Ballet Company Delights a Big Audience." *Detroit News,* February 7, 1941.

Moore, Lillian. "'America Dances' Gaily In the Park." *New York Herald Tribune,* September 4, 1963.

"Music: Dancing Philadelphians." *Time,* July 19, 1937.

"Music: Sleeping Beauty." *Time,* February 22, 1937.

Pollack, Robert. "American Ballet Comes of Age." *Chicago Daily Times,* October 7, 1938.

Sanli, Sevgi, "Madame's Turkish Company." *Dancing Times,* April 1994.

Shanley, John. "Dancing Flirtation." *New York Times,* January 11, 1959.

Staver, Frederick Lee, "San Francisco's Ballet Goes Touring: A Log Book of a Young Company's First Extensive Travels." *Dance,* June 1940, 14–15.

Staver, Frederick Lee, "San Francisco's Ballet Goes Touring: Part Two." *Dance,* July 1940, 7.

Taylor, Carol. "Sunbeam of Ballet Back to Shine on City Center." *New York World Telegram,* February 13, 1957.

Terry, Walter. "Dance: A Joyful Comeback." *New York Herald Tribune,* February 3, 1957.

———. "'The Still Point,' A New Ballet Hit." *New York Herald Tribune,* April 15, 1955.

Tobias, Tobi. "Bringing Back Robbins's 'Fancy.'" *Dance,* January 1980.

Secondary Sources

Aloff, Mindy. "Lake, Prairie, Pillar, and Park: The Landscape of Janet Reed." *Encore Magazine of the Arts* (Portland, Oregon), November–December 1978.

Amberg, George. *Ballet in America: The Emergence of an American Art.* New York: Duell, Sloan and Pearce, 1949.

Anawalt, Sasha. *The Joffrey Ballet: Robert Joffrey and the Making of an American Dance Company.* New York: Scribner, 1996.

Balanchine, George. *Balanchine's Complete Stories of the Great Ballets.* Garden City, NY: Doubleday, 1954.

———. *Balanchine's Complete Stories of the Great Ballets.* Revised by George Balanchine and Francis Mason. Garden City, NY: Doubleday, 1977.

Beaumont, Cyril W. *Supplement to Complete Book of Ballets.* London: Putnam, 1952.

Buckle, Richard. *George Balanchine: Ballet Master.* London Penguin Group, 1988.

Chazin-Bennahum, Judith. *The Ballets of Antony Tudor: Studies in Psyche and Satire.* New York: Oxford University Press, 1994.

Chujoy, Anatole. *The New York City Ballet.* New York: Knopf, 1953.

Cohen, Selma Jean. *The American Ballet Theatre: 1940–1960.* Dance Perspectives no. 6. [Brooklyn, NY]: Dance Perspectives, 1960.

Collins, Nicole Dekle. "A Hero of Dance Preservation." Interview with Nancy Reynolds. *The Dance Enthusiast,* June 14, 2016. Accessed July 20, 2020. https://www.dance-enthusiast.com/features/the-dance-enthusiast-asks/view/Nancy-Renolds.

Copland, Aaron, and Vivian Perlis. *Copland: 1900 through 1942*New York: St. Martin's Press, 1984.

Craine, Debra, and Judith Mackrell. *The Oxford Dictionary of Dance*. Oxford: Oxford University Press, 2000.

D'Amboise, Jacques. *I Was a Dancer*. New York: Knopf, 2011.

Denby, Edwin. *Dance Writings*. Gainesville: University Press of Florida, 1986.

Duberman, Martin. *The Worlds of Lincoln Kirstein*. New York: Alfred A. Knopf, 2007.

Dunning, Jennifer. *"But First a School" The First Fifty Years of the School of American Ballet*. New York: Viking, 1985.

Farrell, Suzanne. *Holding On to the Air: An Autobiography*. New York: Summit Books, 1990.

Fisher, Barbara Milberg. *In Balanchine's Company: A Dancer's Memoir*. Middletown, CT: Wesleyan University Press, 2006.

Gottlieb, Robert. *Avid Reader: A Life*. New York: Farrar, Straus and Giroux, 2016.

Garis, Robert. "Agon." In *International Encyclopedia of the Dance: A Project of Dance Perspectives Foundation,* vol. 4, edited by Selma Jeanne Cohen. New York, NY: Oxford University Press, 1998.

Haggin, B. H. *Ballet Chronicle*. New York: Horizon Press, 1970.

Harris, Andrea. *Making Ballet American: Modernism Before and Beyond Balanchine*. New York: Oxford University Press, 2018.

Hastings, Baird. "Todd Bolender." *Chrysalis: The Pocket Review of the Arts* 3, nos. 5–6 (1950).

Hayden, Melissa. *Melissa Hayden: On Stage and Off*. Garden City, NY: Double Day, 1963.

Jackson, Teague. *Encore: The Private and Professional Triumph of Emily Frankel*. Englewood Cliffs, NJ: Prentice-Hall, 1978.

Jowitt, Deborah. *Jerome Robbins: His Life, His Theater, His Dance*. New York: Simon & Schuster, 2004.

Kirstein, Lincoln. *Ballet, Bias and Belief: Three Pamphlets Collected and Other Dance Writings of Lincoln Kirstein*. Edited by Nancy Reynolds. New York: Dance Horizons, 1983.

———. *Thirty Years: Lincoln Kirstein's The New York City Ballet: Expanded to Include the Years 1973–1978, in Celebration of the Company's Thirtieth Anniversary*. New York: Knopf Doubleday Publishing Group, 1978.

Krokover, Rosalyn. *The New Borzoi Book of Ballets*. New York: Knopf, 1956.

Lobenthal, Joel. "A Conversation with Betty Nichols." *Ballet Review* 41, no. 3 (2013): 56–60.

———. *Wilde Times: Patricia Wilde, George Balanchine, and the Rise of New York City Ballet*. Lebanon, NH: ForeEdge, 2016.

Lawrence, Greg. *Dance with Demons: The Life of Jerome Robbins*. New York: G. P. Putnam's Sons, 2001.

Mason, Francis. *I Remember Balanchine: Recollections of the Ballet Master by Those Who Knew Him*. New York: Doubleday, 1991.

Maynard, Olga. *The American Ballet*. Philadelphia: Macrae Smith Company, 1959.

Mead, Margaret. *Blackberry Winter: My Earlier Years*. New York: Morrow, 1972.

Perlmutter, Donna. *Shadowplay: The Life of Antony Tudor*. New York: Viking, 1991.

Reynolds, Nancy. *Repertory in Review: 40 Years of the New York City Ballet*. New York: Dial Press, 1977.

Reynolds, Nancy, and Malcolm McCormick. *No Fixed Points: Dance in the Twentieth Century*. New Haven, CT: Yale University Press, 2003.

Sagolla, Lisa Jo. *The Girl Who Fell Down: A Biography of Joan McCracken*. Boston: Northeastern University, 2003.

Siegel, Marcia B. *The Shapes of Change: Images of American Dance*. Berkeley: University of California Press, 1985.

Sowell, Debra Hickenlooper. *The Christensen Brothers: An American Dance Epic*. Amsterdam: Harwood Academic Publishers, 1998.

Steinberg, Stephen Cobbett. "America's First Swan: A Conversation with Willam Christensen and Janet Reed." In *Why a Swan? Essays, Interviews, & Conversations on "Swan Lake."* compiled by Janice Ross and Stephen Cobbett Steinberg. San Francisco, CA: San Francisco Performing Arts Library and Museum, 1989.

———. *San Francisco Ballet: The First Fifty Years*. San Francisco, CA: San Francisco Ballet Association and Chronicle Books, 1983.

Teague, Jackson. *Encore: The Private and Professional Triumph of Emily Frankel*. Englewood Cliffs, NJ: Prentice-Hall, 1978.

Terry, Walter. *Star Performance: The Story of the World's Great Ballerinas*. Garden City, NY: Doubleday, 1955.

Tracy, Robert. *Spaces of the Mind: Isamu Noguchi's Dance Designs*. New York: Limelight Editions, 2000.

Vaughan, David, and Melissa Harris. *Merce Cunningham: Fifty Years*. New York: Aperture Foundation, 1997.

Villella, Edward. *Prodigal Son: Dancing for Balanchine in a World of Pain and Magic*. New York: Simon & Schuster, 1992.

West, Martha Ullman. "Pioneer on Point: Janet Reed, the Early Years, 1916–1941." *Dance Chronicle* 30, no. 3 (2007): 471–493.

———. "Todd Bolender: Kansas City, The Early Years." *Ballet Review* 37 (Summer 2009): 49–56.

———. "Todd Bolender with American Ballet Caravan." *Ballet Review* 38 (Winter 2010–2011): 72–89.

Index

Note: Titles of ballets are followed by the name of the choreographer in parentheses.

MARTHA ULLMAN WEST is an arts writer specializing in dance and visual arts, based in Portland, Oregon. She has written for the *New York Times*, the *Oregonian*, *Dance Magazine*, *Dance International*, *Ballet Review*, *Dance Chronicle*, and the *Chronicle Review*.